THE PATHWAY

Rick
DePepe

THE PATHWAY

Follow the Road to
Health and Happiness

LAUREL MELLIN

ReganBooks
An Imprint of HarperCollinsPublishers

The Solution, like any psychosocial, behavioral, spiritual, or health program, is not without risk and may be unsafe or ineffective for some people. If you have any psychological or medical problems, we suggest you consult with your physician and/or mental health professional before beginning this program. The research on the method is based on subjects who, in addition to reading a book on this method, have used the complete Solution course (six Solution Kits), and the program may be significantly less effective and/or pose greater psychological or medical risk for those who do not complete the entire course and use only the resource of this book. In addition, using this method with others in self-help Solution Circle groups or with Solution Buddies may pose more risks, as using the skills may arouse intense feelings or aggressive or other negative behaviors in some people. Those who have behavioral excesses associated with significant medical risk are advised to seek additional supportive interventions to change their behavior and decrease their medical risk in the short term in addition to using this method. For most people, mastery of the method to the point of spontaneous improvements in high-risk health-related behaviors such as overeating, smoking, or substance use may not occur for two or more years, so without that support their medical risk is higher. The author, publisher, Institute for Health Solutions, and Sweetest Fruit Press disclaim all liability for any adverse effects that may result from the use or application of the information contained in this book.

Some profanity is used in this book to more accurately reflect the actual use of the method. Some people find that the intense, primitive feelings that using the cycles arouses prompt them to use profane language, even individuals who normally refrain from using such expressions. If you believe you might find this language offensive, please read this book with caution.

The characters discussed in this book are composites of several individuals and the names of any individuals involved in creating a character have been changed to maintain anonymity.

The Solution™ and the nurturing and limits symbols are trademarks used under license by The Institute for Health Solutions, a nonprofit organization.

A hardcover edition of this book was published in 2003 by ReganBooks, an imprint of HarperCollins Publishers.

First paperback edition published 2004.

Designed by Brenden Hitt; graphics by Teka Luttrell; drawings by Martha Weston

The Library of Congress has cataloged the hardcover edition as follows:

Mellin, Laurel.
    The pathway : follow the road to health and happiness / Laurel Mellin.
      p. cm.
    Includes bibliographical references.
    ISBN 0-06-051402-7—ISBN 0-06-051403-5 (pbk.)
      1. Self-defeating behavior. I. Title: The pathway. II. Title.

BF637.S37 M35 2003
158.1—dc21

2002031916

04 05 06 07 08 WBC/QW 10 9 8 7 6

FOR MY FAMILY

Mackey and Papa, Haley, Joe, and John

Steve and Viv, Sarah, Lisa, and Michael

When the solution is simple, God is answering.
—Albert Einstein

All happy families resemble one another;
each unhappy family is unhappy in its own way.
—Leo Tolstoy

Contents

Acknowledgments

The Solution was developed over the last two decades and is the integration of the work of many generous individuals and institutions. Without the structure, inspiration, and guidance of many researchers and clinicians associated with the University of California, San Francisco School of Medicine, this work would never have been done. I am particularly grateful to Jonathan E. Rodnick, M.D., chair, Department of Family and Community Medicine; Marion Nestle, Ph.D., M.P.H., chair, Nutrition and Food Studies, New York University; and Charles E. Irwin, Jr., M.D., director, Division of Adolescent Medicine; for their support at various key points in the method's development. Mary S. Croughan, Ph.D., professor of family and community medicine and epidemiology, Department of Family and Community Medicine, and Larry L. Dickey, M.D., M.S.W., M.P.H., currently Chief, Office of Clinical Preventive Medicine, California State Department of Health Services, have been instrumental in conducting research on the method.

Many others have offered this wisdom, particularly Jim Billings, Ph.D., whose spiritual essence colors every page of this book and whose courage in facing life's challenges will forever inspire me. Carl Greenberg, M.S., guided my understandings of the family system; John Foreyt, Ph.D., Ken Goodrick, Ph.D., and Elizabeth Brannon, M.S., contributed to program research; and Susan Johnson, M.D., Velia Frost, M.S.W., Marna Cohen, M.S.W., Jane Rachel Kaplan, Ph.D., Dennis Styne, M.D., and Lisa Frost, P.N.P., gave essential support early on. I am grateful for the work of Hilde Bruch, M.D., Dorothy Baumarind, Ph.D., Salvador Minuchin, Ph.D., Wayne Dyer, Ph.D., Thomas Lewis, M.D., Fari Amini, M.D., and Richard Lannon, M.D. John Gray, Ph.D., developed the natural flow of feelings and graciously allowed me to adapt it for inclusion in this method.

The staff of the Institute for Health Solutions, the organization that provides professional training and client support for the method, has made the writing of this book possible. I am particularly grateful to Bernadette Payne for her loyalty, Kelly McGrath for her perseverance, Sabrina Geshay for her enthusiasm, Barbara Krohn for her thoughtfulness, and Sean Maher for his many ways of being helpful.

Nancy Bates, Dr.P.H., R.D., C.H.E.S., has been generous with her time and talents in conducting research on the method, and Bryant Young, Bill Taggart, and Larry Townsend have provided wise counsel to the Institute. Noam Birnbaum, Tracy Weir, Tom Temple, Robert Cho, and Tylor Bohlman all supported our Internet community and website. Karen Marie Richards gave of her time and considerable talents to the development of our support tapes. Bruce Payne, Bonnie Kamen, Sarah Hill, Susan Eisgrau, Kim Reneau, Mary Sue Jackinsky, Barbara Mahoney, Joe O'Hehir, Kara Menghini, Christina Didier, Barbara Reuscher, Dawn Galbo, Lily Fournier, Lisa Herzstein, Harry and Lee Elefther, Susan Sharp, Seleda Williams, M.D., Robert Wilson, Rise Cherin, Eric Maisel, and Corinna Kaarlela have all contributed to this work in important ways.

Over the years, financial support has been provided by the American Cancer Society, the Preventive Medicine Research Institute, the American Dietetic Association, the U.S. Department of Health and Human Service's Bureau of Maternal and Child Health, Balboa Publishing, and Michael Henman. Without each of these sources of support, the work would not have evolved.

My editor at ReganBooks, Cassie Jones, has advocated for this book and carefully ushered it through the publishing process. Kristen Salvatore has been exceptionally supportive and meticulous in editing this book, often improving my writing considerably. My agent, Bob Tabian, has been a source of thoughtful advice throughout this process. I feel grateful to Teka Luttrell for his graphics and philosophic advice and Martha Weston for her drawings.

Many Solution Providers have given support and feedback along the way, as have providers from the Shapedown pediatric program based on this method. I am particularly indebted to Deanne Duvall M.S., R.D., and Barbara McCarty, R.D., C.D.E., who have been providers for more than fifteen years and have been true shepherds of this work. In addition, the contributions of Anne Brown, Ph.D., Kai Frykman, M.F.T., R.N., Alia Witt,

M.F.T., R.D., Susan Stordahl, L.C.S.W, Carra Reichling, R.D., and Jill Shaffer, R.D., have been greatly appreciated. The program participants who were involved in this work during the early days of the Institute were patient and offered suggestions that shaped our growth. To each of them, I am very grateful.

The closeness and love of my family have sustained me. My father, Jack McClure, is a realist and joy catcher, and our chats about life and work and our laughter over lunches have done so much to shape my life and this method. His sparkle and wisdom show up often in the pages of this book. My mother, Rosabelle McClure, is tireless in giving love and support to me, including jotting ideas down on paper, one of which led her to come up with the name of the method. She is a devoted grandmother and has taught me a great deal about the importance of quietly doing what you came to Earth to do.

My children have lived through the ups and downs of this work, and each of them has contributed to it in special ways. They are my greatest joy in life. I am particularly grateful to my daughter, Haley, for her passionate creativity and her sharing of her wisdom and love with me. This work began when she was born, and now the method and my daughter have come of age at the same time. My son Joe brings his kindness, general optimism, and ease with him wherever he goes. I am deeply grateful to him for his good heart, his many ideas, and our closeness. My son John has shot up three inches during the writing of this book, and his loving presence as well as his music and laughter have made the writing of this book far easier. If it had not been for my first child, Riley, this work might never have been.

I can always count on my brother, Steve McClure, for his honesty, pure heart, and humor. He is the best brother anyone could ever have. I am grateful for the closeness of his family, my sister-in-law, Vivian McClure, and their children, Sarah, Lisa, and Michael, and grateful for my memories of my grandmothers. Rosabelle Driggs was a descendant of a California land grant family and a complete rascal, and she *loved* lemon meringue pie. Laura McClure sewed my children's christening gown even in her nineties and wore out her Bible from reading and the paint on her stove from scrubbing.

I have been blessed with an extended family of support during the development of this work, particularly Daniel, Andrea, Sophie and Sarah Sharp, Emily Kearney-Begg and Jock Begg,

Deirdre Taylor, Andria Knapp, Tom Morrison, Donna Fletcher, Marguerite, Jim, Stephanie, and James Patrick Moriarty, Colleen Mauro, Kathleen Flickinger, Ann Squires, Janice Echenique, Lou Thoelecke, Kathy McHenry, Gail Altschuler, M.D., and Sister Marina Ioki.

Brett and Jena Walter have generously shared their remarkable talents and their caring during some of the Institutes's most vulnerable times, and my gratitude to them is boundless.

Many have lent important support earlier on, including Lili Fournier, Karen Schanche, Pat Cherry, Tom Martin, Pat Randolph, Kela Cabrales, Lisa Reyes, Ty Garafalo, Jean Vecchiet, Nora Monfredini, Mary Gregory, Janis Eggleston, Patty McManus, Mel Lefer, Doug and Joan Emerson, Don Thompson, Caroline Maniego, Pascal Ruimy, Brigid Flagerman, Mary Lane, Diane Merlino, Suzanne Danielson, Susie Brown, Peter Marguglio, Laurie Gregory, Regina Deihl, Jo Madrid, George and Liz Girvin, Dorothy Reinhardt, Sheila Larsen, Jan MacDougall, Dina Zvenko, Colleen Sevigne, Serena Puga, Hawley Riffenburg, Janeen O'Donnell, Bonnie Hoag, Margery Greenberg, Sharon Neilsen, Travis Hayes, Emile Mulholland, Shilo Kantz, and Sharon Le Shack.

I am grateful to Dan Rosenthal, who has given me thoughtful advice and encouragement along the way. Bob Mellin originally nudged me to return to graduate school and published my early books. Without his support, this work would never have begun.

So many people have contributed their ideas, caring, and spirit to this work that the method is a reflection not only of grace but also of their collective wisdom. I am deeply grateful to each of them.

THE PATHWAY

I. A SOLUTION TO LIFE

1. What Do You Most Want?

I must have been about six years old when, during a summer heat wave, I stood at the base of our family's towering apricot tree and looked straight up. At the top of the tree, there was one huge, blush-red, honey-sweet apricot. I didn't just *want* that apricot. I *yearned* for it and, in a flash I scrambled up the tree, risking life and limb, undaunted by a twig's scratching or my fear of falling. Finally, the branches parted, and I was at the very top of the tree.

Now, more than four decades later, my memory is still vivid of picking that sweetest of fruits, biting into its sun-warmed flesh, and letting its honey slip down my throat. There at the top of the tree, I remember glancing around to discover not just one plump apricot on the branches, but a whole bushel of them—and they were all mine. Sure, it was good to have apricots, and certainly I felt the immense pride and deep delight of *knowing* what I most wanted, and then *getting* it. But what so electrified the moment was the sheer unexpected *abundance* of what I was receiving, something I never could have even *imagined* when I started the climb.

The purpose of this book is to introduce a new method that offers us a simple, effective way to experience *knowing* what we most want in life and *getting* it. And when we do, finding that life is far different and much better than we have ever known before. This method is called The Solution.

It's really about fruit. What you most want in life, we call our *sweetest fruit*. It may be to end an excess that has troubled us or simply to have more of life's richest rewards. Either way, our sweetest fruit is something that has stubbornly eluded us over the years. No matter what we have done and no matter how hard we have tried, we haven't been able to get it. Other things we can do with ease, but not this!

That yearning is perfect for it motivates us to pop the hood of our inner lives and go inside often enough and well enough, making the small but important adjustments within, to reap what we most want in this world. When we do, more often than not, we experience a true Solution, that is, a life in which we are free from common excesses and have an abundance of life's sweetest rewards: integration, balance, sanctuary, intimacy, vibrancy, and spirituality. Life is still difficult, but having a Solution is about as good as it gets.

In nature, the sweetest fruit is invariably at the top of the tree. So, too, in human nature what we most yearn for, the one thing that has so maddeningly eluded us, is invariably furthest from our reach. For what we most want turns out to be the touchstone of our development so if we make the subtle shifts within that enable us to reach it, we will have the full abundance of health and happiness that our particular life can bring.

Which is perfect! Our yearning for that goal motivates us to take ourselves by the hand and guide, nudge, and cajole ourselves until we have mastered the powerful inner skills often missed in childhood that complete our development. What seemed to be a curse—that we couldn't turn off our deepest cravings or get the rewards all the *other* people seemed to obtain so effortlessly—turns out to be a blessing. The design of human development is *that* elegant, for getting what we most *want* brings us precisely what we most *need*.

It is almost like a fairy tale, except this story is true.

The Solution is to master the two simple skills—self-nurturing and effective limits—that, other than genetics, form the bedrock for human health and happiness. These skills are not genetic. They are learned, and you can learn them. Yes, even you.

Self-nurturing is the skill of checking our feelings and needs throughout the day, so we know and honor ourselves and meet our needs more often.

Effective limits is the skill of having reasonable expectations and following through with them, so we can take action and have more power and greater safety in our lives.

When the two skills are woven together, it is much like implanting within ourselves a good parent who never leaves us. As a result, those who have mastered these two skills, more often than not, have a life of health and happiness. Unfortunately, those who have not mastered them, more often than not, do not.

The basics of these skills can be learned rather rapidly. In fact, most people can learn them just by reading this book, and by doing so, they will catch a glimpse of the effects they can have on their lives. However, it is only when these two skills are used over and over again and integrated into the belly of our brains that a myriad of seemingly magical changes begin to occur. At that point, many people notice that the whole range of common excesses starts to fade and the full spectrum of life's sweetest rewards appears.

The most basic ideas of this method, that people should do a better job of nurturing themselves and setting limits with themselves and others, has been in the scientific literature since at least 1940. These ideas are consistent with current understandings of developmental psychology, family systems theory, medical science, and brain research. *The trouble is that current methods to help us accomplish these goals aren't very effective.* Try as we might, we simply can't seem to nurture ourselves better or set more effective limits in our lives.

The reason is no mystery, for our patterns of nurturing and limits were implanted in us early in life and are so deep that various healing methods, particularly those that focus on insight, knowledge, or analysis, do little to change them. The Solution molds nurturing and limits into skills that can be learned much as one would learn to type or speak a new language—by practice. Using the skills in the moment makes people feel better, but using them repeatedly over time adds up so that self-nurturing and effective limits begin to penetrate the very core of their being and become automatic and spontaneous. When they are, what often follows is nothing less than a personal transformation.

This method began with support from a federal grant on adolescent health in 1979. Still, until recently most people were not aware of the method, and those few who used it would often say, "This really works! Why doesn't *everyone* know about this?"

In a sense, the relative obscurity of the method has been a blessing. It has given us time to learn. Hundreds of people from diverse walks of life have been trained in the method at the university, and health professionals from around the country who are certified in the method have trained far more. Some research has been conducted, which has given us additional insights as well. We know more—and will continue to learn more—about how to make mastering the skill to nurture and set limits from within easier, quicker, and safer.

I will do my best to share these understandings with you, and to make your journey with this method as easy, quick, and safe

Above the Line and Below

Life *above* the line:
in balance
excesses fade
many life rewards

Life *below* the line:
out of balance
excesses flourish
few life rewards

as possible, even though it is not always easy, rarely quick, and not completely without risk.

What I ask of you is to be as persistent as you are able to be and to draw upon your courage—particularly the courage to begin, to stand at the base of the tree and look straight up until you spot your sweetest of fruits, then to put one foot in front of the other, sometimes climbing by taking baby steps and sometimes long strides, using the skills over and over again. At some point, you will find yourself at the top of the tree where, to the extent that genetics, circumstance, and grace allow, you can pluck from the branch what you most want in this lifetime.

It is as simple as that.

There are two worlds . . .

As people use this method, they typically become acutely aware that there are two worlds: the world *above the line* and the world *below the line*.

The point of this training is to pump up our nurturing and limits skills so that we spend more moments of the day above the

The next part of the book is about the skills themselves, self-nurturing and effective limit setting. As we walk along this pathway, we use them in four ways: to cultivate a nurturing inner voice, to stay balanced in the present, to take out "emotional trash" from the past, and to do the "lifestyle surgery" that makes it easier to stay in balance.

The last part of the book highlights the specific tools that allow the common excesses to fade and enable us to reap more of the rewards of personal balance. You may be inclined to read only the chapters on the excesses or rewards that most interest you, but all the chapters, including those that sound as if they wouldn't pertain to you, include ideas, tips, and suggestions that may be important to your mastery of the skills.

The "Method Research" appendix includes a brief review of Solution research, including a new survey of program participants by a University of Illinois researcher and a small six-year follow-up study conducted at the University of California, San Francisco. All research is based on the experiences of participants who completed the entire course based on The Solution Kits. Use of this book alone would be unlikely to produce these results. The book concludes with a plan for making lifestyle balance easier to achieve and a list of recommended readings.

It's about joy . . .

This is joyful work. When you begin to put one foot in front of the other and walk along this pathway, using these skills, you will be likely to laugh more often than you cry and apt to find yourself thoroughly fascinated by using them. Fewer than 10 percent of those who join groups sponsored by the Institute for Health Solutions drop out before they complete their training. This unusual retention rate seems to come from both the power of the method and the excitement of the process. Most people find it enthralling to watch themselves and others take out their tool kit of these skills and predictably "pop" themselves from a state of imbalance to balance, disconnection to connection, and craving to satisfaction.

That said, it's important to note that the skills are not always easy to apply. The emotions that arise from using them sometimes feel incredibly strong, or even overwhelming. Should you experience this, please keep in mind that the feelings that surface are *just* feelings; they will fade, and when they do, you will feel emotionally lighter and far stronger. If at any time you do not feel safe using this method, be sure to stop using it and seek support from your physician or from a mental health professional.

Although the full benefits of the method take time to receive, you are likely to notice impressive changes right from the start, particularly in the area of emotional balance. When you have used the skills enough to feel emotionally balanced most of the time, please remember that you are only halfway through the journey and the best rewards are yet to come.

Some people ask, "How long does it take to reach a Solution?" My answer is, "It takes as long as it takes." The more often you use the skills and the more effectively you apply them, the less time it requires. Most people who enroll in The Solution training—groups and telegroups led by Certified Solution Providers—require about 18 to 24 months to experience the full benefits of the program. Some take longer, some shorter.

Instead of trying to figure out how long it will take you, consider focusing on what you most want in life, then start taking the small but important steps day by day until you get it.

As you read this book and use the skills, please keep in mind that the results you begin to see do not come from the method. They come from you, for The Solution is based on a very simple truth:

On the day that you were born, you had all the inherent
strength, goodness, and wisdom that you would ever need.
All that you required was the tools to access it.
These two skills are those tools.

Introduction

This book is about two timeless tools that offer a universal pathway to acquiring the power to make our lives better. Using them enables us to go to the very roots of our health and happiness and make those roots stronger, so our lives get better, not by chance but by choice.

The two steps of the method are self-nurturing and effective limit setting; in essence, the internal workings that naturally result from having been parented well. Most of us weren't parented perfectly, but instead of slipping into self-pity, hostility, or numbness, we can grieve our losses, then use this method to take the baton from our parents and give ourselves what they could not. When we do, we experience better health and far more happiness and what amounts to a new life.

Here's how it works: we use these two immensely powerful skills over time and, at some point, they become automatic, much like riding a bicycle or typing by touch. When they do, we spontaneously soothe and comfort ourselves *internally* so we no longer need the common *external* solutions to distress—such as overeating, overdrinking, overspending, or overworking. We stop *wanting* them! What's more, mastery of the skills brings us an abundance of the full spectrum of the rewards of life—integration, balance, sanctuary, intimacy, vibrancy, and spirituality. Having no external solutions and an abundance of all six of these rewards is what we call a Solution.

The theories on which this method is based have found support in the scientific literature for at least sixty years, and the method itself has been used for nearly twenty years and by more than 100,000 people. Through the early testing at the University of California, San Francisco School of Medicine and later, in the community, we learned a considerable amount about how to make the method easier and safer to use and how to prompt significant improvements sooner. To draw upon some of what we've learned, please consider turning to the following appendices before reading further:

- **Getting Started**
  Easy ways to begin using the skills with success.

- **The Solution Pocket Reminder**
  A small card you can take with you, as a reminder of the skills.

- **Solution Support Options**
  A summary of support choices, including how to find a "Solution Buddy" with whom to practice the skills, joining a free Solution Circle in your community, or enrolling in professional support, either in groups or through personal coaching. If you like to connect through the Internet, there is an interactive members' section of our website (www. sweetestfruit.org). If you prefer telephone support, there are Solution TeleGroups and TeleCoaching. All professional support is provided by Certified Solution Providers who are licensed health professionals with at least eighteen months of additional professional training in the method. They have mastered the skills personally, and have learned ways to bring others to a Solution as quickly, easily and safely as possible.

- **Solution Circles**
  How to form and conduct a successful free Solution Circle in your neighborhood, through your church or temple or at your work.

The flow of this book

This book provides information on what the method is, how it works, and why it is effective. However, its central story is about three people—Emily, Tom, and Drew—and each of their journeys to reach their Solution. You are likely to see yourself in one or more of these people.

The book begins by explaining the theory and practice of the method and the biology that appears to underlie its effectiveness. Two self-tests will help you identify what you most want in life and guide you in finding the right pace and support you will need to receive it.

line. That is the state in which we feel emotionally balanced, spir itually connected, and intimate with others. What's more, those pesky drives to go to excess—what we call "external solutions" to distress—have faded. They are either abjectly *gone* and we have no interest in that extra glass of wine, that bedtime snack, or another pair of shoes, or their power has been so deflated that with a little bit of care, we can achieve moderation. Life above the line is still difficult, but we glide through life's necessary pain and graciously sidestep the possibility of creating a life that man- ufactures misery.

Without enough of these skills, we spend more moments below the line, and that life is not a pretty picture. We may find ourselves on an emotional roller coaster—way high and way low—or we steer clear of emotions altogether and opt for per- sonal numbness, which means we miss out on passion and the accuracy of the personal radar that balanced feelings can bring.

Moreover, when we are below the line, our relationships are fraught with difficulty. We lose ourselves in others or try to rescue people or distance from those we love and inadvertently persecute them. We may even stir up the hot cauldron of power struggles and have nightly fireworks of a very sad sort. There is also the iso- lation of the world below the line, of feeling lost or abandoned. The grace and mystery of life seem far removed, and the drives to go to excess have little mercy. They bully us and preoccupy us, which only disrupts our balance more and draws us further away from the true solution that, of course, comes from within.

There is an immense difference between these two worlds. If we are above the line, our dreams are apt to come true. If we are below the line, the nightmares seem to have their way.

If you've lived life below the line much of the time, you may make harsh judgments of yourself that are far from accurate. Being below the line is not wrong or bad. It is *not* a reflection of a character flaw, poor willpower, or laziness. *It is a direct reflection of having fewer of the skills to nurture and set limits from within than the realities of your life require.* The good news is that these skills are not genetic; they are learned, and you can learn them.

When we become aware that we don't have the skills we need, we might turn to blame. After all, who *wants* to do this work and gain these skills? Why couldn't *somebody else* just handle it? Why wasn't it taken care of long ago so we wouldn't have to deal with it now?

The truth is that if we don't have all the skills we need, it is probably not anybody's fault. Although it is extremely important to grieve the very real losses of not having the skills, it's hard to point the finger at anyone when you understand the nature of these skills:

More skills are needed in modern life—First, most people have a good supply of these skills but are still out of balance because of the realities of modern culture. In the past, communities were more nurturing; there were fewer choices and less change in life. A lot of the nurturing and limits were *external*; they came from the warmth of our families and the stability of our communities. In modern life, there is simply more chaos, more choices, and less nurturing. To live a life of balance, we need more of the *internal* skills to nurture and set limits. It is not that we are unskilled, but that we have fewer skills than our environment demands.

Parents can't give skills they don't have—These skills are not something you acquire the way you would a new bicycle or a pair of shoes. They are unconscious and buried deeply in our emotional brains, planted there by our parents in the early years of life. No matter how much they loved us or how strong their intentions to raise us well, if they did not have these skills, they could not give them to us. The sad fact is that because these skills are transmitted early in life and harder to come by in later years, the legacy of imbalance often carries on from one generation to the next.

The question is, *how do you stop it*? How do you stop the cascading of life below the line from one generation to the next? Any way you can. If any one person, in order to stop smoking, have intimacy, or lose weight, chooses to master the skills, nearly everyone around that person is affected. The skills are "catching"!

It is tremendously powerful to have the capacity to stay in balance when those around us are down there, below the line, in the emotional playpen being hostile, depressed, self-pitying, rebellious, or numb. Have you ever acted like a four-year-old in the presence of someone who is perfectly balanced and empathetically mature? It is tremendously embarrassing—enough to make most people want to try to pop themselves above the line, too.

Although those around us may be unsettled by our choice to

master the skills, many of them will be delighted and will also change. A man whose wife went through The Solution once called our Institute because he, too, wanted to start using the method. His wife had lost fifty-five pounds and regained her interest in kayaking, lovemaking, and traveling the world. He said, "I want to get into a Solution Group. My wife used The Solution, and I *want* what she *got*."

Some people, like this man, become directly involved with the method, but others move above the line unconsciously because of their proximity to someone who is in balance. Many notice that their kids stop squabbling and start saying "I feel angry" or "I feel sad." Our controlling mother may still be controlling, but since we won't go down there below the line with her and snipe back, it stops being fun for her. There may start to be moments when the warm mother we always wanted begins to appear. As we stay above the line, we often find that work relationships are more intimate and effective, with fewer fierce battles, less infighting, and more cooperation, productivity, and peace.

These questions are universal

Nurturing and limits are clusters of questions that we ask ourselves over and over again until they become automatic. It is only with repeated practice that the questions become spontaneous, the perfect reflection of having a "good mother" and a "good father" within.

The questions of the nurturing skill are:
- How do I feel?
- What do I need?
- Do I need support?

The questions of the limits skill are:
- Are my expectations reasonable?
- Is my thinking positive and powerful?
- What is the essential pain? What is the earned reward?

The nurturing cycle enables us to access our feelings very deeply, so we know ourselves better and honor ourselves more fully. The limits cycle *contains* our feelings and "grows them up" to deal with the realities of the world, creating safety in our world and the power to follow through. The magic of the method comes from the *interweaving* of the skills to nurture and set limits from within. The symbol of the method is an infinity sign in motion:

This symbol suggests both this intermingling and our commitment to keep our fingers on the pulse of our inner lives and stay with ourselves, using the skills, until we are in balance. In our early lives, our parents may not have had the skills to stay with us through our upsets until we were back in balance. With the method, as the symbol suggests, we stay with ourselves until we are back in balance. We feel secure that we will never abandon ourselves again.

At first, we use the skills intentionally to move ourselves from a state of imbalance to balance. When we find ourselves below

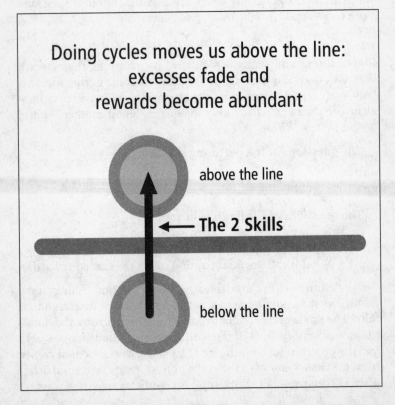

Doing cycles moves us above the line: excesses fade and rewards become abundant

above the line

← **The 2 Skills**

below the line

the line, we ask ourselves the questions of both skills, which we call "doing cycles." With practice, we find that these skills become integrated and spontaneous most of the time, somewhat like knowing how to touch-type and automatically pressing the little finger of your left hand to type the letter "a." You don't have to think; the "a" just appears on the monitor. In much the same way, at some point we just *know* how we feel and what we need, and it wouldn't occur to us to not be aware of it.

As incredible as it may sound, the fact is that the method works for most people. That's why 90 percent of the people who use it in the group programs that we sponsor complete the training. They don't stop because they can see the method working in their own lives. Plus they can look around the room in their group and see that those who have been involved in the training longer have more rewards.

It works right from the start

Most people see an effect that is rather thrilling right from the beginning. Consider Carmen, a petite, red-haired woman who was prone to depression and coped by shopping for clothes and snacking on chocolate. Her house was cluttered with *things*: three closets full of clothes, a garage stuffed with special objects that she couldn't bear to part with, and stacks of magazines literally *everywhere*. She told me how it felt to pop herself above the line for the very first time.

"I got home from shopping and was so furious at myself. I have no willpower; I take out my credit card and buy things I'm not sure I even want. It's so depressing. I was in my normal groove of having just been bad, settling into feeling guilty and depressed. I was thinking about the chocolate ice cream sandwiches in the freezer when I decided to do cycles."

"Great!" I responded. "How was it?"

"Clumsy. I felt awkward. I didn't know how I felt or what I needed, but I kept asking the questions. I started to feel the feelings. Then I used the limits cycle. The second time I asked myself, 'What is the essential pain?' I felt myself pop above the line. It was so incredible! My body relaxed and I felt . . . balanced. I was sad, but the sadness felt like true sadness, not depression. My body didn't feel leaden and achy; I didn't have that abandoned feeling. After a few minutes, the sadness went away, and I felt proud. I had done my first real cycle on my own."

"Congratulations. Then what happened?"

"I felt in balance for about an hour. Then my husband came home, and we started talking about his mother coming to visit. There I went, below the line. It was horrible."

"Perfect," I said.

"What do you mean, perfect? It felt awful."

"It's perfect for where you are in your use of the method. Your inner life is enormously comfortable with being depressed. It may not be pleasant, but to your inner life it is extremely familiar. You can slide into a blue mood just the way you slip into your favorite soft, cozy bathrobe. How long has your inner life been accustomed to feeling depressed at times?"

"Forever. I've never been seriously depressed, but even as a child I had this rolling malaise and tendency to feel depressed at times."

"So doing one cycle is a great start, but it's just a beginning. Think of it this way: When you did one cycle to pop yourself above the line, it was like what happens when you catch a snowflake on the palm of your hand. What happens?"

Carmen shrugged. "It melts."

I nodded and went on. "You pop yourself above the line, which may well strengthen the neural networks in your brain that favor emotional balance. Nevertheless, the dominant pathways that have long favored imbalance soon take over, and there you go, plop, right below the line."

"That's just what it felt like—as if I got dumped back into confusion and disconnect," Carmen said, wincing.

"Did you like your moment of balance?" I asked.

She smiled and said, "I loved it."

"Great. The more you use the cycles, the sooner the neural networks in your brain that favor balance will become stronger, and your mastery of the skills will begin to 'snowball.' Your feeling brain does not learn by having an epiphany, gaining insight, or figuring it out. *It learns by repeated experience.* The more you use the skills, the more dominant the neural networks that favor balance become."

Carmen had accomplished the hardest part of this method: beginning. Once someone experiences popping themselves above the line—out of depression, hostility, rebelliousness, panic, shame, or numbness—they rarely stop this work. The experience is that empowering. Carmen didn't pop a pill, call her therapist, whine to a friend, pour a drink, go shopping, or suck on a candy bar. She simply used the skills to access her inherent strength, goodness, and wisdom and created that balance *all by herself*. Moreover, once she has mastered that skill, nobody can take it away from her. She has it for life.

What we most want brings us what we most need

This method has two parts: Decide what you most want in this life—whether it is to end an excess or to receive a particular reward—then use the skills to climb the tree and reap it. But there is more to it than that. When we reach the top of the tree, we don't just pick our sweetest fruit. Rather, we find ourselves surrounded by more abundance than we possibly could have imagined before we started the climb. We have mastered the skills so deeply that we have created a Solution for ourselves—*no excesses, and an abundance of the most cherished rewards in life: integration, balance, sanctuary, intimacy, vibrancy, and spirituality.* Some would say that we have it *all*.

Dave came to the method because his physician all but forced him to. He was a fifty-four-year-old contractor, the kind of man who had built a great big wall around himself to protect his sensitive inside. Dave had been married to Margaret for thirty-one years, although the union had not been a happy one for some time. Their five children were grown and gone.

Dave said to me, "I don't want to be here. I *hate* groups, and I'm not good at feelings. The last thing I want is to expose my dirty laundry to strangers, people I don't even know."

I could see that Dave already had a strong skill in feeling and expressing anger. He was off to a good start.

"Tell me more," I said.

"I've given up smoking a dozen times, but I've never quit for more than a day. Last month, my partner at work went to the doctor. He's a smoker, and they found a spot on his lungs. Then I saw my own doctor, and he said I had to quit smoking. So here I am."

"So quitting smoking is your sweetest fruit?" I asked.

"I don't care about this sweetest fruit baloney. All I know is that when I decide to do something, I do it . . . except with smoking, that doesn't work," Dave said.

I asked, "How much do you want to stop smoking?"

Dave answered, "If I don't quit, it will kill me." His blue eyes looked a little sad and very scared.

"Are you willing to practice these skills over and over again, even though at times you may hate me, be sick of doing cycles, and be tired of your group?"

The sweet side of Dave emerged, and he said, "Why would I hate you?"

I laughed. "It's like writing a book. It gets so intense at times that you hate the book, you hate your publisher, and you hate yourself. Then it passes, the book is done, and you love your book, your publisher, and yourself. Like anything you do that is important, it is not easy."

"I won't hate you," he said.

"Dave, I'm happy for you to hate me if it makes you mad enough to use the skills so often that you . . ."

Dave interjected, ". . . save my own life?"

We were both silent for a moment.

"Yes," I said, "save your life, and have more joy."

Dave was visibly moved.

In a quiet voice, the one that was under his crusty facade, he said, "Okay, I'll do it."

Dave soon settled into using the method and what he noticed first was how balanced he began to feel, which is to be expected. Emotional balance typically arrives long before the excessive appetites or "external solutions" fade. One study published in the *Journal of the American Dietetic Association* (see note 1 in the appendix "Method Research") showed that on the average, depression scores decrease about 60 percent in the first three months of using the skills.

Once emotional balance is reasonably secure, the skills become more effective, and more of the method's other rewards begin to appear. There is no kicking, scratching, or forcing to turn off the excess. There is certainly no analyzing of "why" one uses external solutions or gaining of insight into the origins of the problem. For most, all that is needed is an eye toward reaping their sweetest fruit, and a certain devotion to doing cycles, which in time causes all the excesses to fade.

I remember speaking to Dave as he was reaching the riskiest point in the training, which is not at the top of the tree but in the thick of the branches in the middle.

Dave said, "I'm so much happier now. My wife and I are closer than we've been in years, and I'm exercising and enjoying my life. The only thing that bothers me is that damned craving I have for the cigarette. What's wrong with The Solution? Why hasn't it turned off my desire for a smoke?"

I smiled to myself, because this was where the power of his "sweetest fruit" becomes most apparent. If it weren't for that last excess, Dave would have stopped using the method and would not have:

- gone into the darkness within, healed his deepest hurts, and felt the emotional lightness and freedom that follow
- honed his skills to true mastery so that no matter what the situation, he could regain his balance
- done enough cycles to secure spontaneous personal balance most of the time

Chances are that his skills would have unraveled and he would somehow have found himself stalled in the middle of the tree or back at its base—not all that different from how he was before his climb.

"Dave, that craving for a cigarette is a blessing, not a curse. When people get close to the top of the tree, there is always one last thing that eludes them. I can almost guarantee that you will crave cigarettes until you get mad enough to give yourself the rest of what you most need in order to have a life of lasting balance—to have a true Solution."

Dave muttered and grumbled during that session. At the following week's meeting, he was still muttering and grumbling, even as he used the skills more deeply. After many more meetings of grumbling and cycling deeply, one evening he arrived at our group beaming and announced:

"I stopped smoking. It's the strangest thing, but I don't even *want* a cigarette, and it isn't even hard. It's just not an issue anymore. I've seen that happen to others in the group, but I believed that I was different and that it would *never* happen to me."

Oddly enough, Dave didn't need to announce to us that he had his Solution. It was obvious. People *look* different when they are solidly in balance. I asked him what I ask others when it is clear that they have their Solution:

"Dave, do you have any external solutions, any at all?"

Dave smiled and said, "Not one."

"Do you have the reward of *integration*; that is, do you feel whole, authentic, and self-accepting?"

He answered, "Yes!"

"Dave, do you have the reward of *balance*? Are you emotionally balanced most of the time, not way high, way low, or numb?"

He answered, "Yes. I feel very balanced nearly all the time."

"What about *sanctuary*? Do you have a nurturing inner voice, a safe place within even when life is very difficult?" I asked next.

"Absolutely," Dave said, nodding.

"*Intimacy*. Instead of control struggles, losing yourself in another, or staying too distant, do you have the warm closeness and intimacy in your life that you need?"

Dave thought for a moment and said, "My relationship with my wife is much, much better, and I am closer to my kids. Yes, I have intimacy in my life."

"An abundance of it?" I asked.

He thought about it, then answered, "Yes, an abundance."

"What about *vibrancy*?"

"I'm not watching *SportsCenter* very much anymore. I'm out riding my bike, and I have lots of energy."

His vibrancy was clear. The facial muscles are attached to the feeling brain. When people are solidly above the line, it is quite visible in their face, as well as in their body and voice.

"*Spirituality*. Do you have a deepened appreciation for the grace and mystery of life?"

Dave said, "I'm not religious now and never was, but there is a change in me. My spirituality is deeper—in fact, much deeper."

I smiled, "You did it! I am so happy for you and so amazed by how you kept putting one foot in front of the other, doing cycles, until you reached your Solution."

This did not mean that Dave would never again go to excess or feel out of emotional balance. It did mean that when he went to excess or fell into an emotional low, he would not judge himself or panic. He would take a big, deep breath, bring up his nurturing inner voice, and in his own time and in his own way, use the tool kit of these skills to return himself to personal balance.

Was your parenting permissive, depriving, or both?

The inspiration for this method was a relatively overlooked study published in 1940 by the late Hilde Bruch, a psychiatrist at Baylor College of Medicine, and her colleague Grace Touraine. This study summarized the results of in-depth interviews with the families of obese children, which concluded that the roots of the drive to go to excess, apart from genetic factors, were parenting styles that were permissive and/or depriving. On closer look, the medical literature since then has corroborated Bruch and Touraine's findings, showing that that various problems are more likely to arise when parents are permissive or depriving. The literatures on eating disorders, substance abuse, affective disorders, and health promotion were particularly consistent with this paradigm.

We've already talked about parents' not being able to give their children the skills they don't possess, but what really happens when they don't have them? Since deprivation and permissiveness are two sides of the same coin, it is clear. If they haven't mastered these two skills, they will deprive and/or indulge, but they will not hit the sweet spot of responsiveness as often as parents who have these skills.

We usually know when we are being depriving or indulging, but it is so hard to change the pattern. Teaching parenting skills doesn't help much because the foundation of these parenting styles is deep; extremes of parent-child closeness, being overly close and "merging" with the child or being overly removed and "disengaged." These patterns are etched into the feeling brain early in life, then tend to be passed along from one generation to the next. The children of parents who indulge or deprive grow into adults who tend either to indulge or deprive and have no nurturing inner voice to draw upon or skill to be responsive to themselves.

Merging and disengaging may sound far less toxic than shooting up heroin, spending to the point of bankruptcy, or eating until you can't fit into your clothes, but it's not. For those of us with deep patterns of merging and distancing, built inside us is a sturdy foundation that supports all the excesses:

- When we merge, it's not just with people but with food, alcohol, possessions, work, you name it! We lose ourselves in the excess so our normal common sense and biological cues that could temper our behavior completely escape us.
- When we distance from others, we distance from ourselves and tend to balance that distancing with merging, too, and filling that emptiness with another drink,

another bowl of ice cream, or a moderate spending spree.

- Which excess we choose or whether we dabble in many external solutions or a few is often a matter of various factors such as genetic propensities, social context, and environmental availability and cues.

There has been a trail of studies since 1940 that supports these ideas and the theories of many of the most revered developmental psychologists—including Alice Miller, Eric Erickson, Marion Woodman, Margaret Mahler, Mary Ainsworth, and Virginia Satir—echo them. The importance of having a nurturing environment with dependable limits to support optimal human development is well accepted by most psychologists.

Moreover, theories of psychological development are based on adolescents accomplishing the "developmental tasks" that separate child functioning from adult functioning, such as separation and individuation and acceptance of body and self. Virtually none of them could be completed without the skill to nurture and set limits from within. We need to be fed these skills early on so we can successfully make developmental leaps in adolescence and the adult years.

This dovetails nicely with the clinical and personal experience of being below the line, using external solutions. Most of us don't feel fully adult and truly responsive to ourselves when we eat the whole pizza, light up a cigarette, or open another can of beer. We feel as if we are four years old or even younger. There we are, below the line, in the playpen kicking and screaming, being endlessly needy and wanting what we want when we want it! We are disengaged from ourselves and fully ready to merge with whatever satisfier happens to come our way.

Since self-nurturing and effective limits are integral to psychotherapy and family therapy, it seemed as if those treatments must have developed ways to teach them directly. Yet I found no mention of such strategies in the literature, at least not ones that taught the full complement of inner shifts that a blend of nurturing and limits suggests. It seemed so *logical* to teach nurturing and limits just the way you'd teach someone to touch type or drive an automobile, something that, in time, becomes automatic.

I began to play with the idea that patterns of nurturing and limits were just skills that amounted to clusters of simple questions. With my colleagues Susan Johnson, M.D., and Lisa Frost, P.N.P., I taught the skills to families who had children with weight concerns at the university as part of a family-based pediatric obesity program, Shapedown, which is still provided by health professionals nationwide today.

There is something about nurturing and limits that seemed so "vanilla"— so warm and wonderful and . . . *boring*—that I was not at all prepared for the results I began to see, not just in one "star" participant but in most of those who used the method over the long term.

The first little girl whom I saw reach her Solution was ten years old. A cherubic child with curly brown hair, she had been obsessed with food since kindergarten. She and her parents had been practicing the skills for about fifteen weeks when her mother came to me, alarmed, incredulous, and grateful. She said, "I don't know *what's* going on, but this is *not* the same child. She doesn't even *want* the extra food, and she's so happy." The mother shook her head. "Weight and food are no longer issues in her life."

When adults began using the method, it took far longer for them to reach a Solution, but the quality of their experience was identical to the little girl's. It is amazing, even somewhat frightening to me that people who reach their Solution tend to use the *exact same words* to describe their experience: "It's the strangest thing, but I've stopped wanting it. It's not even hard. In fact, it is no longer an issue in my life." Since then, the method was adapted to adults with weight problems, then to those with any of the common excesses or who simply wanted more of life's sweetest rewards.

Retraining the feeling brain

I knew that the rather odd changes occurring for many of the people in our groups—emotional balance, relationship intimacy, spiritual connection, and letting go of one excess *without* taking up another—had to have a biological explanation. Emerging understandings of the way the brain works offered a potential one.

Most adults are familiar with the concept of a right brain and left brain, but few are aware of the triune brain, the three "brains" inside our skulls that form our central nervous system. They are the *thinking brain*, the *feeling brain*, and the *brain stem*. All three brains interact, but they have discrete roles.

The brain stem is what keeps people alive when they are "brain-dead," making the heart beat and the lungs work. It is also the seat of temperament, such as one's tendency to be depressed rather than hostile, to be introverted rather than extroverted, or to approach rather than withdraw.

The thinking brain is the seat of knowledge, insight, abstract thought, planning, intention, and decision-making. Most interventions designed to make us healthier or happier rely on insight, knowledge, decision-making, and planning, all of which are processed primarily by the thinking brain. Unfortunately, *there is no significant relationship between the most primitive human behaviors and what is processed by the thinking brain.* That's why one can have a Ph.D. in nutrition and also have an eating disorder, be a priest and have an affair, or have perfect insight into one's childhood but keep repeating its patterns. *Knowledge, insight, planning, and decisions are simply not enough.*

The feeling brain is our emotional core, responsible for our feelings and our emotional balance. It is also the seat of relatedness, as the resonance and harmony between two people is the work of the feeling brain. Since our passions are the impetus for every act

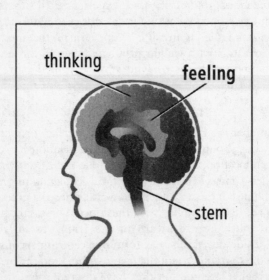

more complicated than a knee jerk, the feeling brain is key to our excessive appetites. As if that weren't enough, the feeling brain may also be the center of the soul, the bodily home of spirituality. It processes our experiences of transcendence, mystical union, and spiritual awakening.

If any intervention, no matter how well intentioned, does not affect the feeling brain, then lasting, broad-spectrum change is unlikely to occur. Transformation appears to be predicated on reaching into and revising the feeling brain, something that is not easy to do after the early years of life.

The feeling brain appears to be "programmed" early in life by *repeated contact* with the environment, typically between parent and child. The wiring is strengthened or weakened by the repeated experiences with those who take care of us. In other words, those close to us contribute to shaping our neural circuitry.

- **Parents with nurturing and limits skills are** *responsive*— If a parent has the skill to nurture and set limits from within, their repeated contact with the child is apt to be responsive. The neural networks in the child's feeling brain may be likely to favor a life of *balance*.
- **Parents without nurturing and limits skills are** *permissive or* depriving—Parents who love their children dearly but do not have the skills to nurture and set limits from within are likely to miss the mark of responsiveness and instead be permissive or depriving. The neural networks in the feeling brain may favor a life of *imbalance*.

When puberty arrives, the thinking brain develops more, and we preferentially process our lives by thinking and analyzing. Our thinking "shields" our feeling brain from the repeated contact with a responsive environment that could readily revise these neural networks to favor a life of balance. That is why most psychotherapists believe that, though adults can learn to cope better, a personal transformation after adolescence is unlikely. More often than not, change in adults is generally modest, short-term, and uneven, or there is an improvement in one area that is offset by more difficulties in another.

If we were raised in an environment that was depriving and/or indulging rather than responsive, and we have a feeling brain that is prone to imbalance, what are we to do? How can we reach into our emotional core and change it to favor a life of balance? The idea that limbic revision occurs remains controversial, but several potential avenues for revising it have been explored:

Drugs—Prescription drugs such as Prozac are used to promote emotional balance because they affect the feeling brain. Psychopharmacologic research is very active now, and some findings have been promising. However, both the results and side effects of these drugs are variable, and their long-term toxicity is not known.

Responsive partners—Love can heal, and the repeated contact with a responsive partner may revise the neural networks in the feeling brain to favor balance. Although it is comforting to think that our struggles can end by finding the "right" mate, this rarely occurs because we usually choose partners and close friends who are as below the line as we are. As a result, our partner often inadvertently reinforces the neural networks that favor imbalance.

Responsive therapists—What's more fascinating than seeing a therapist and gaining insight into why we do things or better understanding our childhood? Although therapy may be interesting, reassuring, and helpful, it is unlikely to penetrate the "thinking brain barrier" and soak into the feeling brain enough to revise it. Some therapists sidestep "figuring it out" and simply offer a loving relationship to their clients. Four to six years of that kind of therapy may supply the repeated contact with a responsive environment that can revise the feeling brain.

The skills of responsiveness—Another way to revise the neural networks in the feeling brain may be the training in this book. Just as repeated contact with a responsive environment early in life programmed the feeling brain for balance, repeated contact later in life with the skills of responsiveness can reprogram the brain to favor balance. Several observations support this possibility:

- **Children require less practice than adults**—Children, whose feeling brains eagerly soak up experiences from their environment, seem to reach a Solution rather rapidly. Adults require more repetition and take longer.

- **Adults who practice more see results sooner**—Progress in adults appears to be a function of how often and how effectively they do cycles.
- **Thinking-oriented adults require more practice**—Those who tend to *think* rather than *feel* take longer to reach a Solution. And those who are very smart by conventional standards, highly educated, or trained in an analytical field take even longer.
- **Changes often appear unconscious**—Changes don't appear to come primarily from willpower or intention, but from an unconscious change that decreases the drive to excess.
- **Progress appears to be broad-spectrum**—The repeated use of the skills typically affects many areas of emotional, behavioral, and spiritual life. The order in which those changes occur is not completely within an individual's control.
- **Improvements seem to have staying power**—Most traditional interventions rely on providing external sources of nurturing and limits. When that support is removed, rebounds often occur. When nurturing and limits are strengthened from within, the changes are more apt to last.

These days, astonishing quantities of resources are being devoted to research on altering genes and identifying designer drugs. Even more resources are allocated to taking medications and seeing counselors in hopes that they will help us solve our problems.

The implication is that *external* sources of nurturing and limits are the solution. The answer for eating too many potato chips is to take a pill that blocks fat absorption or suppresses our appetites. It is to rely on a counselor, diet coach, or support group to encourage us to stop eating. What happened to the concept of mastering the *internal* skills that enable us to encourage ourselves to curb excessive appetites? What about the idea of creating within ourselves such a capacity to nurture and set limits that we naturally close the bag *all by ourselves*?

What's more, human imbalance spawns many symptoms, and it's exhausting, expensive, and ineffective to treat them one by one. Life is anxiety-provoking, and what my mother calls "nerves" can readily prompt stomachaches, headaches, marital spats, and spending sprees. So we take one pill for anxiety, another to quiet our stomach, and a third for that pounding headache. We go to a group for our spending problem and see a counselor for our marital difficulties. It sounds exhausting, doesn't it?

There must be a better solution. What if we stopped focusing on the symptoms, stopped thinking about what is *wrong* with us, and stopped relying so heavily on external support? What if we simply trusted the inherent strength, goodness, and wisdom of the human spirit? What if we strengthened the skills that enable us to access what is *right* with us, then watched the symptoms, one by one, fade away?

Emotional, behavioral, and spiritual balance

A recent phone call from Donna, a heavyset nurse living in Silicon Valley who had reached her Solution, is typical. She called, eager to tell me of her experience that morning.

"I went to see my physician today. Dr. Marshall has been my doctor for ten years. He's a disagreeable little man who dislikes people who are overweight, including me. I've always felt invisible around him.

"Well, when I went to see him today, I changed into a paper gown, sat on the end of the examination table, and figured that he would come in and treat me as he always had before. True to form, Dr. Marshall strode briskly into the room, said hello, and shook my hand without even looking at me. He read my chart for a couple of moments, then looked up abruptly, peered straight into my eyes for the first time in a decade, and demanded, 'What's *happened* to you?'

"I felt flustered, and for a minute I didn't know what he was talking about. I said, 'I used The Solution and I lost 35 pounds.'

"Dr. Marshall shook his head, visibly upset, and said, 'No, no, that's not it. It has nothing to do with your weight. Donna, you are not the same person. *You* are a *different* person."

Donna gasped and so did I. It wasn't because Dr. Marshall had finally seen her or because she had lost weight, but because we both understood that her transformation was so profound that even a rather removed, excessively busy physician could not only see it but understood that it was not of this world.

One has to have some compassion for Dr. Marshall, for the

options he had to offer Donna to feel better and lose weight were limited. Pills and surgery weren't right for her, and any information or advice he could give would be processed primarily by the thinking brain.

That is a problem for Dr. Marshall as well as for all of us. If most of the available treatments designed to make us feel healthier and happier are aimed at the part of the brain that is *not* primarily responsible for emotional balance, relationship intimacy, spiritual connection, and excessive appetites, results would not be expected to be impressive.

When we use those therapies we pour into them not only our time and money but our opportunity and hope and often are not only disappointed, but may blame ourselves rather than pointing our fingers at the inadequacy of the methods. We might even begin to believe that somehow we are different, that the joys and freedoms others experience were somehow crossed off our list before birth or soon thereafter. We may believe that our particular dreams are not important and will *never* come true.

My experience has been that most people aren't disappointed with the results they experience with The Solution. Most call the skills "life savers." Not only do they feel better, but they are relieved from the burden of thinking something is inherently "wrong" with them. The method is not based on *dependency*, on ongoing use of a group, a therapist, a pill, but on *freedom*. We practice the skills, and when we have mastered them, *we are done*. The skills live inside us, and our attention can turn to going about our lives, doing what we came to Earth to do, and enjoying various pleasures—flying kites, making love, or eating strawberries in bed. Whatever nourishes our spirit.

To begin to access the power of this method, consider developing a vision of yourself more like the child you were than the adult you have become. Imagine yourself standing at the base of your particular tree, with all your innocence and inherent goodness, and looking straight up until you see quite clearly what you most want in this lifetime. In other words, begin by being willing to have a dream.

2. The 2 Skills

I t's not that I intentionally stopped dreaming," said Emily, a blonde in her midforties with red spectacles perched halfway down her Anglican nose, "but my life got busy, and the years went by in a flash." Emily lived in an affluent area in the heart of San Francisco with her husband, Clay, an orthopedic surgeon, and their three children, all of whom had serious physical or emotional difficulties.

Emily's childhood dream was to be a pianist. She was schooled at the local conservatory and continued to study piano after college, but the birth of their first child, Rob, who had developmental disabilities, changed everything. Her whole day became focused on caretaking, much as it had been when she was a child and her father would come home in the evening exhausted from his factory job. Her mother was chronically ill with migraines and asthma, and Emily had virtually raised her sister and herself, all while fetching dinner for the family and folding laundry late at night.

Now that Emily's children were older and more independent, on the advice of her closest friend, she enrolled in our group. But she wasn't completely sure what she most wanted from using the method.

No time to honor her passions

During Emily's first meeting, she told the group, "Between Rob's speech therapy, my daughter Nicole's asthma, and Angela's learning problems, there hasn't been any time to dream my own dreams or honor my own passions."

The room was quiet. For many, Emily's words could have been their own.

Emily continued, smoothing her blond hair and adjusting her glasses. "I love my family. I want them to be happy, and I do everything I possibly can for them, but I'm afraid that I've lost my own spirit in recent years. I'm scared to death that when I finally wake up, it will be too late."

Like Emily, most of us wanted *something* as children. That sweetest fruit turned up in our fantasies and daydreams. As adults, many of us, out of necessity, replace those purest longings with the more sobering preoccupations of mature life. In that sad shift, our passion for life in general, and for our own lives in particular, may well be lost.

"Emily," I said, "you don't have to know what you want right now. In time, you will need to know . . ."

"The reason I'm doing this work is to regain my life as a person, apart from taking care of everyone else's life. I'm here to wake myself up."

I nodded.

She continued, "It bothers me that I don't have anything more specific than that. How do I know what I most want?"

"That's easy," I answered. "You use the skills."

"I don't know how to do that."

"It's not hard, and you can start slowly. You might want to start asking yourself the first question of the nurturing cycle: 'How do I feel?'"

The conventional marks of success don't help

Emily seemed to be thinking-oriented and smart, an unfortunate combination. She would have a strong proclivity to think her way out of problems, a surefire way to avoid emotional maturity. It was only by being willing to take a big, deep breath and surrender to the hotbed of feelings under those well-crafted thoughts that she would progress.

What's more, she was pretty, with silken blond hair containing neither dark roots nor stray hairs of gray; perfectly groomed; well-educated; and worst of all, charming. She had been lulled into relying on these qualities to get her way, yet in this training they were of no use of all.

Another disadvantage for Emily was that although her life had been difficult and she had always taken the caretaker role, she was, quite frankly, a little spoiled. The flip side of deprivation is indulgence, and to balance her hardships, Emily had developed a way of being far too easy on herself. When life became difficult, she sank into eating sweets, spending money, or the comfort of self-pity. What's more, as the wife of a wealthy man who loved her, she had been spared some of the grit of life, such as worrying about grocery money or awakening in the middle of the night feeling bone-chillingly alone. Moreover, I would come to learn, those close to Emily saw her as highly sensitive and very vulnerable, so they spared her some of the normal confrontations that take place in close relationships.

I was worried about Emily. I wondered whether she would stay on the pathway until she reached her Solution, or become so mollified by her many blessings that she would miss out on reaching her Solution.

I suggested again, "Emily, consider asking yourself, 'How do I feel?'"

She said, "How do I feel? I feel . . . I don't *know* how I feel. I know how Clay feels and how Rob, Nicole, and Angela feel, but I don't know a *thing* about how I feel."

I shrugged. "It's okay. You don't need to know. Just keep asking yourself that question, and in time, the answer will pop into your mind. I promise. It's only a matter of practice."

Emily said, "My natural state is to be numb or depressed. I've learned not to feel my feelings because when I do, I get depressed. It's better for me to shut them off."

Several members of the group let out faint murmurs of understanding.

"Is it really better?" I asked.

"Yes."

"Yes?"

"No, but it's better than feeling depressed."

I nodded. "You're right. Feeling your feelings is dangerous until you have the other skills to keep them from going off an emotional cliff into depression."

Emily nodded in appreciation.

"I wouldn't ask you to feel your feelings unless I planned to give you some safety nets to keep them balanced."

"Good," she said.

"Would you be willing to try again? 'How do I feel?'"

She opened her mouth, but nothing came out. "I hate this. I feel so *stupid*. I'm an accomplished person. I compose music. I am fluent in Japanese. But when it comes to knowing how I feel . . . I flunk!" She was wide-eyed, part scared, part furious.

The man sitting next to her chuckled.

"What feeling are you feeling right now?" I asked.

"Scared to death," she said.

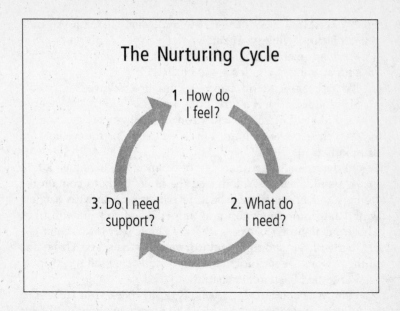

The Nurturing Cycle

1. How do I feel?

2. What do I need?

3. Do I need support?

"What is the basic feeling under that? Angry, sad, afraid, guilty?"

"I feel . . . afraid," said Emily.

"Excellent. You're already getting it."

She nodded, half frowning.

Feeling the feeling and letting it fade

I continued. "You feel afraid. All you have to do is feel that feeling and let it fade. Don't censor it, figure it out, or cut it off with a thought. You can do this."

Emily sat still for a couple of moments, then her face went blank. "It didn't fade. I just went numb."

"That's fine. The feeling arose, right?"

"Yes."

"Then it shut down?"

"Exactly," replied Emily.

"Instead of panicking or telling yourself that you can't possibly ever learn to feel and that you are already a tremendous failure at this work . . ."

"How did you know?" She smiled, slightly.

". . . just take a big deep breath and wait. There's no rush. In time, a feeling will arise again."

She was quiet for about two minutes.

"It's starting again. It's a good feeling . . ."

"What is it—grateful, happy, secure, proud, loved?"

She nodded. "I feel a little bit . . . proud."

"Fabulous. But you've had stronger feelings . . ."

"Much stronger feelings. I'm either numb or the feelings are dripping off me."

"If the feelings were more out of balance, when you felt a feeling, it wouldn't fade. You'd need the limits cycle to contain the feelings and bring yourself back to balance. Otherwise, sadness would fall into depression and anger would fall into hostility. Those unbalanced feelings—either way high, way low, or numb—dig in their heels and turn on the drive to go to excess. This is one of the reasons the nurturing and limits skills are used together."

She settled back in her chair.

"Emily," I continued, "do you want to check your feelings?"

With exasperation, she said, "No! I want some limits! I have *none* whatsoever. I can't say no to anyone; that's why it's so hard

The Limits Cycle

1. Are my expectations reasonable?

2. Is my thinking positive and powerful?

3. What is the essential pain and the earned reward?

for me to have any control over my life. And I'm a quitter. I start things and don't finish them, and I'm not at all sure that I will finish this training. Besides, I know that I will fail. Other people in the room will get their Solution, but I know for sure that I will not."

Emily was showing perfectly normal feelings for those starting their climb. She was right to have fears. After all, it is unsettling to not be "good" at something; there is always the risk of not doing it "right." It takes time and work to build these skills, and Emily wasn't used to committing time and hard work to her own personal development. But I was less worried about Emily now. She was upset enough that she would probably start using the skills and once she was using them, her passion for the work would likely carry her up and over the various challenges on the climb.

The skill to get above the line

I offered, "Emily, are you below the line?"

"Yes. Very."

"Would you like to do your first cycle and get above the line?" She was eager to get some relief. "Definitely."

"What you're going to experience is being thoroughly out of balance, below the line . . ."

"Yes."

"Then you'll take out your tool kit of these skills, use them, and watch yourself pop above the line, into a state of balance."

"I don't know how to do that," said Emily.

"You don't have to. That's why I'm here. Just pretend I'm your hairstylist. You sit in the chair, and I'll help you use the skills."

"Good, I'd like that."

"You are upset about a lot of things. Why don't you choose one of them to do cycles on?"

"What do you think I should do them on?" Emily asked.

"Only you know."

"No, I don't."

"There is no rush, Emily. Take all the time you need."

She was quiet for several minutes.

"Okay, what disturbs me is that I'm so emotionally fragile, and such a wimp, that I don't have any backbone. I just do what I *should* do rather than what *I* want to do. I just keep rolling along in my life, taking care of everyone, then feeling depressed and powerless. I have so many things to be grateful for—my husband, my children, my home. Why can't I just be happy? I hate it!"

The Natural Flow of Feelings . . .

"Emily, your thoughts are moving into feelings. You're off to a good start. Start the Natural Flow of Feelings, feeling each feeling, then expressing it. Start with anger, then sadness, then fear, and finally guilt."

Her face was full of feeling, and I pushed on.

"Emily, focus on your body and wait for each feeling to rise up from your belly. Express it in the most basic way. Don't say it like a teacher or composer. Just use the simplest language: short, chopped sentences. Empty out an entire feeling, and when it has faded, go on to the next feeling."

"Okay, but I don't feel anger, I feel sadness," she responded.

"That's fine, but please take all the time you need. There is no rush. If you will, take a moment and double-check for anger, just in case."

Emily paused, then her eyes widened, "There it is . . . I feel *angry* that my mother was so needy. . . . I *hate* it that my dad was not there. . . . I feel *angry* they didn't give me these skills. . . . I hate it that I get so depressed . . . which makes me sad . . ."

"Beautifully done, Emily. Go into your body, check for sadness, then spit it out. 'I feel sad that . . .'"

"I feel sad that I get so depressed. . . . I feel sad that I am not happier. . . . I feel afraid that I'll *never* be happy. . . . I feel afraid there is something very wrong with me. . . . I feel guilty . . ." Emily stopped. "I don't feel guilty. I don't feel guilty at all. This is *not* my fault."

For many people, the feelings that are the hardest to master are anger and guilt.

"Emily," I suggested, "guilt is very different from shame. Consider thinking about guilt as *what my part of it was*. Knowing your part of it gives you power, for you could do it differently next time."

"I don't like being wrong," said Emily.

"How sad," I said.

"What do you mean?"

"If you don't like being wrong, it means that as a kid, it wasn't safe to make a mistake. You didn't get the message that you were loved regardless, even though your parents set limits with your behavior."

"I don't think my parents set limits. My situation set limits. I had to take care of everyone, and I had to do it right or there was trouble."

"The 'I feel guilty' skill will be healing for you. You can treat yourself differently than you were treated early in life. Let's make this easier; there is no one right way to use this method. Instead of saying, 'I feel guilty that . . . ,' you might prefer to say, 'In the best of all worlds, I wish that I had . . . ' "

Emily jumped in. "In the best of all worlds, I wish that I had screamed and yelled at my parents and gotten their attention. . . .

Doing Cycles

When you are out of balance, this particular way of using the skills is very effective.

1. **The Thinking Journal:**
   Prepare to use the skills by stating the facts about what is upsetting you. Include *no* feelings, only *facts*.

2. **Use the first part of *Step 1, the nurturing cycle*, by expressing the Natural Flow of Feelings:**
   "I feel angry that . . ."
   "I feel sad that . . ."
   "I feel afraid that . . ."
   "I feel guilty that . . ."

3. **Use *Step 2, the limits cycle*, to pop yourself above the line:**
   "Are my expectations reasonable?"
   "Is my thinking positive and powerful?"
   "What is the essential pain?"
   "What is the earned reward?"

4. **Now complete *Step 1, the nurturing cycle*:**
   "What do I need?"
   "Do I need support?"

Congratulate yourself on completing your first cycle!

In the best of all worlds, I wish that I never got depressed."

"Emily, the power of the 'I feel guilty' skill rests on your saying precisely what your contribution was, not what the situation is."

She nodded. "I feel guilty that I take a certain passive joy in feeling bad. I wallow in my depression and relish my self-pity rather than pulling myself out of it."

Emily was quiet for a moment, then said, "Also, I feel guilty that I have so many blessings but don't appreciate what I have."

Emily grew quiet. Usually when we finally express the feeling we block the most, it gushes out—just as it did for Emily.

"Are you done?" I asked.

She nodded.

"You did a great job! Your first Natural Flow of Feelings. Do you feel better?"

Emily smiled meekly and nodded. "Yes, somewhat."

"When you're ready, we can move over to the limits cycle. Effective limits create power and safety in our lives."

"I know, and I told you I have none."

"How do you know?"

"I just know."

How happy do you expect to be?

"Okay, what is the unreasonable expectation at the root of the feelings you just expressed?"

"I take it back. I do have limits. It's just that my expectations are nonexistent or incredibly harsh, as if there is only *one right way* to do something: perfectly."

Several people in the room groaned or smiled with understanding. "So," I said, "under all those feelings that you just expressed, what is the unreasonable expectation?"

Emily's face turned blank. Then she said, "My unreasonable expectation is that I should be perfectly happy all the time and should *never* be depressed."

That made her laugh. Then Emily turned sober: "Can you imagine how mean that is? My expectations are even harsher than those my dad had. I can't *believe* I'm doing that to myself."

"And the reasonable expectation, the expectation that is reasonable for who you are right now?" I asked.

"What is reasonable for who I am? I don't know."

"Everyone is different," I said. "It may be a reasonable

expectation that you are happy sometimes and depressed sometimes."

Emily immediately responded, "My reasonable expectation is that sometimes I'm happy and sometimes I'm depressed."

"Emily, just because I threw out that expectation doesn't mean it's right for you. It's important to me that you go inside yourself and find what is reasonable for who you are at this time. The power of the method is based on intimacy with yourself. All The Solution does is give you the practice that enables you to build that intimacy, brick by brick by brick. The method is the questions, but only you can answer those questions."

Emily continued with her cycle. "It's a reasonable expectation, given the skills I have now, that I will be depressed much of the time. But as I increase my skills, it's a reasonable expectation that I will stop being depressed."

"Emily, is it a reasonable expectation that, even after you master these skills, no circumstance—not death, sickness, job losses, or world events—will ever trigger you to be depressed again?"

Emily shook her head, smiled at herself, and said, "No, that's not reasonable."

"So the reasonable expectation, again, is . . ."

"It is a reasonable expectation, given my skills, that for now I will be depressed sometimes. But as I master the skills, I will be happy more of the time."

"Fabulous. Now, you need to nail down that expectation and make it strong. Just use the rest of the questions of the cycle."

"Okay. Is my thinking positive and powerful?" Emily thought. "Absolutely not! Do you know what I say to myself automatically? 'I'll never be happy.'"

"No wonder you feel so awful. What could you say to yourself that would be positive and powerful, that would support and encourage your new, reasonable expectation?"

Emily said, "My positive, powerful thought is: 'I am capable of creating more happiness in my life.'"

"That was wonderful," I said with a smile. Several people in the group responded with nods of encouragement. What a great expectation for her very first cycle!

"Emily, the last questions of the limits cycle are the most powerful; you can feel the developmental shift. If you answer those two questions from the bottom of your heart, from a deep sense of knowing yourself, you will pop yourself above the line. It's an amazing experience, one you will create over and over again as you use the method. Your blood pressure will drop, your body will relax, and you'll feel a rush of peace, joy, and power."

Feeling the essential pain pops us above the line

The essential pain is the downside, the risk, the reality of the human condition you must face to follow through with your reasonable expectation. The earned reward is the upside, the advantage, the blessing of life you will receive if you follow through. Experiencing them over and over is how we retrain our feeling brain and grow ourselves up from the inside out.

The longer you use the method, the more you will notice astonishing patterns in yourself. For example, you will recognize the same essential pains coming up over and over again. These essential pains are typically the realities of life and the truths about the human condition that your early environment did not prepare you to accept. Examples are: I'm not in complete control. Some people will reject me. Life is difficult. I can't always get my way and, most important, I am alone.

If you feel that essential pain over and over again by *practicing* the method, you will, at some point, accept that reality of the human condition—not just intellectually but emotionally and spiritually. Life begins to change. You accept and move gracefully through the unavoidable pain of life and sidestep the avoidable pain. Examples are: I have some control, and I can use it. Others may not like me, but I like myself. Life is difficult, but there are tremendous joys. I can't always get what I want, but sometimes I can! I am alone, but I have myself (and if it is my belief, I have the spiritual).

When I first explained this to Emily, her response was clear.

"That," she said determinedly, "is precisely what I want."

"You're doing the perfect thing, Emily, just by being willing to do your first cycle. They will get easier and easier to do. So, for you, Emily, what is the essential pain that you will have to face to follow through with your new reasonable expectation?"

"I am a person who is prone to depression. Now I get depressed a lot. As I gain these skills, I'll be depressed less often. That makes me depressed."

"What is the essential pain you would have to face?"

"That I am not perfect."

"That you are not perfect."

"Yes."

"Emily, say it again, and as you do, notice that feelings arise from those words, like steam rising off boiling water. See if you can feel the feelings in your body and just stay with those feelings until they fade, which they naturally will."

Emily nodded and a minute or two passed. When I saw the expression of her face shift and lighten, I said, "Now check for the earned reward, the natural benefit of following through."

She closed her eyes for another moment, then a warmth and joy spread over her face. "The essential pain is that I'm not perfect. The earned reward is that I don't have to be."

Emily was smiling more widely than I had ever seen. She had popped herself above the line, and everyone in the room was moved by her work. When you listen to someone do cycles, the questions and the responses feed you as well, strengthening your skills and awakening the spirit within you.

Yet Emily was not done.

Now that you're above the line . . .

"Emily, you've used the Natural Flow of Feelings to know and honor yourself. You've used the limits cycle to pop yourself above the line and create safety and power. Now that you are above the line, you can identify what you really need and ask for the support to make it easier to meet that need."

"What I need is . . . to be more compassionate with myself and to remind myself that I don't have to be perfect to be wonderful. I need to do the best I can to begin using the cycles."

"Do you need support?"

"No."

"I know you're accustomed to doing everything yourself, but if you're willing, please consider what support you could ask for that would feel safe to you."

"I could use some support from Clay. I could ask him to listen to me do cycles on this."

"How do you feel, Emily?"

She thought for a moment. "Great. I feel happy and relaxed . . . and proud."

I was happy, too. She had done her first cycle and done it

well. She took out her tool kit of skills and popped herself above the line. Yet the dominant neural networks in her feeling brain did not favor this state of balance, and I knew that she would soon find herself below the line again.

Several weeks later, Emily was still searching for what she most wanted in this life. She was frustrated and expressed her exasperation to the group:

"I can't *stand* it that I keep forgetting to check how I feel. I know I should be checking, but I don't. I just go numb or go into my own world of feeling sorry for myself, content to feel blue.

"I'm noticing these patterns in myself that I was never aware of. Already I can see how often I am not just depressed, but off in a fantasy world, and how frequently I numb out and have no feelings at all. What I hate about it the most is that I am not in complete control of when it will be clear to me what I really want. This is really hard!"

I responded, "Of course it is, but it becomes easier and easier in time. I'm not concerned about what answers you come up with right now. The most important thing to me is that you keep asking yourself the questions 'How do I feel?' and 'What do I need?' In time, the answer that is true for you will become clear."

Emily's sweetest fruit: Balance

It took about three weeks of asking herself these questions before Emily thought she knew what she most wanted in life. She arrived early to the group meeting, and the words spilled out of her exuberantly.

"I did it!" she told me. "I know what I most want in life, and it is not to be a concert pianist or a perfect mother. It is something much more basic that that. It is emotional balance.

"When I was a child, my mother always told me that I was too sensitive, and my husband is often frustrated with me because I take offense so easily, so I think that my basic personality is prone to having my feelings hurt and having emotional problems. My sweetest fruit is definitely emotional balance. I truly believe that if I have enough of these skills to be emotionally balanced, the rest of my dreams—whether they have to do with mothering, piano, or who knows what—will fall into place."

Emily had accomplished a great deal: being willing to dream, identifying that dream, and jumping in and using the skills for the first time. She had already started the climb.

3. A Simple Pathway

Unlike Emily, Tom had identified what he most wanted in life when he was four years old. Yet several decades later, after he had vigorously pursued and then reached that goal, he came to the crushing realization that the dream he had followed was empty.

When Tom came to his first session with me—he was not willing to consider participating in a group—my first impression was that he was a very attractive man who had a certain charming ease about him. He had very dark brown hair, a boyish grin, and a tall, slender build and was immaculately attired in what must have been an Armani suit.

He settled into the chair across from mine and said, "I'm here to see you only because I'm desperate and confused. I don't know how I got from having a pretty good childhood to a life that has so many problems. I want to figure out what happened."

I said, "In this work, we don't try to figure anything out." He stopped for a moment, met my eyes with a menacing stare, then continued.

"I have a half-dozen problems that I could name off the top of my head."

"You don't need to do that, Tom. They are all just problems, which I would encourage you to think of as apples on a tree."

At this point, I supposed that Tom was both worried I was crazy and mildly intrigued by this metaphor. In this method, we use a lot of basic images because it is the concrete-thinking kid in us, not the sophisticated, abstract-thinking adult, who requires our tending. Intellectualizing only impedes progress toward a Solution.

"When apples are very ripe," I continued, "they naturally fall off the tree. Your job is to feed the tree by watering the roots. Each time you use the nurturing skill, it splashes a little water on the tree. Each time you use the limits skill, another splash of water goes to its roots. Just focus on feeding the tree, then step back and watch the apples drop off. That is what I can help you do."

Tom fidgeted in his chair, then seemed to relax, but only slightly. "You still want to figure it out," I observed.

"Right."

I shrugged, he said. "I can help you this much: There is a simple and clear pathway into a life of disappointment and an equally simple and clear pathway out."

"You don't know my background, and if you did, you wouldn't say that. I'm not an easy case, and I'm very slippery," Tom said coldly.

You can't buy the skills, you can only earn them

I smiled to myself, wanting to give this man a hug. How brave he was to show up and talk about the method, and how wonderful it was that he was willing to be so direct. Of course he was slippery! Why would an overly intelligent, highly successful man want to go into the hot cauldron of his feelings over and over again and bring them back to balance? In the back of his mind, Tom was likely to be holding out hope that he could buy relief from his troubles—a new sound system, a better car, a younger, more fit woman—or that if he could just analyze things well enough, the problems would disappear and he wouldn't need to do this work.

"I grew up as one of a handful of smart kids in a small community in rural Georgia," he told me. "I knew from the age of four that I didn't like being poor and that what I wanted most in life was what people on television had: money. So I had a good time in school, but I made sure that I did well enough to get into the University of Georgia, then found my way into Boalt Law School and eventually passed the bar exam."

As Tom patiently laid out the details of his early life, I was struck by the contrast between the image of the scruffy poor boy from rural Georgia and the man before me with not one hair out of place, nor one piece of lint on his dark blue suit.

"I went right to work for a law firm that I am still with now, twenty years later." He named the firm, one that was quite large and well respected.

Tom continued. "With the billable hours I was putting in, I began to make more money than I had ever dreamed possible, but the price I paid for it over the years was high. I worked 60-hour weeks and spent half my time on the road, so I couldn't be as involved as I wanted to be with my children.

"On the day that I finally made partner in my firm, I had more money than I would ever need. But I awoke that morning feeling alone and sick. I wasn't hung over or sleep-deprived—I just felt terribly alone."

Tom paused then, seemingly filled with the pain of that memory. Finally, he went on.

"My sons were in college, and the younger one, Nick, was so mad at me that we hadn't spoken in months. As it is, they both tend to call me only when they want money. I live alone—my wife, Karen, and I parted two years ago. She complained about my drinking and accused me of being emotionally detached. Finally, she said that if I didn't get help for my drinking, she would leave. By that time I was fed up, too, so I let her go. I essentially bought her off, hoping she would not hold a grudge or badmouth me to the boys, particularly about my drinking."

His face was sad.

"The truth is that I was probably more lonely than she was. I had stopped trying to communicate with her long ago, and she slept so far on the other side of the bed that she almost fell off the edge!"

Tom looked at me beseechingly, as if to be sure that I understood his frustration and pain.

"It sounds as if you were thoroughly miserable and in a totally impossible situation," I said.

"That's right; I felt like I had nowhere to turn. Part of me wanted to get in my car and drive to Alaska and never come back. The other part of me didn't want a divorce because I still loved my wife. But I had no idea how to deal with her. Yes, I drank a bottle or more of wine at night or sometimes had some scotch, but I did it after the boys were in bed, and it was the best I could do to deal with a stressful situation."

His anguish was palpable. "Tell me more," I said.

Spinning new dreams . . .

"The morning of the day I made partner, I realized that my childhood dream had come true, but I also knew that it wasn't the right dream for me. The moment that it was clear to me was intensely painful but oddly pleasurable," he said.

Someone knocked on my office door, but I didn't respond. Tom went on.

"I allowed myself to feel as bad as I've ever felt, and the

underbelly of that pain was having a vibrant, almost electric sense of being alive. It was then that I asked myself in the deepest possible way, 'What do I *really* want most in my life?' "

Tom was quiet, seemingly lost in the emotional memories of that riveting moment.

"What was your answer?" I asked. "If you could have anything in the world, Tom, anything at all, what would that be?"

Again, he was quiet for some time, then his face softened and he said, "Intimacy. That is the one thing that would complete my life."

Tom could easily have said that what he most wanted was to stop overworking or to drink less. Indeed, turning off those drives may be necessary for him to secure more intimacy in his life. Yet those changes may only be midway up the tree, not at the top, the touchstone of his personal balance.

It was extremely important that Tom identify what he most wanted in life, for those who reach the top of the tree are typically motivated by both a clear vision of what they want and an intense passion to get it. Tom may *know* that he should work less or *think* that he ought to cut back on his drinking, but it's unlikely that those goals would prompt him to practice the skills often enough and deeply enough to reach the top. Tom's face still looked strained as he said, "I can't believe that this is happening to me, that I have this big mess on my hands."

When our dreams don't come true, sometimes the hardest part is the confusion. Understanding how one walks into these difficulties and how one retraces those steps and walks out of them can be an enormous relief.

In the beginning,
there was balance.

"Tom, may I tell you a story?" I asked.

Tom nodded. He was very ready to listen, for he had disclosed so much to me yet hadn't received what he really wanted.

"I promise you that there was a time in your life when there was balance, a time when you were fully aware of yourself, connected to the inherent strength, goodness, and wisdom within you. There was a safe place inside for you to go, a sanctuary.

"Perhaps this state of balance only occurred when you were in the womb, or it may have lasted after birth for a few years or for many. It's important for you to envision yourself being in balance, because it's a semblance of that state of balance to which you will return when you have mastered these skills and have intimacy in your life."

Tom blinked. "I really don't know. I had a pretty uneventful childhood, and I lived in a small town, which was ideal for memories of baseball games and neighborhood barbecues. I was president of the student body and a jock. It's hard to remember the first few years."

"All I ask is that you keep that idea in mind."

"Okay."

"Another way to think of that inherent balance with which you were born is that it was like a cord of pure gold in your very core that runs through your entire body. Everyone has one. Even you."

Tom blinked. Seemingly struck by the idea that he was no different. He had the capacity for a warm, nurturing inner life, too.

"As we grew up, each time we were touched by a nurturing act or word, another golden thread wrapped around that cord within us, making us stronger, more capable of staying in balance and better able to soothe and comfort ourselves from within. Each loving limit that gave us just the safety we required wrapped another golden thread around that cord, too. As we came of age, we were strong and secure inside with a strong, flexible golden cord within had mastery of these skills."

"That wasn't my childhood," said Tom abruptly, his eyes wide.

"It wasn't?"

"No. When she talks, my mom doesn't say anything. My dad was critical and not close to me. He was a good man and my mom loved him, but he wasn't a source of . . . ," Tom looked for the right word, then said, ". . . love in my life. He was the night watchman at a factory near town. For fun, he would go fishing, and he was good at it, but he never took me with him or taught me how. In fact, most things guys learn from their fathers. I don't know."

Tom shrugged, still looking sad.

"Not too many golden threads," I said quietly.

"No, not very many," he said.

"I am sorry."

"My parents were hardworking people," he said. "They did the best they could."

I took a deep breath. This work was painful but the alternative was worse.

Tom shifted in his chair, and I feared that I would lose him. "Without nurturing and limits, we don't develop nurturing and limits skills, so more bad things happen, and when they do, there is no tender touch, understanding ear, or loving tone to heal those hurts. The feelings go underground, mount up, and form emotional trash inside."

Tom cut to the chase. "Baggage?" he inquired.

"Lots of it. Emotional upsets from the past plus whatever upsets there are now . . ."

"Like dealing with a hostile ex-wife, greedy children, and demanding clients?" he said with a slight snarl. Now the sharpness of his hostile side was appearing.

I smiled, purposely relaxing in response to his tightness. "Precisely."

Tom unbuttoned his jacket and sat back in his chair.

We both paused a moment, waiting for the air of tension to clear a bit.

"I want you to understand how you walked into this problem," I said.

He nodded.

"Without the nurturing and limits you needed in your early environment and with the unhealed hurts going underground, the emotions piled up. At some point, they piled up so much that it was no longer soothing and comforting to go inside yourself. There was no sanctuary within. The distress from the current upsets and from the stockpile of emotional trash was too much."

Tom leaned forward in his chair, listening intently.

I continued. "It only makes sense that if you can't soothe and comfort from within, you would . . ."

He shot a response ". . . soothe and comfort from outside."

"Precisely. You use external solutions to feel better. It could be overexercise, overdrinking, overeating, overworking, whatever. There are no judgments, because the drive to go to excess is perfectly logical. If you can't go inside, you go outside. What external solution you use is not completely within your control."

Tom's face clouded. "I don't share your view. I think what I do is wrong."

"Is that what Karen told you?"

Tom was startled. "Yes. She told me I was an alcoholic and that I was killing myself."

"Were you?" I asked.

"I was killing our relationship."

Tom and I were both silent.

*With few skills and more emotional
trash, distress mounts.*

"Tom, only you know about your drinking, but apart from the alcohol or any other external solutions you used . . ."

". . . working, television, having the best materially . . ."

". . . there were worse losses."

He listened.

"When we abandon our pipeline to our own common sense, emotional intuition, and spiritual grace, we lose a lot. There are at least four things that happen. One is that . . . you enjoy wine, right?"

"Yes, I've always enjoyed fine wine."

"A source of pleasure becomes a source of pain. A pleasant spending spree erupts into a financial disaster, an appetite for a couple of cookies becomes a craving for the whole bag, and those lovely sips of wine turn into downing the entire bottle."

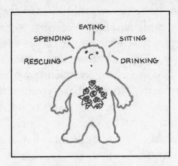

*At some point, balance is lost,
rewards are few, and excesses flourish.*

Tom asked, "Where is the line between wine as a source of pleasure and wine as an external solution?"

"When it causes you to disconnect from yourself."

"So how many drinks can I have?"

"I don't know. How many can you have without abandoning yourself?"

Tom thought, then responded, "Two, maybe three."

He appeared to be mulling that number over in his mind.

"Tom, the second difficulty that comes from using external solutions is that the problem causes hurts.

Tom turned irritable. "I already know that."

I was quiet.

"Arguments, rash words, smashed plates, loneliness . . ." Tom sighed, then nodded, as if to signal me to continue.

"So you have more unhealed hurts, more emotional trash. The more emotional trash you have, the more readily present upsets trigger you to go below the line."

"As if I'm sitting on a keg of dynamite."

I nodded.

"Third, most people try to control their behavior. They put a lot of energy into trying to figure out why they do what they do, obsessing about how bad it is, which draws them further away from connecting with themselves, further away from that which will lead to a Solution."

Tom rubbed his chin. "I do that. I either completely block out what's going on or obsess about it. I wake up in the night, obsess about what's wrong, and plan how to fix it."

The last effect is the most important one and the least pleasant."

"So far, nothing you've said has been very pleasant," said Tom, now beginning to tease.

I pressed ahead. "The last effect is that we stop maturing."

"I wish I hadn't come here," said Tom, only half musing.

"Once we take our fingers off the pulse of our inner lives, we do not grow, change, or evolve. We keep repeating the same patterns, working hard but not getting anywhere."

"Why?" he asked.

"When we're below the line, using external solutions, we're high, low, or numb. There isn't a balanced feeling in sight. In essence, we're detached from the current reality, so we don't experience the moment, feel the true pains and the joys, and learn, change, and grow."

Tom was excited. "That's me. I look like I'm grown up, and I feel grown up in certain circumstances—in court, when I'm with my buddies, and when I work out at the gym—but when it comes to relationships, I feel like I'm about twelve years old."

I smiled. "Twelve?"

"Yes, twelve."

"You might find it interesting to pinpoint when your maturation slowed, when you went from soothing and comforting yourself from within to using external solutions."

Tom shifted in his chair, leaned back, and rested his head against the backrest. He closed his eyes for a few moments, then said, "I'm not sure. When I was a kid, I coped by leaving, and that was at about the age of seven. That's when I decided that I wasn't going to stay at home if I could help it. I played outside all the time, baseball games and shooting hoops with my friends. When I started smoking dope in college, I smoked what must have been thousands of joints, thousands! When I started with my firm, I switched to wine, but only a few glasses at night, rarely more."

He thought for a while, then said, "I don't know if I used external solutions during those years. You could probably call working an external solution, but I don't think it was at first. I tried to make money in a driven sort of way, but given my background of poverty, I think that was normal. At some point, I think the power and money became external solutions, but I'm not sure exactly when."

"When we had our second child, Nick, that's when Karen and I started having problems. I began to drink more and work more . . . and obsess more. I didn't sleep well, between the boys waking up and worrying about cases."

"So," I said, "you're beginning to form a picture in your mind of how you walked into this situation. You didn't get the nurturing and limits you needed. Emotional trash built up, and at some point, you could no longer go inside to soothe and comfort, so you went outside."

"Right," said Tom.

I shrugged. "So that's all there really is to know. You walk out of these difficulties by retracing your steps into them. Taking out emotional trash, muscling up on the skills, and, in general, wrapping your own golden threads around the cord within you."

Tom said, "You don't understand. I don't have a clue where to begin. I have absolutely no capacity to do what you're talking about. I'm not an inside kind of a guy. I not only can't do this, I don't *want* to do it. I don't have time for threads."

"I completely understand. Why would you?"

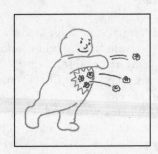

*When you increase the skills and
take out emotional trash,
distress subsides.*

Tom went on. "I don't have many memories from childhood, and certainly not any huge traumas or horror stories. I remember spending most of my time outside playing ball. In a way, I had a great childhood, even though I was never particularly close to anyone."

I nodded and waited.

"The last thing I want to do at my age is to treat myself like a 'project' and excavate my inner life looking for garbage from my past. Who knows what ugliness could come out? I don't want to deal with it!"

"If you don't want to deal with it, then don't deal with it. The only reason people bother to take out emotional trash is to be less controlled by their past. If the past doesn't impact on your drive to drink or your love life, why bother?"

Tom looked perturbed. "Okay, just tell me. How do you take out emotional trash?"

"You use the two skills."

"I don't know what you mean," he said.

"When you're out of balance and you know that it's out of proportion to what's really happening in the present, it's probably emotional trash cropping up. For example—"

Tom interjected, "When Nick calls from college and wants to borrow five hundred dollars to go with his girlfriend to Mexico for spring break, like he did yesterday."

"Right. What happened?" I asked.

"I started hollering at him right there in my office, with my partner sitting across from me. I tore into him something awful."

"Then what did you do?"

"I hung up on him. I told him I was busy."

"You solved that problem!" I mused.

Tom went on. "Last night I called him back and gave him one thousand dollars, no strings attached."

"The lion became the lamb?"

"The marshmallow is more like it," answered Tom.

"Was your anger only from the present or from the past, too?"

Tom said, "He makes impossible demands of me, I flip out and scream at him, then completely buckle and give him more than he asked for to start with."

"So you were out of balance from what was happening right then?"

Tom was struggling. "No, it reminds me of something from before."

"What?"

"Lots of things."

I was quiet, and after a moment, Tom continued.

"My mother. I feel sorry for her. She always worked so hard.

I always did what she told me to do, even if it was cleaning up after my little sister or peeling a crate of apples for pies to take to the picnic. I could never say no to her. I really did love my mother. Her life, always scrimping—it was so hard. I couldn't say no to my mother, and I can't say no to Nick."

"Did what happened with Nick bother you?"

"Of course it did. I could kick myself around the block. He's greedy and spoiled, but I keep giving in to him."

"To change how you respond to Nick, you might need to muscle up on the skills so you stay in balance in the present. You might need to take out emotional trash, too."

Tom nodded. "I can see that. But how do you take out the trash?"

"That's a fair question," I said. "I can guide you in taking that piece out about your mother, or I can show you by taking out a piece of my own."

"I'd rather you show me."

"Do you feel safe listening?" I asked.

"I do."

"There are safety guidelines that I need you to agree to."

"What are they?"

"No interrupting, no judgments, no advice-giving, and no chitchat. Just be a loving presence as I use the skills."

Tom hadn't expected me to open up to him, but that is how this work is done. You can't teach the skills safely and effectively unless you can model them.

"Okay, I agree to all that you just said."

I nodded, acknowledging his pledge, then went on.

"Let me think of a piece of emotional trash that I feel safe taking out with you." I thought for a moment, then said, "Okay, I've got it. First, I'll just tell you a smattering of facts, just enough to get my feelings churned up so I can launch into the Natural Flow of Feelings. I could write this out in what we call a Thinking Journal, or just say it, which is what I will do right now. Okay?"

"Okay."

"Here are the facts: We have a great big brown dog, Bo, who has huge brown eyes and is so gentle that he defers to the cat if they are both trying to come into the house at the same time. He is a tremendously important member of our family, and my children and I love him unconditionally.

"Bo and I went for a hike on the mountain near our house. He heard a noise in the canyon below the trail. I saw his ears perk up, he peered straight at me, and I just knew he was going to go right off the cliff after that creature. I shouted, 'No, Bo, no!' and of course Bo shot straight down that 50-foot cliff and the chase was on! About 20 minutes later, and only after tremendous struggle, Bo, whose muzzle has grayed in recent years, made the grueling climb back up the cliff and onto the trail.

"Within a day, Bo developed this horrible twitch, like a seizure, where his whole body shook every so often. I took him to the vet, who did extensive tests and told me that it was probably a brain tumor and that Bo would probably die. I felt devastated, and my children were so upset, but I went to another vet a week later. She properly diagnosed the problem as a back injury. Since then, with chiropractic treatment, Bo has healed pretty well.

"That's my Thinking Journal."

Tom nodded.

"I know there is emotional trash there because I still feel so much fury, irrational fury way out of proportion to what happened. Tom, would you listen to me take it out?"

"Sure," said Tom, settling back in his chair. He seemed to be enjoying listening.

"What happened with the vet reminds me of . . ."

Tom was doing well—not interrupting, just listening—but all of a sudden, I knew I was taking out a big piece of emotional trash, not a little one.

"Actually, it reminds me of something I don't feel safe revealing to you. When you do Community Connections, or cycles with others, it's not as if the door to your inner life is flung wide open. You can set limits about what you say. I don't feel safe telling you the incident involved, but it reminds me of something that happened a long time ago. A physician, let's call him Dr. Gallon, gave me the wrong diagnosis, and it changed my life. As you listen, remember that I will be totally irrational and say things that I would never say in normal conversation, which is why it's important that you do the best you can to stay in balance and not judge or interrupt me."

Tom nodded. "Okay."

I waited for the anger to come up in my body. It took a

minute or so. Then it was there, pin prickles on my arms and a mound of red-hot rage in my chest.

"I *hate* that doctor's guts. I hate him for lying to me. . . . I feel angry that he hurt me. . . . I am furious that I allowed him to hurt me. . . . I feel sad that I was in so much pain. . . . I feel sad that I felt so alone. . . . I feel afraid that other doctors will lie to me. . . . I feel afraid that I will trust them when I shouldn't. I feel afraid that bad things will happen when my family gets sick. I feel afraid that I will be powerless to protect my family and myself. . . . I feel guilty that I was passive. I feel guilty that I didn't ask for another opinion. I feel guilty that I lost my boundary to him. . . . I feel guilty that I was so ready to believe what he said."

I took a deep breath. I had done the Natural Flow of Feelings, honoring my feelings about what had happened . . . my anger, sadness, fear, and guilt. Now it was time to move myself above the line, to move that trash out of my body, to see myself and the situation with an accurate eye through the tool of the limits cycle.

"What is my *unreasonable* expectation? That when I was ill and had fewer skills than I have now, I would have known whether or not to trust him, and would have advocated perfectly for myself."

I let out a little gasp, almost a chuckle. Tom smiled slightly, but remained silent.

"What is a reasonable expectation? A reasonable expectation for who I was then was that I would trust more than I should have, and may not advocate for myself perfectly.

"Positive, powerful? What do I most need to hear? *I did the best I could.*

"The essential pain? Bad things happened. I didn't take care of myself. A doctor hurt me. I wasn't perfect. I can't change the past."

I took a moment to feel the essential pain rise up like a bell-shaped curve, then fade. It hurt, but then the pain began to lift.

"The earned reward? I have learned. I am not overly trustful of doctors anymore. I am better at taking care of myself now. I can change the future."

I felt better, let out a sigh, then smiled at Tom, feeling proud of myself.

Tom said, "Incredible. That was amazing. I can do that!"

"I have no doubt that you can," I said.

"What happens now?" he asked.

"I feel a little bit emotionally lighter. The incident doesn't have so much pain for me. That's the whole point, my feeling freer from the pain of the past rising up and zapping me today."

Tom nodded.

"When I started this cycle, I didn't know that the emotional trash was this sensitive. It's not as if one cycle is going to heal a big hurt, but each cycle helps."

"I don't know what my big hurts are."

"That's fine. In time, you will, and maybe you don't have a lot of emotional trash."

Tom smiled slightly and said, "I think I probably do."

"Then you can slowly begin to take it out. But only part of the work is taking out emotional trash. You'll be using the skills to stay balanced with whatever happens right now in your life."

"How do you do that?" asked Tom.

"How many times are you tossed below the line each day?"

"I'm always below the line," said Tom glumly.

"Fabulous. You'll have lots of material on which to do cycles."

Tom gave me a disgruntled look.

"It's a simple pathway, Tom. Think of your left foot as the nurturing cycle and your right foot as the limits cycle. Just keep walking, in your own way and at your own pace."

I checked to see if I had lost him, but he seemed to be listening.

"That's it—just one step at a time, until you have taken out enough emotional trash and muscled up enough on the skills to stay so balanced in the present that you have no external solutions and all the rewards of human life—including your sweetest fruit, intimacy."

Tom sighed. "That's why I came here. I want intimacy."

"Do you have any reservations about the truth of the method—that other than genetics and chance, most of the unnecessary pain we cause ourselves and the way we block the normal joys of human maturity come from not having these skills solidly within us? Does that seem like the truth to you?"

"I know I don't have the skills, but the changes . . . it's hard to believe they could happen to me."

"Tom, if you walk along this pathway, at some point, as you have less emotional trash and more skills, you will have a semblance of the balance you had early in life."

Balance is restored.
Excesses fade and the rewards
of life become abundant.

Tom crossed his arms over his chest, his suit wrinkling. "It's hard to imagine that happening for me. Right now I feel very old and very tired," he said. He thought for a moment, then said, "Would there be a time when I could stop using the skills?"

It seemed that Tom would either sidestep the training altogether or come to it kicking and screaming, which is not uncommon.

I responded, "No. The skills become spontaneous, but there will always be times when you'll need to use them intentionally, perhaps to take out a piece of emotional trash or when there is a loss or a surprise."

"What about my drinking? I don't want to give that up."

At that time, Tom's primary attachment was to wine. Of course he didn't want to give it up. Most people don't let go of an external solution until they have no choice, or until the skills are strong and letting go becomes a nurturing act, not a depriving one.

Wealth and success also hampered Tom. He could use money and position to fly under the radar and roll along with a life that appeared more successful than it was. His relationships would be more like parallel play than mature love, but he could find an equally out-of-balance woman, so he would look as if he had adult intimacy in his life. Or he could buy himself something when he was blue and drink at night, and nobody would know. Even if they did, nobody he would allow into his life would dare bring it up to him.

I shrugged. "In this method, nobody makes judgments about your behavior, but the more you use external solutions, the harder and slower the journey will be. Also, safety is extremely important in this training. If you're drinking and you come to the meeting or call another member to do a Community Connection and you don't stick with the safety guidelines, you'll be asked to leave the group for at least one year. If you have any worries about staying within those guidelines, it is important to use the method within a more structured alcohol program rather than in community-based groups."

Tom said nothing.

"Tom, this might not be the right time for you to do this work. Even if it is the right time, this might not be the right journey for you. If you decide to make the climb, I'll do my best to make it as easy, quick, and safe as possible, even though it is not easy, quick, or completely safe. I'll stay with you until you have what you most want in this lifetime . . ."

Tom said, "Intimacy."

I responded, "Yes, intimacy."

As I watched Tom leave, I wondered if he yearned for intimacy enough to disrupt inertia, separate from the familiar, and start the climb. Would wanting his sweetest fruit be enough?

4. The Threshold of Need

I f you saw two people walking down the street, one heavyset and the other lean, could you make any assumptions about which person had more nurturing and limits skills nestled within their brain? What if it were a matter of smoking—one had a cigarette in hand and the other did not. Or mood—one appeared despondent while the other seemed jubilant. Could you rightfully assume that one had more skills than the other?

The answer, of course, is no. It is not how much skill a person possesses, but how much skill they *have* compared to how much skill they *need*. The precise amount needed at any moment to stay in emotional, behavioral, and spiritual balance is called the *threshold of need* for the skills.

Of course, life is not fair, and the threshold of need for the skills varies widely among individuals:

> **A low threshold of need**—Some people have a generally low need for the skills; they have a cooperative biology, an easy temperament, little situational stress, scant emotional trash, a supportive environment, and a natural resistance to external solutions. They have a "vanilla" life, one in which balance is relatively easy to come by, even with a modicum of skills.
>
> **A high threshold of need**—Unfortunately, many of us have the opposite situation: Our threshold of need for the skills is so astronomically high that to live a life of balance, we must possess immense skills and use them with symphonic precision.

As you approach this work, it helps to be aware of your threshold of need because it affects your climb. The higher your threshold of need for the skills, the more time and practice it will take to get what you most want in your life. Being aware of that can help you settle into the process without wondering at every moment, "Am I done yet?"

If you know that your threshold of need for the skills is high, you may have a clearer understanding of your past and feel more compassion for yourself. You might say to yourself, "Now I know why the kid next to me in school—or at work or play—sailed through life while I had a harder time of it. Their threshold of need was lower than mine. My challenge was greater." This is not a view designed to rationalize faults and justify excesses, but a way of seeing the problem accurately as a prelude to taking action—engaging in the hard work of building inner skills that resolve the resolvable parts of faults and excesses.

"Oh, I get it. I'm not crazy. My threshold of need is just high."

Your threshold of need is always changing. As you make this climb, there will be times when it is very low and you feel very balanced. You might even feel like you have a Solution early in the training, as some people experience a "honeymoon" of balance before the real work begins.

At other times, your threshold of need for the skills may be extremely high. You're likely to feel as if you're missing a few memory chips or that your inner life has just "crashed." Neither is likely to be true. It's just that your threshold of need for the skills is "up" so you go below the line. You are not crazy or delusional—just a bit below the line, and still successfully engaged in the process of transforming to a new and far more wonderful life.

Recently, Kevin, a real estate broker who was relatively new to the method, called the Institute for a coaching session. In the session that followed, I learned that before his training, his emotional inner life had been rather numb, and that using the skills enlivened him almost immediately. He was amazed and delighted at how life had turned from black-and-white to brightly colored.

He said, "I felt so great. I had no interest in external solutions and felt more in control than I had in many years. I read that the skills were catching, but there was an *epidemic* in my house! The kids stopped fighting, and my wife and I were making love with more desire than we've had in years. Life was so good, it crossed

---

When you have *fewer* skills than you need, you are *below the line.*

Threshold of need for the skills

**Your Need
for the Skills**
- body
- temperament
- situational stress
- emotional trash
- the environment
- external solutions

**Your
Skill
Level**

---

my mind that I had mastered the skills, that I was something of an exception and had gotten fully above the line in a matter of days, not months or years.

"Then, last Wednesday morning, I arrived at the office to discover that two of my biggest deals of the year had fallen apart and that my office manager, who does *everything* for me, had quit in a huff. With all that chaos, I knocked over a giant cup of scalding-hot coffee on my desk, which not only burned my hand but also destroyed a pile of important letters and documents. In a period of twenty minutes, I went from a balanced life to a disastrous one.

"Immediately, I reached for a cigarette, which helped. But I knew that I was also about to lash out at someone, so I left the office and took a walk. Of course I went straight to the doughnut shop, where I stoked up on caffeine and sugar, including two chocolate cake doughnuts. My stomach started to hurt from all that grease, but what hurt me the most was the realization that *nothing in my life had changed*, that I had no more skill than I did the day I started doing cycles."

I said to Kevin, "Below the line is below the line. It doesn't matter if you're an inch below or a yard below, it feels awful.

You have more skill, but your threshold of need went up, so the switch flipped and you went from above the line to below."

He shook his head and said, "I *hate* it that I could get so out of control."

"If you were a computer and had only a *thinking* brain, you would be in far more control. As a human, buried in the belly of your mind is a *feeling* brain that is passionate, emotional, and driven. When it's out of balance—which can happen in a flash due to factors beyond your control—you may well feel totally irrational, utterly insatiable, terminally miserable, and . . . completely lost. Your time horizon may be so distorted that it seems you always have and always will feel as dreadful as you do right at that moment, which is enough to depress anyone!"

"That's oddly reassuring," he said.

"Given that none of us is in complete control of our threshold of need, it's a reasonable expectation that for the rest of our lives we'll be above the line sometimes and below sometimes."

"So I have to expect to be below the line . . ."

"Of course. It's not that bad. In time, when you notice that you're below the line, you'll just take a big deep breath, use your

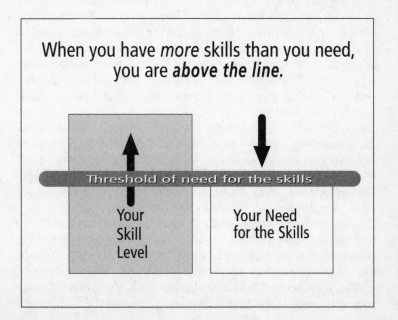

When you have *more* skills than you need, you are *above the line*.

Threshold of need for the skills

Your Skill Level

Your Need for the Skills

tool kit, and use it. Sooner or later you pop yourself above the line. The goal of this training is to spend *more of your moments* above the line, where dreams are more likely to come true. The Solution is not a concept but a practice."

Even though the feeling brain changes at a tortoise's pace, life itself often moves like a jackrabbit on amphetamines. Your threshold of need for the skills can move all over the map: Sometimes it's minuscule, often it's formidable, and periodically, it's gigantic. It's not unusual to keep flipping the switch, going above and below the line dozens of times a day. With all that turmoil, it can be reassuring to understand that the threshold of need varies as a function of six factors.

1. Body Factors

If you have a genetic propensity to seek external solutions, you will need more skills to maintain personal balance. It's important to think of genetic tendencies in shades of gray, or in terms of how much *genetic loading* you have for one excess or another, such as obesity or alcoholism. There are at least 50 genes that affect obesity, for example, and an individual can have none, some, or many of them.

Genetic differences also impact emotional balance and can pump up the need for the skills. For example, depression has been linked to elevated glucocorticoid levels, or hyper-secretion of glucocorticoid by the adrenal glands. Anxiety disorders have been associated with an overabundance of circulating catecholamine, epinephrine, and norepinephrine. To what extent such differences result from genetic rather than environmental factors is not known.

Gender also can affect the threshold of need. For example, the woman who is prone to depression because of fluctuations in her estrogen and progesterone levels has a higher threshold of need. The testosterone-related hostility that can fuel a man's rages does not destine him for a life of conflict, but he may need more skills to minimize the effects of these tendencies.

Apart from genetics, there are biological differences we *create* that influence our threshold of need for the skills. Smoke for long enough to become addicted to nicotine, and up goes your threshold of need to turn off those cravings. Overeat for long enough, and at least seven biological changes will occur that increase your propensity for weight gain.

The more a person uses substances such as alcohol or cocaine, the more the dopamine receptors in his or her brain become altered. As a result, the person may develop an "addicted brain" that needs more and more of the substance to feel gratified. Fewer of life's normal gratifiers, such as exercise, are satisfying.

A wide range of other biological factors can affect the threshold of need, including almost anything that throws you out of balance—the common cold, a sleepless night, an upset stomach. Participants with attention deficit hyperactivity disorder (ADHD) have difficulty concentrating, making it more difficult for them to gain these skills and, once they are gained, to use them.

The biological changes associated with mood problems can also have a variety of effects on balance. If people are so depressed that they can't access their feelings, it is difficult to do this work. Taking antidepressants may or may not help—if the medications numb their feelings excessively, checking their feelings may be impossible.

The factors are so multitudinous and varied that it is often best simply to ask yourself, "Does my biology increase my need for the skills?"

2. Temperament

Your natural emotional tendencies, or temperament, is genetically determined, and the seat of temperament is in your brain stem. There are vast variations in how people naturally respond to daily life. Each individual has a different ease with which they experience the triggering of each emotion, as well as its duration and intensity.

Various temperaments have been associated with certain external solutions, such as the passive, depressed person turning to food for comfort, or the person with a short fuse turning to alcohol. Temperament may be associated with the willingness to engage in a specific external solution, and the ease with which one becomes dependent upon it. In particular, the tendencies to be sensitive, to be emotionally labile, to withdraw, and to have difficulty reading internal signals have all been associated with the use of external solutions.

A difficult temperament is not bad or wrong, but it does mean that you will need more of these skills than the person next to you, who, by the flip of a coin, has an easy temperament and finds persistent emotional balance easily.

You might ask yourself, "Does my temperament increase my threshold of need for the skills?"

3. The Stresses of Life

Life's situational stress is the most universal factor that pumps up the threshold of need for the skills. We all have the best of times and the worst of times. Many years ago, during a tumultuous period of my life, Yolanda Gutierrez, a nutritionist and nursing faculty member currently working at Stanford, said to me, "Don't worry, Laurel. Everything is fine. Things happen in clusters, and you are just going through a 'bad cluster' right now. Before long, a 'good cluster' will come along."

In retrospect, how different that stressful time would have been for me if I had possessed enough of these skills! Just the simple act of using the nurturing inner voice to say, "Laurel, these things happen. You're not wrong or bad, and you're not going down the tubes into the pit of an impossible life. It's just that your threshold of need for the skills is a little high right now. In time, it will come down, and you will feel better."

Please ask yourself, "Does the situational stress in my life right now increase my need for the skills?"

4. Emotional Trash

If you don't have an abundance of these skills, when bad things happen, the feelings go underground and form emotional trash within, and if a lot of bad things happen, you'll have a lot of emotional trash. You may not be aware of those leftover, unhealed hurts. The emotional trash may be sitting there quietly, creating a lesser or greater amount of tension. However, periodically it can burst forth in a gush of anger, sadness, fear, or guilt without your conscious triggering it to do so.

It doesn't take a great stretch of the imagination to be aware that if you have more emotional trash, you will have a higher threshold of need for the skills in order to keep the lid on your emotional life.

Check for deep hurts, particularly early ones, and ask yourself, "How many unhealed hurts do I have inside? Is my threshold of need for the skills higher because of my emotional trash?"

5. The Environment

My grandmother Grannie Driggs had a cherrywood teacart with a glass top that held a sterling silver tea set full of Hershey's kisses. We visited her for a week every summer, driving in our family's Oldsmobile the length of our state to Santa Paula, which took a whole day. My brother Steve and I would sit out on the side porch and eat Hershey's kisses and pick oranges from the tree in her backyard. Once in a while, we would go to Uncle Earl's little store around the corner from Grannie's house to get a jawbreaker. There was a swimming pool at the high school two blocks away, and we went swimming there once or twice each week. Other than that, we just played.

For most people, life isn't like that anymore, and the ways it has changed have increased our threshold of need for the skills. Virtually everything that Alvin Toffler predicted in *Future Shock* has already come true, and life, we all must admit, is very different than it was. If the threshold of need for the skills rises and is unmitigated by an increase in the population's skills, rates of various behavioral excesses and emotional problems will be likely to increase. Such may be what we are observing now, worldwide, as a result of modernization.

On a personal level, please consider how your environment affects your threshold of need for the skills. Do the people in your life, the schedule of your day, and the community and world in which you live make it easier or harder for you to stay in balance?

6. External Solutions

Go on a spending spree, and you find your credit card over the limit and the cashier at the drugstore telling you that your card has been declined. Scarf down two Polish hot dogs and a beer, and you feel more numb, more depressed, and more out of balance than you did before.

What happens to your threshold of need for the skills when you use external solutions? It goes up. When the normal joys of life are distorted into external solutions that hurt us, it affects our balance. I can tell when people come to a Solution Group after they've binged on cookies and candy. They can't access their feelings—the external solution has left them numb. How can you keep your finger on the pulse of your inner life if your feelings are turned so low that you can't perceive them? It's a situation in which the problem is the problem: We're out of balance, so we use external solutions, which take us further out of balance. Not only are we more numb, but we are also more troubled. We obsess about the problem and how to fix it, which shunts our focus from thoughts to feelings, separating us further from ourselves.

When I first began doing this work, my view was that people are adults, and they should do with their excesses what they want to do and wait for the drives to turn off so that the excesses will fade. I did not fully appreciate that the excesses themselves make it harder for people to make the climb. Now the program gives people support to nudge themselves to stop using external solutions early on in the training so the journey will be more gentle and more rapid.

Please ask yourself, "Do my external solutions increase my threshold of need for the skills?"

Some people have a higher need than others

Emily, whose sweetest fruit was emotional balance, had a relatively low threshold of need for the skills, and Tom had a moderate one. Many who are drawn to this method have an exceptionally high need for the skills, as was the case with Drew.

Drew was a fifth-grade teacher in her late thirties, with curly brown hair pulled back into a ponytail and a very round face. She looked so sweet that the words that poured out of her mouth surprised me:

"I've been an addict my whole life, and this is my last stop. I'm here to save my life," she said. "My childhood was very loving until age eight, when my twin brothers were born. At that very instant, I was deserted, no longer the cute, cherished only child, and virtually ignored. It was devastating! I figured that if I was better, they would love me again, so I acted very good—too good, really—but I expressed my outrage by finding secretive ways to be as bad as I could possibly be.

"First, I stole candy from the drugstore. Then I sneaked cigarettes from my mother's purse and dollar bills from my dad's wallet. My mother was very overweight, and even though she ate whatever she wanted, she put me on a diet, so I retaliated by taking candy from the cupboard. I can remember taking prepackaged frozen brownies, the kind with the chocolate frosting, right out of the freezer—still brick-hard—and hiding them under my bed, then gorging on them when nobody was watching."

Drew caught my glance, seemed reassured, then continued. "I found a passion for teaching by chance, when I volunteered as a tutor at the day-care center near my home when I was fourteen, and that passion has been the best thing in my life. I'm not close to my family, and I live a rather solitary life. I have lots of acquaintances, but by the end of the day, I'm so tired from giving to the children all day that I don't socialize much."

As she spoke those words, Drew's face came alive and a slightly devilish grin took over her face. "I take care of myself in other ways. I smoke, I'm a hopelessly compulsive eater, and I binge-drink, but I'm also addicted to more benign things: television, the Internet, computer games, and even mystery novels. I collect stuffed animals and old furniture." As if it were an afterthought, she added, "Oh, and I'm a spender and a hoarder, too."

Drew had done what most of us would do if we found ourselves with no nurturing inner voice to rely on: We would go outside ourselves and patch together a life that includes the external solutions we need in order to get us through the day.

"What you've done has made perfect sense," I said.

Drew was startled. She had expected me to either judge or pity her. "You could say I am creative about making myself happy," she went on, "but the life I lead is difficult. I stay away from other people because it makes me sad to see what I'm missing, and it's not that I haven't tried to change things. In fact, I've had six years of psychotherapy and I've tried various drugs, but they just make me emotionally numb or so wired that I can't sleep. I've tried to stop smoking, but I've never made it for more than three days without a cigarette."

Moving from one external solution to another

"About two years ago," Drew went on, "my weight topped out at two hundred pounds, and I couldn't stand myself anymore. I went on a strict diet and lost about forty pounds, but I still craved brownies and pizza, so to keep the weight off, I started running before work. Now my knees have started hurting, so I've had to stop. I feel like I'm in a cage and have no way to get out."

Drew looked scared. In fact, she looked desperate.

I said, "I'm sorry it's been so hard."

"Thank you," she said, then paused. "I have three problems now. One is that every time I get control of one problem—say, I stop overeating—another one, usually spending or drinking, crops up."

I nodded.

"The second problem is that I spend all my time and nearly every penny of my discretionary income on trying to stop one bad habit or another. *I hate it!* And this struggle has invaded my mind. All I think about is what I ate, whether I should have a cigarette or not, whether I'm over my limit with my credit card . . . and I feel so ashamed that I can't control myself. If the children at school knew about my personal life, I'd be mortified. What I want most in life is to get to the bottom of *all* the excesses and stop them. I want to be free from all those drives."

"I understand. Wouldn't it be wonderful to be free of them?" She nodded.

"I'm wondering what the third problem is. You said there were three."

Drew answered, "Yes, and this one is hard to put into words. I think that I am so used to obsessing about my problems that if I ever stopped, I don't know what I'd do. I'd have nothing to think about. In an odd sort of way, I'd miss it."

"It would be a loss."

Drew said, "Yes, it would."

"It sounds as if you're ready to hear the truth," I said.

She nodded. "Yes, I am."

Filling in the gap

I began. "It seems that you have a high threshold of need for the skills and not a lot of skills, even though you've tried so hard."

She said, "That's true."

"The gap between the skills you have and the skills you need is a magnet for excesses."

Drew was impatient. "I understand that. That's why I'm here. I want to fill in that gap."

"Would you like to check your threshold of need for the skills?"

"Yes," she said.

"The first factor is your body. Think of your genetics, the way your body handles changes, any medications, anything about your body or health that makes you need more of these skills."

"My mother is heavy and so is my aunt, so I know I have a tendency to gain weight. I'm very affected by my cycle and get really hungry and depressed right before my period. I'm a smoker, and I know that I'm nicotine-addicted. My father is a binge drinker. I don't know if my grandparents had any excesses."

"Your need for the skills on account of body factors is . . . ," I prompted.

"Off-the-charts high, I think."

"Good. What about your temperament, your emotional tendencies, having an easy temperament versus a difficult one?"

Drew started to laugh. "I don't think you've ever met anyone who has a more difficult temperament than me. I'm so sensitive that a child can drop his crayon and I'm emotionally wiped out for the day. When there are problems, I run away and withdraw, and I have almost no awareness of my body. I don't know when I'm hungry or when I'm full and, in general, have a difficult time reading my body's signals, even when they're blaring!"

"Situational stress?"

Drew shrugged. "I don't think my current life is any harder than anyone else's, but I do know that when my stress level goes up—there was a threatened strike at work last year—my drives to go to excess increase. I gained twenty-five pounds during that time, and I know a lot of it was the conflict at school."

"Emotional trash?"

"I went to therapy, and it was so incredibly painful to dredge up the past. I went through such agony, but to be perfectly honest, I didn't feel much relief. The ache inside me has never left," said Drew.

"Of course it didn't. Bringing up the pain without the skills to heal it makes you feel virtuous—you are working so hard at healing—but it does not heal."

Drew and I both took a deep breath. "I can't face that pain," she said quietly. "Therapy didn't help, and I don't want to go into that again."

Taking small but important steps, day by day

"You don't have to, Drew, but my experience has been that unless people do all four things—bring up a nurturing inner voice, take out emotional trash from the past, use the skills to stay in balance now, and do the lifestyle surgery that brings down their threshold of need—they don't reach a Solution. Just take the smallest steps, day by day."

She looked discouraged.

"Drew, it's not so bad. You just have a huge pileup of hurts from the past the pain is like overcooked spaghetti, all mooched together into one big, unappetizing lump."

She smiled. "That's what it feels like. A big fat lump."

I took my right hand and put it on my left shoulder and began stroking my arm, a gesture we use in the method to suggest the need to be gentle and nurturing with ourselves.

"The idea is to be gentle with yourself. You don't take out the whole lump at once. Just take out one small strand of spaghetti at a time and use the skills to heal that, then another and another. The goal is not to get rid of all of your emotional trash—just the part that makes life excessively difficult for you."

Drew looked more content.

"What about your environment? How does it affects your need for the skills?" I asked.

"I live alone. I like my job and my home. I have no complaints. I am sensitive to the media. If I read about a car crash or a bomb exploding, I go numb, sometimes for days. I'm a reactive kind of person."

"What about external solutions? How do they affect your need for the skills?"

Again, Drew gasped. "Paralyzing. That's the only way I can describe it. I'm so connected to my addictions that there is no space for me to use the skills and connect with myself. None."

"So if you added it all up, what is your threshold of need for the skills?"

"I told you. Off-the-charts high. I'm furious. Why does this have to happen to me? Why am I the one who has to have everything be difficult and sick and hard? In fact, I'm not just angry, I'm furious. I'm furious that my brothers were born and ruined my life. I hate it that I had such lousy parents, and I feel sorry for myself that I'm here talking to you. I don't want to be here. I want to be healthy and happy and not have to deal with any of this!" said Drew.

"You sound right on track."

"I don't trust you."

"I'm sad that you don't trust me, but I wouldn't expect otherwise."

Drew looked unsettled. "Why?"

"These are the skills of trust. If you don't have the skills, you're not likely to know who to trust and who not to trust, including yourself."

"That's true," she said thoughtfully.

"Drew, I know that you are perfectly capable of reaching your Solution, but I do not know the precise shape your Solution will take. For example, if your genetic tendency to gain weight is strong, you may decide that you want to keep a weight that is stable and healthier, but not slender. If you get above the line emotionally and still binge-drink, you may decide to use your skills to avoid alcohol rather than to drink socially. I'll have no idea, until you reach your Solution."

"I can live with that, but I still feel as if I am defective."

"I feel sad hearing you say that," I said.

"You do?" she said.

"Yes! Here you are, with a high threshold of need, and you're not the only one in that situation, but you have so little compassion for yourself! I know you'll get that compassion in time, but it makes me sad that you are so hard on yourself."

Drew said, "I'm the first person to have compassion for my kids and the last to have compassion for myself."

"Your threshold of need being high is a blessing."

"Why?"

Keeping an eye on your sweetest fruit

"Because you will need to keep that vision of your sweetest fruit . . ."

"Freedom from all excesses . . ." said Drew.

". . . that vision of freedom from all the excesses that have plagued you, and focus on your feet. Think of your left foot being your nurturing skill and your right foot being your limits skill. Just making the climb by taking baby steps. First use the nurturing skill, then the limits skill, then nurturing, then limits . . . and make the climb.

"The drives to go to excess are very primitive and very deep, so you must tolerate not knowing which excess will fade when. But they will fall away, one by one. The payoff of having a high threshold of need for the skills is that when you reach the top of the tree, you'll have an immense amount of skill inside. So when other difficulties arise, which they do for all of us, you'll have the security of knowing that you can handle virtually anything. You'll know that you built these skills inside you, brick by brick by brick and that nobody can take them away from you."

"It's hard to believe that could happen to me," said Drew.

"It will only happen if you practice. Practice, practice, practice . . ."

5. Life's Sweetest Rewards

When Emily first started using the method, she had what I call a "split" expectation:

"I know I'll never get this," she said. "I'm petrified that there is something wrong with me and that somehow, I'll *never* be able to master these skills and have these rewards."

Whenever a totally irrational expectation gets stuck deeply within, it's often because there is a "phantom" expectation lurking behind it, something equally unreasonable but totally the opposite of the first one.

I asked Emily, "Could there be another, equally unreasonable expectation lurking behind that one?"

She thought for a moment, then her face lit up and she said, "Ahhh. Yes! My other unreasonable expectation—the phantom one—is that this will be easy. If other people take a couple of years to do it, I can do it effortlessly in two or three months."

Then she starting laughing, and so did I.

For many of us, it's hard to imagine having these rewards, but equally hard to imagine *not* being able to snap our fingers and get them. Moreover, it is a stretch of the imagination to think that the source of all the rewards and turning off all the excessive appetites, other than genetics, are one in the same. If you have the skill to nurture and set limits from within, the spigot opens and out the rewards flow. If you don't, not only is the spigot shut off, but it's hard to imagine that water could ever flow from it.

The idea that the good things in life follow from nurturing and limits isn't a new one. Developmental psychologist Margaret Mahler writes about children who do not receive that blessed blend of warm caring and effective limits, and so never learn to trust and express their own feelings. Virginia Satir points out that children who are not raised with hugs and a welcoming ear begin to feel that they don't matter. Alice Miller observes that a lack of nurturing can echo from generation to generation. And according to Marion Woodman, "If children do not receive the

Life's Sweetest Rewards

Integration

The sense of inner chaos lessens and you feel whole. You accept yourself and know that you don't have to be perfect to be wonderful.

Balance

The extreme highs and lows and the emotional numbness are replaced by a more balanced and stable emotional life.

Sanctuary

You have a nurturing inner voice and a warm, secure place within, a sanctuary that is always there no matter how difficult life becomes.

Intimacy

Your relationships are more intimate. You can be close to another without merging, distancing, or control struggles. Love and desire deepen.

Vibrancy

The joy you take in being alive and the vitality that comes from better health and a more balanced lifestyle show. You look your best and feel radiant.

Spirituality

You experience a greater awareness of your inherent goodness, a deeper connection with the spiritual, and a new appreciation for the mystery and grace of life.

sweetness of love, they eventually settle for a 'sweet,' " whether that is a cookie, a cigarette, or a bottle of beer.

These theories, the research on the method, and my own journey, though reassuring, are not what convinced me that implanting these skills within ourselves would result in receiving an abundance of life's six rewards. I was convinced by hearing it with my own ears and seeing it with my own eyes, over and over again, from the participants in my groups. These are the six universal rewards of human maturity:

Integration

For Drew, whose sweetest fruit was to live with no external solutions, integration was near the top of the tree. She described what it was like for her: "I'm completely chaotic. I'm such a good person all day. I am the best teacher, the most empathetic person, and so nice—unbelievably nice. That's the problem. When I go home at night, I have no restraint. I am totally bad. I eat. I smoke. I drink. I do whatever I damn well please. The see-saw back and forth makes me feel crazy!"

Drew's experience of feeling "split" started a long time ago. "The Child in the Safe Role" shows a healthy family structure. The parent is in the parent role and the child is in the child role. The horizontal line, called the "separation of the generations line," is the sacred boundary that parents establish so that children can be children and get more of their needs met.

Parents keep children in the child role by giving them the nurturing and the limits they need. When parents are successful, children feel safe. They feel the essential pain that they need to feel in order to grow into healthy, happy adults but miss much of life's avoidable pain.

As you can imagine, Drew didn't spend much of her younger life in the child role. Her parents were occupied with taking care of the twins, so she got little nurturing and was left to take care of herself, which rarely works out for the best. She was not seen for who she was, and she felt invisible, lost, and abandoned. She put up a good front by not being herself, instead taking on the role of the little girl who was too good to her mother's face and very, very bad in secret. Her sense of being whole and authentic was lost.

When Drew took on the good girl role, she turned herself into a pretzel, trying to please everyone, being overly polite and per-

The Child in a *Safe* Role

parents in the
"adult" role

Separation of the generations line

child in the
"child" role

Parents keep the child below the "separation of
the generations line" in the safety of the child role.
They do this by giving the child the nurturing
and limits that he or she needs.

fectly sweet to her parents. When she took on the bad-girl role, she was outrageous! She stopped at the corner store for as much candy, chocolate, and ice cream as the money she sneaked from her father's wallet would buy. She had made the shift first to being a peer to her parents, then to becoming a persecutor. It was as if she were saying, "What do I have to do? How *outrageous* do I have to act to get your attention, so you will give me the nurturing and limits I need and put me back in the safety of the child role?"

Because the human spirit is remarkably resilient, even those of us who found ourselves parenting ourselves early in life usually grow up and do reasonably well. In adolescence, Drew threw off the shackles of being the good little girl and was purely and delightfully bad. She had too much sex, smoked too many joints, and nearly flunked out of school, and her parents hardly noticed. The twins were superstars, and Drew . . . wasn't. Then something quite fortunate occurred. Drew discovered that she had a passion for teaching.

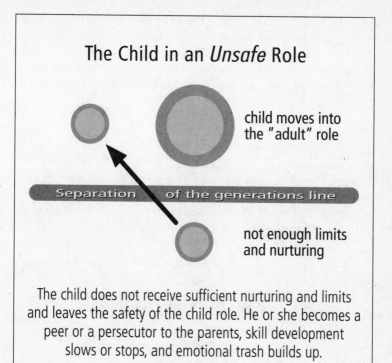

The Child in an *Unsafe* Role

child moves into
the "adult" role

Separation of the generations line

not enough limits
and nurturing

The child does not receive sufficient nurturing and limits
and leaves the safety of the child role. He or she becomes a
peer or a persecutor to the parents, skill development
slows or stops, and emotional trash builds up.

She returned to college, got her teaching credential, and
started her first job. The trouble was that part of her was still
down there below the line—the part that had not received the
nurturing and limits she needed as a child. By acting up in the
evenings after the long day of being overly good, she felt divided,
chaotic, and false, but it was comforting as well. The pattern of
being too good *and* too bad was a familiar one.

As Drew began to develop the patience and persistence to go
inside, bring up a nurturing inner voice, and use the cycles, she
would start to feel seen by herself, even though she had never felt
seen by her parents. She would begin to know and honor and even
delight in her good qualities, her light side. Equally, she would
know, accept, and even love her dark side, the part of her that
didn't have enough skills, tended to go out of balance, and engaged
in behavior that negatively affected her health and her happiness.
She would use the skills in a loving, self-protecting way to minimize

some of the unnecessary pain her dark side caused her. In other words, she would feel whole, self-accepting, and integrated.

Integration is not the easiest of the rewards; it tends to come late in the training, for it requires that you truly see and honor yourself—light side, dark side, and all—and accept yourself so deeply that you feel whole.

Balance

Acquiring emotional balance is the work of the first half of the climb to the top. Until emotional balance is relatively predictable, the other rewards—all five of them—do not begin to accumulate. Balance is far easier to achieve than turning off a primitive drive to go to excess, but it requires a certain devotion to the use of the skills.

The Adult Feels Divided

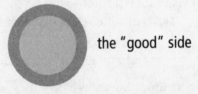

the "good" side

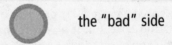

the "bad" side

The child grows into an adult with many successes; however, the part of him or her that didn't get the necessary nurturing and limits remains below the line. The adult feels divided between the "good" side that is balanced and the "bad" side that is out of balance.

What is emotional balance? In this method, it means that you are feeling the balanced feelings that come naturally when you are above the line. These are the feelings that are mostly accurate responses to your environment in the present moment. You feel them, then they fade.

- You feel the *earned rewards*: grateful, happy, secure, proud, and loved.
- You are aware of the negative internal messages that direct you toward meeting your most basic needs: hunger, fatigue, illness, and so on.
- You feel the *essential pain*: angry, sad, afraid, guilty, and lonely.
- You are aware of the positive internal messages that assure you that your most basic needs—e.g., food, sleep—have been met.

The Adult Feels Whole

neither all "good"
nor all "bad"

Separation of the   generations line

As nurturing and limits are mastered, the "bad" part below the line moves above the line. The adult feels integrated: whole, authentic, and self-accepting.

When we are out of emotional balance, we are separated from the moment. Our true feelings do not register; instead, our feelings are distorted and tend to persist rather than fade. There are three types of unbalanced feelings: *false highs, unnecessary lows*, and *emotional numbness*. Most of us spend much of our time in one of those states or ping-pong back and forth between the two.

With a false high, instead of feeling happy, we are so elated that we forget to attend to our child or pay the light bill. An unnecessary low means that rather than feeling sad, we feel depressed, or instead of feeling angry, we feel hostile. Emotional numbness means turning off feelings altogether.

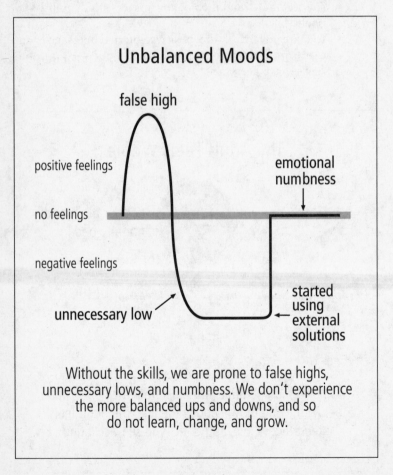

Unbalanced Moods

false high

positive feelings

emotional numbness

no feelings

negative feelings

unnecessary low

started using external solutions

Without the skills, we are prone to false highs, unnecessary lows, and numbness. We don't experience the more balanced ups and downs, and so do not learn, change, and grow.

Although these three unbalanced mood states feel different, they have the same effect on the drive to go to excess: They turn it on. When we're not connected to ourselves and our balanced feelings, we look for something else with which to connect, and it's often an external solution. What's more, we don't get the emotional messages we need—the balanced feelings—if we are going to grow, change, and mature.

Emily, the mother of three children with various disabilities, whose sweetest fruit was balance, came to the group one evening way below the line. She raised her hand when I asked who wanted to do cycles. She looked depressed and lethargic.

Emily began with a brief statement of the facts of a situation until her emotions were aroused enough to start the Natural Flow of Feelings.

She said, "All I can think about is what I'm going to do after

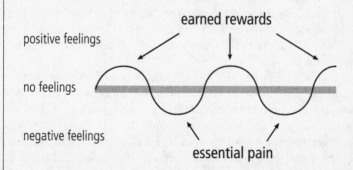

Balanced Moods

earned rewards

positive feelings

no feelings

negative feelings

essential pain

The more balanced ups and downs of life benefit us.
We experience these feelings and learn from them.
We continue doing things that reward us and
seek alternatives to those that cause us pain.

group, which is go and get a big coconut cupcake. Maybe two. The bakery down the street has these huge vanilla cupcakes with sugary frosting and shredded coconut all over the top."

Up to this point, I hadn't yet realized that when Emily was out balance, she craved sweets.

"Are you below the line or above the line?" I asked.

"Below, definitely. I feel depressed and I'm craving sugar."

I asked, "When you are craving an excess, what do you usually do?"

"I try to white-knuckle it and force myself to stop, or I cave in and let myself have whatever I want."

"How does that work for you?"

"Not well," Emily said.

The drives are very primitive and very deep. Your best strategy when you're below the line and craving an excess often is to take a big deep breath, take out your tool kit of the skills, and use it to pop yourself above the line."

Emily's voice was flat. "Okay, I'll do cycles. Our cat's been sick so I haven't been sleeping well, and Rob isn't doing well. With his speech problem, he's still getting teased at school, and I feel so powerless to stop it, and it just breaks my heart . . ."

Emily had done enough talking about the situation to arouse her feelings, so it was time to go right into the Natural Flow of Feelings: anger, sadness, fear, and guilt.

She said quietly, more like a thought than a feeling, "I feel angry that they hurt him."

"Emily, you're below the line enough to want to eat coconut cupcakes. I don't know that you even *like* coconut cupcakes! My guess is that there are some red-hot feelings inside you. I worry that unless you feel them deeply and express them fully, you won't get yourself above the line. Please don't rush. See if you can feel red-hot anger in your body, then spit it out. See the people on the other side of the room?"

She nodded.

"Make your face look angry and your words express your absolute fury so they can see and hear it. This is your son, and he is being made fun of!"

Emily said, "Laurel, it's not *civilized* to be that angry."

"You're right, Emily," I answered. "I'm not sure it is *civilized* to stuff coconut cupcakes in your mouth when you aren't even hungry."

Emily winced, then was quiet for a moment. She closed her eyes, waiting to feel anger in her body. The other members of the group were quiet, but fully anticipating an emotional explosion.

Emily's face soon was crimson. She said, "I feel *furious* that those jerks hurt my son! They are total and complete assholes. How could they be so mean to him?"

She had pumped up her "I feel angry" skills and was spitting mad and well on her way to personal balance.

"Who do they think they are, to pick on someone who is disabled?" she went on. "I *hate* it that they are so mean. . . . I'm so angry that I can't do anything to stop them from harming him. . . . Now I'm sad . . . I feel sad that Rob is hurting. I feel sad that he is different. I feel sad that he may *always* be teased. . . . I feel afraid that he will fall apart. . . . I feel afraid he will stop trying. . . . I feel afraid he will think he is a failure. . . . I feel guilty that . . ."

Common Feelings in the Five Moods

False Highs

rebellious   greedy   righteous   elated   impervious
arrogant   adored   stuffed   manic   immune

Earned Rewards

grateful   happy   secure   proud
loved   satisfied   rested   healthy

Numbness

no feelings

Essential Pain

angry   sad   afraid   guilty
lonely   hungry   full   tired   sick

Unnecessary Lows

hostile   depressed   ashamed   panicked   powerless
abandoned   starved   exhausted   miserable

She stopped and appeared confused.

"Feeling guilt is hard for you, Emily?" I said.

She nodded. Emily had been raised in a home in which you had to be perfect or you risked not being loved. Openly stating that she did something *wrong* was completely foreign to her. It seemed dangerous.

I suggested, "It's not shame and blame, it's just what you contributed to the situation. 'I feel guilty that . . .' or, 'In the best of all worlds, I wish that I had not . . . I regret that . . .'"

"I regret that I feel his pain more than he does. . . . I feel guilty that I always want to rescue him from his hurt. . . . I feel guilty that he sees me crumble emotionally, which doesn't help him."

The group quietly listened.

"Great work, Emily. That was the best 'I feel angry' that I've ever heard you do. Are you ready to go to the limits cycle?"

"I'm ready for the limits cycle, but I don't know where to begin."

The nurturing cycle is easier for many people to master than the limits cycle. You can learn to feel your feelings, even though it takes more practice and effort for thinking-oriented people than for those who are feeling-oriented. The limits cycle is harder for many people because the expectations we hold are often totally unconscious. We *don't know* what we expect and even when we find out, it's hard to figure out what a more reasonable expectation is. Sometimes we ask ourselves, "What is my expectation?" and we come up completely blank.

Building an effective limits skill is like trying on shoes. It helps to develop a sense of curiosity and keep trying on expectations until one seems to fit. There's no need to worry about "getting it right." The idea is to just start playing with the questions and seeing what answers arise. There are lots of unreasonable expectations buried inside, so if we don't uncover one today, we can always uncover it tomorrow.

"Under all those feelings," I continued, "are many expectations, some of which may be unreasonable . . ."

"My unreasonable expectation is that I shouldn't feel sad and angry when my child is ridiculed," she replied.

"Great! Keep going."

She let out a small laugh. "That's ridiculous."

"Okay. My reasonable expectation is that when my son is ridiculed and feeling sad, I will be sad, too."

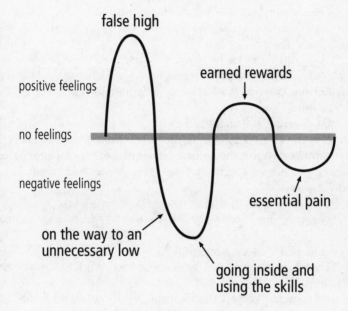

The Skills Return Us to Emotional Balance

false high

positive feelings

earned rewards

no feelings

negative feelings

on the way to an unnecessary low

essential pain

going inside and using the skills

Using the skills return us to inner balance.
We experience the balanced feelings that help
us learn, grow, and change.

"Good. Positive and powerful?"

"The positive, powerful thought that will help me stick with my new expectation is: I have a right to my feelings."

Emily's face began to change. A look of power and peacefulness was beginning to appear.

"Terrific. The essential pain and earned reward?"

Emily said, "The essential pain is that it hurts. It really, *really* hurts."

She allowed the pain of that realization to wash over her. It hurt! A minute or so later, she continued.

"The earned reward of allowing myself to feel my feelings is that they will fade. I won't torment myself about it, so I'll have more balance."

"Excellent. Are you above the line?"

"I feel better, but no, I'm not above the line."

"Let's keep going. Would you be willing to go around the limits cycle again?"

"Yes, but I don't know where to start."

"As I listened to your Natural Flow of Feelings, I wondered whether one of your most basic expectations is that it is bad for Rob to hurt."

"Of course it is," snapped Emily.

"Hurting doesn't feel good, but if you do a quick limits cycle in your head, what is the natural consequence, the essential pain, of having a life in which you don't hurt when bad things happen?" I asked.

Emily shot back, "I don't know."

"What is the earned reward of having hurts and feeling them?"

She smiled. "More strength, I guess."

"That expectation, that Rob should have no pain, may be very deep."

Emily said, "Very! I didn't want my mother and father to have pain. I don't want my children to have pain, and I don't want myself to have pain. I think I'm a big baby, always worrying if someone is going to be hurt. It's horrible."

"So, when you build a new reasonable expectation, you'll need to practice it, just like practicing the scales on the keyboard. Your brain learns by repetition. You say the reasonable expectation over and over again until it is part of your bones and totally integrated."

"So you want me to say to myself all the time, 'I expect myself to allow Rob to feel his feelings so he will get stronger.'"

"Precisely."

She gasped. Then she shrugged and said, "I expect myself to allow Rob to feel his feelings until they fade, to help him understand that everyone has pain and that from his pain, he will grow stronger."

"Wow, Emily. That was so beautifully done! Say it again. Make it as simple as you can."

"I expect myself to let Rob feel his feelings and tell him that feeling his pain will make him stronger."

"Excellent. Positive and powerful?"

"It's not my job to rescue him."

"Essential pain?" I asked.

Emily paused and thought for a moment. "The essential pain I'd have to face if I let him feel his feelings is: This is difficult for me. I can't rescue him. He will have pain."

"The earned reward?"

"The earned reward is: I will be stronger. *He can rescue himself*. He will heal his pain . . . amazing, I just popped!"

The other members of the group were right with her, feeling that emotional surge when people move above the line.

"So what you need is . . ."

Emily smiled. "What I *don't* need is a coconut cupcake!"

The group laughed.

"What I need is to practice that expectation over and over again. The support I need would be from Clay, asking him to listen to me do cycles on this."

That is emotional balance. It is developing a commitment to emotional balance, to keeping your finger on the pulse of your inner life, using the skills to take out emotional trash and stay balanced in the present, and doing any lifestyle surgery needed to make it easier to stay above the line.

Sanctuary

The reward of sanctuary is more than having a nurturing inner voice, more than accepting ourselves. It is knowing that we have a safe place within, a personal internal refuge, where we deeply connect with ourselves and, if it is our belief, the spiritual. It is knowing that we are skilled enough to go there, process our lives with the tools, and return ourselves to balance, no matter what.

Drew said she had almost no sanctuary and both Tom and Emily offered that they had some, but could use more. It's not a worrisome reward because, with enough practice, it eludes few people. Practice is key for having a sanctuary rarely comes from having an epiphany or finally "getting it." It comes from being in the trenches, doing this work. Sanctuary grows out of the use of the skills and we build it brick by brick by brick for ourselves as we use the skills more and more often and more and more effectively over time.

When we have that sanctuary within, many things change. When we are alone, we find we do not feel lost, but, in fact, we find we are in good company. When people reject us or life turns on us and walks away, we feel sad, but we know we won't reject or walk away from ourselves. For sanctuary is not a thought or a concept but an experience, moment to moment throughout the day, a palpable, solid sense of love, connection, and security from within.

For most people, sanctuary comes later in the training, definitely during the second half of the climb, long after emotional balance is reasonably secure. For those who do not have a spiritual base when they enter training, it comes long before a deepened spirituality and having it is integral to progressing well during the second half of the climb. For those who start the training with a spiritual base, it may arrive somewhat earlier.

Intimacy

Just as everyone wants another baby but few want another teenager, most of us want love . . . but intimacy? That's another matter.

For Tom, the successful lawyer whose wife had left him, his sweetest fruit was intimacy, though ending his propensities to work too much, think too much, and drink too much were near the top of the tree. Although he yearned for intimacy, during our first session I feared he would be too afraid to go inside and do this work. However, to my delight, he came to see me the very next week. During our first session, he spoke of his need for intimacy; by our second session, he was talking sex.

"I hate it that my wife deprived me of sex for all those years. Karen was so critical of me and completely ungrateful for what I did for her. But I loved her and when our marriage was good, so was the lovemaking, I could have sex with the women I meet now, but I don't just want sex. I want a relationship, and I don't know where to start."

"Well, you could always try doing cycles."

Tom looked pale and not at all happy, but he waited for his anger to arise—which took about five seconds—then he began. "I hate it that she left me. . . . I feel angry I don't have a complete relationship in my life. . . . I feel angry that I have no sex. . . . I hate it that this is so complicated. I hate it that even finding someone is hard, let alone knowing if they are going to take me to the cleaners and rip me up one side and down the other like Karen did . . ."

"Short, choppy sentences, Tom."

"I feel angry that Karen left me. . . . I hate her for not loving me. . . . I can't stand it that she took so much money from me. . . . I am furious that she criticized me. . . . I feel sad that I let her down. . . . I feel sad that I don't have a relationship. . . . I feel sad that I don't know how to get one. . . . I feel afraid that I'll screw things up again. . . . I feel guilty that I was such a bastard to Karen at times . . ."

He paused, then went on. "That brings up anger again. I feel angry at Karen for blaming me for everything. . . . I feel angry that she's convinced me that I'm a bastard. . . . I feel angry that I am so hurt. . . . I feel sad that my marriage failed. . . . I feel afraid that there is something very deeply wrong with me. . . . I feel afraid that I'll always be alone . . ."

Again, Tom paused. ". . . I feel guilty . . . actually, I don't feel guilty. What man could withstand her constant criticism . . ."

" 'My part of it was . . .' 'In the best of all worlds I wish that I had . . .' "

Tom cleared his throat. "I feel guilt that I was insensitive to her. . . . I feel guilty that I didn't respect her. . . . I feel guilty that part of me doesn't take women seriously. . . . I feel guilty that I can be . . . arrogant and . . . controlling at times. I feel guilty that I didn't listen to her and try harder in our marriage. . . . I feel guilty that sometimes I acted like a jerk."

Tom took a deep breath.

"That was exceptional," I said, "but if you're more specific, your cycle will pop you above the line even more effectively. With fear and guilt particularly, it helps to be very specific."

Tom looked perturbed, but responded anyway. "I feel guilty that sometimes I'm rude, and sometimes I don't take what they say seriously. Sometimes I tune women out, even my wife. I feel guilty that I loved my wife, but that when it came to my drinking, I treated her as if what she wanted didn't matter."

We were both silent, seemingly appreciating his vulnerability.

I was amazed at how quickly Tom was learning the method. It may have been that all those years of therapy taught him the "I feel . . ." skill to use on demand, even if the skill wasn't integrated and part of his moment-to-moment awareness.

"Tom, you just did a quick Natural Flow of Feelings. If you like, you can move from nurturing to limits."

"I'm ready," Tom answered. "My unreasonable expectation is that I cannot listen to women and not treat them with respect but still have profound love and great sex in my life." At this point, he seemed startled, then began laughing. "That's a good one, isn't it?"

I was smiling, too. "Yes, it's a good one." Tom was more above the line than I had realized.

Tom said, "A reasonable expectation? Let's see . . . I expect myself to do the best I can to stay above the line and have intimacy with myself and to be open to having intimacy with others . . ."

"Wonderful . . ."

". . . and be open to developing a warm, intimate, sexually exciting relationship with a woman."

"You did it, Tom." He looked pleased. "That is a big shift from your other expectation."

"I know," he said.

"It will only 'stick' with lots of repetition, saying it over and over."

"I know."

"Would you try it?"

"Okay, I expect myself to do the best I can to use the skills to stay above the line and have intimacy with myself, and in time, I will be open to intimacy . . ."

I smiled. ". . . and hot sex . . ."

". . . and hot sex with the right woman."

His face relaxed.

"Better?" I asked.

He nodded.

"What would be the words of encouragement you most need to hear? What would be the positive, powerful thoughts that would support that new, reasonable expectation?"

Tom replied, "I can build the skills."

"What is the essential pain?" I asked.

"The essential pain is that I can't have everything I want right now."

Tom's face blanched. He looked at me somewhat sheepishly. "That's hard for me to face."

I nodded. "And the earned reward?"

"I will have it in time. I will be open to having an intimate, erotic relationship in time."

"Are you above the line?"

He nodded and smiled. The color was back into his face—a new aliveness, really.

Tom finished his cycle. "What I need is . . . to practice the skills, to begin to deepen my intimacy with myself."

"And the 'Would you please . . . ,' the support you will request?"

"I don't need support."

Making a request is difficult. I said, "Not asking for support is part of the problem, not part of The Solution."

"Okay, the support I will ask for . . . I don't know. I do cycles with you, and I talk about my feelings with my therapist, but I'm not in a group, and I can't go to a deposition and start crying or start telling my partners how sad I am. That's never going to happen."

"What about getting a Solution Buddy, someone to connect with by phone and do cycles with several times a week?"

"I wouldn't do that. Who could I trust? It's personal information. You remember, I keep the door to my inner life totally shut. It's not even open a *crack*."

"I know. That makes me sad, because I want you to reach your Solution, and I worry that the support you have now is not enough. My fear is that you'll get off the pathway, because it will take twice as long for you to reach your Solution unless you're doing lots of Community Connections. A minimum of three per week is required in this training. It's just a matter of picking up the phone and listening to someone's cycles or having them listen to yours."

"I'd rather do it alone," said Tom.

"I know. But if there was one person with whom you would feel somewhat safe, it would be . . ."

He thought for a full three minutes. Then he said, "Carol. She's an old friend I have lunch with a couple of times a month. I'll talk with her about it. She might be interested."

"That's a great start, but I'm worried that you might not find it enough. My group starts again in a month. Would you please think about joining it?"

Tom nodded.

He was on the pathway to more intimacy in his life, but the road to this most precious reward is not a short one. It's the reward that nourishes us in ways external solutions never could, and it is often near the top of the tree. Intimacy with others rests on a strong foundation of intimacy with ourselves, which only begins to develop after emotional balance is our norm. Intimacy with the spiritual makes that foundation stronger, with the forgiving tones and loving notes that spiritual grace affords. Although connection to the spiritual can come early in the training, at the base of the tree, it is more likely to come at the very top, when the last early hurts to the heart have healed.

The dance of intimacy requires our boundaries to be flexible and responsive to a situation, becoming instantly paper-thin when closeness is safe and vault-thick as needed when there is danger. This requires a fair amount of skill in any relationship, but more so when sexuality and commitment are involved. Up goes the threshold of need for the skills once the "honeymoon" is over! We may nurture ourselves from within less because we become accustomed to relying on our partner's nurturing. The partner we choose is apt to bring up emotional trash from our parents, and the interdependence and sexuality make it harder to keep our boundary intact.

In his book *Passionate Marriage*, relationship expert David Schnarch, Ph.D., speaks about the need to hold on to ourselves in intimate relationships, to validate *ourselves* and to recognize that adult love is conditional. The model of relationships based on unconditional acceptance, gooey with incessant love and non-stop validation, is not necessarily a healthy one. It is the blend of having the capacity to be separate but close that defines intimacy and protects us from the treachery of merging, distancing, and control struggles. The only way we can stay separate but close to another is to keep our finger on the pulse of our inner lives and stay above the line. *By this way of thinking, intimacy is not a concept but a practice.*

Adult love that sidesteps the below-the-line patterns of merging, distancing, and control struggles is the foundation for lasting desire. Bertrand Russell wrote, "In the union of love, I have seen, in a mystic miniature, the prefiguring vision of the heaven that saints and poets have imagined." Certainly, love, passion, desire, and good old-fashioned "great sex" are often woven into the daily lives of many of those who are fully above the line.

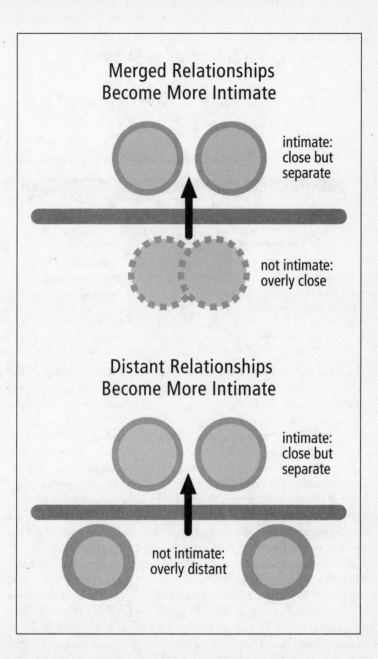

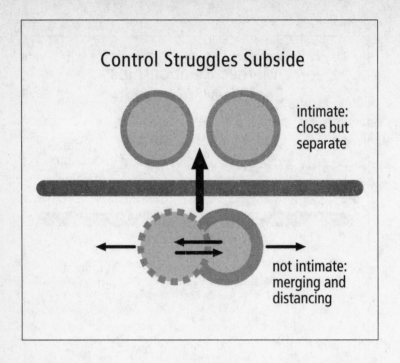

However, when we are below the line, and when we break bread with those who are down there with us, our romantic lives are likely to wander in less heavenly directions that sound more like:

- "I want sex. Why won't she give me sex? What do I have to do, beg for it?"
- "I really want to make love with you. It's just that my body has no desire. I hope you won't take it personally."
- "Sex is overrated. A good sitcom is more satisfying."

Our deepest needs are not for orgasm but for desire. We want to *desire* another, and in turn to be the object of their desire. Nearly anyone with a healthy libido can desire another, but it is only the adult in us that can do our part to make desire last. After the "in love" phase passes and there is more interdependence, the bar is raised. The threshold of need for the skills goes up, and our emotional trash flies in our face. Our tendency to merge, distance, or get into control struggles mounts. It is then that our true compatibility with that person becomes apparent and we test our skill at holding on to ourselves, staying above the line, and being close but separate. The "carrot" that desire provides may be the ultimate motivation to hold on to ourselves and stay in balance, for if we fall below the line, our sexual experience suffers.

The answer, of course, is to do what any good yoga teacher would tell you to do: breathe. After you take a big, deep breath, say to yourself, "My job is to do the best I can to hold on to myself and stay above the line. If I'm able to do that, it is far more likely that far more of my needs for sexuality, sensuality, and passion will be met, in my own separate life and also with my partner.

The greatest risk of this training, in my mind, is not that you might hurt when you take out a hideous piece of emotional trash, or that you could discover that you are in the wrong field and quit your job and go back to school. The most treacherous part has to do with relationships. Most relationships improve with Solution training, as the skills are "catching," but there are no guarantees. Moreover, the developmental shift involved is more like moving to a different world than to a new neighborhood. You lose interest in those who are still down there in the playpen, merging, distancing, and getting into control struggles. You stop wanting to hang out with people who enjoy drowning in self-pity, powerlessness, negativity, or rage.

Compassion for your partner—stopping short of rescuing—is often in order. After all, you are getting a straight injection of these skills, while your partner may be learning them from repeated contact with you, producing a far slower change and far more uncertain outcome. It may be that your focus would be better put on intimacy with yourself, with the idea that in time, improved intimacy in relationships will follow. People in abusive relationships who come into Solution training often do lifestyle surgery to separate themselves from that abuse, so they can decrease their threshold of need to a manageable level. If lifestyle surgery is not in order, consider simply focusing on the moment, staying above the line in interactions with their partners, and watching the changes in your relationships that naturally occur.

Many couples do cycles together. If it is a reasonable expectation that something good can come from your doing cycles with a friend, partner, or spouse, consider asking that person to listen to you do cycles. Maybe your partner will want you to return the favor and listen to his or her cycles as well.

Vibrancy

Vibrancy also arrives when you near the top of the tree. That doesn't mean that you won't look healthier earlier if you are eating well, sleeping enough, and exercising daily, but vibrancy is more than that. People have a vibrant glow when they have a warm sanctuary within, when they are emotionally balanced, spiritually connected, taking care of their bodies, and surrounded with loving relationships.

I usually know when it's time for someone to leave the training because they glow with vibrancy, so I know that they have mastered the skills and reached their Solution. It's wonderful, but it's also something that separates them from others in the room and why The Solution is not a program of dependency. The others are still struggling, using the skills, taking out emotional trash, making Community Connections, and doing lifestyle surgery. Vibrant people are not doing those things. They have their tool kits, and they feel secure inside, and although they go about their business of creating personal balance, much of it is *spontaneous*. They have such a deep commitment to living life above the line that there is little fear they will abandon themselves and end up at the base of the tree.

Chances are that when people comment that you look vibrant, that you glow, you'll be close to having your Solution.

Spirituality

There is no "God talk" in this method, and if you don't want to do the spiritual piece of this work, by all means, don't. In this method, *you* determine what spirituality means, in terms of your connection to the spiritual forces that be. Call that God, the universe, nature, the collective consciousness, or anything that pleases you. It is not about religion, dogma, or rules, but about *connection,* that moment-to-moment awareness of that which is *more*.

Many of us who did not get the nurturing and limits we needed early in life do not have an appreciation of the spiritual. If our parents weren't there for us, how could there be a God? Some of us had parents who made religion a substitute for a spiritual connection, and the result was various forms of personal harm. Those dreadful experiences may have caused us to cross the spiritual off our list at the same time that we nixed religion.

With this method, most people who go more deeply into themselves through using these skills become so intimate with themselves that they bump into the spiritual. By that time, often they have taken out their emotional trash about religion and have separated the darkness of dogma, ritual, and harm from the lightness of spiritual grace.

You can choose to avoid the spiritual rewards that come with using the skills, but if you do, you may not be able to use the skills as well as you need to in order to pick your sweetest of fruit. The tight fist of overcontrol may only open when there is an appreciation for grace. The nurturing inner voice may remain halting and thin when the flow of spiritual love fails to feed it.

Perhaps that was the design of life all along, that we draw upon whatever motivation we choose—whatever pain we want to stop or whatever pleasure we want to receive. We then use the skills until our connection with the spiritual is so strong that we have a blissful appreciation for the grace and mystery of life. When we do, perhaps everything else begins to take care of itself.

6. The 8 Common Excesses

During an orientation on the method that was being held in a stone-cold basement classroom at the university, a woman who looked to be in her seventies sat in the very front row with a big red purse on her lap. She had three pairs of glasses stacked on the knot of auburn hair atop her head. A full inch before the scalp, her hair was pure white.

There were a dozen or so people of nearly every age, race, and shape in the room, and as in most Solution Groups, some of its members would be highly accomplished individuals struggling with one excess or dabbling in a few. There would be others with no excesses but with a deep desire to reap more of life's rewards. A few would say that this was their *last* stop, that they had tried everything else. If this didn't work, they didn't know what they would do.

It was the last group that I felt most confident would reach their Solution without dallying or stopping midway through the journey. During this orientation, they were apt to say how *furious* they were that they *had* to do this work, and how *scared* they were that they *wouldn't* do it—statements that were music to my ears. I knew I would stay with them and help to make their journey safer, easier, and quicker, and that their steely resolve, their willingness to *do whatever it took*, would ensure that they reached their sweetest fruit.

As the session began, several people asked questions. The entire time I was trying to answer them, the woman with the red purse never stopped moving! She wiggled in her chair, then stood up, adjusted the cushion she had brought for her back, then sat down again. Then she dropped her purse on the floor, spilling out cigarettes, lipstick, and crumpled receipts. As she scrambled to push them back into her purse, I wondered what had brought her to this room. Her legs looked painfully swollen, and a thick brown cane rested next to her chair.

Anything can be an external solution

I asked the group, "What can be an external solution?"

Someone in the back row said, "Spending."

Another person said, "Drinking . . . drugs."

A man in the first row offered, "Sex."

Then someone called out rather stridently, "Anything can be an external solution. *Anything* at all."

It was the woman with the brown cane.

The room grew so quiet, I could hear the buses on the street outside. It seemed like everyone in the room was mentally playing with the idea that external solutions are not limited to vices, compulsions, and pathologies, that the potential for excess germinates in a person's every act, thought, and feeling.

"You're right," I said, noticing that the letters on her name tag spelled Della. "When we're out of balance, virtually anything can become an external solution."

Della smiled with a certain satisfaction. Her body became still, and she seemed to settle into the session. I admired this woman already, for she had found her way to this cold basement classroom and was fully prepared to say what was on her mind. She seemed like a person who could latch on to the method and not let go until she had what she most wanted in her life.

Since *anything* has the potential to become an external solution, the tools in this book must be adaptable to them all, and my experience has been that they are, at least as much as genetics, fate, and chance allow. During the first half of this journey, people focus on acquiring the basic skills that will enable them to feel emotionally balanced much of the time. During the second half, they use the skills more narrowly and deeply to end a particular excess or reap a specific reward.

Some of these excesses, when taken to the extreme, are addictions with substance abuse, and require more comprehensive treatment than this method alone. The changes that occur in the "addicted brain"—including alterations in nerve cell membranes and receptors and in neurotransmitters—make the excesses more tenacious and relapse more likely. Using only this training to treat substance abuse is not recommended, particularly during the acute phase of abstinence, when withdrawal symptoms may be the most challenging. Although problem drinkers often rely on this method alone to cut down on their alcohol intake, alcoholics require more intensive, interdisciplinary treatment. Likewise, emotional overeaters use the program alone, whereas those with eating disorders require more comprehensive support; some smokers readily quit without additional support, but others use a nicotine patch and group support.

Getting some nurturing and limits from outside

Some excesses, whether they are considered addictions or not, pose significant medical risk. Since the feeling brain changes very slowly, *spontaneous* changes in such primitive drives as eating, drinking, and smoking often do not occur right away. It is only sensible that if medical risk is high, behavior is best changed immediately in order to decrease that risk.

Think of the skills as being *internal* sources of nurturing and limits that, because of the way the feeling brain changes, can only be increased so rapidly. Consider that having a structured exercise or food plan, arranging for personal training, taking medications or having a coach are all *external* sources of nurturing and limits.

If we use both sources, internal and external, we can often pop ourselves above the line with a high-risk behavior sooner in the training, thus prompting a more rapid decrease in medical risk. That's why the professional training offered by the Institute includes both group training and the option of arranging a form of individual coaching that is for high risk participants. As they progress with the training and their internal nurturing and limits become automatic and spontaneous, the external support is usually no longer necessary. In the meantime, their medical risk has decreased!

What follows are brief descriptions of the eight common excesses. Some of us have been trained to accentuate every freckle we have and to assume that we must work to be perfect. So please keep in mind that most of these patterns are *normal*, that the essential pain we must face is that we are *not* perfect. And the earned reward? We don't have to be. We are human! *It is only when we engage in these patterns frequently and to our significant detriment that they are considered external solutions.*

Having a Solution means having all the rewards of human maturity and *no* external solutions but it does not mean that we

Eight Common Excesses

Eating Too Much

overeating   binge eating   mindless eating

Chemical Pleasures

drinking   smoking   store drugs   street drugs

Working Past Six

overworking   work preoccupation
career as identity   stress highs and numbness
busy-busy-busy

Spending

overspending   excessive materialism
hoarding and clutter

Rescuing Others

emotional merging   expecting too little
being a savior

Putting Up Walls

distancing emotionally   expecting too much
persecuting

Too Much Thinking

obsessive thinking   analyzing everything
avoiding feelings   getting it perfect   overcontrol

People-Pleasing

fear of rejection   approval seeking
being too good

never take a drink, eat too much pizza, or shop until we drop. In fact, a sign of having a Solution is that we do not rigidly contain our behavior or act excessively judgmental about ourselves. We understand, on the very deepest level, that we don't have to be perfect to be wonderful and that there are pleasures in life that are to be enjoyed—even by us. The drives to go to excess are so diminished that we can dabble in excesses without worrying that we will "fall off a cliff" into rampant excessive appetites. At last we can relax and know that we can trust ourselves!

Eating Too Much

overeating—binge eating—mindless eating

The most common external solution is overeating, and given the environment in which we live, I have no idea why the epidemic isn't even more severe than reported. A Hollywood scriptwriter bent on creating a world of overeaters would include:

- total dietary chaos and confusion
- limitless high-fat, high-sugar foods
- social isolation and little intimacy
- highly sedentary occupations
- the obsolescence of walking for transportation
- a frightfully fast lifestyle

In other words, life today! Fortunately, this environment is powerless against an inner life that is soothing and comforting. Food only becomes excessively alluring when intimacy with ourselves, others, and the spiritual is missing.

For example, in working with obese children, the most surefire way to end their excessive appetites is to give them parental love—nurturing and limits. A child will always choose the sweetness of love over having a sweet. The same is true for adults.

If you have any doubts about this whatsoever, have lunch with a friend, lover, or mate. Split a sandwich, but don't eat your half—your partner must feed it to you. You must ask for a bite, and that person must put it to your lips. This little activity, developed by John Gray, Ph.D., seems to be a brilliant one, because almost nobody finishes their sandwich! Most of us are satisfied just by the love.

If we are getting our need for nurturing and love met, it's not hard to set limits with ourselves and eat healthier food or less of it. Nurturing is like putting money in the bank and limit-setting is like withdrawing. If there's not enough nurturing in our lives, we're bound to encounter rebellion, misbehavior, and excess when we set limits. No wonder so many of us have difficulty setting limits with food. It's not that we have a problem with self-discipline, but that we haven't developed the inner skills to nurture ourselves so well that we don't *need* the extra food. In fact, cutting back on how much we eat and pushing away less healthful foods seems like a nurturing act, not a depriving one, for we feel so much better and take such pride in our bodies. Eating better seemed a small price to pay.

Except for rare syndromes, genetic factors, the biological propensities for weight gain brought on by overweight, and the effects of certain diseases and medications, all overeating is *emotional*. The stereotypical picture of emotional overeating is of a premenstrual, hysterical woman eating a quart of fudge brownie ice cream because she is depressed. The controlled, stoic man ordering a second hamburger is seen as a victim of habit.

Yet they are both out of emotional balance. Food soothes the emotional lows, but how numb does a person have to be to down two hamburgers and all those fries, have a bellyache afterward, fall asleep in the chair, then keep overeating the next day? It's not just emotional lows and numbness that fan the flames of our appetites but also false highs. People eat when they are happy, elated, or rebellious and eat just to celebrate *anything* or reward themselves for *anything*.

In these three mood states—false highs, unnecessary lows, and numbness—we are not sensitive to the subtle signs of hunger and satiety, so we don't stop when our body has had enough. Also, in these states, we don't think about the consequences of our actions. In a face-off between body hunger and emotional hunger, emotional hunger nearly always prevails. If we *want* the food, we will get it, even if it is not what we truly *need*.

The most common form of using food as an external solution is plain old overeating—that is, disregarding our inner cues of hunger and fullness and eating anyway because we *want* it, because we *deserve* it, or because it is *there*. There may be a cultural or familial tendency to overeat that never has been overcome. Some of us have eating binges, quite parallel to drinking binges, and others of us are so disconnected from ourselves that we eat mindlessly, in a state of near numbness. We roll along, giving our bodies far more food than needed, often not even knowing that we are doing it.

Overeating is not bad or wrong, but for some there are health consequences, and for most it adds to our imbalance, taking us further from the strength, goodness, and wisdom at our center.

Chemical Pleasures

drinking—smoking—store drugs—street drugs

The most common chemical pleasures are smoking cigarettes, drinking alcohol, and popping pills. Marijuana has its place in this category, as do other chemical cocktails found at your local drugstore. Some people use caffeine so heavily that it becomes a formidable external solution.

Chemically medicating ourselves seems to carry far more stigma than it rightly should. After all, every time you down a plate of pasta, your serotonin levels increase and that sweet, calming feeling rushes through your body. Whether the manner of regulating mood comes from food or from drugs, whether it produces calming effects or offers the increased brain activity and euphoria of dopamine, it is still personal mood regulation. In a world in which most of our pain is psychological, it only seems fair that people have the right and need to modulate their moods. However, when we don't have the skill to stay above the line and modulate our moods with exercise, sleep, laughter, prayer, and sex, we go below the line, and turn to using chemical pleasures.

When it comes to using chemicals, some people are dabblers, taking small amounts of several of them. Dabbling can be a choice to avoid social stigma or the health effects of any one excess, or it can arise purely by chance. Others are loyal to one external solution. For instance, many people *only* soothe with overeating or stick *strictly* to marijuana. Others become devoted to one excess, give it up, then fully devote themselves to another.

Some people who've had substance problems themselves or who have been raised in homes where substance use has led to painful losses view abstinence as their goal. This may be the best choice for those whose emotional trash about substances is high or whose bodies, due to genetic or acquired differences, make them vulnerable to excessive substance use. However, for others, moderation is the ultimate sign of balance and for them, being able to take a drink without needing the whole bottle is a sign of mastery of the skills. This is much the same as for overeaters. A sign of living life above the line is having a cookie or two without fear of sliding down that slippery slope into needing the whole bag.

Working Past Six

**overworking—work preoccupation—career as identity—
stress highs and numbness—busy-busy-busy**

People work more today than they did twenty years ago. Many need to do so in order to meet their basic financial responsibilities, much less save for college, retirement, or the down payment on a house. My mother played bridge, spent afternoons with the kids at the pool, and had time to make meat loaf, mashed potatoes, and chocolate pudding for dinner. Perhaps you do the same in your home, but for most of us there just isn't the time, primarily because of work. What's more, work can fill so many deep needs— validation, power, meaning, and security, not to mention paying the light bill. Working more than we should is relatively easy to justify.

The problem with overworking is that it distorts our capacity to meet our true needs. We get love from the job or people at work, not from personal, intimate relationships. We get so tired that we can't do the myriad things that make life good. We bore into work so deeply that the rest of our lives become rather superficial. It's no wonder that working to excess is associated with other external solutions, particularly drinking, eating, spending, and sitting.

Since it is so easy to rationalize overworking, it may help to be very concrete about it.

- Do you work more than fifty hours per week?
- Do you find yourself preoccupied with work and not present in your relationships or do not have time for the basics of life, such as doing the wash, paying the bills, or diapering the children?
- On your deathbed, would you look back on this time in your life and be happy that you worked as much as you do?
- Do you use staying "busy-busy-busy" all day as a way to stay numb or to tap into an epinephrine-cortisol high?

The most common pattern of those of us who overwork is checking our inner lives like we would our coat when we arrive at work, then racing through the day focused on everyone and everything *but* our own inner lives. When we leave at night, we put that coat on, and it is a mess! It is covered with so many unfelt feelings and unmet needs that it is overwhelming. It's far too difficult to tease apart the feelings and needs and even begin to meet them. Most of us opt instead for plopping on the couch, turning on the tube, going to the fridge, or pouring a drink.

The research on the method has shown that most people who master these skills report less work stress and higher work productivity. When we don't "check our coats at the door," but use the skills to stay above the line all day, we are apt to be more productive and less stressed. We may even work more hours with less detriment to our health and our happiness.

One last note: Some people use the method to deal with underworking or being underemployed. Or they may find that they flip-flop back and forth between binge working and not working at all. These patterns may be the result of needing more of the skill to nurture and set limits from within as well.

Spending

overspending—excessive materialism—hoarding and clutter

When there is not enough love to go around, one of the most common things children do—other than overeat—is steal money from their parents. When we don't have the genuine article of a nurturing inner voice and the compassion and warmth of deep love, we often develop wants and desires that are expressed through spending.

We spend more money than we have, get an emotional fix from acquiring, focus excessively on material wealth, or become overly attached to *things* and can't give them up, so clutter is *everywhere*.

I first began to understand the relationship between the skills and overspending when participants in my groups spoke up about having *stopped* their habit. One of the most dramatic stories involved a fine artist, Clare, who lived in a Victorian in Pacific Heights. Her husband's family was quite wealthy, and she and her husband lived well, but although they had raised four children together, they were far from close. He spent most evenings attending board meetings or social events, and she spent most Saturdays . . . shopping. Stopping her shopping need was not Clare's sweetest fruit but turned out to be about halfway up the tree. After Clare had been involved in the training for about a year, she came to the group one evening, radiating enthusiasm about her recent breakthrough:

"I went shopping last Saturday like I do every week. I took the curved escalators up to the top floor of Nordstrom and got ready to go to work, picking up various things I needed on each floor. I went to the bath shop and realized that I didn't *need* anything. Then I went down one floor to lingerie and found nothing I wanted, so I went on to shoes. I stopped on each floor, fully expecting to have that small but meaningful thrill of purchasing something that I really wanted, but finally, when I reached the first floor, I realized that my hungering for things was gone. I didn't try to be good and not shop. Spending simply didn't do it for me anymore."

Rescuing Others

emotional merging—expecting too little—being a savior

When we are below the line, most of us have a tendency to be either rescuers or persecutors, or to seesaw between those unfortunate patterns. When we see ourselves merging with others or distancing from them, we sense that the pattern is very deep and very old, and it is both. These patterns are laid down so early in life that they underscore our every interaction and affect our happiness and health in profound ways, so attending to them can be both important and humbling.

Emotional merging means being significantly more aware of another person's feelings and needs than our own. We expect too little, have tissue-paper-thin boundaries, are overly sensitive to others' pain, forget ourselves too easily, and deny others the opportunity to learn from the consequences of their choices. In a relationship between two mergers, the implicit agreement is: "I will take care of you if you will take care of me. Then neither of us has to grow up, face our aloneness, and take care of ourselves."

The reason rescuing leads to persecuting is that we can only stuff our feelings for so long. Another way to think of it is that you can only tell so many lies, do more than you can do, and abandon yourself more than you should until there is a backlash. The well is empty and something has to give, which is usually when persecuting moves in. We either persecute others with rages, verbal assaults, or aloofness or take it out on ourselves by eating or drinking or sinking into the muck of depression, self-pity, and powerlessness. What started out as angelic behavior and oversweetness inevitably turns dark and sour.

Putting Up Walls

emotional distancing—expecting too much—persecuting

In order to persecute another, our boundaries have to be very thick, and our tendency must be to distance emotionally. How else could we withstand the pain of another's hurt? A person's boundaries are thick for various reasons, including basic temperament, early training, vicious experiences later in life, or even because behind that big wall is a very sensitive individual who would surely surrender if those bulwarks were not kept firmly in place.

Rescuing sounds so sweet and persecuting so nasty that it is important to remember that they are simply flip sides of each other. All of us have aggressive tendencies, and even in the healthiest of relationships, there can be subtle strains of hate, aggression, masochism, and revenge. We are not angels, just humans!

Emotional distancing means being significantly more aware of *our* feelings and needs than those of the other person. We expect too much, have vault-thick boundaries, are relatively insensitive to others' pain, forget them too easily, and grind into their soul the negative consequences of their choices. In a relationship between two distancers, the implicit agreement is: "I will take care of myself if you will take care of yourself, and neither of us will take care of our relationship, or face our fears about intimacy and learn how to be close."

In relationships between rescuers and persecutors, there can be horrendous arguments. The most common relationship pattern between two people who are both below the line is to have distancing, merging, *and* control struggles. The fabric of the relationship can become so tattered and torn that the only joy left is the sweetness of revenge. Becoming preoccupied with getting even becomes an external solution of its own.

Too Much Thinking

obsessive thinking—analyzing everything— avoiding feelings—getting it perfect—overcontrol

Those who are drawn to this method are usually excessively thinking-oriented or highly feeling-oriented. That is, their first response to what occurs in life is a tendency to either *only* feel or to *only* think. Unfortunately, balance requires a blending of both, something that evolves as people master these skills.

Those who are very thinking-oriented need, more than anything, to feel. Years ago, graffiti artists revised Descartes' "cogito, ergo sum" (I think, therefore I am), spraying a colorful "I feeeeel, therefore I am" on a brick wall near campus. Clearly, they were right.

The natural fallout of avoiding feelings or not yet knowing *how* to feel deeply is for thoughts to run rampant, going round and round and becoming repetitive and obsessive. It is only when thoughts are infused with feelings that their meaning becomes clear, decisions are made from the heart, and balance and peace are restored.

Most of us create a life that builds upon our strengths, so naturally, people who are thinking-oriented gravitate to educations and jobs that draw upon their talents to recall information, analyze situations, and figure things out. Unfortunately, those choices tend to accentuate their tendency to think rather than feel.

Thinking too much brings its own discomforts, such as:

- "I wake up in the middle of the night and think about how the day went, analyze what is not working, and figure out how to change things."
- "I hate the fact that my mind won't stop racing. No matter what I do, my mind keeps obsessing about the same situation."
- "I live in a world of figuring everything out. It gives me the illusion of control."

Excessive thinking is often related to perfectionism, overcontrol, being judgmental, and difficulty forgiving. The assumption is that if we could just get it right, everything would be fine, that people will love us or we will finally love ourselves. The sad part is that all that trying to figure it out and get it right just separates us further from what we want. It is like a "crossed wire," which we will read about in chapter 10, "Step 1: The Nurturing Cycle." The feeling does not correspond to the need. It is: "I feel scared that I am not enough. I need to be perfect." More accurate would be: "I need to bring up a nurturing inner voice and realize that I don't have to be perfect. I am only human."

Regarding control, the essential pain that must be faced is often "I am not in *complete* control." The earned reward varies from "I don't have to be; there is God," to "I do have some control, and some responsibility to use it." Often, excessive thinking has the secondary gain of relieving the person of a responsibility to take action. In other words, "If I can be busy thinking, I don't have to get busy doing."

You might be aware that too much thinking hurts you and may recall the sleepless nights, the endless confusion, and the painful indecisiveness. But the most important downside of too much thinking is that it separates us from ourselves. If we are incarcerated by too much thinking, there is no room to have the depth of feeling that creates a secure and lasting intimacy with ourselves.

The good news is that thinking too much is not completely genetic; it can be learned. As we muscle up on the "I feel . . ." skill and use the cycles, the drive to think too much begins to fade away.

People-Pleasing

fear of rejection—approval seeking—being too good

The woman who sat next to me on the plane trip to Denver was all of nineteen. She sported a blond ponytail and was so overly cheerful that I knew something must be very wrong. As we spoke, she volunteered:

"I've always been a people-pleaser. That's all I think about: How do other people see me, do they like me, are they mad at me, what do they think about how I look? I have to try on ten different outfits before I go to a party because I have to think about what other people will think. I want people to like me, and when they don't, I feel so insecure."

That girl was so young that it seemed perfectly reasonable for her to be reliant on the approval of others and to be so open about her relentless pursuit of their validation. When we grow older, we may look more self-assured and reveal less about our insecurities, yet inside, we may still be that blond kid with the perky ponytail, constantly seeking the praise, attention, and approval of those around us and being willing to completely abandon ourselves just so we are liked.

People-pleasing doesn't *look* like candy-bar binges, heroin injections, or too many martinis. But it *acts* much the same, as it sends us soaring on treacherous false highs of hoping and dreaming that others will love us, admire us, and see us for the good person we truly are. Oh, the bittersweet joy of *seeking* . . .

Yet, even if that person whose approval we most covet utters every word of unconditional love for which we yearn, and even if virtually everyone *likes* us, we feel more out of balance than ever! It's only when the nurturing from outside is greeted by the nurturing voice within us that we can receive that love. Without it, their approval bounces off us, leaving us with a special kind of hangover that is free of headaches but full of heartaches. Feeling more fragile, more dependent, and more aware of the emptiness within, we fear the rejection of others because if they reject us, we have nowhere to go, so we exhaust ourselves with worry and trying to be far too good.

Della's sweetest fruit: Spirituality

Della, the woman with the three pairs of glasses stacked on her auburn hair and the large red purse on her lap, listened to a brief description of each of the excesses and the list of life's sweetest rewards. When I asked the group to consider their sweetest fruit, the touchstone of their development, and to name two of the excesses or rewards near the top of their tree, each person in turn spoke up.

When it was Della's turn, she said, "I have a lot of bad habits, and I am at odds with a lot of people. But what I most want is to have peace in my life, which for me means having the feeling that I had as a kid, that there was a grace and mystery to life, that I was never alone, and that life was good because God was good."

I winced inside when she said that, fearing that those new to the program would think it was evangelistic, that God would be forced on them. As people venture within and use these skills, a spiritual deepening often evolves, but there is no religion or required "God talk" in the method.

Della continued. "Instead, I have this deep ugliness in me that makes me have a short fuse with people. I can easily hold a grudge for a decade or two, and I've managed to alienate almost every friend I've ever had. I've done the same thing to my one child, my daughter, Beth, who lives in Spokane. I'm constantly finding fault with her and trying to control what she does. I could say it's just because I'm old and have had my share of hardship, but I don't want to do that. I want to face it straight on and see if I can use the skills to clean out that ugliness and put inside me a feeling of . . . grace. I want the loving connection with God that has eluded me since I was a little girl."

The pain that showed on her face was akin to a knife in the heart. I felt sad for her but reminded myself that her yearning for a greater awareness of the grace and mystery of life would provide the perfect motivation for her to use the skills. If she had the courage and persistence to master them, her dream would come true, and to the extent that fate, genetics, and personal history allowed, she would have the full bounty of life's sweetest rewards.

Della adjusted the pillow for her back, then continued. "I have lots of bad habits, but the worst one is smoking. My doctor has all but disowned me as a patient because I smoke. But I can't stop. I go through this emotional dip, and I feel myself sinking— not fainting, but sinking into this feeling of being lost. I don't want to feel it, so I reach for a cigarette, inhale the smoke, and I feel such relief. I don't know what I would do if I couldn't smoke when I needed to."

Della had captured my heart already. I thought, How many people at seventy-four years old are willing to do this work? She could be home on the recliner, gently snoring with the television blaring and her cat curled up on her lap! I've learned since how many people over seventy use the method. Often, they work harder than those younger and reach their Solution relatively quickly. There is an urgency about their use of the skills, as if they are secretly saying to themselves, "If not now, when?"

"So," I said to Della, "a spiritual connection is what you most want. The other excesses or rewards that are near the top of the tree are smoking and . . ."

Della paused, smiled a slightly devilish smile, and said, "Putting up walls. In my case, it's needling people and even persecuting them! I've always been a bit of a troublemaker, and although I can cite how many good acts I do, I take a certain delight in aggravating people. My daughter is not an exception. I love her dearly, but I must say, I know just how to infuriate her with a mere look. There is a dark side of me that takes a little bit of joy in stirring up trouble!"

A slow laughter came from the group, the kind of delicious chuckling that suggests a shared secret. Or perhaps they just appreciated her candor. Several members of the group clapped.

Della had made it through the orientation. She knew that her sweetest fruit was a deepened appreciation for the grace and mystery of life and that turning off the drive to smoke and put up walls would be near the top of the tree. She was ready to begin the climb . . .

You now know quite a bit about the method, including what the skills are and much about the journey: the threshold of need, the rewards, and the excesses. Yet, you might wonder how this simple method could produce such remarkable rewards. What is the biology that could explain how The Solution works?

7. The Biology of Transformation

Something about using this method occasionally seems strange to me, even eerie. It is not that people pop themselves above the line by using the cycles. It is that when they have popped themselves above the line so often and so well, they quite often experience nothing less than a personal transformation.

Of course, these dramatic emotional shifts—both the immediate effect and the long-term one—are wonderful and exciting to see. But somehow, *it just doesn't seem right*. How could such ethereal changes come from asking oneself questions as simple as "How do I feel?" and "What do I need?"

Last evening, my friend Kate called just as my children and I were finishing dinner. It was a warm summer evening, and my younger son put Bo on a leash and took him for a walk while I settled onto the sofa to chat with Kate.

She was so depressed that her voice was leaden and her speech halting. Her boss was criticizing everything she did, loading so much work on her that she had left work that day with a migraine. She is supporting her mother, who lives in Florida and is knee-deep in credit-card debt, so she is in no position to quit her job. On the other hand, she couldn't stand the thought of going back there another day.

Kate asked me to listen to her do cycles—something she had never done before—then proceeded to do the Natural Flow of Feelings, to set reasonable expectations, to face the essential pain, and to feel the earned reward. In three minutes flat, my friend who had been depressed, powerless, and immobilized popped herself above the line. Now happy and empowered, she began talking about going for a bike ride. It was astonishing! *Do a cycle and get personal balance*—much like: *Put a quarter into the gum-ball machine and get a gum ball.*

The bread dough becomes the loaf

Although seeing Kate pop above the line was thrilling, it was *nothing* compared to the riveting experience of watching someone use the skills over time and then finally . . . be transformed. Though the skills grow slowly, there is often a moment when that last stubborn drive to go to excess vanishes and the experience of living becomes *different*. The person doesn't feel like the same person, and to them, the world doesn't seem like the same world. Moreover, the change feels *cellular*, as if the bread dough has become the loaf and there is no going back.

What's more, those who approach the top of the tree find a lot of "angel dust" in the air. What they experience is not a simple emotional shift, but a stirring of their soul. The person who was cloaked in neediness suddenly has no particular needs—they all seem met. Before, their fist was tight with overcontrol—*wanting* what they *wanted* when they *wanted* it. Now they willingly open their hand to the will of the spiritual. There is trust that the universe will provide them with precisely what they *need* when they *need* it, and that life will unfold as it should.

Kyle, a man from Idaho in one of our telegroups, was distraught during a recent session. He had participated in a local Solution Circle and had later sought support from a telegroup as he completed his Solution. On this particular day, Kyle was incredibly agitated.

He said, "I *need* a consultation. I don't know whether I should talk with my therapist or go to the doctor or ask you, but something is *very wrong* with me and I'm really scared."

"Tell me more," I said, half smiling inside, knowing what he was likely to say.

In a big, blustery voice, Kyle said, "I'm a chef. My whole life is focused on food. I love recipes. I love to prepare food and talk about food. I love to eat food, and I've been overweight since I was a kid.

"Ten days ago, the strangest thing happened. Everything seemed to change. I didn't know what was going on, but I stopped caring about food. Now I eat . . . whatever, strawberries, some turkey, I don't know, but it balls up in my mouth. I've lost my appetite and my fascination with food."

"It sounds like the love affair is over," I suggested.

"Do you think I'm ill?"

"No. I think you're normal," I said with a chuckle of delight. "I think that you've used the skills for long enough to be at the top of the tree. The psychological drive to overeat is gone, right?"

"Yes, it's gone . . . for the first time since I was nine years old," replied Kyle.

"And you still have a fair amount of extra weight in the middle of your body?"

"Uh-huh."

"The energy from that weight goes right into your blood and keeps your blood sugar reasonably stable, so you're not experiencing a lot of body hunger."

"No, I'm not hungry at all," Kyle said. Then he was quiet, perhaps beginning to understand that something momentous had begun to change in him, and that there was no going back. Life *below the line* held little interest for him now, and an entire world of life *above the line* was before him.

"So what am I going to do? I'm a chef!" he said, exasperated.

"It might help to check your feelings," I suggested.

Kyle was agreeable. "Okay, how do I feel? Happy and proud . . . and scared as hell."

I was overjoyed for Kyle and mused, "Yes, scared as hell seems about right."

"It's not *normal* for me to not be totally focused on food. It's not normal for me to feel so . . . alive."

Again there was quiet for a moment, as everyone in the group took in Kyle's words.

"Kyle, you have worked so hard and have done so many cycles . . ."

"Zillions of them," he interjected.

". . . until you have woven that personal balance into the emotional and spiritual core of your being, where the primitive drives reside. You have *earned* this feeling. You have done the work."

He paused again, then said, "It's odd, but it doesn't seem hard now."

"I know . . ."

"It's a different world."

"Yes, I know."

Every clinician has a few star patients, but the change Kyle was beginning to experience is more the norm than the exception for those who use this method with persistence and dedication. Everything comes down to chemistry, and after I had seen stories like Kyle's unfold over and over again, I knew that there had to be a biological explanation for the *unconscious* changes that often occur when the method is used over time.

Several years ago, my colleagues and I submitted a research article on the method to a scientific journal. The journal's editor, Elaine Monsen, Ph.D., a faculty member at the University of Washington, called me and said, "Laurel, I understand what The Solution is, but how does it work?"

I answered, "Elaine, *I don't know* how it works."

I knew that various scientific literatures were consistent with it—psychological development, family systems, addictive behaviors, and health promotion—but the mechanism of transformation was unclear to me. Today my response would be similar, but I would add, "All I can tell you about is the emerging brain science that seems to explain it best."

A bramble bush of cells

The human brain is a bramble bush of a hundred billion cells called neurons, with countless electrical currents and chemical signals between them. Despite the enormous attention neurobiology receives these days, relatively little is known about the brain, and there is controversy about even the basic ideas that follow.

Our brain is "triune," that is, it includes three brains, each of which evolved in phases. The brain stem, or the reptilian brain, grew first. Next, the feeling brain, or the limbic system, developed. Finally, the thinking brain, or neocortex, evolved.

How do these three parts of the brain figure into creating a transformation? After all, a Solution is more than a blip on the screen, a brief period of relief from troubles or a short foray into good behavior. Instead, it is substantial and lasting, something that involves broad-spectrum change in our emotional, behavioral, and spiritual lives. What part of the brain can give us that change?

Although all three of our "brains" interact, each has different powers and roles. The brain stem is relegated to basic body processes and responses—not a likely locale for personal transformation.

The thinking brain is traditionally considered the most powerful part of the brain, but this is not so. In fact, *feelings are more powerful than thoughts.* We can't "think our way around" our most primitive drives and deepest longings. Nor can we sensibly

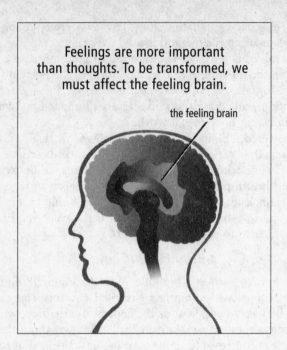

Feelings are more important than thoughts. To be transformed, we must affect the feeling brain.

the feeling brain

act on the rational ideas of the thinking brain when we are highly emotionally aroused.

Although the thinking brain can easily capture our attention and take us on various intellectual escapades, it is our feeling brain that orchestrates our actions and forms the hub of emotional balance, primitive drives, spiritual connection, and relations to others. If there is no change in the feeling brain, there is no transformation.

Let's focus briefly on each part of the triune brain:

The **brain stem** controls basic bodily processes. It keeps our hearts beating and our lungs working and is what would keep us alive if we were "brain-dead." It is also the seat of our temperament, the emotional backdrop of our lives, and our *emotional hardwiring*. It was Kyle's brain stem that made him sensitive and more apt to be hostile than depressed. Temperament is genetically determined and can have a significant effect on our threshold of need for the skills.

The **thinking brain** is the seat of knowledge, understanding, planning, intending, problem-solving, strategizing, and generally, *figuring it out*. It is the largest of the three parts of the brain, consisting of two symmetrical hemispheres—the right brain and the left brain—each of which influences the opposite side of the body. The senses, conscious motor control, and the capacity to speak and write reside in the thinking brain.

Most current healing methods are processed primarily by the thinking brain. For example:

- Therapists help clients gain insight into their problems.
- Behavioral therapy charts the triggers of negative behavior and rewards positive behavior.
- Motivational tapes encourage us to act differently.
- Books give us knowledge, insight, and understanding.
- Groups provide information about shared problems.
- Physicians give medical advice and information.
- The clergy reflect on what is right to do and why.

All these methods have their merits, but the scientific literature suggests that they don't work very well. Many prompt only the smallest changes. Others stimulate change that recedes soon after the treatment ends. Most are narrow in effect because the roots of the symptom have not been addressed, so even if changes are substantial and persistent, the development of another symptom in its stead is likely. In the health community, this is referred to as "symptom substitution."

That's not to say that the thinking brain isn't important. Knowing *what* to do is important, and understanding *why* we should do something can be motivating. Changing our thoughts with cognitive therapy can affect our emotions to some extent, and analyzing what triggers us to go out of balance can, at times, result in changing those behaviors, if only in the short term.

Cognitive approaches suggest that if we just change the internal "computer" of our thinking brains through insight, knowledge, planning, or intending, that would be enough. Unfortunately, our thoughts *rule* neither our heart nor our soul, and quite often, when those powerful forces within us are not attended to, they have their own will and their own way.

When emotions are aroused, knowledge isn't enough

Kyle's catering business put him in contact with an inordinate number of impossibly demanding clients. At one session, he told the group of a disastrous evening. He had catered a large dinner party for a couple whose photographs appeared regularly in the society page of the *San Francisco Chronicle*. According to Kyle, the wife, Audrey, was impossible to please.

"There I was," he said, "sweating bullets to make everything *perfect* for this woman: crispy lamb chops, bright-green asparagus, and long-stemmed strawberries dipped in dark chocolate with just the tip double-dipped in white chocolate.

"What did she tell me at the end of the evening as she wrote out a check that included a five percent tip? That she was *disappointed* the rolls were not piping hot! It was all I could do not to physically assault that woman, but I stuffed my feelings, went home, and ate myself into oblivion."

When emotions are sufficiently aroused, the way they were with Kyle that evening, the power of positive thinking is simply not enough. Even the most sensitive and precise information about what one "should" do or how one "ought" to feel is instantly forgotten.

The **feeling brain** is the seat of emotional balance. It is in charge of our response to the world, orchestrating what our senses reveal of the outside world and the signals from our internal milieu. It settles on an emotional state, then sends messages to the thinking brain and brain stem, which respond in our best interests. Although much technical information has been written about the feeling brain (see Recommended Reading), apart from the diagrams of outputs, arousal systems, and neural activation, the central role of the feeling brain appears to be *connection*:

> **Connection to *ourselves***—The feeling brain is the seat of emotional balance. It is our emotional core, the neural system that encompasses our connection to ourselves, and the storehouse of our dreams, intuitions, and emotional memories.
>
> **Connection to *others***—The feeling brain is also the center of intimacy. Relatedness, attachment, sexuality, and com-

munion appear to rest comfortably within its confines. It is responsible for our instinct to take care of our young and to restrain ourselves from harming others.

Connection to the *spiritual*—The limbic system has been called the seat of the soul, as the experiences of spiritual connection—transcendence, mystical union, and spiritual awakening—appear to be housed there as well.

Connection to *external solutions*—If our feeling brains are wired to not connect effectively with ourselves, others, and the spiritual, we may seek substitutes for the human connections a balanced life affords. The drive to use external solutions may increase, as they offer what seems like a glimmer of relief from the incessant longing within.

Through all of this—connection to self, others, and the spiritual, and a natural resistance to external solutions—the feeling brain offers hope for a transformation.

The feeling brain develops . . .

If the feeling brain is *that* important, how do we access the unique feeling brain that rests right now within us? Of course, both genetics and the environment play a role, but our early environment has the greatest effect. The feeling brain is shaped by *repeated experiences* with the environment, especially during the first few years of life. It is somewhat easy to affect in childhood, but quite difficult to reach and affect after adolescence. The pruning and clipping of neural structures early in life, and the neural networks that are formed in childhood, have a strong tendency to persist throughout life.

Memories are connections between neurons—Memories are formed when neurons fire concurrently, a process that was first identified soon after World War II by Canadian psychologist Donald Hebb. One neural flash activates a string of others, leaving behind a shadow of weak connections. Each time the triggering neuron is activated, the networks become more dominant, the memory grows stronger, and competing networks inconsistent with the dominant one receive inhibitory messages and weaken. *Repetition causes the simultaneous strengthening of* *certain neural networks and weakening of those inconsistent with them.*

Implicit memory stores emotional learning—There are two kinds of memory: explicit memory—what you *know* you know—and implicit memory, the intuitive knowledge that is often beyond awareness. It is often what *we don't know that we know* that is both most helpful and most hindering to us.

Implicit memory is most helpful to us because it is the distillation of the truths of repeated experience. It is one better than a computer, equipping us with the knowledge and intuitions that are our most sensitive and accurate guideposts in life. Implicit memory is beyond our consciousness, so changing those memories—the guides of our emotional learning and our patterns of relating—is quite difficult.

Moreover, the strongest neural networks in our implicit memory are apt to have been laid down early in life by those who may have loved us but did not spawn networks within us that favor balance. The covert power of the implicit memory is astonishing! We deal with work, love, and play based on basic learnings that we are not aware of and did not create, but that unconsciously affect our responses.

Emotional learning is laid down early in life—If the neural networks of implicit memory are created by experiences early in life, for most of us, that means contact with our parents. The resonance between parent and child, the repeated contact that either is or isn't attuned and responsive, shapes the neural networks of a child's feeling brain one synapse at a time.

The inner balance—or imbalance—of the parent leads to the inner balance or imbalance of the child. Those parents whose inner workings are abundant with the skill to nurture and set limits from within are more likely to experience the emotional balance that enables them to quiet their own thoughts, set aside their own needs, and use their emotional sensing to regard their child. They can stay better attuned to the child, perceiving and meeting more of his or her myriad needs and giving abundant messages that the child matters, that his or her feelings are important, and that people and life are good.

The resonance between a child and a parent who has the skills to nurture and set limits from within and who can be repeatedly *responsive* to the child, downloads into the child's feeling brain the circuitry that favors a life of balance. Beyond the effects of genetics, grace, and chance, this parent-child transmission—one limbic brain to another—appears to explain why some children are remarkably resilient whereas others are not. It can account, to some degree, for resilience that travels from one generation to the next. Conversely, and unfortunately, the extent to which the parent's inner life is *out* of balance may well lead him or her to unknowingly download to the child the neural circuitry that favors a life of imbalance.

The developing thinking brain impedes emotional learning— Although much of this limbic shaping occurs in the first few years of life, the feeling brain remains accessible throughout childhood, with emotional learnings finding their way rather readily into the neural networks of the feeling brain. With puberty, the thinking brain develops more; the adolescent engages in abstract thought, planning, and analysis in far more sophisticated ways. At the same time, the door to the feeling brain begins to close.

It's not that the feeling brain does not remain plastic and open to change. But after childhood, we tend to process what happens in our lives by trying to *figure it out*. This has a way of shunting the experience away from our feeling brains and toward our thinking brains. The thinking brain, in effect, blocks our feeling brain from receiving the repeated responsive contact that could revise our earliest learnings.

The fact that it is so difficult to reach into and revise the feeling brain after adolescence explains why many psychologists believe that after adolescence, the inner lives of most people are "set." *Without emotional learning, profound and persistent change is not likely.* Although adults can feel better and make some progress in their lives, the probability of experiencing a true transformation is low.

Emotional learning guides personal balance—Feelings are neurons excited to the point of emotional awareness. Much like a bell that rings, they mount and fade—if they are balanced. Feelings can also open with a ring and then move in unpredictable directions, magnifying in disconcerting ways. An innocent wave of sadness plunges into a blue mood, or a spark of anger ignites a rage that has a life of its own. The course a feeling takes after that initial ring is affected by many things, including:

- The emotional reverberations
- Thoughts and imaginings from our thinking brains
- The real events in our lives that trigger more feelings or thoughts
- Our temperament and how prone it is to certain emotions
- Our health status and the medications we take
- Our behaviors: the food we eat, the air we breathe, the sleep we get
- Explicit and implicit memory in our feeling brain

The implicit memories from our early lives are stirred by feelings, not thoughts. For example, we feel sad in the present and it arouses feelings of sadness from the past, from the knowings, expectations, and intuitions gleaned from a lifetime of experience. Those memories can either contain and balance those feelings or, in a flash, send them into the stratosphere of imbalance. When Audrey criticized Kyle's rolls, certain dominant neural networks in his feeling brain were immediately activated. He could not describe them, explain them, or even recognize them, but the emotions they aroused, the eruption of intense anger, fear, and sadness that they triggered, was very real.

As Kyle's anger aroused emotional memories, Audrey's comments triggered intense emotional distortions. If Kyle had had a hard day, perhaps skipping breakfast or missing a full night's sleep, or was already irritable from being pulled over for a speeding ticket, his emotional imbalance could be more intense or might last longer.

On the other hand, what if Kyle's implicit memory *contained* rather than inflamed the feelings? If his early life had been fraught with less hostility and criticism, and his unconscious knowing was that people accepted him, that note of anger would sound and then fade. Even on a hard day, Audrey's comment would have led to some hostility, but not enough to lead him to numb himself with external solutions or fly out of the house in a rage.

Kyle's story

Kyle's mother adored her little curly-haired, towheaded son, already roly-poly by the age of five and fully the light of her life. She stayed home with Kyle, her only child, while her husband went off during the day to his position as district sales manager for a business supply company.

According to Kyle, "My parents couldn't have loved me more, which troubles me. There was nothing wrong, so why have I had such struggles? We had what all the neighbors would say was a classically happy family, but something was *missing*, and I don't know what."

I said, "It doesn't matter how the family *looked* or what the family *did*. What matters are the unspoken harmonies and discords between you. The capacity your parents had to be attuned to how you felt and what you needed would be low unless they knew how *they* felt and what *they* needed."

"Well," said Kyle, "they never said how they felt or what they needed. I was confused as a kid. My mom seemed to consume me with her love, then turn on a dime and leave. Not physically, but emotionally. She turned critical and detached. I hated her at times, and I know she hated me on some level, but we were also like one."

Kyle had been born with a difficult temperament: extremely sensitive, with emotions that fired easily and often. His mother apparently had the same tendencies. That made for a regular pattern of merging and distancing, indulgence and deprivation, and little intimacy and responsiveness between them. Kyle's father was far more responsive to him than his mother, but his work took him on the road most weeks, so Kyle's repeated contact with a responsive father was eclipsed by circumstance.

If Kyle's early environment had been supremely attuned to him—if he had received the repeated contact with people who were responsive to him, neither indulging nor depriving—the neural networks in his feeling brain would have calmed his extreme emotional volatility. His parents' responsiveness to his needs, maintaining intimacy rather than merging or distancing, would have laid the neural groundwork for intimate relationships later in life. Moreover, there would have been such a sanctuary created for Kyle that his sanctuary with the spiritual would have felt intuitively real. Connection to *self*, connection to *others*, and connection to the *spiritual* would have been fostered.

Instead, though Kyle's parents loved him dearly and thought of themselves as a "good family," the neural networks in Kyle's feeling brain favored a life of imbalance. Kyle developed many strengths during his early life, but he also developed an array of expectations that would have plummeted even those with a cheerful temperament off the cliff into imbalance. His most basic expectations, of which he was *fully unaware*, were that he was unworthy, that people would reject him, and that happiness would forever be beyond his reach.

Unfortunately, these patterns did not slip away with time. Instead, they tended to become more entrenched. Kyle's parents had laid down the emotional patterns in his feeling brain, but he unknowingly continued and reinforced them.

Reaching into the feeling brain

If Kyle's opportunity to create a world in which he has no external solutions and an abundance of life's sweetest rewards rests on affecting his feeling brain, how can he do that?

First, little is known about how to "revise" the feeling brain. Newer brain imaging methods that use PET scans, or positron emission topography, have been helpful in showing changes in various areas of the brain, including the limbic system. More research has been done recently that compares various treatments—from drugs to psychotherapy—on psychological problems thought to be reflective of the functioning of the feeling brain. Any passage of importance typically has many entrances, and although relatively little is currently known, it appears that this is true of limbic revision as well.

The use of drugs to affect the feeling brain has become very popular. Certain drugs seem to be of particular help when a person has serious imbalances, particularly when there are structural as well as functional brain abnormalities. Moreover, psychotropic drugs appear to have a beneficial effect on the feeling brain for various less serious psychological problems and addictive behaviors, such as the use of Wellbutrin for smoking or binge-eating and Prozac for depression.

The downside of drug therapy is that its effects may well end when the prescription runs out, and there is no evidence that

drugs are safe when taken over the long term. No long-term tox-
ilogical studies have been conducted. Drugs can also be costly
and have unacceptable side effects. No doubt drug research will
continue to escalate, and it may be that in the future, drugs alone
or in combination with other therapies will enable us to shape
broad-spectrum, persistent changes in our emotional brains
without worry of long-term toxicity or side effects.

Certainly, human contact can be a route to limbic revision.
Parents can transfer the neural networks that promote balance to
their children. Because the door to the feeling brain does not
appear to be shut completely in adults, repeated contact with
others later in life may well lead to transformation. That human
contact can be from personal relationships or professional ones.

Psychotherapists who offer repeated, responsive contact with
patients, rather than an excessive reliance on insight or analysis,
say that their clients appear to be transformed in ways consistent
with revision of the feeling brain. There is emerging research that
suggests that drugs and talk therapy have similar effects for some
conditions and that both change neural connections in the feeling
brain.

However, there are risks that therapists' own neural networks
may favor imbalance, and that they may inadvertently transmit
those to their patients. The job of a therapist is to stay above the
line when the client is below, to connect with his or her own balance when clients have lost theirs. You know the feeling, for you
may well have it when a friend is in distress and you do what you
can to be responsive to your friend rather than respond to yourself and run as far away and as fast as you can. That is hard
work, and how would you know that a therapist has what it
takes to do that? To be close to you in your imbalance yet stay
loving and balanced. When choosing a therapist, how does one
go about interviewing them based on the balance within their
feeling brains?

Although insight-oriented, analytic psychotherapy can have
some benefit in some situations, my experience has been that the
more analytical the therapy the more stalled in his or her development the program participant may become. It's hard to play
both on both sides of the fence. You either decide that you're
going to figure it out or you decide that you are going to hold
yourself accountable for doing the best you can to stay in balance
in the moment. It's very hard to do both.

The truth is that people *like* to gain insight into their problems. It gives them a sense of security and control, and doing so is far easier than mastering the skills. Their assumption is often that if they just *understood* the problem, it would somehow change. This is much like people believing that if they just knew what to eat, they would eat it, or if they just knew why they got angry, they could stop their rages! As my dear friend Jim Billings, a gifted minister and psychologist, says, "If you have a nickel and a truckload of insight, you only have five cents."

Another route to revision of the feeling brain is to discover love. In the wordless harmony between two people, the resonance of their emotional cores, is a potent balancing force that we unconsciously seek when we are hurting, lost, or alone. Because one mind has the power to revise another simply by its repeated regard for the other, our relationships can either heal or harm us in ways that we may not fully appreciate. When we look into the eyes of a loving other repeatedly, we become attuned to that person and find our emotional balance improves as that repeated contact has the power to change our feeling brain one synapse at a time. Moreover, our closeness with someone for whom we feel the emotion of love but who is not responsive to us can have an equally powerful effect that fosters imbalance in us.

Yet many people find precisely what they need in the arms of a loving, responsive spouse, partner, or dear friend. What could be better than receiving love from another and finding that it nourishes your spirit and retrains your feeling brain in ways far beyond what you could ever have possibly imagined?

Years ago, Debbie Boone recorded a beautiful ballad, "You Light up My Life." When I heard that my favorite radio personality, Gene Nelsen, was going to interview her, I tuned in. He asked her whom she thought about when she sang that luscious love song. I listened carefully, fully anticipating that she would name her husband or her child. Instead, I recall her answering, "God."

In the view of some like Debbie, the ultimate love is spiritual. It's interesting that emerging understandings of the brain's biology suggest that the center of spiritual transcendence and bliss resides in the feeling brain, but the question remains: How could a spiritual shift cause a retraining of the limbic system?

I don't know the answer to that question, but I do know that when people in my groups experience a spiritual awakening or deepening, their use of the skills changes rather radically. It seems to galvanize a persistently nurturing inner voice and to not only deepen their "I feel . . ." skill but increase their awareness of the blessings, the earned rewards, of life. What's more, that shift seems to allow them to accept the essential pain of life far more easily, perhaps because they are receiving nourishment that transcends this life.

Perhaps the most common way to affect the feeling brain is the old-fashioned way: learning from the lumps and bumps of life. Many people patch together their own way of arriving at a life of inner balance, just as a physician from Spokane did.

After giving a talk on The Solution at a regional continuing-education program for family physicians, I raced to the elevator to catch a plane and avoid being gone from my children another day. A small woman with short, curly, brown hair and a wiry build raced after me and grabbed me by the arm.

She said, "I could never understand why I stopped overeating, but after listening to your talk, I know why."

The elevator doors opened and closed, but I kept listening to her.

"I had this busy medical practice, and my husband and I weren't getting along. My children were both teenagers and behaving badly, and I had finally *had* it. I decided to go to a therapist and do something for myself. My therapist, God love her, was wonderful, and what I learned from her was nurturing . . . to honor my feelings and needs.

"By that time, I realized that my limits were completely out of balance and that I could *never* live a nurturing life until that changed. I was too hard on myself all day long, doing everything for everyone and being the perfect physician, then all night I would be too easy on myself, eating and sitting as much as I wanted.

"It took a long time of going inside myself in a nurturing way, bringing up all the harsh expectations I learned early in my life, and switching them to something more sensible. In time, being nurturing to myself and having good limits became natural. When that happened, things *really* started to change."

A cluster of friends from the meeting approached, and she waved them on and continued. "I began caring more about how I looked, not to be a good example to my patients or to please my husband, but because I wanted to enjoy my own appearance.

I started to take better care of my health, and I began exercising more and eating less. The weight, maybe twenty pounds, came off and has stayed off without dieting. My life feels balanced and . . . very happy. I just *had* to tell you that!"

The elevator door opened, she waved good-bye, and off she went.

Making the climb

Not everyone is like that physician, able to nudge their skills up a little bit and reach a Solution. Among those of us who want or need more, some have sought Solution training as a more direct route to mastering the skills and bending our neural networks to favor a life of balance.

The rationale for why the method could affect the feeling brain is simple: If repeated contact with a responsive environment *creates* the neural networks in the feeling brain, then repeated contact with the skills of responsiveness may *revise* them.

I can only speculate about the mechanism through which the method has its effects and draw upon what I've observed in my clinical practice over the last fifteen years and the research that has been conducted on the method (see "Method Research" in the appendices).

As the skills are practiced more and more often and more and more effectively, the dominant neuropathways that favor imbalance seem to fade. Those that favor balance appear to become dominant, one by one by one. Although the resulting "developmental shift" appears sudden, it has long been building. It seems to come from the slow strengthening of neural networks that favor balance. When they become dominant, balance is naturally favored and seems easy, even though it is the result of repeated firings of the neural networks over time. It may be that when enough neural circuitry has shifted to favor a life of balance, people experience a Solution, having no significant excesses and an abundance of all the rewards of human maturity: integration, balance, sanctuary, intimacy, vibrancy, and spirituality.

Feelings arouse implicit memory

The journey begins with the "I feel . . ." skill, which must be taught to mastery—not just a vague awareness of feelings, but the capacity to pinpoint each of the most basic feelings that represent important needs or encompass the healing process.

If your feeling brain is a jumble of imbalance, it's not safe to feel, so as you experiment with feelings awareness, it's best if you do cycles as well. The limits cycle contains the feelings, so that you are less likely to go out of balance, and the remainder of the nurturing cycle guides you in taking action to meet the needs the feeling suggests.

The first half of the climb appears to open the door to the feeling brain. Implicit memory is aroused by feelings; only when it is aroused often and well enough to reach consciousness can the thinking brain do its work of altering it and laying down knowings, expectations, and awarenesses that favor a life of balance. Those who don't develop a devotion to deepening the "I feel . . ." skill will not see transformation.

When Kyle started, he felt clumsy with the method, intending to use the skills but not doing it. He wasn't lazy or wrong but was learning to appreciate the power of the dominant neural networks in the feeling brain. *They are very strong and prefer the status quo.* A spark of a new neural pathway, one that favors balance, is like a blip on the screen. It goes away and the dominant patterns return. Cycles prompt balance, but that sense of balance is usually short-lived. Most people comment that the skills seem superficial, but they deepen with practice.

Kyle was used to being out of emotional balance—hostile or numb. Keeping his finger on the pulse of his inner life was not within the realm of his emotional learning. Progress is slow at first, with lots of stops and starts along the way, which is perfectly normal. It is even more challenging for those who are thinking-oriented, for until the "I feel . . ." skill is deep enough, profound change cannot occur.

Limits revise emotional learnings

As Kyle progressed with the method, he was able to practice the skills more easily and more deeply. The old neural networks that staunchly favored imbalance weakened, and the new neural networks that supported balance appeared to strengthen, bit by bit, cycle by cycle:

Awareness of Feeling—Perhaps Kyle goes inside and notices he feels depressed. He does a Natural Flow of Feelings, with red-hot anger, deep sadness, a fair amount of fear, and some guilt. He has cut through the thinking-brain barrier and is in the feeling brain.

When You Begin

networks that favor balance

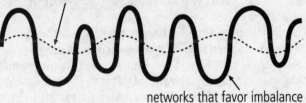

networks that favor imbalance

As You Progress

When You Reach Your Solution

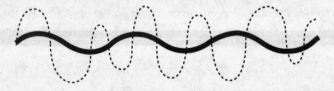

Neural networks in the feeling brain affect emotional, behavioral,
relational, and spiritual balance. Using the skills repeatedly may
weaken networks that favor imbalance and strengthen those
that favor balance, offering a pathway to transformation.

Implicit Learning Awareness—Under all those feelings, he becomes aware of a very basic expectation that makes him laugh. Until then, he had *no idea* that such an impossibly *unreasonable* expectation was at his emotional core. "I expect people to reject me. Really? That's interesting."

Consciously Changing Emotional Learning—Then his thinking brain has an effect: What is a reasonable expectation? He may not know, but he may give it some thought, analyze what is reasonable, and decide on a new reasonable expectation, such as, "I expect that some people will reject me and some will not."

Strengthening New Emotional Learning—That new thought is fragile and needs to be ground into the feeling brain, not just once but over and over again. The stuff of maturation, the emotional learnings, must be *felt*. Kyle says, "The essential pain I must face in order to follow through with that new reasonable expectation is: People may reject me." What he says is a thought, but the feelings that course through his body when he thinks it are the flash of neural networks in the feeling brain. The feelings fade, and the earned reward appears. "I won't reject myself." Again, the thought triggers feelings that further strengthen those networks. So changes may well occur, one synapse at a time, in both the feeling and the thinking brain.

The first half of the climb up the tree toward your sweetest fruit focuses on the nurturing cycle with some limits, for once emotional balance has been secured, the capacity to reach into the feeling brain is enhanced. During the second half of the climb, the focus is on limits. When the emotional learnings from early life are brought to the conscious level and changed through repetition, when those new learnings are ground in, transformation begins to occur. *It is not based on brilliance, but on sweat.* Certainly, the feelings continue to deepen, but it appears to be the repetition of the new, reasonable limits, and change in the most basic expectations about self, others, and the world, that create a transformation.

The sweetest fruit guides transformation

This is where the special role of the sweetest fruit comes in. Whatever is the touchstone of our development leads us right to the pieces of emotional trash that most need to be healed. The desire to reach it guides us to subtly use the skills we most need in order to bring ourselves what we most yearn for in this world. As people approach the top of the tree, they often feel mad as hell.

About two months before Kyle reached his Solution, he came to the session very, very angry. When I asked who wanted to do some in-depth work that day, he spoke up immediately:

"I do. I'm sick of coming here. I'm sick of The Solution, and I don't think this stuff works."

"Good. Tell me more."

"I have emotional balance. I have most of the rewards, but not all of them abundantly. I've stopped smoking, but that damned drive to overeat won't turn off and I'm *sick* of it."

"Not having your sweetest fruit is a blessing, not a curse. You will get it when you have given yourself what you most need, getting rid of the last pieces of emotional trash and mastering the final subtleties of the skills. Your sweetest fruit will give you just the motivation and guidance you need."

"What do I do?" he asked, still mad.

"I don't know, but I will sit with you while you look right down to your very roots and use your tool kit of skills to decide what you most need. Nobody can do this for you but you, although I know you very well now, and I will do all I can to be of support."

I heard someone in the room shuffling papers, probably taking out a pen to write notes.

"It won't help to write down the work Kyle is about to do. The last parts of each person's climb are intensely personal, and they are only apparent at the very end. The changes are only effective because of all the weakening of the old neural networks and strengthening of the new ones. You can't buy your way to the top of the tree; you can only earn it."

The room was quiet again.

"Kyle, think about your skills and emotional trash. What do you still need in order to reach your sweetest fruit?"

What Kyle began to do was what your mother made you do as a kid: make a list, then check it off. He was so sick of doing the work and mad enough at not having his sweetest fruit that his use of the skills became exponentially more effective. At this point, he had the depth of skill to be effective. The neural pathways had been destabilized enough to ease the climb, and he yearned for his sweetest fruit now more than ever.

That week, he *practiced* the most basic expectation, "Life can be happy," over and over again, until it "stuck" and became integrated and part of his bones. He deepened his "I feel sad" skill, accessing the sadness that further cooled his tendency toward hostility.

The next week, he worked on using the skills to separate from his mother, over and over again practicing the essential pain—I can't rescue my mother—and the earned reward—I can save myself—and so on.

Week after week, Kyle cleared away the emotional trash and muscled up on the skills. He could have been home eating pizza, sitting on the couch feeling sorry for himself, or furious with his clients. Instead, he was doing the work of giving himself that which, on the day he was born, his parents most wanted to give him but could not. He had taken the baton from his parents and was completing his own development, mastering the skill to nurture and set limits from within. He had gone a long way toward embedding, in the emotional core of his being, reasonable expectations of himself, of others, and of the world, acceptance of the essential pain of life, and a capacity to receive life's earned rewards.

At some point, odd things started happening to Kyle. As people reach their Solution, there is often a crescendo of change, as if more neural networks of imbalance are surrendering to those of balance. It was at that time that Kyle noticed that his drive to overeat vanished.

To this day, the process is hard for me to believe, and time and research may or may not elucidate the precise mechanisms involved. But ultimately, that may not matter. The diagrams of neural networks don't seem so important compared to Kyle's saying, "It's the strangest thing . . ."

II. YOUR PERSONAL PATHWAY

8. Your Sweetest Fruit

S tanding at the bottom of the tree, looking straight up to the top, and squinting to see your sweetest fruit is not the easiest thing. You are really asking yourself:

What do I most want in my life?—You are separating from what you used to want when you were a child, quieting the voices of others and their desires for you, and shutting out society's "shoulds." You are listening to yourself ask, "What do *I* most want in my life?"

What is the touchstone of my development?—There are many things you might want. Perhaps you'd love a trip to Tahiti or, like Janis Joplin, you yearn for a Mercedes-Benz. Yet your sweetest fruit is that which you most want that your soul most needs. It is the touchstone of your development. If you could reach that, you could reach anything and your life would be complete.

You may not have a vision of what you most want, which is fine, too. Chances are, it will become clear to you in time. It may require you to separate from others, to find a safe place where you can have privacy and to go deeply within yourself. For some people, that means taking a weekend drive by themselves, going out into nature, or staying in bed all day. Others just carry this question, "What do I most want in my life?," with them through their commute to work, the carpools with kids, during meetings, and while grocery shopping. At some point, what you most want will become clear to you.

Your sweetest fruit may be something very specific such as, "I want to have everyone in my family be healthy and happy." But since we're not in complete control of everything that happens to everyone, it's more helpful to shift that goal to something more general, for example, "I want more intimacy in my life." "I want to weigh 140 pounds" might become, "I want to turn off my drive to overeat and reclaim my genetic body build" (which may be 160 pounds, not 140). Look for the enduring rewards of life and the major emotional appetites that get in the way of your health and happiness.

When you are ready, just read the following list and check off some of the rewards and excesses that are important to you.

Ending Common Excesses Checklist

❏ **Eating too much**
overeating, binge eating, mindless eating

❏ **Chemical pleasures**
drinking, smoking, store drugs, street drugs

❏ **Working past six**
overworking, work preoccupation, career as identity, stress highs and numbness, busy-busy-busy

❏ **Spending**
overspending, excessive materialism, hoarding and clutter

❏ **Rescuing others**
emotional merging, expecting too little, being a savior

❏ **Putting up walls**
distancing emotionally, expecting too much, persecuting

❏ **Too much thinking**
obsessive thinking, analyzing everything, avoiding feelings, getting it perfect, over control

❏ **People-pleasing**
fear of rejection, approval seeking, being too good

Then read the list again and look for those goals that seem furthest from your reach. Look again, and find the one for which you most yearn. That is your sweetest fruit.

You might also consider a few more rewards or excesses, the ones you think are near the top of the tree, difficult for you to reach but important to reaching your Solution.

Reaping Life's Sweetest Rewards Checklist

❏ **Integration**
knowing yourself, feeling whole and authentic, accepting yourself

❏ **Balance**
emotional balance, fewer false highs and unnecessary lows, less numbness

❏ **Sanctuary**
a nurturing inner voice, a safe, warm place within

❏ **Intimacy**
closeness with others, less merging and distancing, fewer control struggles

❏ **Vibrancy**
physical vitality, enthusiasm for living, a healthy, happy glow

❏ **Spirituality**
connection with the spiritual, awareness of the grace and mystery of life

---

My Sweetest Fruit:

_____

Near the Top of the Tree:

_____

_____

You have just identified what you most want in this world, and a few of the other rewards or excesses that are important to the success of your climb. That is an important first step!

You are poised to begin your journey. The next chapter will help you plan your journey, find the pace that is right for you, and decide what support would best meet your needs.

9. The Solution Inventory

Now that you have your eyes set on what you most want in your life, please turn your attention to getting it. This inventory is designed to help you make this journey as rapid, safe, and easy as it can be. It includes:

- **The Skills**—A self-test of your skills, determining how much of the skills to nurture and set limits from within you already have.
- **The Threshold of Need**—You will identify your need for the skills, given your body, temperament, situational stress, emotional trash, environment, and external solution.
- **The Pathway**—You'll create a plan for reaching your Solution, including the pace of your climb and the support you will likely need along the way.

The Skills

For each statement, please circle the number that best describes you. When you are done, add up the points for each group of statements to assess your skill in that area. Add up all the points to find your total skills score. Then go on to the next self-test.

	always	often	sometimes	rarely
1. Strong Nurturing				
I am aware of my feelings.	3	2	1	0
I recognize and meet my needs.	3	2	1	0
I ask for help from others.	3	2	1	0
			Total___	

	always	often	sometimes	rarely
2. Effective Limits				
I set reasonable—not harsh or easy—expectations.	3	2	1	0
My thoughts are positive and powerful.	3	2	1	0
I accept life's difficulties and follow through easily.	3	2	1	0

Total____

	always	often	sometimes	rarely
3. A Nurturing Inner Voice				
I am aware of a safe place inside me.	3	2	1	0
I feel empty, numb, or lost.	0	1	2	3
My inner voice is nurturing and warm.	3	2	1	0

Total____

	always	often	sometimes	rarely
4. Staying Balanced				
I stay balanced throughout the day.	3	2	1	0
In the evening, I use external solutions.	0	1	2	3
When life is hard, I soothe myself from within.	3	2	1	0

Total____

	always	often	sometimes	rarely
5. Emotional Trash				
I shut out my bad feelings about the past.	0	1	2	3
I can feel the pain of the past and let it go.	3	2	1	0
The losses in my life have also brought blessings.	3	2	1	0

Total____

	always	often	sometimes	rarely
6. Lifestyle Surgery				
I am physically active and eat a healthy diet.	3	2	1	0
I take time to restore my body, mind, and spirit.	3	2	1	0
My body is as healthy as possible.	3	2	1	0

Total____

Total *Skill* Score _____

Each of the six skill areas has a possible score of 0 to 9.

The higher the score, the greater your skill. Your areas with higher scores are your strengths or *accomplishments;* consider taking a moment to appreciate them. The areas with lower scores are your *challenges.* Pumping up these skills is likely to have the most significant impact on your progress.

Please add up all the totals in this self-test, find your total skill score, and determine your skill level. Circle your skill level below.

Your Skills	
Total Score	**Skill Level**
less than 18	Low
18 to 35	Moderate
more than 35	High

The Threshold of Need

For each statement, please circle the number that best describes how much it affects you. Add up the points to estimate your threshold of need for the skills.

	a lot	some	a little	not at all
1. Biology				
How much do your genetics and your health make it harder to stay in balance?	3	2	1	0

	a lot	some	a little	not at all

2. Temperament

How much does your
temperament make it harder
to stay in balance? 3 2 1 0

3. Situational Stress

How much does your
current level of stress
make it harder to stay
in balance? 3 2 1 0

4. Emotional Trash

How much do past hurts,
particularly early ones,
make it harder to stay
in balance? 3 2 1 0

5. The Environment

How much do your
physical environment and
those around you make it
harder to stay in balance? 3 2 1 0

6. External Solutions

How much do your
external solutions
make it harder to stay
in balance? 3 2 1 0

Total *Skill* Score _____

Please add up your total score in this self-test and determine
your threshold of need level. Circle it below.

Your Threshold of Need of The Skills	
Total Score	**Threshold of Need Level**
less than 7	Low
7 to 12	Moderate
more than 12	High

The Pathway

To begin to develop an idea of the pathway that is right for you, please check the chart below:

- **Circle your threshold of need level:** low, moderate, or high.
- **Circle your skill level:** low, moderate, or high.
- **Find the number that corresponds to both:** This is your pathway.

Although this chart may suggest the seemingly best pathway for you right now, please use your own judgment. If you need

Your Pathway

Threshold of Need

Skills		Low	Moderate	High
	High	1	2	2
	Moderate	2	2	2
	Low	2	2	3

more or less support, by all means consider changing to that. Your needs may also change during the course of the journey, so the most reliable way to determine what is right for you is to keep your fingers on the pulse of your inner life and keep asking yourself, "How do I feel?" and, "What do I need?"

Pathway 1: A Gentle Journey

Your pace:	Brisk
Your support:	Little or none

If there is only a small difference between the skills you have and the skills you need, you may only need to read this book and practice these skills on your own in order to reach your Solution. Your journey may be relatively rapid, and you are apt to reach a Solution within one year. You may notice as you read this book that you start using the skills almost unconsciously. Your journey will be likely to move at a brisk pace with little or no support. Some people on this pathway want community support because it can be fun, interesting, and helpful; that support may be nice but not necessary for you. If you run into a challenging part of your climb, you can always choose to get more support, community or professional, as needed.

Needing just a few more skills than you already have can have a downside. There is a risk that you are so comfortable, you won't bother to reach your Solution. If you are a rather driven, goal-oriented person, you probably will not stop using the skills until you have no external solutions and an abundance of all six of life's sweetest rewards. However, if you tend toward complacency, are too easy on yourself, or have such a seemingly good life that you may not be aware of the pain inside, you may be apt to abandon the climb before you reach your goal. If you think you might be at risk of drifting off the pathway, be doubly sure that your sweetest fruit is something about which you are *passionate*. Draw on that passion to develop a personal commitment to reaching your Solution. Then use the skills over and over again, climbing that tree until you have what you most want in life.

You might also focus on gaining enough skills for the times ahead when life may not be so forgiving. There is a certain security in having more skill than you need so that when there are losses, changes, or upsets, you know that you will continue to accept life's unavoidable pain and open your hand to appreciating its tremendous rewards.

Pathway 2: A Good Climb

> Your pace: Moderate
> Support: Community

You will be likely to walk along this pathway at a moderate pace, taking something more like a sturdy hike than an easy stroll. This journey will take some persistence and some time, typically about eighteen to twenty-four months, if you practice on most days often and well.

Be sure to get community support to help you practice the skills more often and create a journey that is pleasurable enough so you'll stay with it until you reach your Solution. Community support through Solution Circles and Solution Buddies can be gained at no cost.

Some of you on this pathway will find that your journey is safer and easier if you have professional support, especially about three to six months after you begin the journey and again during the last months of your climb. These are the periods when you are likely to experience a developmental shift, when you may feel depressed, hostile, or sick and need support to move through that transition. The last six months of the training are the most amazing time; having some individual coaching to pinpoint the emotional trash that most needs taking out and the most basic expectations that need to be ground into your feeling brain makes this part of the journey far easier and faster.

On this pathway, it is important to complete the same course that is used in all solution training. Those on pathway 1 may only need the resource of this book to reach their solution, however, those on pathways 2 and 3 who use only this book are unlikely to reach their solution. It makes the journey safer and easier and takes much of the guesswork out of building the skills. The course is made of six Solution Kits, one for each part of the climb. You use them *in conjunction with* this book to help you build the skills layer by layer and take out emotional trash gradually and effectively until you reach your Solution. All our research that shows program effectiveness is based on participants using these kits, not just the book alone.

In the middle of your journey, you may be happy with your results and tempted to stop your journey. I encourage you to continue, as the best is yet to come, and "halfway" solutions often unravel.

Toward the end of your journey, you will probably come to a time when you feel very angry. You want a Solution, and you want it now! Use that anger to go deeper into yourself and use the skills with more precision until you have an *abundance* of each of the rewards—integration, balance, sanctuary, intimacy, vibrancy, and spirituality—and no external solutions.

Enjoy your journey!

Pathway 3: A Challenging Pathway

Your pace: Nice and slow
Support: Professional

You are fortunate, because it is probably clear to you that you really need these skills. Perhaps you sense that it is a matter of life and death. If that is the case, settle into your journey recognizing that it will be nice and slow, that at first you won't find it easy but that you are committed to reaching your Solution—and you will reach it!

You are better off getting professional support. If you cannot find a Solution Provider in your area, and cannot get into telephone groups or coaching through the Institute, consider seeing a therapist who is willing to listen to you talk about your feelings and needs without trying to analyze your childhood or discover what is wrong with you. Get support on your Solution training from our website or other Solution Support Options (see page 371). Go through all 6 Solution Kits and use that therapist as a loving presence as you do the work, a sounding board for you to use as you check your expectations.

As you begin your journey in Solution Kit #1, you may feel frustrated because you don't know the answers to the questions. You may often find yourself "numbing out," forgetting the questions, or even forgetting to go inside for days on end. *That is normal*; it results from the separation between the skills you have and the skills you need, and it will change more rapidly than you can now imagine.

If you ask yourself, "How do I feel?" and have no answer, keep asking the question. If you ask yourself, "What is a reasonable expectation?" and the answer is, "Beats me," that is fine, too. All your inner life needs is for you to keep asking the questions of yourself and accessing the professional support you need to guide your journey. In time, you will know how you feel, what you need, and what a reasonable expectation is for who you are at that time.

You may find yourself going around and around the cycles and not popping above the line. If so, get some support to use the skills more effectively. (See Solution Support Options on page 371.) Doing cycles from below the line reinforces the old neural networks of imbalance rather than strengthening the new networks of balance. Be sure that you are trying to bring up a nurturing inner voice, feeling and expressing all four feelings (angry, sad, afraid, and guilty) in the Natural Flow of Feelings, and answering the questions simply, more like the four-year-old inside than the intellectual. Most important, cut yourself some slack. Have some compassion for yourself. You don't need to be perfect to be wonderful. All you need to do is to stay on the pathway, doing the best you can and no better. Allow yourself to take small steps, practicing as much as you can *each day* and no more.

It may take a while for you to reach your Solution, typically two to three years. If you have external solutions that affect your medical risk, such as overeating, drinking, or smoking, we recommend getting some support to change that pattern now. In time, as you reach your Solution, those drives will probably turn off from inside. Until then, consider getting some external support—external nurturing and limits—to pop yourself above the line sooner with the excess.

The wonderful news is that if you are on this pathway, the drama as you reach the top of the tree is unlike any other. It is difficult to imagine now, but when you have practiced the skills for so long and so well that the neural networks in your feeling brain *automatically* favor a life of balance, your feelings of pride and joy will be immense! Keep in mind: *The taller the tree, the better the view!*

Whatever your pathway . . .

Regardless of which pathway is right for you, this journey requires you to take very good care of yourself, moving forward rapidly when you are able and taking very small steps when that seems right for you.

It means being *absolutely alone* with the work when that

suits you, and being highly receptive to accessing community support and professional guidance when you need them.

When your heart says that you need to take a break from intentionally practicing the skills, allow yourself the leeway to do that. Use that as a time to see to what extent the skills will percolate and sink in deeper on their own. By the same token, return to the work over and over again until you reach your Solution.

It seems that the best way to treat ourselves throughout this journey is much the way, in the best of all worlds, we would have been treated all along—gently, but with enough of a nudge to ensure our success.

III. GOING TO THE ROOTS

10. Step 1: The Nurturing Cycle

P aul was a lumberjack of a man with high blood pressure, heart problems, diabetes, and overweight, and a penchant for evenings of big dinners and television. He came to our group at the recommendation of his physician, who suggested Paul should get to the roots of his problem. However, Paul wasn't at all happy about joining a group and simply *hated* the idea of nurturing himself.

In somewhat of a huff, he said to the group, "I don't want to nurture myself. Nurturing is for babies!"

Several people chuckled, and I sensed immediately that Paul would soon be loved by the group.

"But Paul," I responded, "if you don't nurture yourself effectively, you're apt to act like . . . a baby!"

A look of recognition crossed his face.

The nurturing cycle is effective in guiding us in knowing and honoring ourselves. Since feelings are deeper than thoughts, it is only by going under our grown-up thinking to the flurry of feelings underneath that we can possibly recognize our deepest needs and have more of a chance of meeting them, and nurture ourselves well.

Some people say, "What good does it do to know what I need? I never get my needs met!"

If that is true for you now, it will change as you use the skills. Besides, we stand a better chance of meeting our needs if we know what they are. The limits cycle—the cycle of power and safety—empowers us to meet those needs far more often. Even if we can't meet a need, that cycle has a way of putting its arms around the pain of the loss and containing it. We may feel sad, but we won't feel depressed. All in all, life gets better.

The nurturing and limits skills work much like a bank account. Each time you nurture yourself and meet your needs, it's like putting money into your account. Each time you ask yourself to do something, in essence you are setting a limit and withdrawing from that account. As long as you are not overdrawn, there is no rebellion, no slowdowns or grinding pain, and fewer external solutions. You just do what you need to do and follow through with relative ease. Life is still difficult, but it feels abusive far less often.

Question 1: How do I feel?

The first question of the nurturing cycle is: "How do I feel?"

When you check your feelings, you pierce the barrier of the thinking brain and move into the world of the feeling brain. You dip into your innate power that comes from passion, intuition, connection, and drive. It is the starting point in using the cycles, and the goal is to check your feelings as often as possible. Not just once or twice a day, but often enough for the skill to become automatic, so that you just *know* how you feel most of the time.

Some people have a sturdy awareness of their feelings from when they start using the method. Others, like Tom, naturally respond to what happens in their daily life by first *thinking* rather than by *feeling*.

When he had just started using the skills, Tom said to me, "I *don't know* how I feel. I'm not even aware of my feelings much of the time. Mostly, I have no feelings."

If you're like Tom, all you need to do is keep asking yourself

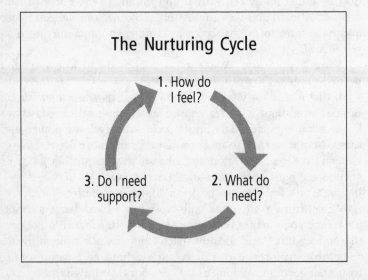

The Nurturing Cycle

1. How do I feel?

2. What do I need?

3. Do I need support?

the question, "How do I feel?" In time, you will notice feelings arising that you can name. It is slow at first, but the skill grows. *Unless we deepen our capacity to feel our feelings, the rest of the cycle lacks the power to pop us above the line.* In order for the feelings to be both authentic and powerful, we must feel them— messy, primitive, unbridled, and deep—before we grow them up with the limits cycle.

Emily was aware of her feelings but found them dangerous. She said, "When I get in touch with my feelings, I immediately get depressed. I'd rather be busy focusing on the kids than checking my feelings. I like feeling numb more than I like feeling depressed!"

If we avoid feelings because they lead to nothing good, we need to use the nurturing and limits skills together from the start. We will be more apt to stay in balance and feel feelings that help rather than hurt.

Drew was somewhat like Emily, but more so. She said, "I have no trouble feeling my feelings; in fact, I have far too many feelings. *The trouble is that I have no limits.* Once the feelings start, they go right out of balance. I'm either the cheerful, saintly teacher who is playing a role and not really feeling her feelings, or this reclusive, dark character whose feelings are on overdrive and out of balance. There is no in between."

Drew also needed to use the nurturing and limits skills from the start. In addition, she needed tips that would help her feel emotionally balanced sooner. Those strategies include:

The Natural Flow of Feelings

The Natural Flow of Feelings mirrors the way emotions naturally cascade from one to another. They are what allow us to find our way to a pool of acceptance, forgiveness, and balance.

There are four feelings in the Natural Flow of Feelings for essential pain: *anger, sadness, fear,* and *guilt.* If you are able to feel all four of them, you are on your way to emotional balance. *Even missing one of these feelings can create emotional imbalance.* The cycles begin with the Natural Flow of Feelings for essential pain. There is also a Natural Flow of Feelings for the good feelings, the earned rewards. They are: *grateful, happy, secure,* and *proud.* The capacity to feel and express all eight of these feelings is central to sustaining emotional balance.

You'll probably also notice that some feelings are easy for you to feel while others are a little more challenging. If you do, remedying this is one of the easiest steps to take in creating a life of personal balance. All you are doing is filling in the nooks and crannies in your emotional repertoire, but it can be very effective.

Emily said, "Of these feelings, all I can feel easily are sadness, fear, and guilt. Anger is not in my repertoire. Also, when I check my feelings, I only look for the bad ones. It doesn't even occur to me to check for the ways I feel good."

Somewhere along the way, Emily acquired two common patterns that fuel emotional imbalance: little skill in feeling and expressing anger, and a relentless focus on the negative feelings. No wonder Emily's sweetest fruit was balance!

Emily was going to feel depressed, self-pitying, and powerless until she took out enough trash and muscled up on the skills enough to be red-hot furious. She needed not only to touch her anger but to feel it in her belly and spit it out—not in a sweet, angelic voice, but in one that honored her fury. Whatever safe way she could find to do that—in the shower, in her pillow, on the mountaintops—that skill had to be pumped up.

As people often do, Emily had surrounded herself with friends who were as below the line as she was. They all were depressed, self-pitying, and powerless, so it was her social norm to talk about how bad things were. Here she was, living a life of privilege with three children and a husband who loved her, and all she could think about was what was *wrong*. She needed to pump up her skill of checking for the earned rewards.

As you experiment with the Natural Flow of Feelings, you'll probably notice that there are several other very basic feelings

The Natural Flow of Feelings

Essential Pain	Earned Rewards
angry	grateful
sad	happy
afraid	secure
guilty	proud

that direct us to our needs: feeling hopeful, lonely, loved, loving, hungry, full, tired, rested, sick, or healthy. Their importance stems from the fact that they trigger us to meet our most basic needs.

Smokescreens and Crossed Wires

"Upset," "stressed," "excited," and "bad" are common ways to express feelings, but they aren't very accurate; they are usually clusters of feelings, not pure ones. Sometimes they are combinations of feelings and thoughts.

There is nothing wrong with smokescreens, except that they don't help us pinpoint our feelings or point us toward our true needs. If we don't know what we need, we are unlikely to meet those needs. If more of our needs aren't met more of the time, we are likely to turn to external solutions more often.

The disadvantage of using a smokescreen is that you might use the same word to describe very different feelings. For example:

- One day you might tell your best friend that you are *stressed*, but if you went under that smokescreen masking your true feelings, you might find that you're tired and scared.
- The next day, you may again say that you are *stressed*, but actually you feel lonely and angry.

You aren't telling your friend how you actually feel, so there is less intimacy between you. You may not know how you feel, so more of your needs go unmet. The needs that correspond to "tired and scared" are very different from the needs that relate to "lonely and angry."

If you check in with yourself and find a smokescreen, there is nothing wrong with that. Just go under the smokescreen and identify your true feelings. When you do, there will be fewer *crossed wires*.

A wire is crossed when a feeling and a need do not correspond, such as, "I feel sad; I need chocolate," rather than, "I feel sad; I need to cry." Most of us have a goodly supply of these crossed wires; we will need to work on uncrossing them as we journey along and use these skills. Perhaps when we were growing up, no one was there to see us attach the wrong need to a feeling. Or maybe we were raised by people who had their own crossed wires, which they inadvertently passed along to us.

According to Emily, "I have dozens of crossed wires. 'I feel lonely. I need to stop at the bakery and get a coconut cupcake,' and, 'I feel sad. I need to keep busy.' What does a coconut cupcake have to do with feeling lonely? When I'm sad, why have I always gone into overdrive, exhausting myself completely?"

It's not a problem—it's just a skill, and a matter of persistently and carefully uncrossing those wires until they are accurate. It will take Emily saying to herself over and over again, "I know that I feel lonely, and what I *think* I need is a coconut cupcake, but that is not very accurate. What I *really* need is some intimacy, someone to talk with, so I expect myself to do the best I can to pick up the telephone and call someone, even if I don't particularly feel like it."

In time, that very old crossed wire will begin to come uncrossed.

Feeling a Feeling

The skill of simply *feeling a feeling and allowing it to fade* may sound very basic to you, but those using the method come back to this time and time again. It is a highly effective part of leading a life of emotional depth and personal balance.

To explore this skill, when you notice a powerful feeling arising in your body, separate yourself from those around you and allow it to rise up in your belly and wash over you, just watching the feeling mount, peak, and then subside. As long as you are reasonably above the line, it will fade—which at first is rather surprising! You weren't overwhelmed, you didn't disincorporate. You just felt the feeling and let it fade. The sense afterward is not unlike when a dog gets out of the tub after a bath. You shake yourself off, then return to what you were doing before, feeling remarkably refreshed and emotionally "clean."

Please keep in mind that this method gives you a tool kit full of skills you can use in your own time and in your own way. For instance, if you use this skill and the feeling doesn't fade, don't keep waiting for it to. Go to your tool kit and take out another tool, such as the limits cycle. Do cycles.

Feeling a Feeling Is:

- Not stuffing it, ignoring it, or distracting yourself from it
- Allowing it to rise up in your belly, burn in your throat, and saturate your being
- Waiting for it to naturally subside, which it will
- Knowing that afterward you will say that it wasn't so difficult and that you are stronger than you knew

---

Question 2: What do I Need

Most of us can learn to identify a feeling, but a need? How does one really know what one needs, and after all, aren't needs bottomless? Do you ever have all you need and is what you have ever enough?

Those are interesting questions, but we are better off staying out of this intellectual territory and allowing ourselves to be four years old and answer the question "What do I need?" moment to moment throughout the day.

If we're above the line, our answers are often surprisingly straightforward. They correspond to the feeling: "I feel cold," "I need a jacket." "I feel happy," "I need to enjoy it," or "I feel guilty," "I need to say I'm sorry." The simple four-year-old response, rather than the adult response, is the most accurate one much of the time. Often the need is to feel the feeling, express the feeling, act on the logical need the feeling infers, or learn from the feeling.

If we're below the line, what we need may be considerably less clear. The way to get some clarity is to pop ourselves above the line with the limits cycle so our *need*, not our *want*, becomes apparent. But how do we know that we are below the line? Often you just *know*, but other times, it helps to use some clues:

- The feeling does not fade but stays and goes out of balance (e.g., sadness becomes depression; anger becomes hostility)
- The drive to go to excess increases

- We engage in external solutions
- We are passive or aggressive rather than assertive
- We are stuck in excessive, repetitive thinking.

Drew had a lot of questions about needs, as she was at a point in her life when she was spending much of her time below the line. She asked, "What does it *matter* what I need? I never get my needs met, and knowing what I need just makes me feel worse."

Drew was perfectly right. What did it matter what she needed when she did not have the skills to meet those needs? Worse, she didn't have the skills to soothe and comfort herself about not having *what* she wanted *when* she wanted it.

Even though Drew had tried so hard to feel better and been so disappointed in the results she experienced, the truth was that she was only just beginning to dig her way out of the emotional trash and personal patterns of her first thirty-some-odd years. Since her feelings were already rather apparent, and she had a hard time identifying her needs because she was so below the line, it was best for her to focus first on the limits cycle. That was the skill that would bring her safety and power.

The limits skill was the cycle that would empower Drew to face the essential pain of life and the unavoidable realities of the human condition. Equipped with that skill, she would be less likely to fall out of emotional balance or duck out of her feelings by turning on the television, eating a pizza, or playing computer games all evening. It would move her through that discomfort of facing, for example, that she is not perfect, that no one will rescue her from her life, and that bad things happen.

She would begin to see the earned reward, the blessings, the payoffs, the lessons learned. In time and with practice, she would master the limits cycle well enough to have within her the power and security to ask herself, "What do I need?" and to have that be a nurturing act.

As you move toward mastery of the method and watch yourself mature in remarkable ways, you are likely to notice that your needs change. When you start using the method, your needs may not be clear. You may think you know what you need, but way down deep inside, you sense that you may not have a clue. As you progress, you will become more accurate in identifying your true needs.

When emotional balance becomes the norm, intimacy with self and with the spiritual follow, and the intensity of those connections may affect what you see as your true needs. Your needs may become less of the flesh-and-blood, immediate-gratification sort. More often, your needs may extend beyond yourself, moving toward deepening your spiritual connection and honoring your personal mission in this world. More and more, life stops being just about you.

Question 3: Do I need support?

The last question of the nurturing cycle is "Do I need support?" It is often the most difficult question of this cycle, for the steps involved are many and the emotional charges attached to them are often red-hot! Making a request involves:

- Knowing how you feel and what you need
- Identifying what support you need and from whom
- Asking for that support in an effective way
- Risking the rejection of the other person
- Risking that you will surrender to that person's will
- Having to receive from another, which arouses emotional trash from the past when there was deprivation or it was unsafe to receive
- Facing the possibility of being turned down, which can arouse more emotional trash

Emily had difficulty making requests because she often didn't know precisely what she needed, so how could she know what to ask for? Tom felt that he should be perfectly self-sufficient and that asking for help showed weakness. Drew was scared to ask for support, as her neediness felt bottomless and she feared that if she starting asking for support, she might never stop.

Yet if Emily, Tom, and Drew did not move themselves above the line enough to make requests of others, fewer of their needs would be met. Perhaps far more important, they could miss the opportunity for the intimacy and healing that only comes with being willing to step off that pedestal of self-sufficiency and into the arena of love and healing. Doing so requires that we tolerate the discomfort of the pregnant moment between the request and the answer. That is the moment in which emotional echoes from early life resound that can shake us to our very depths. Herein lies the opportunity for healing. For if we can hold on to ourselves and feel our feelings during that moment between making the request and receiving the answer, the power of the times before when people deprived us lessens, and the leftover hurts of our earliest exchanges with others begin to heal.

Sometimes when we make a request, we get what we want. The other person say yes. Our specific need may be met: that person washes the dishes, listens to what we have to say, delays a visit from houseguests, or plans our next vacation. Along with those concrete rewards, there may be another gift, which is love. There are times when we may be aware that the meeting of our need says, "I see you and trust you. You matter."

Getting Intimacy from a "Sandwich"?

It's rarely a problem to ask your mate to pass the butter, but to ask your partner to slow down in making love or to quit spending so much money? That's another story, so if anything is at all sensitive, it is often best to wait until you are solidly above the line to make the request.

Even then, the risks diminish by first asking ourselves, "Is it a reasonable expectation that anything *good* can happen for me by making this request?" Only if the answer is yes should we consider giving our partner some empathy, a clear message, and more empathy—what we call giving a "Solution Sandwich."

Making these empathetic but tremendously powerful requests not only maximizes your chance of getting your needs met but also minimizes the risk of being hurt. Moreover, even if you are making these requests of people with whom you're not terribly intimate, such as your boss, your neighbor, or your mother-in-law, you bring the most intimacy possible to the situation. Some Solution participants say that this technique is so powerful it should be *registered*—not unlike a firearm!

Here's how it works: After you have done enough cycles to be above the line, ask yourself if it is reasonable to expect that making this request will bring something good to you, and if you respond yes, you can begin. Try using some soft "white bread" of empathy and compassion, followed by the clear message, or "meat," and then by more white bread of empathy and compassion. The meat is a clear message that emotionally connects and stops short of being controlling.

The honest empathy and compassion need to come right from your heart. Go into the depths of yourself and wait for the empathetic feelings to arise before saying anything. When they do, speak from your heart in a nurturing way, such as: "I appreciate how much you care . . ." or, "I understand that this is very difficult . . ." or other words that are honest and loving and that pertain to the request.

The meat is simply the nurturing cycle: "I feel . . . , I need . . . , would you please. . . ." In our groups, we practice giving Solution Sandwiches because they are not that easy to give, and if you master the skill, life is far better. Often, we role-play using them, which is what Tom did in group. He was practicing making a request of his son Jason.

"Tom, are you above the line enough to give a Sandwich?"

Tom answered, "I think so."

"Is it a reasonable expectation that making this request will bring something good for you?"

Tom said, "Yes."

"Would you choose someone in the group to be Jason?"

"Sure," he said, and turned to Mark, the restaurant owner who was sitting directly across from him in the circle. "Would you role-play Jason?"

Mark said, "Sure."

Tom began with honest empathy, "Jason, you are so important to me and I feel that . . ."

I interrupted him to check with Mark. "Mark, how was that for you?"

Mark said, "More like melba toast than white bread. I could use more of the good stuff."

Tom cleared his throat and turned to me. "What am I supposed to say?"

I answered, "Do you love him?"

"Yes, of course."

"Then tell him that, or say other things that are true and that you believe would be nurturing to him. Take a moment before you say anything just to bring up some warm feelings for Jason. You love this kid. This is a difficult conversation. Imagine how he might feel. See if you can bring up some compassion for him."

Tom paused for several minutes, then looked across at Mark and said, "Jason, I love you and you mean the world to me. I appreciate that it's not easy to be your age and having so many changes in your life."

Mark's smile broadened, and he sat back in his chair. It squeaked.

"Tom," I said, "You're doing great, and now it's time for the meat. Just say: 'I feel . . . ,' and say a feeling. Then 'I feel . . . ,' and finally, 'Would you please . . . ?' "

"I feel that you . . ."

I interrupted. " 'I feel . . . ,' then follow it with a feeling, not a thought. Saying that feeling opens the emotional pipeline between you. He may not connect with your thoughts, but he has had the same feelings about something else. It will arouse feelings in him and increase the chance of emotional connection between the two of you."

Tom went on. "Jason, I feel guilty that I have given you money for so long. I think I was giving you money because I didn't have as much time to spend with you as I wanted to have."

Mark looked as if he were touched by Tom's openness.

"Jason, I need you to know that I'm not going to give you a blank checkbook anymore. You'll have your monthly allowance, and other than that, I expect you to start earning any money for extra things like trips. Would you please know that I am sorry for not being closer to you in the past, and that I'd like to start being closer to you now? You are very important to me, and I love you very much."

It was amazing! The room erupted in applause, and I turned to Mark, who was smiling, too. "How was that for you to hear, Mark?"

Mark said, "Incredible. I wish my dad had spoken to me that way."

"How was that for you, Tom?"

"It was great, but I can't remember what I said. How am I going to remember how to give a Sandwich?"

I looked at him and smiled, then he smiled, knowing what I would say.

"I know. Practice."

I turned to the group. "Good. Who would be willing to do connections with Tom this week to practice giving Sandwiches?"

Mark and two others in the room raised their hands.

If you start asking yourself the three questions of the nurturing cycle, you'll begin to appreciate its power. However, it's important to balance that skill with the limits cycle, which stops nurturing from turning into indulgence. It's only when the skills are used together that we have sensitive inner balance that enables us to be truly responsive to ourselves and others and accepting of the realities of life.

11. Step 2: The Limits Cycle

The limits cycle is the internal skill that creates security and power. This little cluster of questions has an odd way of penetrating our very depths, putting its arms around our wildest emotions, and shaping them into the passionate energy that is our very lifeblood.

Most people who use the method rapidly develop a love affair with this cycle, and for good reason. For example, using the limits cycle will support Emily in lifting herself out of her depression and will enhance inner security and personal control for Drew. For Tom, the intertwining of the nurturing and limits skills will make his boundaries sensitive and flexible. When he is close to someone and there is danger, he can have more trust that his boundary will instantly become vault-thick to protect him. When there are moments of sweet closeness, he will trust it to become tissue-paper-thin, allowing that love to nourish him.

Drew came to a group session soon after she began the program, extolling the power of this cycle. She explained to our group, "There is nothing on this Earth that makes me feel more powerless than being with my mother. When I came home from work yesterday, I found a letter from her. We're not close, but we phone or write every once in a while, and I go home for the holidays every other year. The visit home is always tormenting, because my twin brothers are both physicians, one a pediatrician and the other an internist, and they are both happily married, wealthy, and slender, all of which I am not.

"When my mother's letter arrived yesterday and she mentioned plans for my next visit, she found a way to slip in remarks, asking me when I'm going to lose weight and why I don't get a better job, one that has a 'real paycheck.'"

Several people in the room gasped.

Drew continued. "This was not the first time my mother has been critical of me, but it was the first time that I didn't immediately pour myself a drink or go to the refrigerator afterward. I just sat right there on my fuzzy white couch and felt absolutely horrible, but I didn't eat and I didn't drink. I just held on to one of my white, fuzzy, square cushions, as if it were an emotional life raft, and poured my fury and sadness into it. When the worst of the emotional blizzard passed, for some reason, I had the presence to use the limits cycle.

"I asked myself, are my expectations reasonable? I realized that my expectations weren't *at all* reasonable. My mother has no Solution skills, and she is incapable of seeing me for who I am and giving me the love and cherishing that I've always wanted. I asked myself: 'What is a reasonable expectation?' A more reasonable expectation is that my mother will probably always tend to be critical of me.

"I continued around the cycle to positive, powerful thinking: 'I am not the only person on this planet who has a critical parent.' The essential pain was: 'My mother does not have the skills to love and cherish me.'

"I sat in the pain of that realization, and it really, really hurt, but the feelings did pass. When they did, the earned reward was just *there*. My mother may not have the skills to love and cherish me, but the earned reward is that I am gaining the skills to love myself. I can develop relationships with people who *are* capable of loving me."

Drew explained to the group, "There I was, sitting on my couch with my mother's letter on the floor, all crumpled up and with tissues all over the coffee table. Yet I was above the line, and I felt safe and powerful, and oddly enough, I felt very loved. It wasn't my mother whose love I was feeling, but my own."

Question 1: Are my expectations reasonable?

The first question of the limits cycle is, "Are my expectations reasonable?" Putting into place a reasonable expectation is the first step toward taking action and having power in life.

I hope you have a good sense of humor, because when you start asking yourself this question, you will probably need to either laugh or cry. The most common reactions have been:

- "I have no idea what I expect of myself. None."
- "Can you believe my expectations? I wasn't even aware of them."

The Limits Cycle

1. Are my expectations
reasonable?

3. What is the essential pain
and the earned reward?

2. Is my thinking
positive and powerful?

- "If *that* is really my expectation, then of course I'm out of balance!"

It is such a relief to know that so many negative patterns we've blamed ourselves for are not character flaws or personal shortcomings, but rather the natural result of having unreasonable expectations. Harsh expectations trigger rebellion, procrastination, or self-abuse; expectations that are too easy cause discouragement, low self-esteem, and self-neglect. Realizing this takes away much of our inappropriate blame, particularly because most of our expectations *aren't even conscious* and were implanted within us long before we came of age.

In a sense, this skill sounds easy: Change the unreasonable expectations to reasonable ones. But it is not quite that easy.

It's difficult to find the unreasonable expectation—If you are way below the line, having been raised in a family where there were no limits and little nurturing, when you go to check your expectations, they will be hard to find.

It's hard to pinpoint what is reasonable—When you try to construct an expectation that is reasonable, you may be mystified. Yet each time you do identify a reasonable expectation, you are creating not only power in your life but intimacy as well. In order to identify an expectation that is reasonable for you, you must *see yourself* with the accuracy that your parents did not (though they may have tried).

It's easy to get "derailed"—What's more, you will often get derailed as you move around the cycle: Your expectation may be reasonable, but your positive, powerful thinking has nothing to do with that expectation. By the time you get to the essential pain and earned reward, you will have no idea what the cycle was originally about. If that happens, have compassion for yourself; it is likely to mean that nobody early in life stayed with you through your upsets, so you never learned to stay with yourself. Also, remind yourself that you are in the right place; these skills are what you need.

The reasonable expectation needs to be repeated—Even for those who were raised with reasonable limits and a goodly amount of nurturing, this skill is not easy. Implanting reasonable expectations in the belly of your brain requires that you practice saying them to yourself over and over again until they are ground into your bones and become integrated and spontaneous. The same is true for earned rewards and essential pain. It takes *that kind of repetition* for your feeling brain to soak them in, and this remains true even if you are highly educated and brilliant. *There are no short cuts,* no matter how smart you are.

For many people, the best way to master reasonable expectations is to first be aware of the unreasonable expectations. If you ask yourself, "What is my unreasonable expectation?" your answers may amaze you! Here are some examples of very common but very unreasonable expectations:

- "I expect my spouse to make me happy."
- "I expect to neglect myself and still be healthy."
- "I expect the people I love never to hurt me."
- "I expect to be happy without working at it."

- "I expect myself to be perfect all the time."
- "I expect everyone to like me."

In a sense, it is humorous to think that we have those expectations buried within us, but having even one of them can do much to separate us from a life of balance.

Tom began dating Michelle, a former client of his from several years before. He remembered his attraction to her and decided to call and ask her out. She accepted. After only two coffee dates, she was talking about a serious involvement and he was very aware of their compatibility and of his desire for her.

Within an hour of the time Tom met Michelle for their third date, he found himself below the line in a near panic. His emotional trash from the loss of his first wife had come up so strongly that Michelle even began to look like Karen. It was all he could do not to end the evening midway through dinner. His inner life said: Run!

Tom had first started working with a Solution Buddy, then decided to go into a group as well. He had done a couple of cycles in the group, but this was the first time he had done sensitive work there. In spite of that, he seemed remarkably comfortable.

Tom began. "I feel angry that . . . actually I'm not angry, I'm scared . . . scared that I'm going to get involved with this woman and lose all my power again. Karen made my life miserable. What she did to me was . . ."

I interjected. "Tom, it's important to do a Thinking Journal where you can state the facts. Then, when the feelings are very strong, launch into the Natural Flow of Feelings. Use short, choppy sentences that are pure emotion. If you blend thoughts and feelings, your cycles will not be as powerful and may not pop you above the line. Please take all the time you need."

Tom frowned, then said, "Okay. I can do that. When I was married to Karen, she had me totally controlled. I didn't want to put the boys through a divorce. She denied me sex and affection and seemed to have no libido herself. All she could do was find

> *What is my unreasonable expectation?*
> *What would be a reasonable expectation*
> *for who I am right now?*

fault with me. There was nothing I could do that pleased her. I was so miserable and lonely that I took pleasure in having more wine at night, so she carped on me and gossiped to all her friends about my drinking problem. I hated it!"

"Are you ready to go into the natural flow?" I asked.

Tom launched into his feelings. "I *hate* her for trapping me. . . . I feel *furious* that I allowed her to ruin my life. I feel angry that she hurt me. . . . I feel furious that she controlled me. . . . I hate it that she didn't love me . . .

"I feel sad that our life together was so unhappy. . . . I feel sad that I chose such an immature woman. . . . I feel sad that I didn't take better care of myself. . . . I feel sad that I had no good options . . .

"I feel afraid that Michelle is going to turn into Karen. . . . I feel afraid that she will look loving but turn out mean. . . . I feel afraid that I will get trapped again. . . . I feel afraid that every woman I see is going to turn into a bitch and make my life miserable. . . . I feel afraid that there will be someone who is right for me and that I'll miss out on love because I'm so afraid. . . .

"I feel guilty that I want to run away. . . . I feel guilty that I don't want to deal with this."

Tom may have needed only a simple expectation to pop himself above the line, such as: "I expect that I will have a lot of hurt in relationships." Perhaps the positive, powerful thoughts might be: "It is not the worst hurt in the world." The essential pain might be: "I will hurt." The earned reward: "I will heal."

This cycle was an important one for Tom. At this point, he was in emotional balance much of the time and making the second half of his climb. His sweetest fruit was intimacy, and he needed a very sturdy limits cycle to help him continue toward a life in which he would experience an abundance of that reward. He did three kinds of expectations:

- His most basic expectation
- His expectation of the situation
- His expectation of himself

"Tom, you did a great job on the Natural Flow of Feelings, the best I have heard you do. What is your *most basic expectation* about relationships?"

Tom answered, "I don't know."

"Just pretend you are looking straight down into the water and can see all the way to the very floor of the ocean. What is there?"

He thought for quite a while.

"My most basic expectation is that relationships cause pain," Tom said.

"Is that reasonable?" I asked.

He nodded. "That has been my experience. Look at my history. My sons are doing well, my practice is busy, but it's my relationships that have caused me the most misery in my life!"

"Would you be willing to consider a different basic expectation about relationships, even if it doesn't feel comfortable to you right now?"

Tom said quietly, "Relationships can bring pain and they can also bring joy."

"Terrific."

Tom was silent.

"You may feel like you're in a hole," I said gently.

"That's exactly right."

"So you need to dig out. An effective way to do that is to have a past, present, and future expectation. Do you want to try that?"

"Okay, but I don't know how."

"In the past, did you have enough of these skills to have intimacy with yourself?"

Tom shook his head.

"Intimacy with self is the foundation on which intimacy with others can be built. 'In the past, when I had fewer skills and less intimacy with myself, it is a reasonable expectation that . . .' "

". . . I would have less intimacy with others and my marriage would be unhappy."

"Great. 'Now I have more skill and am beginning to be more intimate with myself, so it is a reasonable expectation that . . .' "

". . . my relationships will still be difficult."

" 'In the future, as I have more skills and more intimacy with myself, it is a reasonable expectation that . . .' "

". . . I will have more intimacy with others and my relationships could even be . . . happy."

What Tom accomplished was monumental. He was willing to experiment with shifting to a basic expectation about relationships that would give him more security. He created an expectation about the situation that closely matched reality and offered hope.

"Great. Are you feeling more balanced?"

"I'm feeling somewhat better, but not good."

"Remember the infinity sign, the nurturing and limits symbol?"

He nodded and said, "You stay with the cycles until you are above the line."

"Correct. You did a basic expectation about relationships, then an expectation about the situation, past, present, and future."

"Right," said Tom.

"You will feel better in a moment, because the last expectation is what you expect of yourself, the way a good parent sees a child so accurately and knows just how much to nudge and no more."

"I get it."

"Try this: 'I expect myself to do the best I can to . . .'"

Tom said, "I expect myself to do the best I can to . . . use the skills to get more intimacy with myself so that in time, I can have more intimacy in a relationship."

He looked at me and said, "I felt the shift. That's amazing. Whooo! I feel so much better."

I said, "Excellent!"

Question 2: Is my thinking positive and powerful?

Tom had created a reasonable expectation for himself, but where would it go? Unless he nailed that expectation down by completing the rest of the cycle, chances were that he would not follow through.

That is where positive, powerful thinking comes in. We all know the value of cognitive therapy and positive thinking, but in my experience, there is no more powerful placement for that than right in the middle of the limits cycle. It provides just the encouragement needed to stick with that new, reasonable expectation. Moreover, the positive, powerful thoughts chase away the negative, powerless ones. If the negative, powerless thoughts, which are often unconscious but relentless, are allowed to remain, the expectation gets lost and the entire cycle shuts down. We do not follow through, and we do not create power and safety in our lives.

When Tom finished saying his reasonable expectation, his face looked serene and powerful. A moment later, nearly in a flash, his expression clouded.

Examples of Positive, Powerful Thinking:

It won't always be this difficult.

I have choices.

I can do this.

I am not alone.

Good things could happen.

My feelings matter.

I am a strong person.

I don't have to be perfect to be wonderful.

"Tom, what just happened? What are you thinking?"

"I don't know what I'm thinking." He paused and his face went blank. Then he said, "I'm thinking: 'I'll never do it. I will fail.'"

I was quiet.

Tom said, "That's a helluva thing to say to myself."

We both paused.

I asked, "Tom, can you turn it into something positive and powerful, the words that you most need to hear to follow through with using the skills to create intimacy for yourself so that you can have more intimacy with others?"

"Okay. I can do that. 'I won't fail.' But that doesn't sound honest."

"Create a statement that is positive, powerful, and honest."

"I can do that. 'I will try hard. I am not the only one who has had relationship problems.'"

Tom was back on track, moving around the limits cycle.

Question 3: What is the essential pain? What is the earned reward?

All Tom needed was to finish the limits cycle by facing the essential pain and feeling the earned reward. This was the most powerful part of the cycle, the point at which he would pop himself above the line. These questions are:

What is the essential pain?—What is the downside, the risk, the reality that I have to face in order to follow through?

What is the earned reward?—What is the payoff, the lesson learned, the benefit I will receive by following through?

Answering these questions requires that we both *think* and *feel*, by first thinking about the logical consequence of following through, then feeling the feelings related to it.

"Tom, what is the essential pain of following through with using the skills to create intimacy with yourself so you can have intimacy with others?"

"It takes work."

Tom sat with the thought and allowed the feelings to rise up, then begin to fade. His face relaxed, and he looked vibrant! That man who, when I'd first met him, had tapped his toes and was tight with tension, now looked relaxed and happy.

"What is the earned reward, Tom?"

"The earned reward is that I will have the intimacy I need."

"Are you sure?"

"Yes."

"Are there guarantees like that in life?"

Tom thought, then said, "The earned reward is that I will have intimacy with myself and I may have intimacy with others." He frowned. "That doesn't sound like a good deal."

"Is it reasonable?"

"Yes."

"To be above the line, what is another essential pain you would have to face?"

"That I am not in complete control."

"Great."

"The earned reward is that I'll be using the control I have."

"That was wonderful. Let's just check for one more essential pain."

He thought for a moment, then said, "The other essential pain is that I can't have a loving relationship now."

"Let's go under that to find the essential pain to find what is at its roots, the truth about the human condition that you may find yourself not yet accepting."

"The essential pain is: I can't have what I want when I want it!"

Tom roared with laughter. "My partners would love to hear that! That's what they tell me all the time, that I have to have what I want when I want it."

By now, Tom was enjoying himself and had popped himself above the line.

"Now that you are above the line, what do you need?"

Tom answered, "I need to stop being so selfish. I need to have a crash course in these skills. I need to have more intimacy with myself so I can have intimacy with others. I need to stop dating Michelle for a while and focus on myself."

"The support you need, the 'Would you please . . . ' "

"I want people in the group to do cycles with me, a lot of cycles!"

I was impressed. "You did an incredible job, Tom. Now how do you feel?"

He smiled happily and broadly. "Good. In fact, I feel great."

Tom's cycle brought a visible shift in his emotional balance, but more important, since he was beginning to do deeper cycles, he was beginning to alter his inner life in important ways that had implications beyond his romantic life. Each time he did a cycle of that depth, it seemed to move him a little bit further toward the level of human maturity that would enable him to move through life's pain and open his hand to the goodness that has always been there for him.

Separating Essential Pain from Self-abuse

People often make decisions by thinking about options. They twirl ideas around in their brain, analyzing their drawbacks and benefits and projecting their consequences. The trouble is that all that thinking typically results in compromised decisions.

Making good decisions is like trying on shoes until a pair fits. You check the box to be sure of the shoe size, but also try it on and notice how it feels. The implicit memory in the human brain, intuition, is the result of millions of unconscious experiences that are carefully wired into your feeling brain to provide you with a wealth of information. But to access intuition, we must feel.

Emily came to our group with a knot in her stomach. She had been in pain all week because she couldn't decide what to do about Angela, her youngest child, a teenager who was full throttle in the middle of an adolescent rebellion and had started getting into screaming matches with her mother. This sweet child had suddenly turned into a tyrannical adolescent, totally focused on herself and her friends. Instead of cuddling with her mother, she was mocking her, snarling at her, and flagrantly disobeying her, but it was the arguing that disturbed Emily the most.

When Emily told this story to the group, she did an excellent Natural Flow of Feelings with red-hot, molten anger and strong feelings of sadness, fear, and guilt for allowing her daughter to treat her with disrespect and for getting hooked into Angela's fury. She used the limits cycle to make her decision about what to do.

"I have no idea what is a reasonable expectation. When it comes to my Angela, my mind goes blank. I lose any sense of reason."

I suggested, "What about trying on expectations the way you'd try on shoes? Say one expectation, and then check the essential pain and the earned reward. Wait for the feelings to come up for each."

"Okay," said Emily. "If I looked at my behavior, I'd say that my expectation has been that when Angela screams at me, I expect myself to scream back."

"If you follow that course of action, what is the essential pain?"

"Constant fighting."

"Check the feelings that arise from that statement. Does that feel like essential pain, that is, the unavoidable pain of the human condition, or like abuse or neglect?"

"Abuse and neglect. Abuse of her and neglect of my own needs."

"What's the earned reward?"

"The payoff is that I get to do whatever I want to do. I get to hurt her back. I get to lose my temper. Frankly, it feels good just to have it out with her, but it's not enough to offset the negative consequences, the abuse and neglect."

"Let's try on another expectation. But first, it might help to check on your most basic expectation, about communicating with other people, the basic limit you set on yourself."

She didn't answer. Then she said, "I don't have one. Nothing comes to mind."

"Then reflect on how you act. That may give you a clue."

"Well, based on the way I act, I am passive when I want to be, which is most of the time, and then when I can't stand it anymore, I get aggressive."

"Do you have any limit on your behavior with another person?"

"Well, I don't hit people and I don't call them names, but I do swear. But I want to set a limit with screaming and yelling at each other."

"What is your most basic expectation of yourself?"

"When Angela starts screaming at me, I expect myself to separate from the situation, to not engage with her until we are both reasonably balanced."

"What is the essential pain?"

"I would have to control myself. She might be hurtful. Angela might be mad at me."

"Does that feel like essential pain, or abuse and neglect?"

Emily blinked and said, "Just essential pain. It's not pleasant, but it doesn't feel like abuse or neglect."

"The earned reward?"

"The earned reward of not having screaming matches with Angela? Personal pride. I'd feel more balanced. Less hurt between us. Those are a lot of rewards."

Adult life involves making decisions when there are no good options, choosing what loss, change, or discomfort we are willing to accept in order to receive the corresponding reward. This tool of the limits cycle, particularly when we open our inner life first with the Natural Flow of Feelings, can be tremendously powerful in helping us make decisions in which the gain outweighs the pain, particularly in the most sensitive and challenging situations.

Accepting the Truth About Life

The last benefit of the limits cycle is that its long-term use grows us up into mature adults who see the world accurately and accept the realities of the human condition. It is only when our limits cycle is working well that we can do that.

Please consider the idea that most of the unnecessary pain we cause ourselves in life comes from *not accepting the truth* about the human condition and the realities of our lives. If we could just accept those truths and realities, we could move through our days and decades without so much unnecessary pain.

The more responsive our early environment was, the more the essential pains and earned rewards of the human condition found their way into our unconscious. Responsive parents see us more accurately, and see the world more accurately as well. In

Some Essential Pain and Earned Rewards of Life

Essential Pain	Earned Reward
I am not perfect.	I am human.
I am alone.	I have myself.
No one will rescue me.	I can rescue myself.
Life is difficult.	Life has its rewards.
People may reject me.	I won't reject myself.

the words they say, the life they model, and the lessons they teach us, we learn to accept the good and the bad of the human condition. However, if our parents do not see us accurately and do not view the world in a reasonably balanced way, chances are that those lessons will have been missed, and we may continue to butt our heads against the wall. We will be furious, depressed, and confused as to why other people can cope but we can't. It may only be that we have not yet strengthened the neural networks in our feeling brains that favor a life of balance. Without those networks firing around the clock, whenever we need them to be there, we won't intuitively recognize and accept the truths of the human condition.

It is only during the second half of the climb that most people become so intimate with themselves from doing so many cycles that they can see to their very core. They become aware of their most basic expectations about life that may be unreasonable. They become aware of the realities of the human condition they have not learned to face and the rewards they have not learned to feel.

The way new reasonable expectations become their own is by practicing them one by one until they are ground into their bones. The way the essential pains of life and the earned rewards become part of them is practice, one by one, as well. When all this practice results in changes in the dominant neural networks, the change is so dramatic that it makes every single cycle you have ever done feel more than worth it!

Now you know about what the method is and how it works, and what those two simple steps are. Now it is time to begin walking, or if you prefer, making the climb . . .

IV. CLIMBING TO THE TOP

12. A Nurturing Inner Voice

One January evening several years ago, I did a book signing in a huge mall on the outskirts of Dallas. Unfortunately, a horrendous storm had just come in, and the mall—including the bookstore—was virtually empty. One family had made its way through the downpour and sat in the front row of chairs; the rest of the seats were empty. The husband, an extremely large man dressed in jeans held up with suspenders, explained to me that he had gained and lost hundreds of pounds and had tried everything to lose weight, including fasts and surgery. Clearly, nothing had worked. As he spoke, his children, who were perhaps two and four years old, squirmed off their chairs and found their way to the nearby bookshelves. They began pulling one book off the shelf after another, giggling with delight.

His wife, a very small woman with tiny hands and feet and short-cropped, carrot-red hair, arose from her chair and in a resigned fashion, began putting the books back. The children turned their attention to each other and quickly fell into a bear hug, rolling and tumbling on the carpet.

Amid her reshelving, the woman turned to me and said, "I understand that The Solution is about questions, but who answers them?"

At the time, I was stunned by her question. I didn't know how to answer it without risking embarrassing her, so I said matter-of-factly, "Well, you do."

In retrospect, I was the one who should have been embarrassed. My answer to her was less than accurate. When we start using The Solution, most of us don't answer the questions ourselves. Often, we don't have our own responsive voice, but the depriving and/or indulging voice of our parents.

Unfortunately, asking the questions of the cycles without first bringing up our own nurturing voice is not very effective. The questions don't sound responsive, for just the way a child senses a parent's rejection or love more by tone than by words, if we ask ourselves responsive questions with a harsh tone we end up feeling neglected or unloved. It is only when we use a tone of self-cherishing with ourselves that the cycles offer the nourishment and power we need. Thus, *reaching a Solution requires us to take the baton from our parents and implant within ourselves a nurturing inner voice.*

Neither Emily nor Tom nor Drew had a nurturing inner voice when they started their journey. Each built that loving and honest connection with themselves the way we all must: brick by brick by brick. But the story I want to share with you now is not any of their stories, but Sharon's. She was the woman who first taught me the importance of cultivating a nurturing inner voice.

The skill of "checking in"

Sharon was a successful nonfiction writer in her midforties with chestnut hair and huge, deep-set, brown eyes that were hauntingly sad. She had a high voice that sounded well bred, perhaps tweaked by teachers at a private girls' school, and high cheekbones and full breasts that had probably made her the envy of most of her classmates in high school. Sharon told of having been highly attractive to men during her twenties and thirties and having dated several famous personalities during those years. She had become accustomed, without any particular effort, to being the object of men's desire.

Sharon particularly relished male attention because, throughout her childhood, her father had been such a rejecting force in her life. Oddly, she felt closer to him than to anyone, and her face, build, and temperament bore a striking resemblance to his. But his biting criticisms and grating harshness still echoed within her. There were times when her dad was sufficiently provoked by a bad report card or too much scotch to slap Sharon and her siblings around. So she had learned from a very young age that *feeling* was not safe, and that emotional numbness offered her a refuge.

Her forties hit Sharon hard. One relationship after another had failed, and her striking good looks began to fade. To make matters worse, she began developing various symptoms—back trouble, jaw pain, chemical sensitivities, and hormonal imbalances that made her gain weight and feel bloated and weary. Before long, she was spending most of her discretionary time and money on various alternative remedies that did little to restore her health.

Sharon was extremely attentive during our group meetings. When she did cycles, she was skilled at popping herself above the line. But even after she had been working with the method for quite some time, Sharon did *not* seem to be progressing. She was still depressed, her health was still suffering, and she seemed more isolated and hostile than ever. I asked her about this during a session.

"Sharon, I'm worried. You use the skills so well in group, but . . ."

"I know I'm failing," she shot back. "I've been worried that you're going to kick me out of the group."

I was exasperated. "Sharon, you can't flunk The Solution. But I am worried."

Sharon said, "I have something I want to admit to you. When I'm not here, when I'm at home or at work . . . I don't use the skills. I stay numb. I don't bother to go inside."

"You don't use them?" I was astonished.

"No," she said in a high, somewhat aloof voice.

I was quiet, and so was the group.

Sharon explained, "I don't *like* going inside. I can't seem to make myself do it."

"But, Sharon, going inside can be a nurturing act, like slipping into a warm, soothing bath," I said.

"Are you kidding?" she responded. "I can't find any nurturing voice on my own. I don't find a warm bath. My inner life is like a cold shower."

She continued. "When you coach me through a cycle, I use your nurturing voice. When I do Community Connections on the phone with people, I listen to their cycles, and with people I feel safe with, I use their voice. But I don't use my own voice, ever."

"When you go inside by yourself, whose voice do you hear?" I asked.

She thought for a moment. "It's a mean voice. My dad's voice."

We both sighed.

"Well, that's logical. Who would want to go inside if it meant meeting up with a mean voice?" I asked.

"My father."

"Yes, your father."

Again, we were quiet, and several group members squirmed in their seats, their chairs squeaking.

"Sharon, a nurturing inner voice isn't genetic, it's learned. You can learn to have one."

"How?" she said. "I'm not an easy case. My inner life is as cold and harsh and dry as they come. I'm afraid that will carry me to my grave."

"I understand that you're afraid," I said, "but if you let yourself get below the line about it and feel despair and self-pity, you probably *will* go to your grave with it. You have to plant that voice in yourself—nobody else will."

Sharon sighed. "Okay, tell me what to do. I'll trust that you're right. I'll try it for two weeks. That's it."

"Good. The idea is to trigger yourself to go inside, then to consciously create an intimate connection with yourself. When you do, you can feel your body shift, that warm 'downshift' into the power within. It can feel like a relaxation response, or as if you're finally home."

"I don't know how to downshift," Sharon said, irritation creeping into her voice.

"You bring up a nurturing inner voice and ask yourself the questions of the nurturing and limits cycles. What would you need to trigger you to go inside?" I asked.

"I don't know," Sharon answered. "I don't have a clue."

"Would you like suggestions from the group, or examples of what has worked for them?"

The Skill of Checking In

- Set a watch alarm to go off hourly.
- Post pocket reminders around your home.
- Set your computer to remind you hourly.
- Go inside whenever you take a bathroom break.
- Check in when you wake up and when you go to bed.
- Check in before and after you eat.
- When you exercise, check in.
- Go inside when you take a shower or bath.
- Do whatever works for you!

"I'd love them," she said, her irritation lessening.

A young architect just out of school offered, "I post notes all over the house. They say things like, 'Check in!' and 'How do you feel?' and 'Go inside, dummy.' It works for a while, then I stop seeing them, so I move them to another location."

A woman in her late thirties, the mother of two girls ages seven and nine, said, "I use a watch that's set to go off every hour. When it goes off, my children say, 'Time to check in, Mommy.' It has a double benefit, because now they're learning to check in, too."

A retired nurse who was near her Solution said, "The nurturing voice is automatic now. When I first started, I checked in during television commercials. I have a small brown teddy bear on my bed and whenever I see it, I say to myself, 'How do I feel?' in a loving voice."

A middle-aged man who had joined the group long after Sharon said, "When I first started, I made it a ritual. I would check in when I got up, each time I ate, when I used the bathroom, when I took a shower, and when I went to bed. Now the voice is just there. I don't have to prompt it."

There are dozens of ways to trigger yourself to go inside. It doesn't matter which you use—all that matters is that you use *something* to trigger yourself to go inside many times a day. At first, you may notice that even though you *intend* to go inside, the day slips by and you don't. In time, a nurturing inner voice will come naturally, but in the interim, using external methods to prompt you to go inside can be very effective.

Bringing up a nurturing voice

Sharon left that session planning to check in with herself by using an hourly watch alarm. She intended to take time on her commute to go inside and do cycles. But in sessions during the weeks that followed, she said that she hadn't made much progress. Each week, she tried another strategy, but with little success.

Finally, Sharon came to a session furious.

"I can't *stand* it. I am so frustrated that I'm so resistant to going inside! I know I'll *never* get this. I am a defective person and will go to my grave without a Solution. Everybody else here is getting it and I'm not. What is *wrong* with me?" she practically cried.

I wondered if her harshness toward herself was a pure download of her father's harshness toward her. "Sharon, I feel sad hearing you be so hard on yourself."

Sharon did not respond. She was sitting at the end of the couch in the living room of my home. Her mouth was set in a stubborn frown. Curled up in a ball on the floor next to her was her neighbor's little white poodle, Pinky. The dog was ailing and her neighbors were away, so Sharon didn't want to leave Pinky at home alone. Nobody in the group was allergic to dogs, so Pinky stayed, resting on a soft, woven blanket Sharon had brought for her.

Just then, Sharon reached down and petted Pinky on the head and rubbed her ears. Pinky looked up at her adoringly, and Sharon said to her in the softest voice, "It's okay, sweetie. You'll feel better soon."

I was astonished. Here she was, giving all that softness to the dog when all she gave herself was harshness.

I said, "Sharon, I wonder how it would be for you to use that same voice, the one you afford Pinky, with yourself."

She looked shocked, then said, "You mean go inside, feel the love I feel for Pinky, connect with myself, then do the cycle?"

"Precisely."

She thought for a moment, then said, "I think I could do that."

When Sharon came to group the following week, she looked like a different person. She looked a little bit the way people look when they reach their Solution: vibrant. The feeling brain is attached to the facial muscles, so you can often *see* a Solution in someone long before they *tell* you they are experiencing it. Several people in the group noticed the change in her, her glow and vibrancy, and commented on it. Right after we started the session, Sharon poured out her story.

"I don't know what's going on," she said. "I don't have any trouble doing cycles. I like going inside now, and as long as I can find my 'Pinky voice,' I don't feel lost or abandoned anymore. It's wonderful!"

"What happened to your father's voice?" I asked.

She smiled, "Well, as a matter of fact, I haven't heard it. I guess I crowded him out with a more loving voice."

That was the turning point in Sharon's training. She still had to take out a lot of emotional trash and go deeper with the skills, but that was the moment at which it was clear she would reach

Creating a Nurturing Voice

- Speak to yourself with the voice you afford your pet.
- Use the voice of someone you know who is nurturing but strong.
- Try on the voice of someone famous whom you see as warm.
- Intentionally go deep inside until you connect with yourself.
- Watch for the shift in your body, the relaxing response.
- Bring up a nurturing but strong inner voice and begin to ask yourself the questions of the cycles.

her Solution. Now and then, she would lose her Pinky voice and her father's harsh voice would return, but that harsh voice visited less and less often. In time, even her Pinky voice faded. Sharon still heard a nurturing inner voice, but that voice was her own.

Sharon's experience stimulated me to include going inside and bringing up a nurturing inner voice as one of the four basic practices of the method. This practice is essential to the method but is particularly important if you are very smart and analytical. If you are, you may tend to work hard at answering the questions of the cycles "correctly" and analyzing them thoroughly, almost turning the method into insight-oriented self-psychotherapy. Unfortunately, using the method in that way is not likely to produce a Solution; you would be far more likely to make it halfway through the climb rather than to the very top of the tree.

It may not be your favorite activity, but consider holding yourself accountable for asking yourself the questions of the cycles only *after* you have brought up a nurturing voice, one that is deeply connected to the inherent strength, goodness, and wisdom within you.

13. Staying Balanced Now

When the alarm on Emily's nightstand went off each morning at 6:00 a.m., the first thing that popped into her mind was the list of things she had to get done that day. While showering, she prioritized her errands and obligations. She was halfway through her second cup of coffee before she even thought about whether or not she was above the line.

Staying balanced *now* starts with the decision that since nothing much good happens when we are below the line, your first priority is to keep your finger on the pulse of your inner life and use the cycles to stay above the line. We call that Commitment to Personal Balance.

When you switch your priority from the checklist of things you should do to a personal inventory of how many moments you spend above the line, life gets better. That tight fist of over-control relaxes. You begin to see that it *will* all work out, that things will unfold as they should. Oddly enough, *more* gets done, not less.

When I brought this idea up in group, Emily responded immediately.

"I can't be committed to personal balance—that's selfish. I have lots of people to take care of. I'm not going to sit around all day thinking about my personal balance. How would the lunches get made, the housework get done, and the bills get paid?"

"If the priority is to get everything done, you have no anchor," I responded. "In fact, you could easily imagine all of your external solutions—people-pleasing, rescuing others, staying incessantly busy, being preoccupied about sweets—like balloons, huge balloons with lots of helium in them, with you holding on to the whole bunch of them."

Emily blinked, then laughed. "You think I'm going to float away, don't you?"

I smiled and shrugged.

Emily pushed up her red glasses. "Well, I do feel like I'm floating half the time," she said.

"What if you let all the balloons go and anchored yourself to the ground, keeping your feet beneath you?" I asked.

"I'm not sure I've even tried that," she admitted.

"Your most basic expectation would be that you would do the best you could to stay above the line," I explained.

Emily began. "I expect myself to do the best I can to keep my finger on the pulse of my inner life and to stay above the line."

"Exactly."

Emily thought for a moment, then said, "That changes everything, doesn't it?"

"Yes, it does," I responded.

"It requires that I trust . . . ," she trailed off, and a flash of fear passed over her face. ". . . That I trust myself, my deepest self, and the universe. That I accept the essential pain that I am not in complete control."

I prompted her. "Yes, that you're not in complete control, and . . ."

Emily continued, ". . . and don't necessarily need to be."

She looked at me, her eyes pensive and doelike behind her glasses. I smiled and said, "When you face the realities of the human condition in that way, things change. The weight of the world comes off your shoulders. All of a sudden, you are more curious, you see more of the humor in life, and often you have a renewed sense of the wonder of being intensely alive."

Emily's face hardened. "Would you be practical for a minute?"

"By all means. Try telling me some expectations you have for your life, something very basic, and let's change it to be based on personal balance."

"You mean let's let go of one of those balloons," she said.

"Correct."

"Okay. I expect myself to make love with my husband at least twice a week."

Cultivating a Commitment to Personal Balance:

I expect myself to do the best I can to keep my fingers on the pulse of my inner life and use the skills to stay above the line.

As this was a woman who had hardly ever mentioned her husband, let alone discussed sex, I was somewhat taken aback. I responded, "Okay, that's simple: 'I expect myself to do the best I can to stay above the line and to make love with my husband as often as I have the desire and he is willing.'"

"Hmm," Emily said. "You know, I think we'd make love more often that way."

I smiled. "Perhaps."

"Then again," she said, "sometimes we'd make love less."

"What is the essential pain of making love less?"

"He might have some of his needs unmet."

"What is the earned reward?"

"I wouldn't be having sex when I don't want it. I wouldn't be rescuing him sexually. Perhaps our love life would start to become more . . . honest."

Emily's eyes lit up. This invariably pale woman was looking very, very alive.

"I think that's being too easy on myself," she said.

"It's not at all easy," I said. "In the beginning, staying above the line is one of the hardest things you'll ever do."

Emily said, "All right, it could work for sex, but I have other obligations that are serious because my children have some very serious problems."

"I know," I said. "Give me an example."

"I expect myself to fix Rob's speech problem," she responded.

"Can you do that?"

"I can try."

"And what happens when you make Rob's speech problem more important than your staying in balance?" I asked.

"I get him a better therapist. I take him for treatment more often. His speech gets a little better."

"But there are probably some losses. You may win the battle, but not the war."

"I don't get to play tennis as much as I want to. I'm tired more often. I resort to comforting myself with cookies more frequently."

"I mean losses that have to do with Rob," I said. "When you cut off from yourself, you curtail the emotional connection between the two of you, and other bad things could happen."

Emily frowned. "Yes, there were two times—times I am not proud of."

She shifted in her chair, and it creaked. She shifted back again. "One was when I was exhausted, and Rob was in a bad mood. We were in the car, and I let him have it. I tore into him about his messy room and his laziness with his lessons."

"Your expectation was what?"

"I expected that because I was furious, I had a right to express it . . ."

". . . from below the line," I finished the sentence for her.

"Right," she nodded.

"If your Commitment to Personal Balance had been in place, what would your expectation have been?"

Emily stared at the ceiling for a moment. "I don't know," she finally sighed. "Maybe I would have expected myself not to open my mouth and talk to him until I got myself above the line."

"Perfect."

Emily seemed relieved, then sighed and said, "The other thing was far worse."

"What was that?" I asked.

Deep train tracks appeared between Emily's eyebrows. "Last week, Rob asked me if his speech would ever be normal. We were making dinner. I was stirring the pasta sauce on the stove, and he was breaking up lettuce into the salad bowl and he just blurted it out."

"What did you do?"

"I went right below the line—and I lied to him. I said, 'Of course it will. If you keep working at it, your speech will be just fine.' I immediately felt awful, like I had betrayed him. I had lied to him and set him up for disappointment later on. I didn't say anything else. I just kept stirring the pasta sauce."

I paused for a moment, then said, "If your first priority had been to stay above the line, what would you have done?"

"I don't know," Emily nearly cried. Then she took a deep breath and said, "I think I would have taken a minute to collect my thoughts, recognized that I was too below the line to talk about it, and said to him, 'I love you, Rob, and I'm happy to talk with you about it, but right now I'm frazzled. Can we talk about it later, after dinner?'"

"What would be the essential pain you would have had to face, not giving him an answer when he asked the question?"

"The essential pain would be that I could worry more. Not meeting his need immediately would mean that I'm not a perfect mother. I would have to face the essential pain that I can't make the problem go away."

"The earned reward?"

Emily was stern. "I wouldn't have flat-out lied to my son about one of the most important things in his life."

I nodded.

Emily put her hand on her forehead and started to cry. Drew was sitting next to her. She reached into her purse, pulled out two tissues, and handed them to Emily.

Emily said, "I hate life sometimes. There is so much pain. I wanted The Solution to take away my pain, that's what I most wanted, and now I'm feeling worse."

She simply wept for several minutes.

"I'm sorry you're feeling worse, Emily," I said gently.

She lifted her red glasses and wiped her eyes, and I continued.

"There is always pain and there are always rewards, no matter what path you take in life. The Solution helps you avoid more of the unnecessary pain and gives you more power, but not complete power in determining what essential pain you are willing to feel in order to get the earned reward you most value."

Emily said, "So if my priority is to keep my finger on the pulse of my inner life and stay above the line, I could choose to protect Rob from reality. The essential pain would be that I had lied to him. The earned reward would be that he would be protected from reality."

"And there may be benefits to that," I said. "Only you know what is right for you."

Emily continued. "Or I could choose to tell Rob the truth and face the essential pain that he would feel hurt when he realized his speech would probably never be normal. There would be earned rewards, though."

"What would they be?" I asked.

"He could begin to grieve. He would see himself more accurately. I would have a greater sense of personal integrity and more intimacy with my child."

"Yes."

"They are all hurtful options," she said.

"I know. And each one has its rewards."

Emily nodded again, and the lines between her brows softened. "If I'm committed to personal balance all day long, when I go below the line, I make it my priority to stop everything as much as possible and get above the line. I would make being above the line my foundation for living."

"Precisely."

She looked me straight in the eye and said, "I'm not completely sure that would work for me, but I'm willing to give it a try."

"That's all I can ask of you, Emily. Thank you."

She nodded as if to say, "You're welcome."

14. Taking Out Emotional Trash

Most mornings as I was growing up, my mother would set eggs in an aluminum saucepan, fill it with water, and heat it on the stove until it boiled. When it did, she would set our small white kitchen timer for precisely three minutes. When the timer went off, she would rush to remove the eggs from the heat, scoop them out of their shells, and slip them into little glass bowls. She would serve them with white toast spread with real butter and grape jelly.

Taking three-minute eggs out of their shells is always neat and clean. But this is not at all the case for taking emotional trash out of your inner life. Healing the hurts from the past can be messy, and there are no guarantees that it will take three minutes—or even three years. If you embark on the journey to release the pain of the past, the travel plans must be open-ended, for your pain is unique, and each hurt is different. And it takes as long as it takes.

The good news is that the tools in this method for healing past hurts are effective for most people. They include four steps:

1. Thinking Journals

2. Feelings Letters

3. The Limits Cycle

4. Tender Morsels

In the Thinking Journal, we tell the facts about what happened. Those thoughts trigger the feelings from that past hurt to arise in the present moment. Once the feelings are triggered, the healing can begin as we feel each feeling of the Natural Flow of Feelings—and express it. We can say the feelings aloud or write them out in a "letter." If we write them out, the letter is addressed to the person or situation, then we feel our anger, then express it in writing. Then our sadness, fear, and, finally, guilt.

After we express all four feelings, we feel more acceptance, love, and balance, and some of the emotional trash has been taken out.

Those two tools—Thinking Journals and Feelings Letters—are enough to heal many hurts, but for deeper ones, we also need to use the limits cycle. It has the effect of containing the feelings and keeping them from wandering into imbalance. We can stay in the balanced feelings longer, so we can heal more deeply.

When there is a deep hurt, these tools may be used many, many times without feeling much relief. We keep feeling our anger, sadness, fear, and guilt, and it hurts! Perhaps the only limit that we can set with ourselves after feeling those feelings is that we will be as angry, sad, afraid, and guilty as we need to be for as long as we need to be. But at some point, we will do a Natural Flow of Feelings, then the limit will actually allow us to see the full truth about the situation and we will feel a great deal of healing.

We still may feel some of the deep pain of that loss. But the pain won't be as devastating. We will see that what happened, in its own way, was perfect, or at least that it taught us important lessons or brought some of its own blessings along with it.

1. The Thinking Journal

How do you begin taking out emotional trash? Think of all your emotional trash as a big bowl of spaghetti. You just start taking it out, one piece at a time. The most important thing is to begin. Choose one strand of hurt, one crack in your heart that are ready to begin to heal.

Once you have a hurt in mind, write a Thinking Journal in which you state what happened. Tell the facts without any mention of feelings. The longer you write about what happened, the more feelings are apt to arise. When you can't stand it anymore and feel as if you are going to burst from feeling, it's time to write a Feelings Letter.

2. The Feelings Letter

Fortunately, the feeling brain cannot differentiate between what is happening in the present and the thinking brain's thoughts about what occurred in the past. As you write your Thinking Journal, the feelings that arose during a hurtful situation will arise as you remember that situation. When the hurt

Taking Out Emotional Trash

1. **Thinking Journal**
   - Bring up thoughts about past hurts.
   - Stick with the facts—no feelings.
   - Wait for feelings to mount in your body.

2. **Feelings Letter**
   - Address the letter to a person or situation.
   - Feel each feeling in our body.
   - Express each feeling in writing, starting sentences with "I feel . . . ," until the feeling subsides.
   - Begin with anger, then sadness, then fear, then guilt.

3. **Limits Cycle**
   - If the hurt is not healed, do a limits cycle.
   - For big hurts, the limits cycle will first allow you to stay in the feelings. Later it will allow you to accept, forgive, and heal.

4. **Tender Morsels**
   - Give yourself some praise. Taking out emotional trash is not easy, but it does heal.

occurred, you did not have the skill to feel those feelings and move through that pain. The hurt went underground and formed emotional trash. Now you have the tools to feel and heal it.

A Feelings Letter is the Natural Flow of Feelings in written form. Address the letter to the person, thing, or situation involved in the painful memory. Then bring up each feeling—first anger, then sadness, then fear, and finally guilt.

Feel each feeling in your body. Then express it with words until it subsides and go on to the next feeling. By the time you finish the Feelings Letter, you are likely to experience more acceptance and understanding. If you do, write down what you accept and understand.

The Natural Flow of Feelings fans out potentially unbalanced feelings into anger, sadness, fear, and guilt. Following the steps of

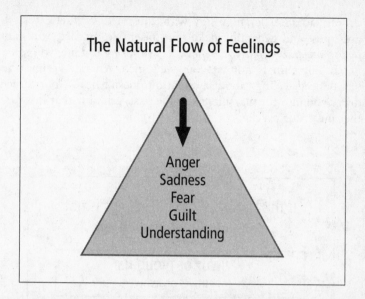

The Natural Flow of Feelings

Anger
Sadness
Fear
Guilt
Understanding

a Feelings Letter will help you avoid getting stuck in any one feeling and watching it go out of balance into a false high or an unnecessary low. For example, if you are depressed, the extra sadness you feel is often not sadness at all, but a symptom of one of the other feelings in the natural flow that has not been felt or expressed. People who are depressed often have not mastered the skill of feeling and expressing anger. If all four feelings are operating well—if the Natural Flow of Feelings is flowing—getting stuck in any one unbalanced feeling is unlikely. All four feelings needed to grieve a loss can be felt.

Feelings Letters can also cut down on the times you find yourself in obsessive, repetitive thinking, since that, too, is just a symptom of the Natural Flow of Feelings shutting down or never having started up. It's important to keep your Thinking Journals factual and relatively brief. Otherwise, you may be prone to obsessive thinking or unbalanced feelings. If you are able to feel the feelings of the past hurt in the present, and to keep them in balance, they may fade and you may begin to heal. The challenge becomes keeping them in balance, for they are apt to be so strong that without a huge amount of skill, they will go right out of balance.

The disadvantage to having those feelings go out of balance is twofold. First, unbalanced feelings tend to stay stuck instead of simply fading. They may stay with you for days, fuel excessive appetites, and generally make you miserable. In fact, *you may feel so miserable that you believe this suffering is doing you some good.* But pain is not virtuous—it's inconvenient. Feeling the unbalanced feelings about a situation doesn't heal it but rather drags you into the marshlands of the past, grinding that loss further into your psyche.

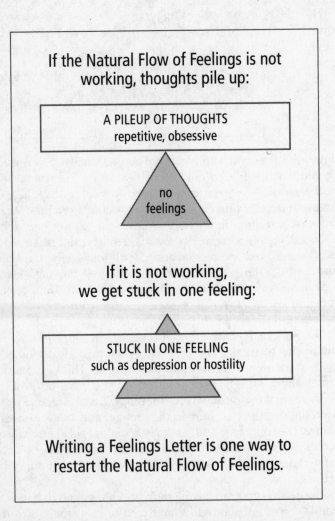

3. The Limits Cycle

When a hurt is so painful that the Thinking Journals and Feelings Letters are not enough to help you heal, using the limits cycle can be very effective.

Drew once told me, "I feel like a walking time bomb. Nearly anything can set off an emotional explosion in me. Yesterday was Valentine's Day, and the second-graders brought cupcakes to school and exchanged heart-shaped cards. It was wonderful!

"But after all the valentines had been passed out, Claire—a student who is particularly special to me—walked up to my desk with her lip trembling and these huge tears in her eyes, and whispered hoarsely, 'I didn't get any valentines. Not *one*.'

"She was so sweet and felt so hurt that I bent down and hugged her. But what happened to me was an intense explosion of sadness inside. It was like *I* was seven years old, having my feelings hurt and being left out and all alone.

"We walked back to her desk and found a valentine with her name on it that had slipped behind the desk. I was so relieved for her, but . . . I was emotionally shaken for the rest of the day.

"I said to myself, 'This is not rational. This sadness is far too monumental compared to what a sensible person would expect. It must be emotional trash.' "

"Drew," I responded, "when Claire's lip trembled . . . what did it remind you of? It feels like . . . seems like . . . something from the past . . ."

Drew's face lit up with recognition. "I know! It felt like all the times that the twins got attention and I was left out."

"Fantastic," I said.

"I can feel it in the pit of my stomach. Right here," she pointed to a spot just above her waist.

4. Tender Morsels

Taking out emotional trash is painful. After you do, be sure to feel the emotional lightness. Think about how much easier it is to stay in balance, and watch the sense of peace, forgiveness, and acceptance wash over your body.

Say something that is kind, honest, and nurturing to yourself, such as, "I had the courage to heal my hurts," "I feel better," or "I did that!" Nourish yourself in ways you were not nourished long ago.

Honoring your feelings

Drew moved right into telling the facts about what had happened. She knew the story, but her inner life needed to hear it again, to bring up those thoughts so the feelings could start firing in her feeling brain.

"I was the adored child until I was eight. When the twins were born, I wasn't the adored child anymore. In fact, I wasn't special. Instead of feeling cherished and the center of my parents' attention, I was a bother to deal with. All four of them—the boys and my parents—were always together, and I was in the other room watching television or playing with dolls. I was all alone, and nobody cared."

"Drew, would you rather write your Feelings Letter or speak it?"

"Speak it."

"Okay; I'll listen."

Drew's face turned slightly red, then she blurted out, "What idiots they are. What fools. How could they possibly bring twins home and make no arrangements whatsoever to take care of my needs? What miserable parents they were. . . . I feel furious that they were so self-centered. . . . I hate it that they were so insensitive to my needs. . . . I can't stand it that they neglected me and ignored me and made me feel less important. . . . I hate them for how they treated me. . . . I feel angry that they deserted me. . . . I feel angry that they didn't care about me."

"Sadness?" I prompted.

"I feel sad that I was so hurt. . . . I feel sad that it was such a surprise to me. . . . I feel sad that I felt so lost."

She segued right into fear.

"I feel afraid that I will always feel lost. . . . I feel afraid that I will always have the scars of that hurt. . . . Now I feel angry again. I feel angry that they deserted me. . . . I feel angry that they didn't love me. I feel afraid that they will never love me. . . . I feel afraid that I will never love myself. . . . I feel guilty that I can't just get over it."

"Drew, you did anger, sadness, fear, and guilt. Do you feel any more understanding or acceptance?"

"No, none. Maybe just a little. I appreciate how painful this was. Is that enough?"

I shook my head. "Drew, taking out emotional trash can't be

rushed. You can't force acceptance. All you can do is feel the feelings until you notice that acceptance and forgiveness arise."

Drew seemed relieved.

"Do you feel in balance now?" I asked. "If not, consider doing a limits cycle."

She said, "No, I don't feel in balance. I definitely need a limits cycle. I expect myself to feel as angry, sad, afraid, and guilty as I need to, for as long as I need to feel that way."

Drew breathed deeply and said, "That feels great. Now, positive and powerful. I have a right to my feelings. These are deep hurts and I am only beginning to heal them. Essential pain? I will hurt. Earned reward? In time, I will heal."

"Great job, Drew."

"Thanks; I feel much better."

The hurt she was healing was deep. She would not be in complete control of how long it would take her to heal it, or how many Feelings Letters she would need to write. However, if she continued, one day, perhaps when she was not even expecting it, she would use the tools, then notice that she somehow felt emotionally lighter . . . and healed. That hurt would lose much of its power over her.

Watching yourself heal

Drew continued to take out emotional trash about feeling left out early in life. About three months later, she came to one evening's session and seemed absolutely vibrant, eager to tell what had happened to her in the car that afternoon.

She said, "I've done dozens of Feelings Letters, and the best I could do for a limits cycle was to say that I was going to be as angry, sad, afraid, and guilty as I needed to be, for as long as I needed to feel that way. Nothing really budged. I just allowed myself to be . . . well, about eight years old, feeling as outrageously upset as I needed to feel.

"Today, I was driving home from school and working on that emotional trash, saying the Natural Flow of Feelings out loud. People must think I'm nuts, but I don't care—I just roll up all the windows and have at it."

Several members of the group chuckled.

"When I was angry, I was shouting like crazy, and when I was sad, there I was, driving down El Camino Boulevard, when tears started rolling down my cheeks. I felt my fear and my guilt. But what shocked me was that when I got to the limits cycle, my vision was perfectly clear."

The room was quiet, as everyone listened intently.

"It was as if, for the first time, I could see myself and my parents accurately. I wasn't revising the story to make myself look better. I wasn't expecting them to be saints. I was seeing the situation with twenty-twenty vision, as though I were a loving but objective observer.

"I said out loud, 'It was a reasonable expectation that they were overwhelmed. It was a reasonable expectation that my dark side that withdraws and tends toward self-pity would make it harder. It's a reasonable expectation, given their skill level and mine, that I would feel left out and unloved.'"

Drew gasped. "That's the truth. It didn't feel like I was intellectualizing it. I felt it as true, right in the pit of my stomach.

"My positive, powerful thinking was: Everyone was having a hard time. The essential pain? I felt lost. I felt unloved. They weren't perfect. I wasn't perfect. The earned reward? I don't have to feel lost now. I don't have to feel unloved now. They don't have to be perfect to be wonderful. And neither do I."

Drew took a deep breath and smiled the smile of youth. She turned to the group and said, "I've heard other people in this room heal a deep hurt, but I never thought it would happen to me. It's *so* wonderful. For the first time, I feel like I can begin to live a new life of my own."

15. Lifestyle Surgery

W hen some people get involved with The Solution, they treat it like a psychological program. But it isn't one. If one's mind is above the line, that's good. But if our entire body isn't above the line, we will not have a true Solution.

Lifestyle surgery decreases your threshold of need for the skills by nudging your body and your behavior above the line. It comes in four forms:

- **Good Health**   enhancing your physical vitality
- **Body Pride**   honoring your body and yourself
- **Balanced Eating**   eating for personal balance
- **Mastery Living**   an active, meaningful, and restoring lifestyle

Some who use the method focus on the nurturing and limits skills and find that lifestyle surgery occurs naturally—the drives to go to excess naturally turn off, and they begin taking care of their health, taking pride in their body, and eating and living in a balanced way.

But if there is a significant gap between your skills and your threshold of need for the skills, your climb will be far easier if you use lifestyle surgery. If your external solution poses a significant risk to your health or happiness, lifestyle surgery may be essential, even if it means getting extra support. Getting a little external nurturing and limits from a counselor, a personal trainer, a friend, or even a food plan or exercise program can be of support for some.

Some two months into using the skills, Drew was feeling out of control with her lifestyle. She came to the group feeling guilty and sick about what had happened the previous evening.

Drew had had three difficult parent-teacher conferences that day. The first parent she met with was the mother of a slow learner who blamed Drew for her daughter's difficulties. Next,

Drew met with the father of Anthony, a boy with behavioral problems who was rarely clothed properly and hardly ever brushed his teeth. Anthony's father was uninterested in his son's hygiene and instead verbally lacerated Drew for playing favorites in class and "rejecting" his son. Finally, Thomas's parents showed up early for their conference and stayed late to berate Drew about her reading curriculum, insisting that there was not enough homework and that she was not doing her job.

Drew said, "I felt so beaten up by the end of the day that I called for pizza delivery right from my car. When I got home and it arrived, I went right to bed. I sat there surrounded by my pillows, watching old movies on television, reading the newspaper, and eating that pepperoni pizza and drinking glass after glass of wine. When I woke up this morning, it was disgusting! I had pizza sauce all over the sheets, papers and napkins strewn all over the floor, and I smelled like day-old pepperoni."

"Sounds like a hard day," I said.

She nodded.

"I wonder if you would like to do cycles or if you'd like to try some lifestyle surgery."

Drew was instantly furious. "If I wanted to go on a diet, I would have gone to Weight Watchers. If I wanted to abstain from drinking, I'd go to AA. I don't want that. I want a Solution."

I shrugged. "I understand you want a Solution . . ."

Drew was quiet. Then she said, "I don't want to do cycles right now. I'm sorry that I was rude. I'm afraid that you're going to try to control my eating and drinking. Right now, I *need* to eat and drink. I'm afraid you're judging me."

"Drew, thank you for telling me that. I'm just a little worried. Would you be willing to listen to my worry?"

She nodded.

"I'm worried because there is a catch-22. You need the skills

---

Lifestyle Surgery:

Good Health
Body Pride
Balanced Eating
Mastery Living

to end the excess, and you need to end the excess to get the skills! If you don't do a little lifestyle surgery to make it easier to cut down on the excesses, it may take far longer for you to reach your Solution. If you only do lifestyle surgery, you won't master the skills, and the changes will be short-lived."

Drew listened thoughtfully. Then, looking me straight in the eye, she said slowly, "I understand what you are saying. But I don't particularly want to change my eating and drinking right now."

I waited to hear her next remark.

She let out a small sigh and said, "But I would be open to hearing something about lifestyle surgery, just in case."

Good Health

The first form of lifestyle surgery is to be sure that we are as healthy as we can be at this time. The quickest way to make our need for the skills skyrocket is to get sick or have a serious accident. The blurring of the body and mind means that most accidents or illnesses bring up a lot of emotional trash and add more situational stress to our lives.

This means checking in with your body, scanning your body daily for both good feelings—and difficult ones. Any signs of tension, weakness, discomfort, numbness, or just plain bad feelings need your vigilance. It means asking yourself throughout the day:

- **"How does my body feel?"**
- **"Am I taking care of my body?"**
- **"Is my health care effective?"**

Many people who use the method get a new doctor right away; we ask you to take your health very seriously, and most people have not established good health-care support. We want you to have a physician who is responsive to you, who not only supports your goal of being as free of disease as possible, but also supports you in having optimal physical vitality for who you are at the time.

We also ask you to be extraordinarily vigilant about your self-care. Even with exceptional health care, nobody takes better care of you than you. Only you can honor yourself so thoroughly that you take the small but important actions to attend to your body's needs.

Drew said, "I have no health problems. I'm young and my body is strong."

"It is?"

"Yes."

"When you come to group, you have such bad allergies."

Drew grumbled, "Well, I have allergies, but I just ignore them."

"And your knees, you often say they hurt you."

Drew grumbled again, "Yes, they do, but I just live with it."

"If you were as sensitive to your body as you're trying to be to your feelings, what would you do?" I asked.

Drew smiled and said, "I'd go to the doctor, and I'd probably stop running as much."

All Drew would be doing is taking the first small but important steps, moment to moment throughout the day, to be sure she had optimal physical vitality for who she was at that time.

Body Pride

Body pride means honoring your body and yourself and developing a commitment to not neglect or abuse your body. It means walking through your day, asking yourself:

- "Am I avoiding external solutions?"
- "Am I using words, not external solutions, to express myself?"
- "Am I honoring my body and myself?"

Because body and soul—that is, the depths of our feeling brains—are intertwined, having body pride usually comes late in this work. It is often the fruit you pick during the second half of the climb and near the top of the tree. Early in the climb, you can do some lifestyle surgery to change the *behaviors* that harm your body. But the essence of Body Pride is to have a true depth of caring for your body, one that makes you committed to not harming, distorting, or neglecting your body or yourself. That, of course, is an inside job.

The first part of Body Pride is simple—avoid using external solutions so often or so much that they get in the way of our health and happiness in ways that matter to us. The second part is not simple. Using words instead of external solutions to express ourselves means that when something is disturbing us, we don't reach for an external solution. Instead, we feel it and express it. We don't allow that need to go underground and reemerge as a behavior that hurts us, such as:

- Reaching for a cigarette instead of saying, "I need comforting."
- Carrying an extra twenty pounds of body weight as a way of saying to our spouse, "I don't want sex."
- Having a chronic spending problem as a way of saying to our partner, "You can't control me."
- Eating our way into oblivion instead of saying, "I don't want to grow up."
- Drinking too much at night as a way of saying to our spouse, "This marriage is over."
- Acting perpetually unhappy as a way of saying, "I need you to rescue me."

Using external solutions as a means of self expression is often chronic, in that continuing a problem may have a hidden "secondary" gain that expresses a covert need. In these examples, the person who "can't" take weight off may unconsciously *not* take weight off because it enables him or her to have a "beneficial" effect without saying anything at all. People who seem powerless over a spending problem may not realize that, unconsciously, they would be reluctant to stop because spending allows them to communicate their anger to a partner without ever opening their mouth.

Drew said, "I don't have a spouse or a boyfriend, but I use external solutions to express myself all the time. My drinking and eating protect me from having to grow up and make a full life for myself. It's an excuse. As long as I'm drinking and eating, I don't have to face myself and pull together a decent life for myself. The words I would have to say out loud so that there wouldn't be a hidden advantage of continuing would be, 'I don't want to grow up.' Wow, just saying that out loud felt great!"

When we start using words instead of external solutions to express ourselves, some of the hidden advantages of using external solutions suddenly become conscious and . . . poof! Sometimes they disappear.

Drew took a few moments to recover from expressing herself with words instead of external solutions. Then she said, "I think my parents didn't give me that 'chip' of having a limit about hurting myself. I don't think I have a floor in my inner life that holds me up off the ground and says, 'There, there, don't hurt yourself. You are too precious for that. Your body is sacred, and hurting it is wrong.' I don't have that sense of Body Pride."

"Drew, you might find that you acquire that Body Pride naturally. It grows out of having sanctuary and limits. Later on in your climb, you can even begin to implant that 'chip' within yourself."

"I can?" she said.

"Yes. What is the expectation, the limit, that didn't find its way into your inner life early on?"

Drew thought for a moment, then said, "Well, there are several, but I think one might be that I have this expectation that my body doesn't matter. So, perhaps the reasonable expectation, the most basic one is, 'My body matters.'"

"Beautifully said, Drew."

"Thanks," she said and smiled.

Balanced Eating

Food is extremely important to personal balance. *If your food is not above the line, you are not above the line.* It is well recognized that the primary way Americans cope with stress is by sitting and eating. Food is palliative; eating makes us feel better, at least in the moment. But the effects of living within a body that is out of nutritional balance are devastating, not just on health and weight but also on energy and mood. For those who use eating as an external solution, the plot thickens, since overeating often causes lethargy and depression that trigger more overeating.

If our bodies are out of balance nutritionally, part of the solution is to pop ourselves above the line with food. It means making our way through a three-day period of feeling ourselves somewhat irritable, hungry, and unsatisfied, to shift your body back into nutritional balance. After that time, assuming that the drives to overeat have been turned off and we are using words instead of food to express ourselves, it will be relatively easy to stay above the line with food. More about popping ourselves above the line with food appears in the appendix (see "The Three-Day Balancing Plan"), but the basic concept involves asking yourself the questions:

- "Do I eat regularly?"
- "Do I eat only when I am hungry?"
- "Is my food healthy but not depriving?"

The rationale for eating regularly throughout the day (breakfast, lunch, and dinner, or something similar) is that bodies are like automobiles. They do better with gasoline than without. Most people function better cognitively, emotionally, and physically if they eat regular meals. Between meals, their thoughts should go elsewhere, to doing what they came to Earth to do, and not be preoccupied with food. Obsessive thinking about food can even trigger changes in insulin levels that mimic hunger, so you feel hungry when you are not. If you are hungry between meals, consider having something to tide you over that has little psychological payoff, such as veggies or a piece of fruit.

Despite all the research on the "genetic" causes of obesity (and some people do have genetic obesity), most people who use The Solution for weight loss recognize that they eat when they aren't hungry. The simple habit of eating when hungry and stopping when satisfied, not full, is basic to being responsive to ourselves with food and avoiding weight gain. The idea is that portion sizes have no power over us. We stop eating when our body hunger is gone, not when our plate is clean. (If we wait ten minutes after eating, we will be full!) The most effective way for some people to eat in a balanced way early in the method is to focus only on hunger. In the complete Solution course, we call this the Nurturing Food Plan.

The last part of Balanced Eating is eating food that's as healthy as possible, stopping short of triggering a sense of deprivation. Eating for emotional balance means eating a variety of whole plant foods (vegetables, fruit, whole grains), lean protein foods (fish, poultry, meat, and dairy products), and some healthy fats (olive oil, canola oil, nuts) and limiting the consumption of "white stuff" (sugar, refined carbohydrates). The most effective way for some people to eat in a balanced way when they start their climb is to eat according to a plan. In the complete Solution course, we call this the Clear Limits Food Plan, which involves knowing how many servings of which foods will give you the emotional balance and nutrition you need.

If you have been using chemical pleasures or overeating and engaging in a sedentary lifestyle, you may want to use the Three-

Day Balancing Plan that appears in Appendix E. This little plan works for many people to jump-start their Solution and makes mastering the skills and turning off external solutions easier.

What's interesting is that when most people reach their Solution, they eat in a healthy way—that is, they eat regular meals, are sensitive to their feelings of hunger and fullness, and move toward a healthful diet. They gravitate to this naturally, as eating this way makes them feel better and they don't need the food to fill the void or block life's inevitable pain.

Mastery Living

Mastery Living means making each day complete, so that we can turn out the light at night and have the satisfaction of knowing that we moved our body, engaged in meaningful pursuits, and took time to restore ourselves physically, emotionally, intellectually, and spiritually. In a world that's focused on meeting deadlines, looking outward, and meeting the needs of others, it means keeping our finger on the pulse of our inner lives and meeting our own deepest needs. Mastery Living means asking ourselves the questions:

- "Am I physically active?"
- "Do I engage in meaningful activities?"
- "Do I take time to restore myself?"

The cornerstone of living a masterful life is exercise. More than 60 percent of Americans do not exercise at all, and we are perhaps the most sedentary generation in the history of mankind.

Everyone knows they should exercise, but part of The Solution is committing to moving our bodies more, not just because it makes us happier and healthier, but because *it enables us to reach our Solution in about half as much time*.

If we don't exercise, we shut down our emotions. That might sound like a good idea when we are in a lot of emotional pain. Unfortunately, when we shut down, we shut off both our bad feelings and our good feelings. Consider that, with this method, we will need to feel worse before we feel better. Unless it is not safe for you to do so, consider turning up the heat, moving your body, and stirring up the negative feelings so you can use the skills on them to bring them back to balance, turn on the good feelings, and feel . . . better. Daily exercise has been shown in some studies to be as effective as psychotherapy or antidepressants in alleviating emotional distress.

If you don't want to exercise and can't seem to make yourself do it, then don't. Instead of pushing yourself, recognize that right now, you do not have enough of the internal nurturing and limits to prompt yourself to exercise. Instead, you'll have to get some of those skills from outside.

There's a credit card company with commercials that tell us some things can't be purchased, but for everything else there's a credit card. If you are not able to exercise on your own right now, consider using that credit card to get a personal trainer or to join an exercise program or a gym that will give you the structure, support, love, and caring you need to get off the couch and move. If you don't have the resources to do that, consider asking a friend to be your exercise buddy, enlisting a family member or coworker to exercise with you, or drawing upon whatever external support you can find. Whatever you do, if you are able to move, please do.

To reach your Solution in a year or two instead of three or four, move for at least one hour per day. And limit sedentary activities in the evening to no more than two hours. It doesn't necessarily mean going to the gym every day—you can create a routine that is a nurturing blend of long, brisk walks, digging in the garden, lifting weights, taking bicycle rides, or turning the music up loud and dancing! The complete Solution course involves a variety of strategies to entice yourself to move. Some people who are particularly resistant to exercising use what we call Nurturing Exercise, in which they do virtually anything they enjoy that gets them moving. Others want what we call a Clear Limits Exercise, a program that gives them the structure and results they want with their particular flexibility, strength, and endurance. Still others use a pedometer with the goal of walking 10,000 steps per day.

Check with your physician before initiating any change in your exercise, and make any increases in your exercise gradual. As you increase your daily exercise to sixty minutes or more, be

---

*To enhance your Solution training,
move your body
for at least sixty minutes daily.*

aware of exercise as a potential external solution. Averaging more than ninety minutes of exercise per day puts you at risk of using exercise as a substitute for low nurturing and limits skills, and may put your body at risk of injury.

The second part of Mastery Living is developing meaningful pursuits that don't just meet our own needs but give back to the world. The isolated, depressed lifestyle and the angry, obsessed world are self-centered. Unfortunately, if we focus too much on ourselves, we seem to implode, so including activities in our day that reach beyond our little world and give back in meaningful ways moves us toward a life of balance.

The last part of Mastery Living is taking time to restore ourselves physically, emotionally, intellectually, and spiritually. It means filling up the well so we can dip into it later on. Most people begin to fall into a lifestyle that is restoring as they reach the top of the tree, but by intentionally making some of these changes earlier in your climb, you will speed your journey.

When I brought up the idea of taking time to restore ourselves during a group session, Drew was the first one to respond:

"I work hard—too hard—all day, then collapse at night. It seems like I have a lot of time to restore, but what I do isn't all that restoring."

"What makes you say that?" I asked.

"Well, I don't get enough sleep, and I watch too much television, which makes for an easy night, but I can't say that watching sitcoms is emotionally gratifying! I haven't taken a college class or read a challenging book . . . well, since graduate school. And I have no real spiritual life to speak of. No wonder my life feels so . . . stalled."

"Drew, it's a reasonable expectation that if you have not had the skill to nurture and set limits from within, the lifestyle you would build would not be restoring. What counts is taking baby steps. What small piece of lifestyle surgery would you be willing to try?"

"To turn off the light at ten-thirty, not midnight," she said.

"Fantastic."

V. WATCHING COMMON EXCESSES FADE

16. Eating Too Much

It's normal to overeat at times. Nearly all people do, in all cultures. But at what point does overeating become an external solution? Why is it so hard for us to push back from the table and prevent our waistlines from thickening?

To a large degree, it's cultural. Our society offers the perfect collision course of emotional deprivation, overwhelming stress, sedentary lifestyles, and an environment bombarding us with cues to overeat. Newer research even shows that stress alone—and the changes in cortisol and epinephrine it heralds—can make us fat even if our lifestyles are reasonably sensible.

With a virtual epidemic of overweight—more than 60 percent of adults weigh more than they should—you'd think there would be more sensible advice available for those of us who find it difficult to push away from the table when we should. Diets obviously aren't the answer, and never has more money been spent on gym memberships that rarely get used.

The answer to weight worries and overeating patterns, as you might imagine, is to stay above the line. But depending on the nature of your problem, where that "fruit" sits on the tree can look a bit different for everyone.

Turning off the drive to overeat may be higher on the tree— or it may be your sweetest fruit—if you have:

- a genetic propensity to gain weight,
- an emotional appetite for food that keeps you bingeing, munching, or stuffing,
- health problems or attendant medications that pack on pounds, then turning off the drive to overeat might be lower on the tree.
- a history of early emotional and food deprivation or emotional, physical, or sexual abuse, or
- a history of food preoccupation, eating disorders, or failed dieting attempts.

If turning off the drive to overeat is lower on the tree, the problem may, in time, take care of itself. You will notice that you feel better when you eat more healthfully, so you will naturally reach more often for an apple instead of a candy bar. As you become more skilled at meeting your true needs, you don't eat unless you are hungry, and you're naturally more physically active, which also curbs your appetite.

If ending overeating is toward the top of the tree, I suggest you appreciate how difficult it is to turn off that behavior. The drive to overeat is very primitive and very deep, and body hunger easily gets mixed up with emotional hunger, sexual appetites, relationship issues, emotional trash, and spiritual longings. Each of those "crossed wires" will have to be lovingly uncrossed in order for you to be at peace with food. In a way, it is a blessing. You can trust that that drive will not let up until you have completed your own development. It won't let up until you give yourself precisely what you most need.

To turn off the drive to overeat, there are some basic expectations that must be ground into your feeling brain until they are

---

Reasonable Expectations: Eating Too Much

I expect myself to do the best I can to:

- Nurture myself so well that I don't need the extra food
- Eat regularly throughout the day
- Start eating only when I am hungry
- Stop eating when I feel satisfied, not full
- Eat mainly foods that keep my energy steady and my body strong
- Eat *just enough* of the less healthful foods to avoid feeling deprived
- Move my body for at least an hour each day
- Use words—not weight or food—to express myself.

---

integrated. There is also some essential pain that you must feel over and over again until you can move through that pain and accept it as an unavoidable reality of the human condition. Of the expectations, essential pain, and earned rewards I've listed, some may apply to you more than others, and some that are important to you I may have failed to list.

The lists that are part of this chapter and the remaining ones in this book are simply common themes, and what is true for you may be quite different. Besides, the bulk of the work remains the same: bringing up a nurturing inner voice, staying balanced, taking out emotional trash, and doing the lifestyle surgery that makes it easier to stay above the line.

If overeating is near the top of the tree for you, you're probably very sensitive about it. The idea of eating differently may bring up cascades of emotional trash, and the four-year-old within you is likely to stomp its foot, stick out its chin, and say, "NO!"

What do you do with a four-year-old who is having a tantrum? You give some love, stopping short of indulgence, *and* some limits. Overeating impedes your progress with mastering the skills because it is so *numbing*. What's more, the eating may cause weight gain that gets in the way of your health, thus making getting above the line more difficult. Nothing pops up one's threshold of need for the skills more rapidly than physical problems.

And so the way to begin resolving an eating or weight problem is gently but firmly using the skills, taking yourself in hand and making it easier to eat and live in a balanced way—and doing it all sooner rather than later. It will probably take a couple of years for your feeling brain to change enough to fully turn off the drive to overeat from within. In the meanwhile, it only makes sense to get a little nurturing and limits from outside yourself, helping you to start eating and moving in healthier ways.

If turning off the drive to overeat is particularly challenging for you, if your weight poses a significant medical risk, or if you simply want to feel better sooner, you can make the shift to balanced eating easier by using these three strategies:

1. **Use the Three-Day Balancing Plan**—Although comforting ourselves with food may seem like a nurturing act in the short term, it has an effect on the body that creates imbalance. The more we eat when we are not hungry or the more we eat less healthful

foods, the more our bodies may crave them and the more our emotional hunger will become confused with body hunger.

What can we do? I suggest spending three days rebalancing your body. Your appetite will diminish, and your sense of power and control will increase. Doing this is not a Solution, but it makes reaching your Solution far easier and quicker. On this plan, you spend three days eating in a way that decreases your insulin and other gut hormone and peptide levels, encouraging your body to need less food. It begins with a "balancing meal," then continues with a plan that has a tremendously balancing effect. If you like, after the three days, choose either the Nurturing Food or Clear Limits Food Plan and continue any other parts of the plan that worked well for you.

After using this balancing plan, you are likely to find yourself "on a roll," feeling far more capable of continuing to eat and live in a way that is reasonably above the line. Use this plan only with the approval of your physician. See the Three-Day Balancing Plan in Appendix E for more details.

2. Arrange for External Nurturing and Limits—No matter how fiercely independent you might be or how much you fear that receiving support will lead you down a slippery slope into total dependency, consider getting external support.

Try putting your right hand on your left shoulder, stroking your arm, and saying, "In time, I will not need external nurturing and limits as much, but for now, I do. It's okay. I don't have to be perfect to be wonderful, and my health and happiness matter."

I am ceaselessly amazed at how much a little bit of external support lifts people up over many obstacles. It's only for a little while, so consider getting support, such as:

- A friend with whom you check in each morning for five minutes to talk about your exercise and food from the day before
- A diary in which you write about what you ate and how much you exercised, or in which you plan what you will do the next day
- A counselor with whom you check in once a week to talk about what you did and how you felt

- A walking buddy with whom you walk and talk about your eating and activity that day or the day before
- Posting on our website under "Checking-In" about your exercise and eating, as well as about how to stay above the line

3. Choose a Nurturing or Clear Limits Food Plan—Obviously, if you could eat in a balanced way, you would! And when you reach your Solution, chances are that your eating will, rather naturally, be reasonably balanced. You will eat when you are hungry, stop when you are satisfied instead of full, and eat primarily foods that make your body strong and your energy consistent. However, when you are at the bottom of the tree, this is not likely to be the case.

I have found that most people have a certain level of strength, and you probably do, too. Perhaps your strength is that most of the time, you can manage eating when you are hungry and stopping when you are satisfied not full—but if someone dared to tell you *what* to eat, you'd go to the moon . . . or the fridge, whichever was handier. You would be a good candidate for the Nurturing Food Plan, which focuses less on *what* you eat and more on eating only when you are hungry and stopping when you are satisfied.

Or perhaps your strength is that if you *know* what you should do, you can do it. If so, you could be a good candidate for the Clear Limits Food Plan. On that plan, you focus on what you eat, being sure to get a wide variety of whole plant foods (read: high in fiber and unprocessed), some protein foods (fish, poultry, meat, legumes, and dairy products), and only enough white stuff (sugars, refined complex carbohydrates, and alcohol) to stave off feeling deprived.

Consider using one of these plans as you begin making your climb. Simply do the best you can to follow the plan, and to follow it in your own way. Even that level of commitment will go a long way toward turning off the drive to overeat and speeding your progress in mastering the skills.

In time, as you reach your Solution, you will naturally integrate both of these plans, eating in a way that is responsive to you. But for now, having a plan can be of tremendous support. On the other hand, continuing to use food from below the line will hold you back.

Any external solution can be used as a means of self-expression. (Please see the information on Body Pride on page 208.) It seems that weight and overeating particularly lend themselves to this dynamic. When people have enough of the skills to maintain emotional balance, the emotional drive to overeat that comes from being on a false high, in an unnecessary low, or emotionally numb abates. It is then that they can clearly see to what extent the overeating or overweight fulfills another purpose, or what psychologists call its "secondary gain."

Those of us who overeat are often "too good." We tend to be passive and depressed; our anger gets expressed through eating. For many, early hurts that have gone underground find comfort in being expressed through staying heavy or eating more. It is not bad or wrong to have a hidden "reason" for staying heavy, but it is inconvenient. After all, the weight gets in the way of having the optimal health and happiness that make life far better.

For example, it is self-abusive to put weight on or maintain a weight that is above genetic body build as a way of saying to our partners, "I don't want to have sex." Why not just *say* it—if not to our partners, then at least to ourselves, so we can be conscious of that drive and decide what to do about it.

Holding on to extra pounds in order to feel safe is also very common. For some people, screaming out about their need for safety brings tremendous relief. Imagine screaming, very loudly and very slowly in the language of a four-year old:

I don't feel safe!
I don't feel safe!
I can't protect myself!
I will let anybody do anything to me!

Unless you still have a great deal of emotional trash about being harmed by others, chances are that screaming will pop you above the line. A place deep within you becomes aware that you are no longer that person—perhaps that child—who had so little power, that you no longer need that extra weight to protect yourself from others.

Ask yourself what your weight says for you. Check on whether maintaining a bigger body size is saying things for you without words. If so, explore saying those things aloud, so that the weight begins to feel "extra" and no longer needed.

Drew was doing well with her Solution. She had climbed about halfway up the tree without too much focus on her external solutions. Mostly, she focused on using the skills to create enough balance to begin the powerful second half of her climb.

But her work was not easy; she had many external solutions, nearly all of which caused her pain and made her threshold of need higher. Smoking, eating, drinking, and spending were all part of her life, as were numbing out with television, computer games, and even mystery novels. A whole bedroom in her apartment was filled with stuffed animals, and nearly every horizontal surface was covered with old furniture and linens from the 1950s. It would only be near the end of her climb that she would spontaneously let go of many of these attachments. For now, they were her lifeblood, giving her the connection she needed since she had not yet pumped up the skills that would enable her to connect more deeply with herself, with others, and with more abiding spiritual forces.

Drew came to group discouraged one day. "I'm hopelessly addicted to external solutions," she lamented. "I'm not making any progress at all."

"Drew," I responded, "I'm worried that you're underestimating your progress. What about all that emotional trash you took out about your mother?" She nodded, and I continued. "What about how you are cultivating a nurturing inner voice?"

"I've made progress," she said.

"Staying balanced?"

Drew answered, "I'm balanced most of the time, but when I binge, it ruins everything. I've been binge-eating lately, and I hate it."

"If you put your energy into forcing your external solutions to fade, instead of creating a safe sanctuary within and muscling up on the skills so you can soothe and comfort from within . . ."

"I know—I'll never have a Solution. But this food is driving me crazy, and I can't do cycles when I'm hungover from eating a whole pint of ice cream. I feel powerless to control my eating, but I know I must. Otherwise, I'll never get these skills. I'll just have to stay home the rest of my life and become this recluse who is an angel by day, saving children, and this devil at night who is so indulgent and hurtful to herself. *Something has to change!*"

I took a deep breath. Everyone in the room was quiet.

"Would you like to do a cycle?" I asked.

Drew nodded and began.

"Okay, my Thinking Journal. I have lots of excesses, and they take me so out of balance that I can't get on solid ground with these skills. I am down to five cigarettes a day, mainly because I can't smoke at work, and my drinking is better except for an occasional binge, but food is the external solution that seems deepest. It was imprinted in me at the age of eight, when the twins were born. It has this primitive quality to it, like I will die before I give up the food. It is the way I nourish myself when all else fails, the thought of which makes me sad . . ."

"When you're ready," I prompted, "go into the Natural Flow of Feelings."

"I feel angry that I am such a baby," Drew began. "I hate it that I have to suck on food like a four-year-old. . . . I feel furious that I can't have whatever I want when I want it. . . . I feel sad that I have to grow up. . . . I feel sad that I have to be responsible for what I do. I feel sad that I am a four-year-old in a grown-up body and trying to fake it. . . . I feel sad that I've waited for so long for someone else to take care of me. . . . I feel scared that I'll never do a good job of taking care of myself. . . . I feel afraid that nobody will rescue me from my pain. . . . I feel guilty that I still want to be rescued. . . . I feel guilty that I haven't been brave enough to . . . ," she trailed off, and I stepped in.

"Great Natural Flow of Feelings, Drew. Are you ready to take all those uncensored feelings that so beautifully honor the depths of your spirit, grow them up, and create safety and power with the limits cycle?"

She nodded. "What is my unreasonable expectation? I don't know. I think I expect that someone will come along and rescue me from this problem. That one day I will wake up and all the pain will be gone."

"I heard another expectation, Drew," I said. "It was a phantom expectation, one that is equally unreasonable but opposite the first. When you are holding two equally unreasonable and opposite expectations, you are likely to be way out of balance."

She sighed and nodded. "The other one is, I expect that I can get no help, that I am alone, lost, and abandoned with my eating."

Drew thought for a moment, then said, "Hahhh! No wonder I feel so bad. It's like I have myself in a vise—no pun intended—where there is no good choice for me."

"That's not genetic, it's learned," I responded. "You can take out your tool kit of these skills and change it."

Drew began to smile. She was clawing her way above the line and could see the light up there.

"I expect myself to use the skills to stay in balance as best I can, but to get some soothing and limits from outside to make up for the skills I don't have right now."

"Great. Positive and powerful?"

Drew's face fell. "All I can hear myself saying is, 'No matter what you do, you will fail.'"

Several people in the room gasped. So did Drew.

"Isn't that awful? It's not even *my* voice. It's my mother's voice."

"Check for anger," I offered.

"I feel angry that I allow that woman inside my head. . . . I hate it that she still lives inside me and I'm not even aware of it."

"Just move that awareness from your feelings to your thinking brain and change it."

"I will succeed no matter what."

Essential Pain and Earned Rewards: Eating Too Much

- I can't eat whatever I want to eat.
- I can eat some of the foods that I like.

- I have to eat more vegetables.
- Some vegetables taste good. I will feel better.

- I must exercise.
- Exercise can be fun. I will feel better.

- I can't numb my feelings with food.
- I can feel my feelings!

- I *must* meet my true needs.
- I *get to* meet my true needs!

- It takes hard work.
- Personal pride. Good health. More joy.

"Drew, are you one-hundred-percent sure, without one shred of a doubt, that you will succeed no matter what?"

"No."

"Positive and powerful statements must be perfectly accurate to be powerful."

"Okay, I *can* succeed."

"Does that sound accurate to you?"

She nodded, and I continued.

"The essential pain for you of using the skills to stay above the line and getting some extra nurturing and limits from outside?" I asked.

"Now I'm confused," said Drew.

"You have a new reasonable expectation."

"Right."

"It means letting go of two unreasonable ones."

"Correct."

"What is the essential pain of not having someone rescue you from your problems? That vision of having some angel drop from the heavens and magically take all your pain away?"

"The essential pain . . . the truth about the human condition that I'd have to face is that I am alone. I am not a kid anymore. I have to grow up. No one will rescue me."

Drew took a deep breath and was quiet. The pain of those realizations was settling into her inner life, and that predictable experience of her thinking deeply and having fireworks of feelings was also occurring. Her face lit up and she said, "But there is an earned reward."

"What is it?"

"The earned reward is that I can rescue myself. I can get my needs met. I can be grown up and powerful."

She was smiling.

"Drew, we're not done. There was another equally unreasonable and opposite expectation. What is the essential pain of giving up that one?"

"I don't remember it."

"The phantom unreasonable expectation was, 'I expect that I can get no help, that I am left to be alone, lost, and abandoned with my eating.' "

"Oh, I don't want to say this because it's embarrassing!" she grimaced, putting her hands over her nose and mouth and half laughing. But she forged ahead.

"The essential pain of getting support and giving up feeling lost is that I have to change. The truth is that I like being lost and abandoned and isolated. I can find comfort there, because it reminds me of when I was a kid. There is a certain familiar misery and self-pity that I would have to give up."

"The essential pain is . . ."

"The essential pain is that I have to change, that I have to give up feeling sorry for myself, that I have to give up the familiarity of being miserable and lost."

Now she was chuckling warmly at herself.

"But the earned reward is that I will change and that I can feel a new pride and joy in life, although that fills me with fear."

"I feel afraid that . . . ," I prompted.

"I feel afraid that someone will take food away from me before I am ready. I feel afraid that changing my food will cause me to binge-eat. I feel afraid that I can't trust someone to help me, that they will try to control me. I feel afraid that getting help will make things worse."

"So what do you need?"

"I need to go slowly. I need to experiment with small changes and to take my time to find out what is right for me, what outside nurturing and limits would work for me."

"The support you need to begin to explore that?"

"I don't know."

"You don't have to know."

"I think that I need to cycle more about this and learn more about my options."

"Great; I can help you with that."

"Good," she said.

"Drew, is it reasonable for you to expect yourself to let go of your primary object of connection, love, satisfaction, and stability—that is, food—unless you have a substitute?"

Drew was indignant. "I have myself. I have myself more now than ever because the skills are starting to become automatic."

"Excellent, but your drive to overeat is near the top of the tree."

"In all honesty, I think it is *at* the top."

"So you may need . . ."

"I don't want to go back to counseling. I fall into this dependent role and start wanting the counselor to rescue me. It brings out the worst in me, not the best."

"What do you need then?"

"What I really want is the group. I want to do daily connections, to cycle with people, but I need more. Maybe checking in with someone for just five minutes a day to say what I did with food the day before."

"Who would be willing to do a cycle with Drew this week?"

Several people raised their hands and Drew took note.

"Who would like to be a daily, five-minute check-in buddy with Drew this week?"

Emily volunteered.

"How would that be for you, Drew?"

"Good. Emily and I have done a lot of connections together."

"This is just five minutes, the same time every day, and each of you can report whatever you want to report, whether it's an excess or . . ."

Emily said, "I want to do a check-in about eating sugar."

"If you each have a plan for support, that's wonderful. Now, you need to figure out what you will use, a Nurturing Food Plan or one with Clear Limits."

Drew said, "Laurel, if you told me how many servings of fruit or bread I needed to have, I'd immediately go to the candy machine and buy three things. I'd eat them all, too."

I smiled. "Drew, it sounds like you're a candidate for the nurturing plan, which means just holding yourself accountable for doing your best to stay above the line. The idea is to keep your finger on the pulse of your inner life, to only eat when you are hungry, and to stop when you are satisfied, not stuffed."

"Yes, that's what I need," Drew said, and seemed very pleased with her plan.

Emily said, "There is no way I could do that. My diet is a mess. I'm on a blood-sugar high or low all the time. Between the caffeine I have and all that sugar, my energy is very fragile. I race through my day, then the bottom falls out and all I can think about is getting something sweet."

"You need clear expectations, so think about lifestyle surgery and balanced eating, eating to keep your energy strong and consistent," I said.

"I don't know how to do that."

"It's not that hard, but you won't like it."

"I'm ready to think about changing. I hate feeling so weak and so emotionally flaky."

"Eat a balanced diet, but keep your emphasis on food that's high in fiber and moderate in protein and good fat, like canola oil and olive oil."

"That sounds appetizing," said Emily, frowning.

"It's not so hard. Eat only foods you like, and if you're willing, I'll listen to you create a plan for what you'll eat tomorrow."

She looked doubtful, but went ahead. "Breakfast, some whole-wheat flakes and nonfat milk."

"Do you like having that for breakfast?"

"Yes."

"Good. Don't plan to eat anything you don't like. It's abusive and it backfires."

"I know. Okay, midmorning, I'll have fruit."

"Lunch?" I asked.

"A big salad, a little bit of dressing. Maybe some chicken or fish on top. Or half a turkey sandwich on whole-wheat bread."

I nodded.

"Late afternoon is my high-risk time. Maybe I'll have a frozen yogurt cone for my sweet tooth or, if not, a glass of milk, or more fruit, or some baby carrots."

"Dinner?"

"Clay comes home late, around 8:00 P.M. By then, I've already had some ice cream and cheese and crackers, then I have a second dinner with him."

"Are you merging?" I suggested.

A flash of anger came across Emily's face. "No, I'm trying to support my marriage. It's important to me that we eat together."

"I feel worried that you're focusing on how he feels and what he needs, not on what you feel and what you need."

Emily pushed her glasses up on her nose and looked pensive. "Maybe. I'll think about that."

"Is it a reasonable expectation for you to not eat dinner until 8:00 P.M. and not eat sugar from five to eight?"

"No. Maybe I'll have my dinner earlier, then have a salad with Clay. That might work, but I'm not sure. I'll try."

As Drew reached her Solution, she would no longer react to limits about eating with sheer rebellion. Emily, on the other hand, would be able to trust her inner signals of hunger and satiety. But for now, they each had a plan that would support them in their climb.

17. Chemical Pleasures

Although external solutions come in an endless variety, many people consider the genuine article of personal excess to be substance abuse.

There is no denying the emotional rewards that come from making the perfect purchase or eating really good chocolate. However, these softer excesses may have fewer emotional pay-offs than lighting up a cigarette, sipping that second or third glass of wine, popping various pills, or even drinking far too much coffee. They aren't physically addictive either.

Those of us who have grown accustomed to taking in significant doses of stimulants, depressants, or opiates suffer withdrawal symptoms when we go without. These sensations are often uncomfortable enough to encourage us to scurry back and latch on to that excess once more—to relapse. The symptoms of withdrawal often amount to experiencing the opposite effects of the drugs. Those feelings can last a week or linger for several, and the tendency to relapse may last months, years, or a lifetime.

If one or more of your external solutions involves chemical pleasures, it's important to pause and acknowledge the fact that your climb may take a little more effort. The tree may be a little taller for you. If you were exposed to various chemicals early in life, were addicted as an adolescent, or have a strong family history of chemical dependency, life at the top of the tree may be somewhat different for you than for others. You might have to forgo social drinking, casual drug use, and the like because your basic biology makes that first sip, toke, or pop a slippery slope into the quagmire of imbalance called addiction.

On the other hand, to the extent that chemical pleasures have felt more like a knife in the heart than a cozy blanket to curl up with, there is an advantage. You may be more motivated than some to reach your Solution, for you so deeply *want* to stop the pain. You will be more likely than those for whom the drive for chemical pleasures is weaker to decide that you will do "whatever it takes" to reach a Solution. That fire in the belly is what we all need in order to complete the climb and not get lost in the middle branches of the tree.

Doing this intense, sensitive, and deep work while we are separated from reality and from ourselves by chemical pleasures is like making a big bowl of raspberry Jell-O and putting it in a hot oven and expecting it to set. The skills are unlikely to "set."

If chemical pleasures have a serious hold on your mind and body, in order to practice these skills deep and often enough to reach a Solution, you will need to abstain altogether. It's hard enough to reach your Solution when you are clean and sober. So if you are alcoholic, drug dependent, or caught in a spiral of multiple chemical dependencies, the best bet is first to get more comprehensive services to stop the excesses. Then use The Solution to create the inner balance that can go a long way toward preventing relapse.

You may be a dabbler, having a few too many drinks now and then, smoking a joint at a party, or sneaking a cigarette in the backyard when nobody is looking. If you are, you may turn off the drive for chemical pleasures simply by climbing the tree without paying special attention to the excess. In fact, you may even be able to use these external solutions now and then without significantly slowing your climb. Some people who dabble are able to continue using chemical pleasures as they journey toward their Solution. Some prefer to abstain. You probably have a sense of which path would be best for you.

Perhaps you are somewhere in between the occasional dabbler and the full-blown addict. If you are, I suggest that you choose abstinence, or something close to it, if you want to reach your Solution in a timely fashion. You might try the Three-Day Balancing Plan (see page 385) to help turn off those drives, plus a fair amount of community and professional support for your Solution training.

If you've been in recovery for long, you may have been exposed to some ideas about addiction and codependency that are at odds with what you learn in Solution training. You won't hear in this book, or in The Solution Kits, anything about being powerless over your problem or dependent upon a sponsor or meetings. It is wonderful to have community, and that's why I recommend getting a Solution Buddy, joining or starting a Solution Circle, or getting professional Solution support via groups, telegroups, or coaching. However, the most profound intimacy to be had is with yourself. Only you can make the decision to go inside yourself throughout the day, to take out your tool kit and practice the skills deeply and often enough to transform your feeling brain. It is a very personal act. When enough of the dominant neural networks in your feeling brain support balance—when you have no external solutions, when you have an abundance of integration, balance, sanctuary, intimacy, vibrancy, and spirituality—you stop going to the group. The skills are solid within you, and you can be independent of any program or any meetings. You are finally free.

If our early years were filled with serious abuse or neglect, or if our parents were substance abusers or those who rescued them, it's particularly hard not to see the substance as the problem. What's more, our early feelings of abandonment may have affected the neural structures in our feeling brain, making it far more difficult for us to keep our fingers on the pulse of our inner lives and to stay above the line. It helps to take heart and recognize that this is just part of our dark sides. The idea is to love and accept our dark side, yet use the nurturing and limits skills with even more intensity and commitment to prevent some of the unnecessary pain our dark side may cause us.

You may not be sure to what extent there was serious neglect or abuse early in your life, but you may notice aftereffects that are with you today. If we suffered far too much early on we may have difficulty feeling. Our minds turn off, or they often go numb. Our "I feel . . ." skill is unreliable, so that feelings will flow freely, then shut off abruptly like a faucet. We also tend to get "derailed" as they move around the limits cycle. For example:

Reasonable expectation: I expect myself to not let anyone abuse me.

Positive, powerful thinking: Life is hard.

Essential pain: People hurt people.

In this case, the stated positive, powerful thought does not encourage the person to continue holding on to the new, reasonable expectation. Moreover, the essential pain confirms an expectation different from the one the person started with and one that is unreasonable.

The good news is that when we hear ourselves getting derailed as we do cycles we have *proof* that we did not have an early environment that was responsive. We may not remember our childhoods, or we may find it hard to think negatively of our parents. Even though our parents may have loved us dearly, our getting derailed in cycles provides strong evidence that we were deprived early in life, for our own internal process mirrors abandonment rather than connection.

If you notice that you derail yourself and have difficulty moving around the cycles and popping above the line, arranging for individual coaching in the method is often important or even essential to reaching a Solution. Going around and around the cycles, working hard but reinforcing rather than revising early patterns, is not productive, and the sooner the cycles are done effectively, the sooner relief begins to arrive.

Tom didn't show up in group for a month, and I worried that I had lost him. I had known from our first meeting that he was slippery, that he would probably "look the part," seem to be progressing, but still be holding back a big piece of himself.

When he finally came to a session, I was relieved and hopeful. His early months in the training had been extremely productive. He had muscled up enough on the skills to be able to get himself above the line with some pretty difficult situations brought on by a serious disagreement with a partner at work. He'd gotten back in balance about an ongoing conflict with a neighbor who had cut the hedges on their property line. Moreover, Tom seemed to be practicing the skills and connecting well with several people in the group, especially Emily.

That evening, we did a Feelings Check and then went around the circle, each person saying a couple of the feelings they had noticed. When it was Tom's turn, he offered, "I feel guilty, that's all. Guilty."

I nodded and said, "There are always good feelings, too. All you need is to access them."

Tom was quiet for a moment. "I guess I am . . . grateful."

"Great. Now, who would like to do some in-depth work today?"

Tom's hand shot up, and I asked him if he'd like to begin. He was squirming in his chair, his face full of pain. He didn't look at all like the arrogant man in the Armani suit I'd met some months ago. Instead, he looked like a man in transition.

"I started a relationship with a woman, someone I'm far more compatible with than I was with Karen."

The group seemed to settle into their chairs, intently listening to his story, relaxing with the knowledge that they would be experiencing Tom's cycle and feeling the shift from the world below the line to the world above, much like he would be.

"It was going pretty well . . . and now it isn't." His words came out forced and painful, like someone reluctantly 'fessing up.

He went on. "I was just beginning to exhale and think that this could be a woman I could have a serious relationship with. We went out to dinner and split a bottle of wine. Toward the end of dinner, she said something about her feelings for me—that she cared for me so much she feared she wouldn't attend to her other relationships enough. She worried that she would slack off on work—she's an architect. Well, I couldn't understand what she was bloody saying. She seemed to *need* me to understand, and I could see that I wasn't getting it. I got so frustrated that we argued in the car all the way to my house. When we got there, I opened another bottle of wine, and things didn't get any better after that. After an hour or so, and the better part of a second bottle of wine, Michelle—who wasn't drinking by then—told me that she didn't feel safe. She up and left!

"She didn't return my phone call that day or the next, and when I finally caught up with her, she didn't have anything pleasant to say. She wasn't like Karen, though, who just gave me dirty looks and brooded. We met for coffee, and she told me that she cared for me but couldn't be involved with anyone who drank when they were upset.

"It was hard to be mad at her. She was so caring but firm about it that I think I have finally found a woman who is—well, above the line. I care for her, and we're incredibly compatible. She even likes watching sports on television, and I love her sense of humor, and we have great sex, and I don't want to lose her. But I won't be controlled by anybody, and I won't have some woman telling me that I have a drinking problem, and . . ."

"When you are ready, feel free to go into the Natural Flow of Feelings," I said.

Tom's face was flushed with anger as he began. "I hate it that I care for her. . . . I can't stand it that she's calling me on my drinking. . . . I feel sad that this problem is coming up again. . . . I'm afraid I will lose her. . . . I feel guilty that I lost it and drank

Reasonable Expectations: Chemical Pleasures

I expect myself to do the best I can to:

- Nurture myself so well that I stop wanting chemical pleasures

- Connect with my nurturing—not depriving or indulging—inner voice

- Put no chemicals into my body that harm me

- Put no chemicals into my body that cause me to harm others

- Use words—not chemical pleasures—to express myself

- Create a happy, healthy lifestyle for myself

too much . . . which makes me angry. I feel angry that I can't just relax and have a good time. . . . The minute a relationship is good and I relax and start enjoying it, a problem comes up. . . . I feel angry that life is so difficult. . . . I feel angry with myself for drinking too much. . . . I feel sad that I treated her badly. . . . I feel afraid that I will never have a relationship. . . . I feel guilty that I don't control how much I drink. . . . I feel guilty that I have such a temper."

Tom was midway through the climb. His courage to go inside himself, to begin using a nurturing inner voice, and to use the skills to stay in balance and take out emotional trash were beginning to pay off in a productive but destabilizing way. This is the stage in the training at which you must let go of one trapeze while you're still in midair, waiting to catch the next. It is the time when the old neural networks favoring imbalance are weakened, and the new neural networks that favor balance are stronger but not yet dominant and firing automatically. Tom was less connected to work, wine, and overthinking, and more connected to himself and perhaps another, but nothing was quite clear. It was all "up in the air."

The most effective course at this point in the climb is to focus on limits, to grind those new, reasonable expectations into your inner life until they become part of your bones. With stronger skills, taking out emotional trash is now far more healing, and the deepening skill to nurture and set limits from within makes for more balance in the present and better follow-through with lifestyle surgery. *But it's the strengthening of limits that offers the most power to transform.*

It seemed rather perfect. Tom's sweetest fruit was intimacy, and midway through his climb he encountered a woman who was above the line enough to hold on to herself in his presence. Given their mutual attraction, if this woman was not solidly above the line, her feeling brain would easily be overpowered by his, and she would join him below the line, crazy in love, merging and distancing, blind to his dark side and, for all intents and purposes, in grave danger.

This woman was apparently above the line enough that just because she cared about him, she did not find herself sucking on his sleeve, merging with his expectations, and forgetting about how she felt and what she needed. She held on to herself, which was very disorienting to Tom.

When Tom drank too much during his marriage to Karen, he went below the line and became aggressive, while she went below the line and became passive. A few hours or days later, they would change roles or one would start a control struggle, then the other would put on gloves and fight back.

Michelle wasn't doing that. Fortunately, Tom had enough mastery of the skills to sense that he could respond differently to her, potentially even join her above the line. At least, that's what he thought one moment—the next, he was ready to drop right below the line and flee.

"Tom, this is an important cycle," I said gently.

"I know," he said.

"Let's experiment with going below all those feelings to your most basic expectations. If you were on a boat in a very clear lake, and you looked over the edge straight down to the bottom and could see your most basic expectations about alcohol or the use of any chemicals in your body, what would they be?"

"I don't know," he said.

"Take a nice deep breath. Match the expectation to your recent behavior. Under all those feelings, there is the most basic expectation that . . ."

"I expect myself to put chemicals in my body if I want to."

"Okay, let's try it a different way. Imagine that whatever your most basic expectations are, whatever emotional learnings you have, they were deeply implanted at a very young age. This pattern is more than drinking. Drinking is just a way that you're doing the same thing you have always done, since being a little boy perhaps."

A wave of awakening passed over Tom's face. He said, "My most basic expectation is that when things are bad, I leave."

It felt as though the entire room exhaled, then was quiet. Tom continued.

"My most basic expectation, the one that is under thousands of cycles and so many conscious and unconscious acts, is that when things are bad, I flee emotionally or physically."

"And how is that for you?" I asked.

"It's shitty. It's awful. It makes my life so . . . limited."

I looked around the room and saw others, including Emily, with tears in their eyes, and still others looking on in awe of the work Tom was doing.

"Tom," I said, "we could do cycles on alcohol that rest on top of this most basic expectation, but let's start with this basic one. When we come up with a very fundamental expectation, it means we slow the pace of our work and increase the intensity. We focus on this one expectation and grind it into your feeling brain by repeating it ten times a day for as many days as it takes for it to become automatic. Most people take three to four weeks until it becomes integrated. When you say that new basic expectation to yourself, it is uncomfortable. The more uncomfortable it is, the more you know that the antagonistic, opposite expectations are firmly entrenched, and that it will take lots of practice to loosen them up and implant the new one."

Tom paused for a moment before he quietly said, "Okay."

"Okay," I said. "Now. What is the most basic expectation that, in the best of all worlds, would have been implanted within you from the start?"

"Ummm, the most basic expectation is the opposite of the one that is there. The most basic expectation, the new balanced one, is that when things get bad, I feel my feelings and do not flee."

"When things get bad, I do not flee," I repeated.

"Yes."

"Does that mean that you let people beat on you?"

"No, it means that I don't abandon myself, I don't disconnect from my feelings, I don't separate from my personal sense of integrity."

"You stay above the line."

"Precisely."

"Where does that leave you with your drinking?"

"I don't like anyone messing with my drinking."

"I don't think anyone really could."

Tom looked angry. We could have done a cycle on lots of things at that point, such as how much he could reasonably drink or what he expected of himself when he did drink, but for now, the most powerful tool Tom could use was to make that new, basic expectation solid within him.

"Tom, I know you could do some beautiful work right now with other cycles, but my belief is that the most effective use of your attention would be to practice that expectation ten times a day, every day, until it is part of your bones—until it is just 'there,' the way it would have been, in the best of all worlds, all along. I don't want you to be brilliant this week. I want you to be focused and persistent, to practice those words in your Community Connections, in the shower, as you drive to the office, or as you work out."

"I can do that."

"Think that each time you do you are accomplishing two things: weakening the neural networks that support imbalance, and strengthening those that support balance. This is not a benign act. A lot of painful emotional trash may come up. When it does, get out your tool kit and use the skills to take it out. But keep practicing at least ten times a day, every day."

"I will, but what do I do about Michelle?"

"What expectation about her rests on that basic expectation about not fleeing?"

"I have to do some cycles, get above the line, and stay with myself. And to the extent I am able, I have to be honest with her about who I am."

I nodded.

Tom looked calm and secure, as if he knew what he needed to do.

There are lots of expectations related to drawing upon the powers of chemical pleasures, and some basic forms of essential pain and earned rewards that help in loosening a dependency or addiction. The expectation that "I will nurture myself so well that I don't need chemical pleasures" and that "I will use words, not substances, to express myself" are core for most people. For some people, the "chip" deep within that enables them to go so far but no further with chemical pleasures is missing. It may be due to a genetic sensitivity to certain chemicals, such as alcohol, or to early psychological trauma or distress. Most people know whether they are the kind of person who has the chip that enables them to have a drink without emptying the bottle. If they don't have that chip, they may decide that for them, a reasonable expectation is to abstain.

Facing the essential pain of life without the numbing or mood-altering effects of chemical pleasures is tougher for some of us than others. When our threshold of need for the skills is high and we can't quite claw our way above the line, chemical pleasures can fill that gap and give an illusion of balance—or at least help us get through the day. That's why, in The Solution, the ideal is not necessarily abstinence.

Adults have the right to choose their pain at times, and there is almost no action you can take that doesn't involve both an essential pain and an earned reward. If you use the skills well, you can figure out what is right for you at the time—not perfect, not angelic, but *right for who you are* at a particular time in the world, in your life, and in your day. In other words, in this method, the philosophy is that individuals make their own decisions and experience both the good and bad consequences of those decisions. Good is not necessarily abstaining, and bad is not necessarily drinking. For example, Tom might decide not to drink in the face of his work stresses and the tentative nature of his relationship with Michelle. But he might also decide to drink on any particular evening and do it from above the line, understanding that the essential pain is that he risks having one drink lead to another. The essential pain may be the potentially higher risk that he will lose Michelle.

When Tom was at the bottom of the tree, it would have been hard for him to do that cycle well. He might have asked the question of the cycles but not popped above the line, and therefore he might have decided on an action that was permissive, such as drinking when he wasn't balanced enough to stop. But with the skills he mustered halfway through his climb, Tom could probably do a cycle, pop himself above the line, and make the deci-

Essential Pain and Earned Rewards: Chemical Pleasures

- I can't do whatever I want to do.
- My life will be better. I will grow up.

- I cannot rely on chemicals for comfort.
- I can rely on myself and on the spiritual.

- I can't escape my life.
- I can create a life I don't need to escape from.

- I am not perfect.
- I don't have to be perfect to be wonderful.

- Life is difficult.
- Life can be very good.

- I can't change the past.
- I can change the present and the future.

- Nobody else will rescue me from my problems.
- I can rescue myself.

sions that were right for him. He might see the risks of having more than one drink as low, and the earned reward of having the pleasure that the wine afforded him as higher or the opposite.

Tom didn't come to the next week's session, or the one after that. Emily said he was out of town on business, but I wasn't so sure. On the third week, he showed up again and had a lot to say.

"Well," he began, "first of all, I said the basic expectation over and over again to myself. It wasn't easy, and it annoyed me to have to repeat it so much. About ten days into it, the expectation that when things get bad, I don't flee started to deepen and have a stronger grip on me.

"Right after the last session, I talked with Michelle. I gave her a Sandwich and told her how much I cared about her, that she was right about my drinking. I told her that I agreed that she shouldn't put up with someone who drank when he was upset, and that I was changing."

"Did she believe you?" I asked.

"I don't know, but since that time, we've still been seeing each other a lot, and this damned expectation is creeping into corners of my life, and is highly disruptive. If I have the basic expectation that I don't flee when things are bad—like the other night, for instance . . ."

"What happened?"

"Michelle was upset because her cat is sick. This cat is like a child to her. Every time it has a stomachache or a hair ball or throws up a little, she takes it to the vet. This time, the vet said that the cat has lost weight and has thyroid disease. So there Michelle is, depressed as hell about her cat and completely sullen. I can't stand sullen people, and I had a long day at work and a hearing to prepare for. What I wanted to do was to tell her I had to work so I could get away from her. What I wanted to do even more was open a bottle of wine or pour a beaker of scotch."

I nodded. Everyone in the group was listening intently.

Tom cracked a smile. "That damned basic expectation just appeared in my mind: My most basic expectation is that when things get bad, I don't flee. So what that meant was that I had to stay above the line, hold on to myself, and be present for her, which was not at all comfortable. I wanted to make an excuse and go into the other room to work, and I really wanted to open a bottle of wine. But somehow, I didn't do it."

Now Tom was beaming. "I don't know that I'll always be able to do that, but I'm . . . I'm proud that this stuff of getting at the basic expectation is affecting so many things in my life."

I smiled at him. "Tom, early in the training you wouldn't have even been aware of your basic expectations. And if you were, without all the emotional balance you've built, saying it to yourself over and over again wouldn't have had much effect."

"I understand."

"So what do you need now?"

"I need to keep doing the work, and I need to stay in balance and see what else comes up."

"That sounds just perfect."

He was smiling, and so was I. There was a possibility that Tom had turned the corner and would complete the climb. Time would tell.

18. Working Past 6

Work solves a lot of problems. I remember, as a woman in my early twenties and in an unhappy situation, going to my job on a Monday morning and thinking, "This is great! I can walk in the door at work and escape my problems at home! What a relief."

Of course, I was not the first person to have made that discovery. Work has an endless array of uses and abuses that have nothing to do with the job. At work, we can re-create our family of origin—see our boss as our mother or dad and the other workers as our competitive siblings. We can get high on the stress, addicted to the numbness, hung up on our position, or seduced by our fantasies of being deeply respected or vastly rich. What's more, we can hide from troubles on the home front, including difficulties with love, troublesome offspring, or overdue bills. Overworking is often intertwined with other excesses: The overworker by day becomes the overeater, overdrinker, or overspender by night.

This is often one of the easier excesses to stop, because it is so concrete. We are either working or we aren't. Even if we aren't directly working but are at the beach obsessed by a deal or upset about our job, we are at work. And it has an effect.

The most successful strategy often seems to be turning up the heat when overwork is an issue. Create a clear, reasonable expectation, such as "I will leave work by six" or "I will not work weekends," then watch the emotional trash arise, the other excesses hit the wall, and the emotional drives to overwork surface. It sounds harsh, but it often is very, very effective. Find a limit and stick with it, then watch the fireworks!

Most people do not attempt this until they are at least halfway through the climb. Those for whom ending overworking is their sweetest fruit don't attempt it until they are near the top of the tree. But at whatever stage you take on this task, the process seems much the same: exciting, not without pain, and *very* effective.

You may not know whether overworking (or underworking) is an external solution for you. Perhaps you are accustomed to working long hours, have unusual financial need, or simply possess a strong work ethic that drives your productivity.

The easiest way to determine if you *need* to work or you *want* to work—that is, if it's an external solution—is to notice if working is something you use to abandon yourself. If you just had a belly full of sanctuary, if you just had a nurturing, strong inner life, you would have someplace to go so you wouldn't have to . . . go to work. If your external solution is underworking—whether that be working too few hours, not earning the money you need, or not having a job that uses your talents—you might ask yourself, "If I had sanctuary, a truly nurturing and strong inner life, would I be working the way I am?"

In different ways and to varying extents, Drew, Emily, and Tom all used work as an external solution.

Drew worked more than she should have on correcting her students' school papers and developing special projects for her class. She was so merged with her second-graders, she sometimes got lost in their needs. Drew spent her weekends on her work, which was the only time she had available for developing her own intimate relationships, exploring a wider range of interests, and attending to the business of building a more complete life. It was the perfect shield from coming to terms with her life. Who could fault her for being committed to the education of the young?

Reasonable Expectations: Working Past Six

I expect myself to do the best I can to:

- Work no more than "x" hours per week
- Do the work I came to Earth to do
- Earn enough to meet my financial obligations
- Avoid self-abuse or self-neglect due to my job
- Get my love from my personal life, not from work
- See myself as having many important roles in the world, not just being a worker
- Create a rewarding life in addition to my career

Drew had long been aware that she used work as a subtle but important external solution, but it wasn't until about halfway through her journey that she committed to stop working weekends. The results were painful.

She came to a meeting and said, "My most basic expectation is that if the children love me, I am good, and that is enough. But it isn't enough. In fact, it isn't *nearly* enough."

Drew had the attention of everyone in the group.

"I didn't work all weekend long because that was my limit. No work on weekends. Do you know what my weekend was like? Awful . . ."

Her lips began to curl in a smile. "I was bored to death, and there was no steady stream of suitors at my door."

Now people in the group were chuckling a little.

"There was no perfectly appointed home with books shelved in alphabetical order and CDs lined up in categories in a row and sweaters stacked nicely in the closets without any cat hairs on them. No, my house was a total and complete mess, with piles of laundry in the living room and a refrigerator in which I had spilled a jar of jam all over the butter dish and the catsup bottle two months ago, and now it was as hard as tar. I had to ask myself, 'What kind of a life have I created for myself? My students are doing fine, but *what about me?*' "

It was clear that Drew had turned the corner and sooner or later would grieve the losses and begin to build a life that rescued nobody other than herself.

Emily wasn't addicted to her work, but her role as caretaker to her family had become an external solution. She had abandoned her own talents with the piano early on because with her husband's needs and her children's various problems, she chose to build a family instead. But at some point, she took her finger off the pulse of her inner life and started using her motherly role as a way out of deeply honoring herself. Then she wondered why there was a near-constant undertone of depression in her life!

The essential pain of doing what she came to Earth to do would be hefty, including giving up being an angel, a savior, and a martyr, all of which are far more delicious for some than any other external solution available. Moreover, she could avoid the essential pain of taking risks and failing or taking risks and succeeding, then potentially superseding her husband, Clay. She had to take the risk of displeasing her husband, who had always expected her to take care of everything.

No wonder Emily had not rocked the boat, and from listening to her, it became clear to me how strong her drive was to overwork as a housewife and avoid dealing with her musical calling. That drive would be unlikely to turn off until she had deepened her skills enough to find herself near the top of the tree, certainly not now midway through the climb.

Tom was a classic "workaholic," and he knew it.

"If you're raised without much money, and everyone around you goes to a factory job and is bored and poor, you're going to be ecstatic if you have a chance to make money and have an exciting, prestigious position."

Mark nodded, and so did Drew.

"When I started with my firm, a whole new world opened up for me. I was out of Georgia, and I didn't have to look back, except to be glad I wasn't there anymore.

"Work wasn't an external solution for me at first, but I did notice that I really enjoyed billing more per hour than I used to make in a week flipping hamburgers. Early in our marriage, when Karen and I were happy, I hated to be away from my family, but as things started turning in directions that weren't happy, it was a relief. I had my own world that I could control, and my partners were happy to see me each morning. When I went home, there was an angry wife and squabbling children. Work became my refuge."

"There was also something about my work that was akin to drinking too much. When I start thinking about a difficult court case, I don't have to feel. I feel this . . . ," he was searching for the right words, ". . . illusion of control from building this house of my arguments and the precedents. My body is in the chair, but I am somewhere else."

From working with other attorneys toward their Solution, I knew that Tom was probably under a huge amount of pressure to produce a certain number of billable hours each month and that there was competitiveness among the partners about who was bringing in how much revenue.

I suggested, "Would you be willing to make an observable, measurable, specific plan that outlined how much you would work each week?"

Tom immediately balked.

"I can't do that. That's not what people in my firm do."

"What is the essential pain of continuing to work like this?" I asked.

He answered, "I don't know. I guess no time to have a life."

Then he paused for a moment, and shrugged slightly. "Actually, it isn't that bad."

I continued. "If it's not that bad, why do you have to drink so much at night? Why do you come home exhausted and irritable?"

Tom glared at me, then said, "I expect myself to leave work by six every night . . ."

". . . and make up for it by working weekends?" I finished for him.

Tom winced. "How did you know?"

Mark shifted his weight in his chair. Emily sighed.

"Tom, this is not easy. How would it be for you to set a limit to try something for three months?" I suggested.

"How about *one* month?" he countered.

"Good, one month. During that time, do all the cycles you can to stay in balance, then reevaluate at the end of that month."

Tom shrugged and said, "Okay. No work on weekends and leave the office by six every day of the week unless there is an urgent need."

I looked at him warily.

He continued. "I'll leave the office by six every day of the week, no matter what."

I smiled.

What Tom wasn't prepared for was how hard he had to cycle in order to stick to his goal. I listened to him do many cycles on this, but one was particularly riveting.

During that particular weekly session, he seemed to be brooding. His face, which was usually rather sunny, looked dark and troubled. I asked him if he wanted to do a cycle. He nodded and began—and wandered right into a very big piece of emotional trash. He started with his Thinking Journal.

"When I was a child, my dad seemed to me to be a powerless person. He had no money. He had a job as a night watchman, and when he was at home and awake, he was either critical or quiet. I know he loved my mother, but I really don't know what she saw in him except that he was the flip side of her, full of quiet instead of full of talk. My dad seemed empty, and . . . he was worse than a tragic character. It's like he was invisible, like a person who wasn't there except for his negativity. It's infuriating."

"'I feel angry that . . .'" I prompted him.

"I feel angry that . . . no, I don't feel angry. Not really. . . . I feel sad that my father was such a colorless man. . . . I feel sad that he couldn't provide for his family. I feel sad that he had such an unhappy life. . . . I feel afraid that my life will be as colorless . . ."

Tom looked at me with a blank expression, then said, "I know this is irrational, but I feel afraid that I won't be able to put the boys through college. . . . I feel afraid that I will let my family down the way my dad let us down. . . . I feel guilty . . . no, I don't feel guilty."

Tom looked at me questioningly.

"Take all the time you need to find it," I said, "because that's where your power lies. 'In the best of all worlds, I wish that I had . . .'"

"I feel guilty that I . . . wasn't born to a different father . . ." His face was contorted with frustration.

"Tom, you might try anger," I gently suggested.

His face turned crimson as he blurted out, "I feel angry that he was such a failure. . . . I feel angry that he was so damn *insensitive* to our needs. . . . I feel angry that he couldn't even provide for us. . . . I feel angry that he was so mean to me . . . and I feel sad that he was such a loser. . . . I feel afraid that I'll be a loser. . . . I feel guilty that part of me hates him . . . can't accept my own father."

Tom grew very quiet, and as he sat thinking, so did I. In that particular cycle, Tom had such a hard time accessing his anger, the feeling that primes the pump of emotional separation, so perhaps in some small way, he was still merged with his dad. If so, he'd tend to do precisely what his dad had done—or something opposite but equally out of balance. The man in the Armani suit couldn't have been more opposite than the image he painted of his dad, the night watchman.

"Tom, under all those feelings there are some unreasonable expectations."

"My unreasonable expectation . . ." I could see that he was struggling to go deeper and find it. He took a deep breath and said, "I expect myself not to be my father. I expect myself not to make his mistakes. I expect myself not to be invisible, mean, powerless, and poor."

I responded, "There may be a phantom expectation, Tom, one equally unreasonable and opposite."

"I expect myself to be visible." He started to smile. "Visible, indulging, controlling, and filthy rich!"

Tom's face was red again, this time from embarrassment. Several people in the room smiled with him.

"That makes perfect sense," I said. "You're getting good at this, Tom. Now, how about a reasonable expectation?"

"Give me some ideas," he asked.

"How about, 'I expect myself to grieve the losses of a depriving childhood, give myself the skills to get above the line, and do what I came to Earth to do.'"

"That's all?"

Essential Pain and Earned Rewards: Working Past Six

- People at work will think less of me.
- I will think more of myself.

- I must stop rescuing other people or my company.
- I can start rescuing myself.

- I can't feel high or numb from overworking.
- I can feel my feelings and enjoy my life.

- I will have *less* love from work relationships.
- I will have *more* love from personal relationships.

- I won't be able to ignore my personal life.
- I can build a rewarding personal life.

- I may lose my job.
- I may lose my job!

- I may not have all the money I want.
- I will have the health and happiness I need.

"That's enough!" I laughed.

Tom put his fist on his chin and took several deep breaths.

"I can't think of anything positive or powerful to say about that."

"Try harder," I said.

He frowned. "I can do all of that."

"The essential pain?"

"If I don't do the opposite of my father, if I don't rebel against him, I'll lose him. I'll be . . . alone. The essential pain is that the childhood drama I've been playing out would end, and then what would I be left with?" His face looked sorrowful.

"The essential pain I'd have to face is . . ." I urged him on.

"The essential pain is that I am alone."

"The earned reward?"

"I have myself. I have myself perhaps for the first time in my life."

The room was quiet. Everyone was aware of what a precious moment this was.

"What I need is . . . to grieve the losses and perhaps at some point begin to understand my father. And to forgive him."

Everyone seemed to exhale at once, but the room was still perfectly quiet as Tom continued.

"What I need is to create a nurturing voice for myself that my father didn't give me. I need to build a sanctuary within so I don't need to escape my life so much. I don't think I need additional support. I want to do cycles with people, but I want to be alone with this, not the way I used to be alone when I was drinking or obsessing, but just . . . alone."

I was surprised that Tom had gone so deep, but reminded myself that at this point in the climb, people often begin a seemingly simple cycle and find treasure troves of emotional trash that they now have the skill to heal deeply.

19. Spending

Sugar highs get lots of attention, but even more common may be spending binges, hoarding possessions, and equating possessions with love or self-worth.

One afternoon in early fall, I was giving a Solution group in my backyard. There was grass all around our circle of chairs, and a flurry of early fall leaves from the plum trees lay at our feet. It was a cozy session with people who all knew each other rather well.

When I asked who wanted to do cycles, a blond woman in her midfifties raised her hand and said that she wanted to do a cycle on her attachment to possessions, on clutter.

I focused my attention on her, asking her to start with a Thinking Journal. She began, and at once there was such commotion! I looked around the circle. Nearly every man and woman in the room had a pen in hand and a piece of paper of some sort on their laps. They were preparing to write down her cycle!

It was at that moment that I began to appreciate how common it is to have some sort of spending, acquiring, or hoarding problem, just as if it were the basic currency of pleasure, love, and mattering.

Of course, much like overeating, overspending has to do with cultural values and emotional vacuums. We're taught to value ourselves not by the good that we do but the shoes that we wear, and even if we don't believe it on a deep level, materialism may haunt us. We attach to things when we cannot attach to ourselves or tap into the spiritual dimension of life.

Often spending problems don't get the respect that drinking or eating problems do. We can make light of them, for after all, aren't we all at least somewhat in debt? The truth is that the basic expectation that "I don't spend more money than I earn" is often hard to come by in our culture.

Digging out of a spending problem may mean getting additional support, from seeking advice on debt consolidation, filing for bankruptcy, closing a business that has long since failed, or pursuing various legal actions. Most of us find a coach to help us cut up our credit cards or a friend or counselor to listen to us mourn our losses and share our regrets. When spending problems are serious, it may be best not to be alone but to create a circle of support to help you weather the inevitable storms.

Neither Drew, Tom, nor Emily had a severe spending problem; however, they each had a subtle one that impeded progress toward their sweetest fruit. In Solution Groups, spending and overworking are excesses often shared by everyone. People may deviate in their chemical pleasures and overeating, some rescue and people-please, and others tend to distance and think too much. But overspending and under- or overworking are nearly ubiquitous.

Drew's spending was the most blatant. She spent just the way she ate and drank: with abandon. Her attitude was, "Give me a credit card and let me have at it. Shopping makes my day." With a mischievous grin, she once said to the group, "When the going gets tough, I go shopping, and I almost don't care what I buy. If I buy something, it means I'm valuable. I get this zing from it, and it doesn't even matter whether or not I really want what I buy. I have at least nine black sweaters. What do I need another black sweater for? But if I went shopping tomorrow, I'd probably come home with one. Or maybe two. Shoes are another favorite of mine. It's totally ridiculous, because I wear flats to work, but I have a closet full of mules, spike heels, strappy sandals, and hiking boots.

"I also collect things. For years I've been collecting old furniture and linens. I get so much of it that I have to either have it hauled away or have a huge garage sale. Twice I've had to hire a man to haul it away out of desperation—there was no room to put my car in the garage."

Drew took a quick bite of air, then continued. "I have so much clutter! I go to other people's houses, and their counters are clean and their bookshelves are neat. There is not one flat surface in my home that isn't stacked with papers, books, children's projects, and memorabilia. It's everywhere!"

I didn't think Drew was far along enough in the training to let go of her spending problem, since that drive was rather deep within her. I knew that as she continued to do cycles, her sanctuary within would grow, and her drive to spend would slowly, naturally decline. She was not overspending so zealously that she faced bankruptcy, so there was no urgent need to stop the flow of cash from her wallet. Instead, we focused on her need to collect things and hoard them, and the resulting visual chaos and personal clutter.

"What do you think of the idea of doing a cycle about clutter?" I asked her.

Drew launched ahead. "I like things. I like to have them around me. I like to look at them. I can't bear to get rid of them. Somehow just seeing them is comforting to me. It's a problem, because there are so many of these things around me that they're stacked everywhere. I can't find things, and there are cobwebs and spiders . . ."

She frowned, and a couple of people chuckled.

"It's revolting," she said, "and yet I can't part with these things. I took a class on clutter, and I made all these goals to clean out one room each week. But I never did. I couldn't bring myself to, which feels sad . . ."

"Go into the Natural Flow of Feelings when you are ready, Drew."

"I feel sad that these things are so important to me. . . . I feel sad that I need them so much. . . . I feel afraid that I won't have enough. I feel afraid that I will be alone. . . . I feel afraid that someone will take them from me. . . . I feel guilty for being so . . . possessive. . . . I feel guilty for being so lazy and not cleaning up. . . . I feel guilty for being such a slob."

"'I feel angry that . . . ,'" I encouraged her.

"I don't feel angry," she answered.

Reasonable Expectations: Spending

I expect myself to do the best I can to:

- Spend less money than I earn.

- Have no debts other than my home or car.

- Nurture myself in ways other than spending.

- Base my self-worth on the person I am, not on what I own.

- Satisfy my need for pleasure in way other than overspending.

- Connect with myself, not with possessions.

"Drew, you need your anger. Otherwise, you're going to find yourself in this puddle of self-pity and powerlessness."

She looked irritated and waited, as if checking for anger to arise in her body. Several very long minutes passed until she started speaking again.

"I hate it that I feel so empty. . . . I hate it that I have no love in my life. . . . I hate that I am so confused. I hate it that my mind is such a mess. . . . I hate it that I never had things as a child. . . . I can't stand it that I was so alone. . . . I feel angry that I feel so unloved. . . ."

Abruptly she stopped. Pure silence followed.

"Wheeeew," she said finally, and loudly, her exhale felt by everyone in the room. Then she looked forlorn. "I'm disgusted with myself," she said.

"Incredible!" I said. "That was a beautiful Natural Flow of Feelings, Drew. That anger was the best you've done! At this point, you can do another Natural Flow of Feelings or head over to the limits cycle."

She said impatiently, "Limits. I need limits!"

I took a deep breath. "Do you want me to try?"

"Yes, pleeease."

Very quietly, I said, "Drew, it's a reasonable expectation that if you can't attach to the love within, you'll attach to the love without. You'll connect with things, and you won't be able to give them up."

Her eyes lit up. "That's right. That's exactly right!"

I continued. "And that expectation prepares you to create another one, one that will give you a safe highway that will take you out of hoarding and clutter."

Drew nodded. "I expect myself to do the best I can to stay above the line and attach to the nurturing inner voice within me. As I am able to do that more and more, I will detach from possessions, stop hoarding things as much, and get rid of some of my clutter."

The room burst into applause.

"Incredible!" I said.

Drew was beaming. "Positive and powerful? I can do that. Essential pain?"

"What is the hard part for you about connecting with yourself?"

"Emotional trash. I'd have to take out a lot of emotional trash about feeling so alone as a child. That would hurt."

"And what else?"

"The essential pain of connecting with myself instead of with possessions . . . eeeek, this one hurts, too. The essential pain is that I would have to face myself. I would have to get the love inside me—and I don't know if I can do that."

"Let's go back to the expectation," I said. "If you will, put your right fingers on your left wrist, and I'll do the same."

We both put our fingers on our pulses.

"I expect myself to do the best I can and no better to keep my finger on the pulse of my inner life, to soothe and comfort myself from within so that I need less soothing and comforting from possessions," I said.

Again, Drew's face brightened. "So, the essential pain is that I must love myself."

"Yes!"

"The earned reward is that I will love myself!"

Again, the room was full of laughter and empathy.

"'So what I need is . . . ','" I urged her.

"What I need is to deepen my nurturing inner voice and practice the skills."

"And the support you will require?"

"Community Connections, lots of them."

I grinned. "I think you have a lot of people who would love to do connections with you on this."

Emily was the first to speak up. "Wow, Drew. I loved your cycle, particularly your anger. I need to do more of that."

Then Mark said, "Drew, I have fourteen saws in my garage. I have no idea why I have fourteen saws, but I do. They are black and greasy, and my wife complains about them all the time. I learned a lot from your cycle. Thanks."

When I asked who else wanted to do cycles, Emily's hand went up immediately.

"I want to do a cycle, but it's a different kind of spending problem. I think it is somewhat sick, and I don't know how to explain it." She hesitated, and as she looked around the room, the fear in her face was clear. It was as though Emily knew she was going to say something very shameful.

"I don't overspend. I think I get some pleasure out of depriving myself. My husband's work makes us somewhat wealthy, and he's always telling me to make myself happy by buying things, and we do go on extravagant vacations, but I get this kind of perverse pleasure out of denying myself things. I don't buy nice underwear, and I skimp on paper towels. My clothes are ten years old, and when my husband buys me jewelry—he bought me diamond earrings for our twentieth wedding anniversary—it stays in the velvet box it came in and I tuck it into my sock drawer. I helped my neighbor with her sick mother, taking her to the doctor several times, and my neighbor gave me a gift certificate for a massage. I gave it to my daughter."

"Well," I began, "you could do cycles or you could use words, not external solutions, to express yourself right now."

Emily was already familiar with this technique, which is based on the idea that when we use external solutions, they are often filling a below-the-line need, "saying" something for us passively. If we could pop ourselves above the line, bring that idea to a conscious level, and say it aloud using very simple words, the drive for the external solution would begin to fade. It's a technique that requires a certain amount of trust between the individual using it and the provider as we work together to find the essence of the words used. Rather than tell you about it, let me show you how it is done:

"Emily, would you please settle back in your chair and take a nice deep breath."

She began to settle back and close her eyes.

"If you will, keep in mind your early life, caring for your parents and sister, your father's exhaustion coming home from his factory job, and your mother's illnesses. Depriving yourself works for you because it enables you to express yourself without using words; however, that expression is from below the line and needs to see the light of day. If you say those words aloud over and over again, you may not need to spend. This is called using words, not external solutions, to express yourself.

"As you say the words, over and over again, those words will be transformed into words that are underneath them, or you may just say them over and over again with no relief. They may even seem to be true to you because they are lodged in a piece of emotional trash that must come out before you will stop underspending. On the other hand, you may say it again and again until it pops from below the line, out of balance and passive, to above the line and balanced. At that time, the words will seem silly, like words that used to hold meaning but now do not. You are apt to pop above the line and stop needing to underspend to express yourself."

Essential Pain and Earned Rewards: Spending

- I cannot buy whatever I want.
- I can buy some of the things I really need.

- I can't change the past.
- I can change the future.

- I cannot numb myself by spending.
- I must feel my feelings and meet my true needs.

- Possessions are not a substitute for love.
- I can create love in my life.

- Security does not come from things.
- Security comes from me.

Emily nodded.

I continued. "Imagine yourself in the house where you live with the husband you have and the children that are your own. Imagine that you could relax and not worry about anyone, that your cupboards were full and nobody had a problem, that everyone was healthy and happy and at peace. Imagine there was abundance of love, laughter, money, food, and repose."

Emily said, "I feel scared."

"That's the start of a cycle. We're going to use words instead of external solutions to say what you need to say, so just keep focusing on that image of yourself living a life of receiving what you need, of abundance, and of joy. In order to stay in that life, to keep from rushing back into deprivation and darkness, you have to say some words very loudly, as if you're shouting from the rooftops. They're just the simplest words, just start somewhere, and we'll work together."

"I don't know what I'd have to say . . ." she trailed off.

"Take all the time you like. There's no rush."

"I was deprived as a child."

"Say it very loudly."

"I WAS DEPRIVED AS A CHILD."

"Let's move under it to its essence. Let's try, I WAS DEPRIVED."

"I WAS DEPRIVED."

"Again."

"I WAS DEPRIVED."

"Louder."

"I WAS DEPRIVED!"

"Let's try, I can't receive."

"I CAN'T RECEIVE."

"Again."

"I CAN'T RECEIVE."

"I can't receive because . . ."

"I CAN'T RECEIVE BECAUSE I AM NOT WORTHY."

"Again."

"I CAN'T RECEIVE BECAUSE I AM NOT WORTHY."

"Try, 'I am not worthy.' "

"I AM NOT WORTHY."

"Again, louder, several times."

"I AM NOT WORTHY. I AM NOT WORTHY. I AM NOT WORTHY."

Emily's face lit up and broke into a wide, gleeful smile. She had popped above the line!

"Of course I'm worthy! That's ridiculous!" She laughed, and the group clapped and gasped.

When someone uses this technique to pop an old, below-the-line expectation above the line, it is extremely emotional. Often, people feel worn out for days, but elated as well. Others in the group can see that dramatic change when the person finally pops that old, early learning from below the line to the present day, and above the line.

I heaved a sigh after Emily had popped above the line. It's always risky to ask someone to go into an old, unbalanced thought, because if that's done too early in the changing of the feeling brain, it gets so stuck in a piece of emotional trash that the statement seems hurtful, too. Even that, though, has its rewards, because the person can relax and know that the excess will not abate until they do enough cycles to loosen and take out that hurt from the past.

Tom was not in the group that evening. Whether it was because of Michelle, because he was back to drinking, or because he was on a business trip, I did not know, but at a later group session, he did a little bit of work on his equating self-worth with expensive objects, especially expensive playthings.

Actually, it was during a session in which someone else, an educational consultant named Claudia, did a cycle on possessions. She had bought a tremendously expensive dining room set—a huge rosewood table, eight chairs, and a sideboard—without telling her husband. When the furniture arrived, and the bill with it, they'd had an explosive argument: he was furious at her furtiveness and indulgence, and she was adamant that she had to have the best and she was going to get it no matter what!

She did a cycle on it, popped above the line, and practiced through role-play giving her husband a Solution Sandwich, the intimacy technique we use in the method I describe on page 162.

When it was time for group members to share their appreciation for the cycle another member had done—that is, to give Tender Morsels—it was Tom who was first to speak up.

"I appreciate your cycle, Claudia, and I understand that you like to have nice things. Having the best is really important to me, and when I listened to your cycle, I understood myself a little better. Thanks."

After a couple of other people gave Tender Morsels, I turned to Tom.

"Do you see having nice things as an external solution or just part of enjoying the good life?"

The look on his face made me know that he was not particularly receptive to this line of thinking.

"Who wouldn't like a BMW instead of a Honda, or a Rolex instead of a Timex?"

I shrugged. "It's not an issue of whether you have a BMW or a Honda, it's whether or not acquiring the best things is an external solution. It's whether it causes you to disconnect from yourself. It's whether you acquire things you want because you don't have the skill to give yourself what you really need."

Tom was thoughtful for a moment.

"Getting nice things makes me feel better about myself."

"You used to use a lot of marijuana, right?"

"Yes."

"Does it feel like a hit?"

He nodded, then laughed. "If it's the very, very best, it feels like a hit. If it's not, it doesn't."

"Do you want to do a cycle to go under it, to see what feelings are there?"

Tom shook his head. "No. I've worked hard. I enjoy having

the very best, and I probably always will. It is a solace to me that I don't intend to give up."

"Wonderful," I said. "My only worry is . . . whether it would get in the way of your acquiring what you most want in this world, your sweetest fruit, intimacy."

Tom looked so perturbed at that moment that I wondered if he was going to get up and storm out of the room.

He grimaced. "You got me, Laurel."

I waited for his next remark.

"I hate it when you get me like that."

Other people in the room laughed. By this time, Tom was seen by most as a little incorrigible but lovable. When he reached his Solution and graduated from the group, I knew that he would be sorely missed.

"Michelle tells me I am arrogant, superficial, and materialistic. That I am like a twelve-year-old boy with his playthings and I must have a deep sense of insecurity to be so tied to my possessions and having them be perfect."

Everyone listened intently.

"Lovely," I said.

"She says that the fact I have to have my Porsche . . ."

"I thought it was a BMW?"

"I have both."

"Oh."

"The fact that I have to have them washed by hand every week and detailed every six months and won't let her drive either of them . . . it's not that I don't trust her, but that . . ."

"What?"

"I don't want anyone messing with my playthings. I don't want anyone scratching them or getting lipstick on the leather seats or eating crackers in the backseat . . ."

The room was deathly quiet. Tom seemed to be digging his own grave.

"I feel angry that Michelle is messing with my program. . . . I feel angry that she doesn't understand how important my cars are to me. . . . I feel angry that she is so critical. I feel sad that she doesn't accept me. . . . I feel afraid she is going to dump me. . . . I feel guilty. . . . I don't feel guilt . . ."

"Is that the cycle you want to do, Tom?"

"Yes, I'm ready to use the limits cycle."

"Whatever you'd like . . ."

"I expect myself to date only women who accept me for who I am."

"Great. It might help to check what's the essential pain of that? If you hold on to that expectation, what is the natural consequence of that choice?"

Tom looked pensive, then he broke into a smile. Finally!

"The essential pain is that I will only date women who are superficial, perfectionistic, and materialistic and care only about what I can buy them, not about me."

The room was jumping at this point. Not one person could contain their mirth.

I waited. Tom took his time.

He said, "A reasonable expectation? I expect myself to be attached to things, and perhaps I always will be and that is not bad. However, as I use the skills and start getting rewards like intimacy more, I will rely less on having perfection in material things . . ."

"Positive, powerful . . ."

"Love is more important than crumbs in my car."

Again, chuckling in the room.

"I am not in complete control. My things aren't perfect. The earned reward? I may be happier and have more love in my life."

Tom's face softened, the sign that he had popped above the line.

"So what I need is . . ."

"What I need is to feel miserable for a while, to mourn the loss of the dream of total control over perfect possessions . . ."

His face looked sad.

"And to start to think about love and caring and intimacy."

"The 'Would you please . . . '?"

"It would be to the group. Would you please do cycles with me about this, and would you please tell me if you think I am a complete jerk?"

Mark spoke up first.

"Your cycle was so great. I'm glad that I'm not the only one who gets obsessed with things being perfect and with material objects. Thanks for the cycle."

Emily, who was always ready to rescue any group member from any shred of pain, said, "Tom, I don't think you are a jerk. I think Michelle is a lucky woman."

That was just what Tom wanted to hear.

20. Rescuing Others

My father once said to me, "What do you mean, 'rescuing'? People *should* care about one another. People aren't supposed to be cold!"

Of course, my dad is right—people should care for one another. But by rescuing, I mean:

- Extending yourself to a person to the point that you've lost your own spirit and feel as if you've abandoned yourself
- Caring for someone to the point that you have developed a clear pattern of neglecting or abusing yourself
- Protecting a person from the essential pain of their choices so they fail to learn, change, and grow.

The flip side of rescuing is persecution. Under the blanket of passivity and rescuing, there is red-hot aggression and persecution toward ourselves or toward others. Tolerate the intolerable and we'll find ourselves headed for the bottle, the fridge, or the credit card. Be sickeningly sweet with someone, and we'll notice the bitter tone we use later on, with that person or with ourselves.

What's more, rescuing people actually hurts them deeply over time, because at its root is disrespect. Why is it that we expect so little of them and continually clean up after their messes? If we truly respected them, wouldn't we expect them to do their share and clean up after themselves, at least sometimes? At the core of rescuing is an unexpressed regressive agreement: If I make you happy and don't mention your external solutions and your serious insufficiencies, then you won't mention mine. I will rescue you if you rescue me. I will be responsible for your happiness if you will be responsible for mine. Then neither of us must face ourselves, be responsible for our own lives, and grow up.

All that sounds rather nasty, but there is no judgment involved, because the pattern is typically completely unconscious, and its seeds were sown very early in life. The pattern of merging with another, rescuing them from their problems, and being unable to tolerate their experiencing the pain they need to feel in order to learn, change, and grow usually has its roots in our family of origin. We did that then, and we are still doing it now.

At the heart of ending rescuing is a capacity to soothe and comfort ourselves so that we are less dependent upon the soothing and comforting of others. We can enjoy the love of others without holding ourselves hostage to it. That intimacy with self involves a deep personal "integration," or self-knowing, as well as an acceptance of the human condition: We all need to feel our unavoidable pain in order to mature. It is only from having a profound sense of personal integrity that we can deeply respect the separateness of another and their need to journey through life at their own pace and in their own way.

The expectations, essential pain, and earned rewards you see in the boxes in this chapter are core to ending rescuing, but these are typically not fully integrated until a lot of emotional trash has been taken out and we are nearing our Solution. The implicit learning in the feeling brain is what sets the stage for rescuing; until those early knowings are revised to favor intimacy and independence, not merging and dependence, the pattern will not fade.

For many of us, rescuing will always be part of our dark side, and when that tendency crops up, we will need to accept that proclivity but also take out our tool kit and use the skills to hold back. Saying to yourself, "I know that my tendency would be to rescue in this situation, but I'm going to take a big deep breath and face the essential pain that the other person will hurt, and I'll see if I can stay above the line, just this one time."

It is also helpful to pump up your boundary when in the presence of those you tend to rescue and say to yourself in a strong, loud voice, "Okay, I know how they feel and what they need, but how do *I* feel and what do *I* need?"

Emily had so many blessings in life, but she did not have an easy climb. She *looked* like someone who was going to have a somewhat easy time of it, but the more I spoke with her, the more I saw the telltale characteristics of someone who would struggle, or even perhaps get perpetually stalled in the middle of the tree.

Emily was too easy on herself and too easy on others. She didn't fully engage in our sessions each week, struggling through the tough parts of the process, growing more and more aware of

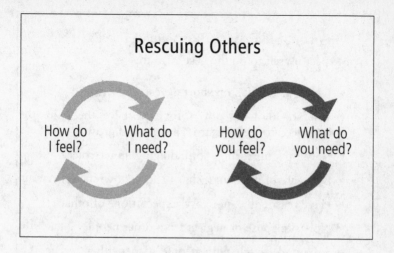

Rescuing Others

How do
I feel? What do
I need? How do
you feel? What do
you need?

how much she needed a Solution—the way, for example, Drew did. Instead, Emily came each week with excuses about why she hadn't practiced the skills. She was taking The Solution only half seriously, the way she took herself only half seriously.

Emily was also very firmly connected to being "good." Most of us who don't get the skills we need early on fall into the "good girl/good boy" role (or the "bad girl/bad boy" role) instead of just being who we are: some good, some bad. Being too good becomes an external solution in its own right, and as the angel of her family, the one who was always sacrificing for others, Emily had no real incentive to stop merging with others and grow herself up.

To make things more difficult, Emily was sickly, just as her mother had been. She took little care of her own health, eating too many sweets and hardly ever bothering to exercise. She was at a reasonably normal weight and was quite attractive, but she always looked rather ill—a little weak, pale, and vulnerable to every cold or cough that came into town. Emily was the kind of person who, if stranded on a desert island, wouldn't make it through the first day.

One evening, we began our group with a Feelings Check. I asked everyone to settle back in their chairs, take some nice deep breaths, and begin to go inside, connecting with themselves and bringing up a nurturing inner voice, then checking on what feelings were within. It's a session beginning that's familiar to anyone who's participated in a group meeting about The Solution,

Reasonable Expectations: Rescuing Others

I expect myself to do the best I can to:

- Love others but stop short of rescuing them.

- Tolerate allowing others to experience the pain they need to feel to learn, change, and grow

- Develop a nurturing, not indulging, inner voice

- Be aware of my own feelings and my own needs

- Have reasonable, not easy, expectations of others

- Not take abuse or neglect from other people

- Surround myself with people who neither rescue nor persecute

and it's followed by a "lightning round," during which each person in the circle briefly comments on what the experience was like or what feelings they noticed.

When it was Emily's turn, she said, "I noticed that I have two inner voices: one that is very harsh and one that is very lenient. I usually only hear the harsh, negative voice, but today I heard another voice, the indulging one."

"Tell me more," I said.

Emily said, "I think that voice is more powerful than I realized. I think I listen to it a lot, and it says things like, 'It's just too hard,' or, 'Rob can't tolerate any pain. If anyone rejects him, he's going to fall apart.'"

"So the voice indulges you and indulges others?"

She nodded. "I think so."

"It reminds me of my mother," she continued. "My mother was such a victim. Everything in life that was bad happened to her. She was so powerless and easy on herself . . . and on me, I think. I've always focused on how hard it was to take care of everyone, but I got a lot of special treatment because of it, and I got myself out of having to deal with certain things."

"Like what?" I asked.

"They didn't push me. I didn't have to enroll in any sports. I didn't even have to go to gym glass. I got a D in seventh-grade gym because I never went, and when I did, I didn't participate. My parents said nothing. Basically, I didn't have to take risks or extend myself. I could just be a good little hermit if I wanted to."

She paused for a moment, then said, "I feel as if I have my mother growing inside me, that passive, victimized, sickly person, and I hate it."

"Do you want to take out some emotional trash?" I asked.

Emily flew right into the Natural Flow of Feelings. "I hate it that she was such a coward. I hate it that she was so easy on herself. I can't stand it that her indulging, self-pitying, weak voice is within me . . . which makes me feel sad. I feel sad that she was such a passive person. I feel sad that she never reached her potential. I feel sad that she had such an unfulfilling life. I feel afraid that I am repeating her pattern. I feel guilty that I have allowed it. I feel guilty that I am her."

"Emily, see if you can sit up really tall in your chair, as if you're physically moving yourself above the line."

She shook her head, her blond hair swinging slightly, then pulled back her shoulders, breathed deeply through her nostrils, and said, "Okay."

I continued speaking. "Some of the most powerful cycles have to do with separating, often separating from the past or from other people. You use the limits cycle to do that, since that's the cycle that creates safety and power."

Emily nodded, and I went on.

"Let's try one way of separating. If that doesn't work for you, we'll try another."

"Okay," she said.

"Before we begin, let me just double-check that you have expressed enough anger to be able to separate from your mother and from her indulging inner voice, that you can toss out that piece of emotional trash."

Emily took off her glasses, dropped them onto her lap, and said, "No, I think I need more anger. *Lots* more."

"Good, but don't bother expressing it until you feel it red-hot in your body, ready to explode. Then express it *loudly*."

"Okay," she said. She waited for about a minute, and I saw red patches appearing on her neck. Finally, she nearly yelled, "I hate it that you are passive. . . . I hate that you are so self-serving. . . . I can't stand it that you are so easy on yourself, such a wimp. . . . All you cared about was yourself. All you thought about was how bad you had it. Didn't you ever care about *me*? Why didn't you have an indulging voice for *me*? . . . I am so angry that you neglected me. I'm so furious that you were so easy on yourself. . . . I hate it that you live inside of me, and I won't stand it another minute!"

"Go right into the limits cycle," I said.

"No," she said. "There's more. I hate it that you rescued my father. . . . I hate it that you couldn't stand up to him. . . . I am furious that you let him ignore me. . . . I feel furious that you didn't tell him he had to act like a real father. . . . I feel furious that you indulged him and never spoke up to him and made it just fine for him to do whatever he wanted, even if it hurt us kids. . . . I can't stand it that you wouldn't stand up for yourself and for us. . . . I feel furious that you were so passive and were so easy on yourself . . ."

Emily looked over at me. "Now I'm ready," she said.

"Go right ahead," I responded.

"I hate that voice, and I won't have it in me. . . . I expect that you will always be a passive rescuer with a self-indulgent inner voice, for as long as you live!"

Emily gulped. She had surprised even herself with her fury.

I nudged her. "What do you expect of yourself, separate from your mother's choices?"

"I expect myself to fire that indulging inner voice, to fire that depriving inner voice, and to stop rescuing everyone and everything. . . . I expect myself not to be my mother. I expect to develop a nurturing, not indulging, inner voice."

"Good. Positive, powerful?"

"I am not my mother!" At this point, she was yelling the words.

"Excellent. The essential pain?"

Her face turned sad. "The essential pain is that I will never have a mother who is loving to me. I will never erase a childhood that was filled with deprivation and indulgence."

Tears rolled down Emily's face. The room was quiet. Several others had red eyes, too.

Emily took a tissue from the tissue box someone handed her and blew her nose.

"The earned reward is . . . I don't know if there is one. No, there is. The earned reward is that I can have a good mother inside me. I can have myself. I can be free of her voice. I do not have to rescue others. I can have a full, free life!"

She had popped herself above the line, but it had been a hard cycle, so I wanted her to be sure that her new limit was nailed down.

"What is the essential pain of having your own nurturing voice instead of your mother's indulging, rescuing one?"

Emily thought for a moment, then said, "The essential pain is that I can't change the past. The essential pain is that I didn't have a good childhood. The essential pain is that I can't rescue my mother. I can't live in the past. The earned reward is that I can make a good future for myself. I am not trapped in the past."

The room erupted with clapping and gasps and laughter. Emily had popped herself above the line, and others had "popped" with her.

"So, what you need . . ." I nodded toward Emily.

"I need to practice that essential pain. In fact, I need to practice the whole cycle over and over again. Did someone write it down for me?"

Essential Pain and Earned Rewards: Rescuing Others

- They will have hurts.
- They will learn from the hurts.

- I can't rescue them.
- They can rescue themselves.

- They won't rescue me.
- I can rescue myself.

- They may be mad at me.
- I won't be mad at myself.

- I am alone.
- I have myself.

- I can't be a savior.
- I can be a normal human being.

Drew had been across the room from her, busily writing throughout her whole cycle. She passed the paper around the circle until Emily had it.

"Thanks, Drew. And I need to start checking my inner voice, bringing up one that is not indulging or depriving."

"What support do you need, Emily?" I asked.

She let out a laugh, then said, "I need my dead aunt Nora's help!"

"What?" I asked, amused.

"My dead aunt Nora was the only balanced one in the whole family, and she had to go and die on us!"

By now, Emily and most people in the room were making joyful noises.

"She did?" I asked.

"When I was about ten, Aunt Nora died in a car accident. She was the only one I had been close to. She had a warmth about her, but she was still strong. There wasn't a self-indulging, self-pitying bone in her body."

"So you want to use her voice, until you cultivate your own."

"Precisely."

Emily's cycle was like a lot of cycles people do at the middle of the tree. It was a little messy, blending different ideas and various issues. That is both fine and good; it's a needed prelude to the clarity that comes in cycles as people near the top of the tree.

As Emily continued her climb, her cycles grew far more narrow and productive, something she could only accomplish near the top of the tree. One day, she came to me feeling especially heartsick. Emily was finally sick to death of rescuing others, and she did a cycle to that effect.

Her cycle was about her husband.

Emily did the cycle in private session with me, as she didn't feel at ease speaking about it with the group. Her husband was known in the community, and she wanted to maintain his privacy, even from group members.

"I don't know that I want to stay in my marriage. I always thought that I loved my husband, but now I'm not sure how I feel. We had a marriage that worked in that he did his role and I did mine, but now I'm not that same person. I realize that I have passions that I've never acknowledged, and I'm mad as hell that I've squandered my dreams while he has honored his. I've been the doormat, and I'm tired of it and I'm mad at him."

"Is that what you want to do your cycle on, Emily?" I asked.

She frowned and shook her head. "No. That's not it. It's not even about my marriage. It's that I've been rescuing everyone and everything and merging with everyone and everything and there's no energy left for myself. I've indulged everybody, and now I'm furious at them . . ."

"I have a quick tool for that," I told her. "How about, 'I feel guilty that I have taught them I will rescue them'?"

She looked glum. "That's right. I've taught them to neglect me. I've taught them to expect me to neglect myself."

At this point, Emily's skills were solid enough within her that they held her in her sadness. A year before, that sadness would have sent her off the emotional cliff into depression. But now, she seemed to just be . . . sad. And she had a right to be sad. It was a sad situation.

At that moment, Emily's anger ignited within her. With steely eyes and slow speech, she said, "My most basic expectation—the most basic expectation that I will grind into my bones—is: I do not rescue other people." Her eyes darted to me. "Did you hear me? I will not rescue other people."

"Say it again. Say it ten times."

It would have been a useless mantra if done near the bottom of the tree, or even at the middle. But now, near the top of the tree, it took on new power. The neural networks that appeared to favor a life of merging and rescuing had been weakened by what felt to Emily like thousands and thousands of cycles. The networks that favored balance were getting stronger and stronger.

She said, "I DO NOT RESCUE OTHER PEOPLE. I do not rescue other people. I do not rescue other people. I do not rescue other people. I do not rescue other people. I DO NOT RESCUE OTHER PEOPLE. I DO NOT RESCUE other people. I do not rescue other people. I DO NOT rescue other people. There. I feel a little better!" She smiled with a certain look of satisfaction.

"Good. Now do that ten times every morning, noon, and night. Do it every day until it has been integrated into your inner life and it is just *there*. Take out emotional trash that arises, be curious about what else becomes apparent as you do it, but keep doing it."

A new security washed over Emily's face. She looked just a little bit vibrant.

"Yes," she said, "I will do that."

I don't remember much about seeing Emily for the next month. The group took a break between sessions, and I recall that she was away with her husband on a vacation after that. But I remember quite clearly what happened at a session about five or six weeks after she started implanting the most basic expectation "I do not rescue others" in her feeling brain.

When it was Emily's turn to say what she had accomplished during the previous week in the training, and the biggest challenge she faced in the following week, she was indignant. It was a posture I had never seen her take before.

"I have two major accomplishments," she said. "One is that I am working very hard at not rescuing Clay anymore, and he just hates it."

Several people chuckled, sharing the semimasochistic counterpart to rescuing: the joy of persecution.

"He hates the fact that I am not willing to make my schedule around his. I've looked into taking a music class at the conservatory, and the only night I can do it is the same night he has a meeting. That's an inconvenience to him. I'm also looking into private lessons with a woman who can take me on Saturday mornings. To him, that time is sacred—but you know, it isn't sacred to me. He and I are two different people. He has his feelings and I have mine. I can tolerate him feeling the essential pain he needs to feel in order for me to be a . . . well, a full human being with a life of passion, not sacrificing my health and happiness to please him!"

By now, everyone in the room was clapping, and I heard a few hoots and hollers.

"After all," she said, now mocking, "I take care of my health and my happiness."

Drew immediately gave her a Tender Morsel. "Emily, you amaze me. What happened? You went from doing a zillion cycles and making a slow climb to taking off into the stratosphere!"

Emily was near the top of the tree. That's how it is after you've climbed all that way and the method is beginning to "snowball." The neural networks that once supported a life of imbalance appear to fall away, one by one by one.

Emily smiled and went on. "Thank you, Drew. It feels great, but I can tell you what doesn't feel great. I'm still not very healthy, and I have a long way to go. And one of the worst things is that . . . well, I can't stand my friends, and I can't stand my family."

Emily had everyone's attention.

"I've taught everyone that I will rescue them, and they're not happy when all of a sudden I have reasonable, harder expectations of them. My children are mad at me that I don't pick up after them and look the other way when they're totally irresponsible and thoughtless. And I have a couple of friends who are above the line, but all of a sudden I'm seeing people differently. There are so many people who are so removed and closed—they're like machines. They're not nice people. I've been thinking they were above me, and now I've realized that they're dangerous. They are probably persecutors, and I can't stand being around them. And then there are the rescuers who are most of my friends. I can't stand listening to all these people complain about their lives and nitpick their husbands and take no responsibility for their lives or their happiness. It makes me sick!"

Now I was the one taking a deep breath.

"Emily, they're not bad people. They have a skill insufficiency."

She looked at me, now embarrassed.

"Oh, I guess I could look at it that way. Insufficient skills. But I don't want to be around them!"

"Then don't be, or take a break from the relationships with those friends. What's a reasonable expectation?"

"I expect myself to remember that I was the one who taught them I'd rescue them, and I expect it to take time for them to adjust to not being rescued."

"That sounds about right."

She nodded. "Okay, I'll give them some time."

Then she smiled.

Life above the line is a new world . . . a very new world.

21. Putting Up Walls

I t would be wonderful if we never needed to put up walls. What if life were truly safe and we could just relax? It would be like forever being in the security of the womb.

Unfortunately, putting up walls, distancing, and having thick boundaries are often learned early in life. If there is no one there to soothe and comfort us, a shell may form around us so we can soothe and comfort ourselves. If those around us are harsh, critical, or hurtful, developing a protective shield may have been essential to our emotional or even physical survival.

The hallmark of putting up walls is shutting down our sensitivity to the feelings and needs of others. We are aware of our own feelings and needs, but their feelings and needs may totally escape us. Perhaps in the back of our minds, we know, but we are even more aware that we cannot focus on them. We must take care of ourselves.

The trouble is that without reaching over and keeping our fingers on the pulse of the inner lives of those we love now and then, we may be apt to neglect their needs or, even worse, be aggressive or abusive to them. We may not even be aware that we are doing it!

Of course, things could always get worse, and when they do, instead of neglecting people, we may persecute them. Alas, rescuing and persecuting are two sides of the same coin, so when we rescue someone, we often later persecute them or ourselves. Sometimes we do it on purpose! Awareness of how they feel and what they need vanishes, and we plummet right below the line and take delight in passively or actively persecuting our partners. It's human nature, in a certain way, for it is the natural backlash of rescuing.

None of this sounds very nice, but those of us who put up walls or even persecute others are often extremely loving in certain ways. Behind that big, thick boundary that lets us roar like a lion, there is a sweet kitten of a person—a little marshmallow, really, that keeps its guard up for fear it will completely melt.

That's why if your external solution is to put up walls, it's essential that you allow yourself to take them down slowly. If your inner

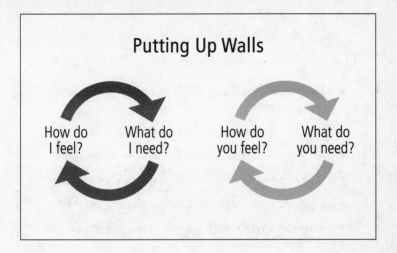

Putting Up Walls

How do I feel? → What do I need? ⟲

How do you feel? → What do you need? ⟲

life is like a closed door, it won't do to fling it open. Instead, it is perfectly fine to open it just a crack, then a bit more and a bit more. Feel the essential pain that others could hurt you. Feel the essential pain that not all of your needs will be met. Feel the essential pain that you are not in complete control. It's just a matter of practicing those essential pains and reaping the earned rewards while you take out emotional trash and recognize that the distance from others you required in the past is not the distance you need now.

Tom certainly put up walls when he started using the method. I was aghast when I learned that David, his best friend and business partner for more than a decade, didn't even know Tom was having marital problems. Tom simply didn't share personal information with others, especially information that could be viewed even remotely as negative. Tom knew everything about David's personal life—his concerns about his wife's spending problem, his thinning hair, and his flagging sex drive. But all Tom spoke to David about was sports.

After some time with The Solution Method, Tom began opening up. He felt his feelings and, at times, expressed them, opening up slowly to both David and Michelle and testing the waters to be sure he could trust them. It was a slow process, but he made progress.

Drew was having more difficulty.

It wasn't that she wasn't working hard on the skills, because she was. But Drew had acquired a remarkably harsh, even persecuting,

> ## Reasonable Expectations: Putting Up Walls
> I expect myself to do the best I can to:
>
> - Honor myself but stop short of neglecting or persecuting others
> - Care about the feelings and needs of others
> - Develop a nurturing—not depriving—inner voice
> - Have reasonable—not harsh—expectations of others
> - Avoid abusing, neglecting, or persecuting anyone
> - Surround myself with people who neither rescue nor persecute

inner voice. In his book *There Is a Spiritual Solution to Every Problem,* Wayne Dwyer discusses the fact that people are like oranges. When you squeeze an orange, you get orange juice—but when you squeeze those of us with deep, bitter hurts inside, nothing sweet comes out. Drew had been deeply hurt when the arrival of her twin brothers knocked her off the pedestal of parental adoration, and she did not have the skill to grieve her losses and heal them.

Instead, Drew's hurts festered, and the abusive excesses to which she gravitated made the infections more insidious and raw. In essence, she was furious at her mother, her father, both of her brothers, and especially God. She hated God for what He had done to her—and she knew it was a "He" because "a woman couldn't be that mean."

Drew had such a hot cauldron of hate within her that whenever one excess faded, two more popped up. Her sweetest fruit was to have complete freedom from excess, but as far as I could see, meeting that goal would be a formidable one.

Finally, I spoke with her about it in group. She wanted to do yet another set of cycles on her eating and why that dastardly drive wouldn't turn off! When a person focuses excessively on the symptom, it's usually a tip-off that the basic work hasn't been done.

"Drew," I said, "I know you want to do cycles about your eating, but I'm worried that may not be the best use of your time."

She looked at me, clearly displeased, but I continued.

"I'll do those cycles with you if you want, but I'm worried that some of the basic skills, the first half of the climb, aren't serving you as well as they might."

Drew was silent.

"Would you please check it with me?" I asked.

She nodded.

"Do you have a nurturing inner voice?"

Her eyes glazed over. "No. I mean, sometimes, but not usually."

"Let's stop everything else you are doing and focus on that."

"I don't want to go inside. I don't want to hear that voice. I don't want to bring up a nurturing voice. It's just not me."

I just looked at her, and she looked at me. The room was silent. "I feel worried that if you don't cultivate that voice . . . If you want a Solution, you do want to go inside," I said.

"I can't stand bullshit," she said. "I can't stand pasting a sweet voice on myself when I feel ripped apart inside."

"Then don't," I said.

Exasperated, she said, "Then what am I going to do? Stay in my house for the next thirty years playing computer games and eating chocolate? I have this tight knot inside me."

"When the knot is tight, you loosen it any way you can."

"But I don't want to loosen it. No, it's not that I don't want to, it's that I can't. I just can't!"

I breathed deeply.

"Take little baby steps."

Drew said, "I can take *one* little baby step. That is it. *Do you understand?* That's it."

I nodded.

"Okay, what should I start with?"

"I don't know. Whatever you are willing . . ."

"What hurts me the most is that I am so fake. I can't stand that I am so sweet all day, then by nighttime I'm living a very different life. I hate it that I want to hurt my brothers. I spend a lot of time fantasizing about how I will get back at them."

"Would you like to take out some emotional trash about them?" I asked.

She looked at me and said, "Maybe."

"Start wherever you want. Tell the story that is eating away at you the most."

"When the twins were born, my life ended, and they got all the attention. They're still getting all the attention. They are good and

I am bad. I harbor intense resentment toward them, and it has always been them against me. I have no relationship with them except at family gatherings. Next month, we're all getting together for my grandmother's eightieth birthday. I know they'll be there, and I know that I'll find some way to get back at them. Either I'll drink too much and get in an argument with them, or I'll find a way to insult one of their perfectly groomed wives."

"So that's the situation. Now what about expressing the feelings . . ."

"I feel angry that my brothers ruined my life. . . . I hate it that they're still doing it. . . . I feel angry that I hate their guts. . . . I feel angry that they don't like me."

"You sound sad," I noted.

"I feel sad that I'm not loved. . . . I feel sad that I'm different. . . . I feel afraid that I will never get over this. . . . I feel afraid that I will make an idiot out of myself. . . . I feel guilty that I still hate them all these years later . . ."

"Okay, Drew. Why don't you just hate them? Why don't you be as angry as you want to be, for as long as you want to be?"

Essential Pain and Earned Rewards: Putting Up Walls

- People could reject me.
- I won't reject myself.

- I must feel other people's feelings.
- I can empathize with them more.

- I cannot be hard on myself or others.
- Life will be easier.

- I cannot focus only on myself.
- I will have more intimacy in my life.

- I have to give as well as receive.
- Giving can feel good.

- I can't be a persecutor.
- I can be a balanced human being.

"That's indulgent."

"That's essential."

"I'm tired of being an infant with them, wanting to get back at them."

"Use the limits cycle to create intimacy with them, to see them for who they are."

"My unreasonable expectation is that my brothers are persecuting me."

"Okay."

"My unreasonable expectation is that their lives are perfect. My unreasonable expectation is that my life is awful."

Each time Drew brought up an unreasonable expectation, it seemed to pop like a bubble and disappear.

Drew seemed to have nothing left to say.

"Are you above the line?" I asked.

"No," she said. "My unreasonable expectation is that I can be rude to them and it will make me feel better."

"That may be true."

She shook her head. "A while ago, it was true. My most basic expectation was that I was going to get back at them. I would go below the line and be aggressive to punish them in any way I could."

"What's reasonable?"

"I expect myself to go to my grandmother's party and do my best to stay above the line and say nothing that is aggressive toward them. If I do go below the line, I expect myself to separate from the situation, to leave and walk around the block. Or not to open my mouth."

"Positive, powerful."

"I can do that when I'm at the party."

"Essential pain?"

"I can't hurt them while I'm there."

"The earned reward?"

"Pride. Personal pride that they can't trigger me to go below the line."

Drew looked more relaxed, but still troubled. Then she said, "But I put up walls all around me, not just with my brothers. I'm so closed at work. I don't tell anybody about my personal life. I'm too ashamed. It's vulgar that I'm thirty-two years old and I don't have a life."

"What about the orange juice?" I asked.

"What?" Drew said.

"Whatever you have inside comes out."

"So you mean, I can't open up about my personal life until I feel at peace with it?"

"Even if you felt at peace with it, it doesn't mean you would tell everything to everybody. That's what a kid does. You only tell if it's a reasonable expectation that something good will happen for you by telling."

"So what do I do?"

"First, get above the line about your personal life, then decide what you will and will not share. The door doesn't have to be locked shut or flung open; it can be in between, whatever is responsive to you."

"Okay, I'll start with a Thinking Journal. You already know this, so I don't know why I should say it."

"So you can hear it. So the feelings can arise. Just the facts."

"I have no personal life. I live like some crazy person. I love to teach and I love my students, but when I'm at home in the evenings and on the weekends, I have no discipline. I eat too much, and I do all these really lazy things, and sometimes I drink and I spend money, and I don't have what you would call a real life. Which makes me feel sorry for myself."

"Self-pity is not a Solution, Drew. Try, 'I feel angry that . . .' Wait for the anger to come up in your body. There's no rush."

She paused, then murmured, "I feel angry that I am alone."

"That sounds like sadness to me," I said. "If you want to express sadness, go ahead, then come back to anger."

"I feel sad that I am alone. . . . I feel sad that my life is so lonely. . . . I feel sad that I hurt myself. . . . I feel afraid that my life will never get better. . . . I feel guilty for being so lazy."

"Anger?"

"I feel angry that I have allowed myself to be such a loser. . . . I can't stand it that I hurt myself. . . . I am furious that I haven't made anything at all of my life. . . . I HATE it that I eat. . . . I HATE it that I am addicted to food. . . . I CAN'T STAND IT that I am so pathetic. . . . I am furious that nothing works. . . . I am angry that I can't seem to change. . . . I am angry that it has gone on for so long . . . "

"Wonderful job. Ready for the limits cycle, Drew?"

She nodded.

"What's under those feelings? What most basic expectation?"

"That I'm a loser."

I breathed deeply and waited.

"You know what I really expect? I expect that with virtually no skill and a dump-truck-load of emotional trash, I should still be able to waltz through my life with joy and happiness and not a shred of protection."

Several people in the group, accustomed to Drew's humor, began to chuckle as she did. She went on.

"I expect myself to be clothed in gossamer and surrounded by angels, and to be a perfectly joyous human being all the time!"

We all laughed a little, then settled back into the cycle.

"What is a reasonable expectation for who you are, Drew, light side, dark side, and all?"

"It's a reasonable expectation that as long as I feel bad inside, I'm going to do bad things, at least some of the time."

"What is positive and powerful about that?"

"I'm doing what I need to do."

"Essential pain?"

"I'm not totally fulfilled. I weigh more than I should. I'm not as healthy as I could be."

"The earned reward of seeing yourself and accepting yourself for who you are now?"

"Peace. Acceptance. A sense of not being the bad person, but just being who I am."

" 'So, what I need is . . .' " I prompted.

"What I need is to begin to accept myself for who I am. That's very hard for me. I've never seen myself accurately, let alone accepted myself. I need to stop being so hard on myself. I need to be willing to bring up a kind voice, one that respects me and cares about me."

"And the support you'll ask for?"

"From the group. Community Connections and a lot of calls this week. Right now, I need a lot of calls."

Tom was the first person to speak up. "Drew, as someone who has a mean side, a dark side that isn't kind or nice, I really learned a lot from your cycle. Thank you."

Drew nodded and smiled.

Mark was next. "Bravo, Drew!"

Finally, Emily spoke up. "I think you're such a wonderful teacher and have worked so hard with the skills. I love seeing you change. Thanks for inspiring me."

But Drew was not done, and I posed another thought to her.

"We were talking about opening the door—just a crack, or as much as is responsive to you. Is it a reasonable expectation that opening your life to anyone at work in any way would bring something good for you?"

Drew thought, then said, "One person. Craig. He teaches second grade, too, and he just had pancreatitis and came back to work three months ago. It came up out of the blue, but he's okay now. Craig is a photographer on the side, and the nicest guy, and has a boa constrictor in his classroom. I could talk with him."

"What would be the essential pain you would have to face in order to talk with him about your life?"

"He could reject me."

"People are inherently irritating to one another. Most people aren't deeply compatible with most people. You're right, he could reject you."

Drew said, "The risk would be that he could reject me, but the earned reward of opening up anyway and having him reject me . . ."

She thought for a moment, then said, "I know what it is. Even if he thought I was the lowest form of humanity and never spoke to me again? I would not reject myself!"

Drew was above the line and on a roll.

I asked, "What would be a reasonable expectation then? What would be reasonable to talk with him about?"

Drew's eyes sparkled, knowing she had me. "I don't know, Laurel. I'd have to keep my fingers on the pulse of my inner life."

Everyone laughed at this point, and so did I.

"How can I argue with you, Drew? If you kept your fingers on the pulse of your inner life, what is the range of possibility?"

"Well, I might tell him about my old furniture and linen . . . no, that wouldn't be that interesting to him. That would take care of how I feel and what I need, but quite frankly, I don't think he'd really be turned on by linen, and he doesn't need to hear about it for hours on end. I'd probably tell him that I don't do much on the weekends and that I'm trying to do more. That's enough."

I nodded.

Anytime an external solution is tight as a knot, it doesn't matter how we do it, but we must do something to loosen it. What Drew did was phenomenal. One small step can lead to another and another, and she seemed to be on her way.

22. Too Much Thinking

If you think well, you probably earn more money and make better conversation than those who don't. The only downside is that thinking can easily become an external solution, a spiral of obsessive thoughts and endless analysis.

All that thinking crowds out room for feeling, and feelings are required in order to connect more deeply with ourselves, with others, and with the spiritual. We may think that as intelligent, evolved people, our lives are complete. But without feelings, there is something missing. And that missing emotional depth shows up in irrational, unintelligent, and regressive ways, such as external solutions. Thinking too much breeds numbness, and numbness triggers emotional appetites.

If you think too much, it's hard to start feeling. Try as you might, the spigot to that wealth of emotion is tough to turn on. So it helps to have some patience with yourself, for you may be a *born thinker*, with a brain stem that keeps the emotional lights low. Perhaps you have such a natural capacity to think and analyze that you chose an education and profession that furthered that tendency. Now you're surrounded by thinking types, which only reinforces the trend.

It's also not uncommon for those who are naturally very feeling-oriented to think too much because they learned that pattern as a means of protecting themselves. Perhaps nobody in your family expressed feelings, or maybe life was so treacherous that feeling your feelings was not safe.

A dear friend who went through Solution training was about a year into the course when we went on a walk together along the bay. She is an attorney, so she advised me on some legal matters, and then we shared stories about our children and work. Eventually, she brought up the fact that she felt stuck in the training. She wasn't changing!

"How well have you pumped up your 'I feel . . .' skill?" I asked. "Has it become automatic to just *know* how you feel?"

"Laurel," she gasped, "it may *never* be normal for me to

feel. My norm is just to think. That's what I've done my entire life."

I thought for a moment, then offered, "How would it be for you to completely set aside the limits cycle and just check your feelings on the hour, every hour, all day long?"

She was alarmed. "You mean, *no* limits cycle?"

"Yes, no limits cycle."

Exasperated, she said, "Why? Why on Earth would you suggest that?"

"Just consider thoughts to be like your own personal form of . . . heroin. There are lots of thoughts in the limits cycle. It might be safe for you to avoid . . ." I searched for the words, ". . . shooting up!"

We both laughed and continued our walk, but what I said had some truth to it. Too much thinking can be extremely addictive, and the only real way to break the addiction is to gently, persistently, and frequently nudge yourself to feel. Thoughts about what could happen or what did, what you could have done differently, how you will handle a situation, and other intellectual mind games are fun—and they are fueled by lots of other external solutions, particularly overcontrol and perfectionism. Often harsh judgments are made easily and forgiveness hard to come by.

As a person who has too many feelings rather than too many

Reasonable Expectations: Too Much Thinking

I expect myself to do the best I can to:

- Feel my feelings at least hourly
- Go under my thoughts to find my feelings
- Avoid analyzing everything and "figuring it out"
- Deepen my feelings until they arise in my body
- Communicate my feelings rather than thoughts to others
- Express my feelings, my caring, and my warmth to others

thoughts, I find it amazing to listen to those who think too much. It all becomes so immensely complex so rapidly:

- "I start thinking about what happened and play the conversations back in my mind over and over again for hours."
- "I have thoughts in my head that nobody will ever know about. I have written at least five novels, all in my mind."
- "I really love to learn, especially about history, and I spend countless hours thinking about all the details of certain events and the people involved. I enjoy it tremendously."
- "I have lots of different parts of me, all speaking at once. One voice is on my left shoulder telling me not to do something, and the other is on my right shoulder telling me to go ahead and do it. I don't know which to listen to!"

The last point is an important one, because alternatives in any situation are simply thoughts. Without a deep awareness of feelings, we can't draw upon our intuition and wisdom. We are more apt to make poor decisions or to be indecisive, then to obsess further about our options or about the decisions we made that were not good ones.

If you're a little resistant to feeling your feelings, know that there is a certain sanity about that position. Learning to feel involves a slow retraining, and you are not in complete control of how that process evolves. The faucet may develop a slow drip of feelings, or it may open a torrent of them, flooding your inner life and overwhelming you for a little while.

It may also bring up some emotional trash. If feeling had been easy and safe for you earlier in life, you'd probably have a well-developed "I feel . . ." skill by now. The hurts of the past that you coped with by pushing them down may come popping up again. As they do, you'll need to take out your tool kit of the skills and take that trash out, piece by piece by piece.

Your inner voice may not be so nurturing at first and might say things to you like, "Get it right, buster," or, "Why can't you figure it out?" That voice needs to be fired and another one needs to be hired—one that is warm, fuzzy, accepting, and deep, that understands that this is not at all easy or safe for you to do.

Tom was accustomed to analyzing everything, but he put a fair amount of effort into checking his feelings during the first half of his training. He bought a watch that went off every hour, to remind him to check his feelings, but he still found that it was hard work and that his patterns of going numb persisted. He was such an incredible thinker; the details of every basketball game he had ever watched, the precise date of Custer's last stand, and the composer and lyricist of "Me and Bobby McGee" were all mere facts at his fingertips. But he struggled with feeling his feelings long into his climb.

In group one evening, Tom volunteered, "I don't think about feeling."

That statement said it all. Several people chuckled with fondness for Tom.

"Every once in a while, I remember to feel . . . ," he continued.

I shook my head. "Tom, you scare me to death."

"I do?" he said.

"Every time you take your fingers off the pulse of your inner life and aren't aware of your feelings, it's like letting go of your toddler's hand when you're walking through Golden Gate Park," I said matter-of-factly.

Tom didn't flinch. I tried again.

"It's like taking your hands off the steering wheel in a Formula One car."

He blinked. That had done it.

"Okay, but how do I stay aware of my feelings?"

"You take that tight fist of overcontrol," I made a tight fist, digging my fingernails into the palm of my hand, and looked over at him, "and you open your hand."

I turned my hand over and cupped it, as if to collect rainwater.

"And you see what occurs. You just keep checking inside, and if you're thinking, go under the thoughts to the feelings."

Tom was looking lost.

"Tell me when you think too much," I said.

"At night," he replied. "I wake up worrying about my cases or the deposition the next morning."

"Do a Natural Flow of Feelings. Go under the thoughts. Did it happen last night?"

"It happens almost every night. Yes, it happened last night."

"Go back to that moment when you awoke and go under the

feelings. Imagine yourself getting a piece of paper and writing a Feelings Letter, or just do a Natural Flow of Feelings in your mind."

"I'll just do the Natural Flow of Feelings. . . . I feel angry that I'm not fully prepared for this deposition. . . . I feel angry that there is not enough time to do everything. . . . I hate it that I can't get it perfect. . . . I feel angry that I can't predict everything that will happen . . . I feel sad that I'm not a better attorney . . . I feel afraid that I will make an idiot of myself. I feel afraid that I won't do a good job for my client. . . . I feel afraid I will make a mistake . . . I feel guilty for not preparing more."

I asked, "Do you feel any more in balance?"

"Actually, I feel like I want to go to sleep."

Several people in the room laughed.

"When else do you think too much?" I continued.

"All day long. As soon as I get to work . . . actually as soon as I get in the car to go to work, I start thinking . . . actually, as soon as I get in the *shower* in the morning. Let's just say that I always think, except when I am relaxing at night, or with Michelle, or sometimes when I'm at the gym."

"What do you need to interrupt your numbness?"

"Michelle would say that I need a blood transfusion."

I didn't get it, but the noise in the room told me that some people did.

"Tom, what would help you?"

"I'll go back to the watch, having it beep every hour, and I'll put an hourly reminder on my computer. With two things beeping me, I should remember to check my feelings."

"Okay," I said. "That sounds like a plan."

But I wasn't satisfied that it would be enough for Tom. It would help, but to the extent that his inner life was putting on the emotional brakes because of emotional trash, it wouldn't be enough. I was also concerned that his work was in the way, along with his external solutions. When he came to group the following week, I checked with him about his progress.

"It went fine the first morning," he said. "I checked my feelings every hour, but after that, I ignored the beeps. Finally, I turned the alarms off."

"Shall we do a quick check on how to make this easier?" I asked.

He shrugged. "Sure."

"Nurturing inner voice? How is that coming along?"

Tom frowned, then said, "Not bad. It's getting stronger."

"Nurturing and limits skills? When you use them, are your skills strong enough so that you usually pop yourself back in balance rather than staying in that abyss of numbness, false highs, or unnecessary lows?"

"Yup, I'm getting better at that."

"Emotional trash?" I queried.

"It's slow. Very slow. I don't like taking it out and can't stand being a whiner and complainer. My parents did all right by me."

"It's not about blaming your parents," I said. "It's about *you*, the leftover feelings *you* have that get in the way of having the most health and happiness possible in your life."

"I take some trash out each week, but I'm not into it. I don't like doing it."

"I don't expect you to like doing it."

"Well, I don't know what to say."

"There was a time when you shut off your feelings."

"No, I didn't. I just went outside and got away from everybody."

"There was a time when you shut off your feelings," I reiterated. "The idea is to consider what was going on inside you, not whether you played basketball or went outside."

Tom was silent.

"I didn't know enough to feel. I didn't have feelings."

"People are born with feelings. It's just to what extent they are aware of them."

"I remember feeling angry at my sister about a toy. I remember my mother telling me to give it back to her. I remember my mother telling me I couldn't go across the street because I wasn't as old as my sister and it wasn't safe. I remember feeling . . . sad about that. Feeling left out."

It was the first I'd ever heard about Tom's sister.

Tom continued. "I recall feeling angry about her. I can't remember feeling angry toward my mother. I felt sorry for her. Toward my dad, I felt nothing really. I really don't remember and don't want to remember. There is nothing to remember."

I was silent.

"Okay, I'll do a Natural Flow of Feelings," he said.

I nodded.

Tom said, "I feel angry that I didn't feel. . . . I feel angry that

I didn't feel safe. . . . I feel angry that I was alone. . . . I feel sad that nobody cared how I felt. . . . I feel sad that I was all by myself. . . . I feel sad that I didn't feel loved. . . . I feel afraid that if I say something, they will be mad. . . . I feel sad that if I talk about what is going on with me, things will get worse. . . . I feel guilty that I shut down emotionally. . . . I feel guilty that I stopped feeling."

Several people in the room let out huge sighs. So did I.

"Create some intimacy with that child you were," I urged. "See him for who he was in that situation."

Tom shrugged and said almost in a whisper, "Well, it was reasonable to shut off his feelings."

"Yes, it was reasonable to shut off his feelings. Positive and powerful?"

Essential Pain and Earned Rewards: Too Much Thinking

- I must be emotionally present.
- More intimacy with myself. More intimacy with others.

- Feelings can hurt.
- Not feeling can hurt even more.

- I won't be able to figure it out.
- I don't need to figure it out.

- In the past, it was not safe to feel.
- Now it is safer to feel.

- I am not in complete control.
- Relief from analyzing everything!

- I must feel.
- I get to feel!

- I must feel my feelings.
- I will be more authentic, present, and alive!

"I protected myself."

"Essential pain?"

"I stopped feeling. I stopped feeling the good feelings."

"Earned reward?"

"I stopped feeling some of the bad feelings."

"Now, what do you expect of yourself? What is reasonable?"

"I expect myself to start feeling."

"Positive, powerful?"

"Feelings don't always have to hurt."

"Essential pain?"

"It takes a lot of hard work. I'd have to face the essential pain that as a child, nobody in my family felt their feelings, including me. Our family was emotionally . . . ," he searched for the word, ". . . challenged!"

With that, several people laughed.

"The earned reward?"

"I will feel. I will deal with the reality of my life. I will be freer from the past. I will feel more alive."

I was exhausted just listening to him, and so were others. I asked for Tender Morsels, and Emily spoke up.

"Tom, that was so helpful to me. I go numb, and the idea that it started young is new to me. Thanks for your cycle."

Drew said, "Tom, I feel . . . happy and proud just listening to you!"

Mark said, "I hate feeling, too, my friend. Thanks for inspiring me. Great job, Tom."

We weren't done. I said, "Tom, one more thing. What about lifestyle surgery? To get your threshold of need for the skills down."

"I'm pretty healthy," he responded.

"Body Pride?" I asked.

"I'm not drinking at all."

"You're not?"

"No. I'm not sure I can drink without drinking too much. When I have a Solution, I'll see. Maybe I'll drink socially. I don't know. Right now, I'm not taking any chances."

"Michelle?"

"Yes. It's going well, and I want to keep it that way."

I was doubtful. The drives to go to excess were still turned on. Perhaps he was getting enough external nurturing from Michelle that he didn't need to drink, but that wouldn't last.

Once the "in love" stage passed, he would need more internal skill.

"Good Health?" I continued.

"I'm in great health. I just went to the doctor, and he says for a guy my age, I'm very healthy."

"Balanced Eating?"

"My diet is fine."

"Mastery Living?"

"Yep, I'm exercising and doing well."

"Tom, may I give you a suggestion?"

"Sure," he said.

"Just keep doing what you're doing. Taking out trash, checking your feelings, and watching for any other excesses to crop up since you're not drinking. It can come up in odd ways, like external solutions we haven't even talked about. Anything you use to excessively detach from yourself—exercising to excess, finding yourself hostile and overcompetitive, obsessive thinking—anything. I'm not saying this to judge, but because my job is to help you reach your Solution."

"I know," he said.

23. People-Pleasing

M ost of us are capable of having an extra glass of champagne at a wedding or an extra blueberry pancake on Sunday morning without spiraling into a state of overdrinking or overeating.

For many of us, people-pleasing is a similar indulgence. Now and then, we dip into our well of neediness for others' approval—sometimes when we least expect it. Perhaps we hear ourselves dropping names, boasting about a success, or saying precisely what we know a person wants to hear, even when the words have no grounding in our own personal truth.

Ouch, you might think, how could I abandon my personal integrity just to win someone's approval? What am I, a four-year-old wanting Mommy to love me best?

The short answer is, perhaps so.

When I see myself doing such things, I have a good chuckle at myself and perhaps stroke my arm in a cherishing sort of way and say to myself, "There, there, Laurel. I guess there's still a little bit of you down there below the line, needing the approval of others. Oh, well—that may always be part of your dark side. Don't worry. You don't have to be perfect to be wonderful."

But for some, the external solution of people-pleasing is no small thing. It runs their lives! It is so incredibly disorienting to be in your *own* mind and in *another's* at the same time. There are outfits that find their way to the floor because, on second, third, or fourth thought, people may not like them. There is constant thinking and rethinking about what you will say or what you should do. The more people-pleasing invades your inner life, the less attached you are to pleasing yourself, and the less able you are to muscle up on these skills. In fact, a day of people-pleasing can slow down your Solution training nearly as much as a morning bingeing on doughnuts or an evening downing a few too many drinks.

Understanding why people-pleasing is an external solution brings, for many, a painful realization. *The root cause of people-*

pleasing is often parental absence, aloofness, or rejection. As adults, we walk through our day looking for the approval we didn't get as a child from our parents. The child we were needed that approval so much we were willing to do handstands to get it, or even to abandon our inner truth. That child needed approval then, and the child within us still needs it now, until we move that part of us above the line. Our job is to take out the emotional trash of that past hurt, fill ourselves with the sanctuary of approval we need now, and muscle up on the skills that enable us to respond to people differently in the present. It takes a real willingness to take people-pleasing seriously as an external solution and to use our tool kit of skills over and over again until the torment of people-pleasing finally ends.

Drew noticed her tendency to yearn for others' approval when she was in teacher meetings. She was a very smart woman with very good ideas, but if she knew her views might offend someone, she'd clam up. She was more willing to seem slow or mediocre than to risk displeasing others.

She brought this up in our group. "I know I'm manipulative when I put on a sweet face and tell people what they want to hear, and I'm starting to find it tiring. So what if they like me? They don't know me. They just know the person who pleases them. If they knew my true character, my honest opinions, my little annoying idiosyncrasies, they'd probably reject me anyway."

Drew was beginning to have enough skill to be aware of the pattern and how it affected her. For Drew, ending people pleasing would be a slow proposition that would probably culminate near the top of the tree. As she used the method and climbed the tree, she would have more intimacy with herself, more sanctuary and integration within, and less tolerance for being held hostage to the approval of others. She had already started to shift to more authentic relationships.

Drew said, "My friendship with Craig, the second-grade teacher whose room is next door to mine, is different. I don't seem to care what he thinks of me. I don't know whether I am less needy in general or if he doesn't bring up my emotional trash, but I'm really enjoying having a relationship that is so easy. All I have to do is stay above the line and be grounded in myself."

Perhaps it has crossed your mind that when Tom stopped drinking in response to his deepening relationship, he was people-pleasing. But after having listened to him do cycles, it seemed this wasn't the case. People-pleasing rears its head when we abandon ourselves to win others' approval, when there is no reasonably steady stream of self-approval within.

Tom had done a lot of cycles on his remorse about his drinking during his marriage. He had felt the anger, sadness, fear, and guilt that come with looking back on things we've done that we wish we hadn't. He didn't want a life of ducking problems through alcohol, or staying the twelve-year-old that drinking allowed him to be in order to escape feeling life's pain and his own evolution. He wanted to be a grown-up in a grown-up relationship, and he met Michelle, a grown-up with whom he was deeply compatible in so many ways. Not drinking to excess would please Michelle, but his ultimate motivations for not drinking were to please himself, to feel a sense of personal pride and balance, and to increase his likelihood of getting what he most wanted in this life: intimacy.

Yet a subtle strain of people-pleasing did find its way into Tom's life, and it had to do with his possessions. He enjoyed having nice things—and who wouldn't enjoy having a Rolex, a Porsche, and a closet full of designer suits? But Tom wanted the best in life not only for his own personal enjoyment but also because of the satisfaction he derived from knowing that *other people* were aware he had these things and that they admired him for his success and good taste. This tendency would probably lessen as he reached his Solution, but on the other hand, who really cares? Having a Solution does not mean we don't have a dark side or various subtle strains of external solutions. Was this tendency really getting in the way of Tom's health and happiness in ways that mattered to him? Probably not. If it ever did, he could always take out his tool kit, use the skills, and have a good chance of watching it fade.

Emily was in a different situation. She would need a huge collection of tools—a crowbar might come in handy—to dislodge the excess of people-pleasing from her inner life.

In addition to rescuing others, Emily incessantly focused on pleasing them. Between the two excesses, she was nearly always "outside" her own body. She gave away her power to others so freely, it was as though she walked around with her purse open and said, to anyone who'd speak with her, "Here! Take whatever you want! All you have to do is love me, and you can have anything I have. Here, take it, please!"

Again, most of us who people-please have very similar stories to tell: an early life in which there was at least one parent who

Reasonable Expectations: People-Pleasing

I expect myself to do the best I can to:

- Know myself so well and accept myself so deeply that I don't need the approval of others

- Develop a nurturing, approving voice within

- Recognize that *their* approval is no substitute for *my own* approval

- Live my life in a way that pleases me, even if it doesn't please others

- Recognize that just because others reject me, it doesn't mean I'm bad

- Take out emotional trash about past rejections

rejected us or withheld love. Or it may have been a parent with whom we had great sympathy, but who was emotionally separated from us in some way; we thought that if we just said or did the right thing, we would win that parent's love and feel peace for the first time. We shifted from looking within for acceptance to looking without.

The plot thickens. As children grow, they think harder about what will please their parents and others. As they contort themselves more, their people-pleasing separates them further from themselves. They become more externally focused and less internally aware. The struggle grows more entrenched, even frantic, and even if they do get the approval for which they yearn, that approval is of a person who is *not them*. What's more, the doors of the heart are closed to true approval of who they are, and will open only when they have grieved their losses from the past and given themselves the approval they did not receive early on.

When I brought up people-pleasing to our group, Emily was the first to want to do cycles on it.

Emily said, "I have no idea where to begin with people-pleasing. There is no one person I can pick out. I lose myself in pleasing my children, my husband, my piano teacher . . . even social friends. This weekend, Clay and I are going to go to a black-tie affair for the symphony. I know I'll try on five different dresses from my closet, then go out and buy another one and fuss over every detail of that. Then I'll go to the party and focus on whether people liked me or not, whether they thought I was attractive or not, and whether what I said was interesting to them or not. I will no doubt comfort myself with too many martinis and too much food and end up feeling sick the next day, still obsessing about what other people thought of me the night before!"

"Emily, when you're yearning for someone's approval, it may be related to emotional trash. When you're doing cycles, be sure to look for emotional trash first. If you can take that out, the cycle will have far more effect. That feeling you get when you're yearning for someone's attention: What does that look like, sound like, feel like from early life?"

"Oh, definitely my mother. It feels just like my mother."

"Perhaps you could do a Thinking Journal about her."

Emily nodded. "My mother had no time for me. She was busy with my father, and she always seemed so unhappy. There were always somber, unhappy noises in our house. I felt like I had done something wrong but I didn't know what. I just kept trying to make her happy and trying to do things so she would smile at me and love me, but it hardly ever worked . . ."

Her eyes widened, and tears glistened at their edges. "I feel sad that my mother didn't love me. . . . I feel sad that I grew up feeling wrong. . . . I feel sad that I was hungry for her love and she never gave it to me. . . . I feel sad that I still feel the pain of it . . . I feel afraid that hole in me will never be filled . . .

"I feel guilty for being such a big baby, still feeling sorry for myself that my mother wasn't loving to me."

"Emily—anger. You need anger," I said.

She looked at me wide-eyed over her red glasses.

"I don't have anger."

"Emily, you have anger. It's just not easy to access it."

"But I can't blame her!" she cried.

"I'm not asking you to. Anger toward the situation, anger toward her lack of skills, anger toward the experience you had growing up or the effect it has had on you . . ."

On Emily's very white neck, blotches of red started appearing.

"I feel FURIOUS that you didn't love me. . . . I feel ANGRY that I was starved for your love. . . . How could you not love me? How could you ignore me? How could you make me feel so small and unimportant? How could you not cherish me? . . . I hate what you did to me. I hate it that I've spent my life looking for love from everyone and everything all because YOU didn't give it to me. . . . I feel angry that you did that to me. . . . I feel angry that I didn't get your love."

Emily took a huge breath. She looked exhausted, but relieved. Everyone in the circle seemed to take a big deep breath, too. Several people reached for the tissue box in the center of the circle and wiped their eyes. Mark didn't use a tissue, but his eyes were moist and his face red.

"Beautifully done, Emily."

Everyone clapped.

"What was your most basic expectation, the one that is under all those feelings?"

"I think what I expected was that if I was just good enough, she would love me. I expected that if she loved me, I was good, and if she didn't . . . I'm not sure. I think my expectation was not that I was bad, that there was something terribly wrong with me."

The blotches on Emily's neck were still very red.

"What is a reasonable expectation?"

"I don't know. I really don't know."

"Let's try out a few and see if any of them resonate for you, okay?"

"Sure."

"Did your mom have these skills?"

"Ha! Hardly," Emily replied.

"Then how about, 'I expected a woman who didn't have these skills to see herself, to see me, and love me for who I am.'"

"That's a good one."

"In your own words . . ."

"It was a reasonable expectation that my mother didn't have the skills to give me the message that she approved of me. It is a reasonable expectation that that would hurt and that I would try harder to get her approval, that I would learn that approval comes from others, not from me."

"Great. Positive, powerful . . ."

"I was taught to people-please."

"The essential pain?"

"The essential pain of pleasing others?"

"If you like."

"The essential pain is that I lose myself. I am invisible to me."

Essential Pain and Earned Rewards:
People-Pleasing

- I can't rely on the approval of others.
- I can approve of myself.

- Other people won't validate me.
- I can validate myself.

- My parent didn't make me feel loved.
- I can mourn the loss and make myself feel loved.

- I have wasted time seeking approval of others.
- I don't have to do that anymore.

- I must face myself.
- I will know myself and learn to love myself.

- The approval of others doesn't fill the void.
- The spiritual and I can fill the void.

"The payoff of continuing to people-please?"

"There is no payoff. It's a painful pattern."

"There is always a payoff or you wouldn't be doing it."

"I've lost you. I'm not sure what you're saying."

"Okay, try it another way. An expectation. 'I expect myself to stop people-pleasing, to get my approval from myself, not from others.'"

Emily was quiet, seemingly thinking about that expectation. She knit her brow and brought her index finger to her mouth, rubbing her lips gently.

"I guess the essential pain would be that I'd have to give up. I'd have to accept that I will never be cherished by my mother. I will never get her full attention and her complete approval."

Emily looked very, very sad. She cocked her head and stayed quiet for several moments.

"But the earned reward would be that I would stop the yearning. I would begin to face myself and, in time, cherish myself."

Her eyes met mine, and she said in a quiet voice, "This is very sad."

"Yes it is, Emily, and it will take some time to grieve it, to feel the feelings and let them fade."

She seemed to perk up. "I can do it, though, and it's time. What I need is to take out emotional trash. And I need to go to that party on Saturday evening and stay above the line and *not* people-please."

At least half the group had the external solution of people-pleasing, so there was lots of interest in giving Tender Morsels.

Mark said, "That was a gargantuan cycle, Emily. You were doing my work for me. I really loved your cycle. Thank you."

Drew said, "Emily, it was so painful to listen to, but I knew you had courage to do it. You are inspiring me to take out some emotional trash of my own."

Emily turned to me. "I'm serious. What can I do so I won't people-please at the party? I'm sick of doing it, and I want to stop!"

Emily was close enough to the top of the tree to do some focused limits work. This work often triggers a shift in the dominance of neural networks, from those that support imbalance to those that support balance.

"Emily, first continue to take out trash. Be sure you feel red-hot anger, not the 'good girl' anger that feels like sadness or a semi-compliment, but good old 'bad girl' hostility. That anger will help you toss out the emotional trash so it loses much of its power over you."

"Okay," she said. "I can do that."

"There are two more tools I will give you. One is to grind into your bones some basic expectations that will create a foundation for a new life free of people-pleasing. What is the most basic expectation, the foundational one, that you would want to grind into the belly of your emotional brain?"

Emily frowned, then said, "I expect myself to get approval from me, not from others."

"Incredible! Say it ten times."

"I expect myself to get approval from me, not from others. I expect myself to get approval from me, not from others . . . I expect myself to get approval from me, not from others. I expect myself to get approval from me, not from others. I expect myself to get approval from me, not from others. I expect myself to get approval from me, not from others . . ."

"Keep going."

"I expect myself to get approval from me, not from others. I expect myself to get approval from me, not from others. Is that ten?"

"Two more."

"I expect myself to get approval from me, not from others. I expect myself to get approval from me, not from others! Phewww. That feels pretty good. That helped!"

"How many times do you think you've consciously and unconsciously had the opposite, competing expectation?"

"About a million."

"So that's a start. My suggestion is to do that three times a day, like breakfast, lunch, and dinner, every day, until it is part of you, until you just know it and it's deeply true for who you are."

Emily nodded. "You said there was one more thing."

"Yes. People-pleasing is a symptom of having skinny boundaries, of losing yourself to others, knowing how they feel and what they need but not how *you* feel or what *you* need."

"Like rescuing," said Emily.

"Correct. So the tool is to change how you respond, in the moment at the party and before. Over and over again, in a big, lumberjack voice, say to yourself, 'How do I feel? What do I need?' "

She smiled and said, "I don't want to do the lumberjack thing. I'll be in Bruno Magli strappy shoes and probably in a black dress that shows every bit of cleavage I have or can create."

"Okay, erase that. How about . . ."

"I know!" Emily piped up. "I could use my dead aunt Nora's voice. I could have her whispering into my ear, 'Now, Emily, how do you feel and what do you need? Don't worry about how they feel and what they need. Who are they anyway?' "

The whole room erupted in laughter, and the session ended.

The following week, Emily started reporting on what had happened before the group even began.

"I did a ton of Community Connections. I practiced saying, 'I get approval from me, not from others,' at least two hundred times. And when I went to the party, I used my dead aunt Nora's voice and kept asking, 'How do I feel and what do I need?' and it worked. I had a great time, maybe the best time I've ever had at one of those events, and the next morning I didn't have a martini hangover or a food hangover. I didn't obsess about everything I had said, what people thought, or how I could have said it better. I just went about my day . . . happily!"

Emily seemed to be nearing the top of the tree.

VI. REAPING LIFE'S SWEETEST REWARDS

24. Integration

For most people, integration arrives near the top of the tree. It is such a relief to know and accept yourself, to leave behind that experience of being held hostage to the chaos of being very good, then, in the blink of an eye, very bad. It is liberating to know that, in fact, we have a safe core of personal authenticity, and that although we have a dark side, so does everyone else. Progress, not perfection, is all that is required.

If you are on Pathway 1, you will probably find that a robust sense of self-knowing, self-acceptance, wholeness, and authenticity comes just as you approach the top of the tree, but well before you reap your sweetest fruit.

If you are on Pathway 2 or 3 and using the complete solution course, a full-bodied sense of integration usually arrives during the fifth kit, after about a year of using the method.

It's important to watch for and work toward integration because that sweet reward is the bedrock of intimacy with ourselves. Its arrival is often followed by a deepened capacity for intimacy with others and with the spiritual. My experience has been that most people need all three forms of intimacy to have a secure, robust, and lasting Solution.

Reaping the reward of integration takes going back in time, back to when you were whole, when you had harmony and balance within, and when you were aware of a true center, a safe sanctuary, a vision of yourself that was singular, integrated, and whole.

It also means being willing to chart the course our inner life has taken since then, and the ways and times that our integration and wholeness were broken. Keep in mind that when we were children, in the best of all worlds, our parents would have supplied us with the nurturing and limits to keep us above the line, feeling integrated and whole. When they were not able to, we went below the line. Although we still were whole, we didn't feel as if we were.

So how do we pick up the pieces and put them back together again? Like all the other rewards, we approach them during the second half of the climb and as the excesses that cut into your rewards begin to abate. You do cycles that offer the "glue" to reestablish that wholeness, particularly some of the expectations and essential pains mentioned in this chapter. In time, you will notice a growing sense of personal integration that ushers in a feeling of security that nourishes you and makes you strong.

It often helps to practice bringing up a nurturing—not depriving or indulging—inner voice. You are accessing not the bad voice or the good voice, but the voice that sees all of you and appreciates both your dark and light sides.

You might start noticing the times when you are below the line and can only see your dark side or, conversely, only your light side. You know you're in trouble when you can see one but not the other.

Perhaps you bring out that nurturing voice and say to yourself, "There I go again, splitting. I can only see what's good about me. Better think of three things that are part of my dark side. That will help balance me."

Or conversely, "My Lord, you'd think I was the worst human being on Earth. I can only see my dark side. There is so much good about me, whether I sense it or not. Better think of three things that are good about me or I will stay split and won't have any of the strength that integration can bring."

These two little tools might sound foolish, but I don't think they will when you are below the line, sorely split, and using them!

How You Act—Unless you have balanced expectations solidly inside you, each time you do something "wrong," it could penetrate your self-image and toss you below the line into identity chaos. In order to feel whole and self-accepting, the most basic expectation must shift from "I expect myself to do everything well" to "I expect myself to do the very best I am able to do. Sometimes I will do things very well, and sometimes I will not."

How You Feel—A simple separation of self from feelings is equally helpful. If your expectation is that to be a good person you must always be happy, you are in deep trouble! The expectation that supports integration is something more like "I expect myself to have good feelings and bad feelings. I am not bad when I have bad feelings or good when I have good feelings. I am

Reasonable Expectations: Integration

I expect myself do the best I can to:

- See myself as not all good or all bad
- Know and accept my body and myself
- Honor and appreciate my light side
- Know and accept my dark side
- Use the skills to minimize the hurt my dark side can cause
- Remind myself that I don't have to be perfect to be wonderful

always the person I am, regardless of my emotions in the moment."

How Your Body Looks—Have you ever had a bad hair day and watched your sense of self-worth take a nosedive? What about gaining a few pounds and being sure that you are a worthless person? How many days each week do we not measure up to our admittedly arbitrary assessment of looking okay? It could be a day or two, or nearly every day. On those days, if we have not separated our self-worth from our appearance, we will go right below the line, and any sense of self-acceptance will disappear.

Here is a sturdy expectation you may want to experiment with on those days: "I expect myself to do the best I can to stay above the line and to take care of my appearance. Some days I will look good, and some days I won't."

When all else fails and you can't seem to feel whole and integrated, consider using one of my favorite positive, powerful thoughts of the method: "You don't have to be perfect to be wonderful."

The first time Drew heard that phrase used in group, her face blanched. I asked her if she wanted to do cycles, and she said yes.

"I don't feel integrated, and I don't accept myself. It's one of my biggest sources of pain because I'm such a big fake. Nobody knows what's inside of me. I go to work and everyone thinks I am happy and have this wonderful life. Everyone buys my facade . . ."

"Drew, are you sure?" I asked.

"Of course I'm sure," she said. "I'm the most cooperative and positive person . . ."

"Drew, is it a reasonable expectation that if someone at work thought you weren't authentic, they'd tell you?"

She frowned. "Well . . . I guess not. Maybe not."

"But that's not the point. The point is, how does not feeling authentic get in the way of your health and your happiness? How does it *matter* to you?"

"Well, it's everything," said Drew. "It's who I am. And when I don't know who I am . . . when I go back and forth from being bad to being good, it's exhausting!"

"How long have you been in training?"

"A little over a year."

"Do you have emotional balance?"

"Somewhat, but I think I'm a remedial Solution person."

Several people chuckled with fondness for Drew. She was the first to point out her failings and always magnified them.

"It takes as long as it takes," I reminded her.

"I know."

"Have you been practicing the skills and taking out trash?" She nodded.

"Doing three or more Community Connections per week?" Again, Drew nodded.

"May I give you a thought?"

"Yes, I want you to," Drew said.

"I think there may be some big pieces of emotional trash that are holding you back, and I wouldn't be surprised if your work on integration will trigger you to take some of them out."

"Good. I'm ready. I'm getting sick of this. I've seen three people in the group get their Solution, and I feel like I'm never going to get mine, that I'll be a retired schoolteacher and I'll still be in this group."

There were more chuckles from the group. Drew was very loved in this circle, and for good reasons—among them, her brutal honesty, her dry humor, and the fact that she always returned connection calls and was an incredibly empathetic listener. She had taken several people who were new to the group under her wing and made several connections with them to help them get started.

"Drew, would you like to do some work today?"

"Yes!" she said.

"I want you to imagine that from the earliest time in your life there was a sense of wholeness . . ."

"I think I did feel whole at one point. I was happy. Then the twins were born when I was eight."

"You've taken out that trash before . . ."

"About a thousand times, or at least that's what it feels like."

"You've done the Natural Flow of Feelings: angry, sad, afraid, and guilty."

"That's only recently, though. Before that, I was in therapy for years, and all I could feel was depressed about it."

"When you're below the line and feeling depressed, it feels bad, but it doesn't heal. Now you have more skill in staying balanced, and you've probably weakened enough of those dominant neural networks that favor imbalance . . ."

"I think that's right. That's what it feels like."

"You can begin to throw that trash out and truly heal."

"I'd like that."

"Drew, the cycles we're going to do together wouldn't have the power they'll have now unless you had made the first half of the climb."

"I know myself better now. I know how I feel and what I need, and there is more of a sanctuary, I think."

"Good. Just start with your Thinking Journal whenever you're ready. Tell the story of losing your integration, of falling away from feeling authentic and whole."

Drew reached for the tissue box and put it on her lap. She took out two tissues and dabbed her eyes, which were already filled with tears.

"Tell the story. Stay in thoughts."

"I was just fine until the boys were born. I thought it was going to be great to have brothers, and I was so excited and happy. And then when they were born, my parents disappeared. I lost my mother's attention, and my dad was busy with the boys, and nobody cared about me. I was totally alone . . ." She looked at me and said, "I think I need to go into feelings."

I nodded.

"I feel fucking furious that they deserted me! . . . I hate them for leaving me, for making me feel so alone and so . . . deserted. I hate them for what they did to me. . . . I feel sad that I was so alone and afraid there was something defective in me and guilty that I kept acting so bad."

She sighed. "There! That's all."

I took a deep breath, then said, "Drew, for a moment, would you please put the fingers of your right hand on your left wrist?"

We both put our fingers on our wrists. "What I meant to ask you to do was to go back to the time when you took your fingers off the pulse of your inner life and abandoned yourself. When you were little, you didn't have the skills to stay with yourself. I want you to grieve the loss of what went on inside you, your change in your relationship with yourself."

Drew breathed deeply. She had a cold, and everyone in the room could hear her breathing.

She squinted and seemed to be deep in thought. Finally, she said, "I stopped seeing myself then. I lost my connection to myself and didn't have one with them, and I hated God for doing this to me, so I was spinning out of control . . ."

She took a big gulp of air, then began. "I feel angry that I was so confused. . . . I feel angry that I tried to do handstands, to be so good and so responsible and so sweet, telling them what they wanted to hear, not the truth. . . . I feel sad that I was so vicious and secretly did whatever I could to pay them back and get at them in ways I could hurt them the most. Stealing, getting fat, doing whatever I could to get their attention . . ." Her face relaxed and looked playful. "I feel sad that I wasn't more effective!"

Drew laughed, and so did a couple of others.

"I feel sad that I was so alone. . . . I feel sad that I had to be too good and then . . . and then too bad. I'm sad that I lost any sense of being whole. . . . I feel afraid that I will keep being too good and then being as aggressively bad to myself as I want to be, and that I will never feel solid." She looked toward me. "You know, solid."

"Yes, I know. Not chaotic. Seeing yourself for who you are, light side, dark side, and all. Knowing and accepting yourself and still being mindful of your need to use the skills to minimize the pain your dark side can cause."

"Yes," she said.

"Drew, I don't know if you're mad enough."

She darted back, "I'm mad. I'm plenty mad."

"You need that anger to separate from that event. You have

needed to feel your anger, sadness, fear, and guilt about that traumatic event, that tremendous loss in your life. You have felt it
enough so that it may well be 'loosened up' enough for you to
heal it, for you to throw that piece of emotional trash out."

Drew listened attentively.

"To do that, you'll have to have implanted in your inner life
enough of the skill to nurture and set limits from within—and
enough that you can see yourself and your parents accurately. It
is only when you see what occurred with the twenty-twenty
vision that comes with doing cycles over and over again that you
can deeply heal."

Drew blinked. "I'm ready."

"Let's go to the limits cycle, the cycle of acceptance and forgiveness."

Drew said nothing; she was going deep within herself. She
sensed that there was a possibility that in this cycle that hurt
could finally heal.

"My unreasonable expectation was that if I was just good
enough, they would love me . . ."

I waited. Drew was skilled now and would know where to go
next.

"My unreasonable expectation was also that if I was just bad
enough, they would love me . . ."

She waited for a moment for those thoughts to sink in.

"The reasonable expectation, given who they were, their skill
level in that situation, and who I was, is that they loved me but
didn't have the skills to show me. I was a child who tended to
withdraw into being overly good or overly bad, instead of just
getting in their faces telling them what was bothering me."

She was doing a fabulous job, and I didn't want to stop her
momentum.

"Positive and powerful . . . ," I prompted.

Drew hesitated. This was an important next step, as she normally would say something negative and powerless to herself,
thereby stopping the cycle. She needed to identify the opposite of
what she normally said to herself.

"What I would normally say to myself is, 'They are bad parents,' and, 'I am not lovable,' or, 'There is something wrong with
me.' "

"Which positive words, the opposite of those, do you need to
hear right now?" I asked.

Drew's face turned pale. "What I need to hear is: 'There is nothing wrong with me.' "

"Good. The essential pain?"

She rubbed her forehead. "There's lots of it. I had an unhappy childhood. But I've said that before. This time the essential pain is different. The essential pain I must face in order to accept those expectations is . . . I'm not bad and neither are they. It was a difficult situation. They weren't perfect and . . . neither was I."

She took a huge, deep breath and calmness swept over her face.

"You can feel the shift in your body?" I asked.

Drew nodded and smiled.

I asked, "The earned reward, Drew?"

She thought for a moment, then said, "The earned reward is that I can forgive them . . . ," she sighed again, now speaking very slowly, ". . . and I can forgive myself." She looked at me straight in the eyes and said, "I guess the struggle, that awful drama of being good or bad, hating them or hating myself, is finally over."

There was total quiet in the room.

Drew looked over at me and said quietly, "So what I need is to be grateful that I feel more peace than I have felt since I was eight years old." Now a smile spread slowly across her face. "And the support I need is what all of you just gave me. Listening to me . . . and the love and safety I felt as I was doing that cycle."

The room was still hushed.

Emily spoke first. "Drew, the way you healed in that moment—I'll never forget that. Thank you for inspiring me to take out my own emotional trash."

Drew nodded.

Mark gave a Tender Morsel, and so did Tom.

As much as Drew had begun to heal her hurt in a far deeper and more effective way, she would not have an abundance of integration until she performed some lifestyle surgery and developed a dependably nurturing inner voice.

Several sessions went by without Drew doing any cycles, just reporting her accomplishments—taking out more emotional trash about her dark side and about the early loss of authenticity—and her challenges. Then one week, she came to the group with a look on her face that suggested she was ready to do some important work. Sure enough, when I asked who wanted to do some in-depth work that day, Drew raised her hand.

"I'm doing well with healing the past, but I want to get rid of the patterns that I still have that came from that past. I want to invade my mind and change it."

I was elated with her comment. Some people only want to deal with the past. Unfortunately, until they revise the internal software that was downloaded into their inner lives at the time of the trauma, the hurt will keep occurring. More and more emotional trash will pile up!

At the point during her childhood when Drew went below the line and split into the little girl who was alternately too good and too bad, there were changes in her abilities to nurture and set limits for herself. Instead of one nurturing inner voice, she may well have found herself with two voices: one harsh and one indulgent. Instead of clear, flexible expectations that would help her to have a coherent, reasonably consistent way of behaving, she might have found herself with a set of wildly unreasonable expectations shooting off in all directions.

As a result, the harsh consequences of her actions—the ones driven by unreasonable expectations—would seem to her to be essential pain, the unavoidable pain of the human condition. Self-abuse and self-neglect would seem "normal" to her. In the meanwhile, she would be missing the "practice" of feeling life's true essential pain and becoming accustomed to moving through that pain and opening her hands to the profound rewards of life.

No wonder Drew felt like such a little girl, a small child in a grown-up body. It was not because her inherent goodness, strength, and wisdom were not there; it was just that her inner workings doggedly avoided listening to them. Time had gone by, but because she had not been exposed to the cycles moving in a balanced way within her, she had not truly matured.

Drew was halfway or more through her climb and far more balanced than she had ever been, so it was important that she begin to fine-tune her skills. That fine-tuning would lead to the more sensitive and effective work that usually comes toward the end of the climb, and that would surely fuel her ability to receive the reward of integration.

"Drew, I'm extremely happy with the way you've been taking out emotional trash, and even more pleased that you are ready to work on how you use the skills in the present! Where would you like to begin?"

She said, "It's my voice. I have two of them, not one. Say anything to me, and I'll tell you what my voices say to me."

"Okay. Drew, I'm so happy you're taking out that really difficult emotional trash. You're doing a great job."

"See, it happened. First I said to myself, 'You did an incredible job!' Then, immediately pops up the thought, 'She's wrong. You did a horrible job. You'll never get this.'"

"There is no singular voice that knows you and loves you and accepts you for who you are?"

"None, and there never has been."

"There was before you were eight, wasn't there?"

"But I don't remember that. I didn't have an aunt Nora, like Emily—not even a dead one. All I've got is a cat, and my cat is always scratching me. She was taken away from her mother too early."

And with that, Drew's eyes began to brim with tears. She put her hands over her face and shook her head, then said, "I don't want to do cycles today. I want to get on with these skills. Nothing is going to change until I get the internal wreckage of my childhood out of my head. I can't stand it anymore. I want advice."

"That pattern of splitting, all negative and all positive, is extremely destructive," I said. "It will take some work, some practice to retrain your inner life to have one coherent voice that knows and loves you. If you don't have that voice yourself, you'll have to borrow one from someone else."

She shrugged.

"Do you want suggestions from the group?" I asked.

"Sure, I'd like that."

Mark said, "Use Ronald Reagan's voice. The way he would always say in that warm, fatherly voice, 'Now there you go again.'"

Emily offered, "What about Mr. Rogers from *Mr. Rogers' Neighborhood*?"

Tom smiled and said, "At first I was going to suggest Howard Cosell, the sports commentator, but I reconsidered. What about Mother Teresa?"

Drew laughed, still somewhat tearful. "Thanks, you guys. Those are all good suggestions. I think I'll go with Emily's dead aunt Nora. I feel like I know her now from all the cycles I've done with Emily."

"How is that for you, Emily?" I asked.

She was cheerful. "Fine. I feel flattered, and I think Aunt Nora would be, too."

"Drew, the change won't happen without lots of practice."

"I know."

"Let's try now. Okay?"

"Okay."

"I'm going to say what I said before. You're going to notice both voices, then bring in Aunt Nora and use her voice to say something that is neither too good nor too bad, but accurate, responsive, and what a good parent would have said all along."

"Okay, let's go for it."

"You did a great job on taking out trash."

Drew was silent.

"What happened?"

"I heard: 'It was great,' then 'She's wrong, you were awful.' Then I brought in Aunt Nora's voice and it said, 'You're doing pretty well with emotional trash, and it is not easy.' "

"How was that?"

"Wonderful. All the tension drained out of my body. It felt like just what I most needed to hear."

"That's what I need you to do. At least three times per day, and more, if you're able. Listen to the two voices that respond to what happens, bring in the nurturing voice of Aunt Nora, and say what you most need to hear that is honest and neither too good nor too bad."

"I can do that, but that's not all."

"What else?" I asked.

She rolled her eyes and said, "I feel embarrassed."

"Embarrassment is a smokescreen. What are the basic feelings under it?"

"I feel sad, lonely, guilty, and afraid."

"Excellent."

"I've been doing limits cycles all along, but now I'm struck with why they've been so hard to do. I can find unreasonable expectations, lots of them. But when I turn to creating a reasonable expectation, all I see is gray cardboard. There's nothing there. I don't have a clue where to begin. Not always, but enough of the time that it scares me."

"Drew, that's true of everyone to some extent, but because that pattern is so deep . . ."

"Yes, it is very deep. The emptiness is huge."

Essential Pain and Earned Rewards: Integration

- I can't continue seeing myself as all good or all bad.
- I will be more authentic.

- I must look at myself and see who I am.
- I may like some things I see.

- I can't continue to hate myself.
- I may even like myself.

- I am not perfect.
- I don't have to be. I am human.

- I can't live in chaos.
- I will have inner peace and harmony.

- I have to grow up.
- I get to be grown up.

". . . there is something good about that."

"Tell me," said Drew, dubious.

"If you go inside to find the reasonable expectation and what's there is the Mojave Desert—with virtually nothing in sight—it's a reasonable expectation that early in life, the experiences you had gave you no roadmap of what is reasonable to expect in life."

She nodded. "That's definitely true."

"So at least you know that it's not in your imagination. It's real."

Drew nodded. "That helps me, but that's not what I want."

"What do you want?"

"I want to be able to have expectations that are reasonable, and not feel like I'm on a fishing expedition every time I go inside myself. I'm tired of not knowing and of going inside and not finding anything reasonable that I can bank on. I feel flaky as hell."

"Well, I agree, you are! As long as your most basic expectations of life, the ones that all the little expectations of your day rest upon, are unclear or too harsh or too easy, you will feel—and be—somewhat flaky."

"Delightful, Laurel. You say the nicest things!"

Everyone in the group laughed.

"The good news," I said, "is that you're above the line enough now, and you know yourself well enough now, that you can start grinding into the belly of your brain those most basic reasonable expectations. I mean really grind them in, until the neural networks that favor imbalance, which have been there since you were eight years old, fade away to sheer threads and the new neural networks that favor balance become as thick as ropes."

"I like that idea," said Drew.

Any neurologist would probably faint or scream at the description I just gave Drew, for we really don't know for certain how The Solution works. But what we do know after training so many people in the method is that that metaphor perfectly reflects how The Solution seems to work.

At this point in the climb, if Drew was not willing to get down and dirty, roll up her sleeves, go right to her roots, unearth her previously unconscious expectations and substitute reasonable ones for them, and then practice those reasonable ones ten times a day, she would take another couple of years to reach her Solution.

If she did this work now, I could see Drew having a Solution within six months. Not a life stuck in the middle of the tree, in which she felt "better" and used external solutions "a little less," but a red-blooded, all-out Solution in which she had no external solutions and an abundance of all of life's sweetest rewards. But she would have to work for it.

"Drew, it's just like spaghetti."

She looked perturbed. "What does that mean?"

"You have this whole bowl of spaghetti inside, a bunch of very basic expectations that favor a life of imbalance. The idea is that you only take out one strand of spaghetti at a time. Lay it on the table, all straightened out and balanced, and just focus on it. Practice it. Stay with it until you have ground it into your feeling brain and it has become dominant and is part of you, part of your bones."

"Okay, I can do that."

"Which one do you want to start with? What's a very basic expectation that is at the roots of your feeling inauthentic, chaotic, and self-rejecting?"

"I don't know."

"Take your time."

"Well, my most basic expectation is . . . I am a bad person. There is something wrong with me. Also, I don't really exist. I am not here on this planet."

"That's a lot of spaghetti."

She frowned. "Okay. I'll take one. I am a bad person."

"That makes me sad when you say it."

She looked straight into my eyes. "Me, too."

"This sounds like a silly little activity, but what I want you to do is find the opposite statement, one that resonates for you, then say it ten times per day until it is integrated into your inner life. The statement you come up with will be so foreign to your inner workings that you will forget it! You must write it down for yourself. Also, saying it will bring up emotional trash, and you'll have to take that out, but that's something you are perfectly capable of doing at this point in the climb."

"I don't know what's opposite of that unreasonable expectation."

"How about suggestions from the group?"

She nodded.

Emily said, "How about, 'I am a great person'?"

Tom offered, " 'I'm not a bad person.' "

Mark said, " 'I am a pretty good person, not perfect, not awful.' "

Drew smiled. "I like that one. I am a pretty good person, not perfect and not awful. That's the one I'm going to grind in."

"Great, Drew."

"I feel better. Thanks."

"Drew, when you're ready, I want you to do Community Connections to get ideas about how to change your lifestyle to make it easier for you to be not all good or all bad, and to have a life that authentically reflects . . . you. Right now, you have enough to work on with this."

"Yes, I'm happy with just this."

And she looked happy—quite happy, actually.

25. Balance

Balance is the reward that comes quite naturally during the first half of the climb; for most people it is the foundation on which the excesses begin to leave and the other rewards of human maturity begin to arrive.

Yet for some, this is not the easiest reward to receive. The simple use of the skills repeatedly over time doesn't seem to open the coffers of emotional balance.

What is the definition of balance? It is not feeling happy all the time. Rather, it is feeling life's true feelings: sad, happy, angry, grateful, secure, afraid, guilty, and proud. It's feeling those feelings as they are attached to the present moment, not when they take us on mental excursions into the past or the future. It's feeling them as relatively separate from the distortions, assumptions, and imaginings of emotional trash. The feelings fade rather than linger, except during times when it is reasonable to have lingering feelings, such as an ongoing situation or a period of mourning a loss. When we are in balance, the drives to go to excess are more manageable, and in addition to bad feelings there are good ones. Though there are those inevitable times when we need to pull the blanket over our head and go to sleep—in one form or another— while we feel our pain, when we are balanced, we more often feel our pain and, at that same moment, are aware of the under-belly of bliss it offers. It's kind of like the kid in the rainstorm locked out of his home, sitting on the curb out in front, soaking wet and miserable, who gazes upward to see the rainbow or, on a whim, turns his face to the heavens, opens his mouth, and drinks in the rain! If the nature of life includes a lot of rain-storms, having the balance to see the rainbow and drink in the rain makes all the difference.

Because life isn't fair, and securing emotional balance is harder for some of us than others, consider double-checking the following if you are finding that emotional balance still eludes you after six to nine months of training or after completing the first three Solution Kits:

1. The Natural Flow of Feelings for Essential Pain—It is essential to be "good" at feeling all four feelings of the Natural Flow of Feelings. If you can't fan out an out-of-balance feeling into the natural flow of anger, sadness, fear, *and* guilt, you will not move yourself above the line. Check each feeling and be sure it is not masquerading in another feeling, turning into an unbalanced feeling, or showing up as a thought.

When a participant says in a flat voice, or even a sad voice, "I feel angry that they did this to me, which was really hard for me," that is *not* an expression of anger. Did the person feel the anger in the belly? No. Did it get so red-hot that it erupted from his or her mouth like hot molten lava? No. The anger was expressed from below the line as numbness or sadness, and there was no four-year-old language there. It was completely adult, which won't get us very far. Until we honor the four-year-old in us, we cannot grow ourselves up into an authentic adult.

Some people have trouble expressing sadness. They need to practice feeling and expressing that feeling, and recognizing that feeling sad cools hostility. Others have difficulty effectively expressing fear and must learn that the idea is to say precisely what you are afraid of. Instead of saying, "I feel afraid that bad things will happen," say, "I feel afraid that I will never be happy again. I feel afraid that I will always be alone. I feel afraid that I will lose my house. I feel afraid that I was a bad parent. I feel afraid that I will lose my job." It is powerful to be specific when expressing fear.

Still others have trouble feeling guilt. You can't sidestep the need to feel your guilt by calling it regret—they are not the same thing. "I regret that the IRS is auditing me" is different from, "I feel guilty that I cheated on my income tax." The Natural Flow of Feelings asks us to check our guilt for a reason, for that is where our power resides. If we know and can express that we did wrong, we can do something differently next time. We can take action toward not contributing in that way in the future.

2. The Natural Flow of Feelings for Earned Rewards—For those of us who have spent our entire lives in that murky world below the line, feeling bad can be comforting because it is familiar. When we go inside, we gravitate immediately toward everything that is bad: our anger, sadness, fear, guilt, loneliness, disappointment, shame, depression, hostility, rebellion . . . you get the idea.

It is all so dramatic, so familiar, and so utterly dysfunctional. If you want to live life above the line, change is in order, and you will have to become kissing cousins with the good feelings. You not only must feel good but must train yourself to access the good feelings whether you feel like it or not.

A helpful tool is the Natural Flow of Feelings for earned rewards. For an entire week, don't even intentionally touch the negative feelings—they will arise of their own accord. Instead, do the Natural Flow of Feelings for earned rewards at least three times each day. Say each feeling five times. It's a form of emotional housecleaning that doesn't have to make any sense at all. Just start the sentence and see what comes to mind or, if you're doing it during a Community Connection, what comes out of your mouth:

> "I feel **grateful** for my cat. I feel grateful that I am alive. I feel grateful that my knee is better. I feel grateful for my wife. I feel grateful for this soft bathrobe."

> "I feel **happy** that the sun is out. I feel happy that my houseguests are going home today. I feel happy that my daughter cleaned out the dishwasher. I feel happy that Steve is coming home. I feel happy that I slept well."

> "I feel **secure** that I will never abandon myself. I feel secure that I can make my credit card payment. I feel secure that God loves me. I feel secure that I have enough food in the house. I feel secure that I do a good job at work."

> "I feel **proud** that I am a good parent. I feel proud that I recycle my newspapers. I feel proud that I told Kevin I was sorry. I feel proud that I didn't yell at the pizza delivery man when he was late. I feel proud that I am gaining these skills."

3. Frequency of Check-ins—I hope you develop a kindly sense of humor about doing this work, because it helps! You will probably be a little slippery in some areas and that's okay—the work is hard, and of course you'll want to wiggle out of doing some of it. A perfect example of this is checking in with yourself.

Are you doing it every hour?

If not, consider getting a watch and having it set for an hourly alarm, or setting your computer to go off every hour—do whatever you must do to check in with yourself often throughout the day. The goal is to check in so often that your awareness of your feelings begins to be automatic and continuous. Checking in more often is often the quickest way to get better results with emotional balance.

4. Body and Lifestyle Balance—If your health is not good and your lifestyle is unbalanced, your threshold of need for the skills will be sky-high. Consider using the Three-Day Balancing Plan, or doing whatever you need to do to encourage a balanced lifestyle. If you are sick, make it a priority to get the self-care and health care you need to feel as well as you are able to feel. If you are taking medication that turns your emotional volume down so low you can't feel, you won't be able to do this work effectively. In fact, if you are taking any medications that affect your libido, energy, depression, anxiety, or mental status in any way, you must be very assertive with your health-care professionals and be sure that you are taking the right doses and the correct medications for you. More is not better. Less may not be safe. Bring your entire list of medications to your physician and go over each of them to determine whether or not you need them, and how they affect your emotional balance. If you need a medication and there are substitutes that will maintain your health but not cut into your emotional balance, consider taking them.

5. Your Threshold of Need—When someone in our group is feeling decidedly awful, I check to see if their threshold of need for the skills is high, which it usually is. If your threshold of need for the skills is high from health problems, situational stress, emotional trash, or external solutions, you basically have two choices: lifestyle surgery or cycles.

I heartily recommend lifestyle surgery. When the earned reward of making a change is greater than the essential pain of making it, action is often in order. Getting out of an abusive relationship, stopping working on weekends, not running yourself ragged all week, not staying up until midnight watching television, and saying no to people who take too much from you will all lower your threshold of need for the skills.

If you've done all the lifestyle surgery you are able to do, turn to using the power of doing cycles—a lot of them. Use "The Instant Connection" on the website. Call your Solution Buddy

> ## Reasonable Expectations:
> ## Balance
>
> I expect myself to do the best I can to:
>
> - Stay above the line in emotional balance, most of the time
> - Feel my feelings and let them fade
> - Use the cycles to stay above the line
> - Fan out my feelings: anger, sadness, fear and guilt
> - Feel the good feelings, not just the bad
> - Take out emotional trash when it arises
> - Face the essential pain of the human condition
> - Reap the sweetest rewards that life can bring
> - Create a lifestyle that supports personal balance

and do a cycle. Join a Solution Circle or Group, but get support in doing cycles.

It's often a great source of comfort to have on hand an expectation such as, "My threshold of need for the skills is high. I expect myself to be as below the line as I need to be for as long as I need to be. In time, I will take out my tool kit, use my skills, and regain my emotional balance."

Life is difficult, and simply seeing accurately both yourself and the difficulty of what you are going through right now can be enough to pop you above the line.

As Emily and Tom neared the top of the tree, each struggled with emotional balance more than I would have predicted, though for different reasons.

There was no question that Emily was far more balanced than she had been when she started the climb, but a few things missing from her skill set held her back from a sense of mastery over the emotional whirlwind of life. A few big things . . .

After I talked at length with her about those "missing things," it became clear to me that one factor was her still-fledgling "I feel angry" skill.

Life above the line includes hefty helpings of anger. Anger, which is another word for passion, is the impetus for escaping passivity, for getting out and *doing something* in the world.

Without it, we fall so very easily into self-pity, powerlessness, depression, rage, and a whole slew of unbalanced feelings. If you don't have a robust "I feel angry" skill—if you can't feel deep and intense anger without falling off the emotional cliff into hostility—you will never master emotional balance.

Emily's pattern was to go through the Natural Flow of Feelings without feeling any deep anger in her body, much less having that immensely powerful, depression-stopping venom spew out of her mouth. She *thought* her anger rather than *felt* it.

Emily said, "I feel angry. At least, I think I do."

"Emily, bad things happen. If you can't muster normal, adult, passionate outrage and upset, I'm worried!"

Emily looked nervous and pushed up her glasses. She shook her head, her straight blond hair swinging a little.

"Anger feels dangerous to me," she said, "like I'm abandoning my . . . femininity. Like I'm being a bad person, sort of . . . uncivilized."

Several people in the room shifted in their chairs. Emily looked as though she'd caught herself saying something abhorrent.

"That's really stupid, isn't it?" she finally said aloud. "I can't have my anger because I have to always be so damn good! I can't be just as furious as anyone has a right to be about all the things that are hard in life . . ."

Her voice turned sad—or rather, it turned self-pitying, powerless, and depressed.

"Emily, see if you can stay in anger, really robust, red-blooded anger. Are you willing to do the Natural Flow of Feelings?"

She nodded.

"What were you thinking about just then?"

"Rob, how unfair it is that he's . . . disabled."

"Go into your body and wait for the anger to arise. Say nothing until it's red-hot, until it overflows and comes out so strongly that the people sitting across from you are startled, until your face looks angry and your body is angry. Allow the feeling to course through your veins and spout out your mouth in a natural flow. Not hostility. Not numbness. Just pure, deep anger."

Emily was silent for more than a minute. Then her pale skin began to flush.

"I HATE IT. I AM . . . FURIOUS. FUCK THEM. . . . How could God hurt my boy like that?"

"Stay out of sadness and go back into anger if you are able."

Her voice deepened into a gully of anger that had never been filled, not since Rob was born nearly twenty years before and she had first realized that her son was different.

"I *hate* that he is different. . . . I *hate* that there is a world that is so evil. . . . I can't stand it that it happened to a child. . . . I hate it that it happened to *my* child. . . . I feel furious that it happened to me. I feel so angry that I am alone. . . . I feel so angry that nobody knows my fear. . . . I feel angry that I can't do a fucking thing about it, that no matter what I do, he can't have a real life, he can't be just what nearly every other kid is—normal."

Then her eyes widened and she screamed. She screamed a shattering, full-body scream. It came from such an honest pool of fury within her that, although the others in the room were startled, somehow her scream was deeply refreshing.

Although Emily's anger was essential, she needed to be equally honest and deep with the rest of her feelings—all of them.

"Emily, I'm going to ask you to skip the limits skill today and instead do both natural flows. Stay with me and be curious. See what happens!"

She nodded.

"'I feel sad that . . .'" I started off for her.

"I feel sad that he is different. I feel sad he will not be normal . . . ever. I feel sad that he has pain . . ."

"I feel afraid . . ."

"I feel afraid that people will reject him. . . . I feel afraid he won't ever be totally independent . . ." Then a look of shock came over her face. "I didn't realize it, but I feel afraid he will never have children, that he won't have a real family life, which is foolish because I believe he probably will."

"I feel guilty that . . ."

Emily was getting better at guilt. "I feel guilty that I am such a drama queen," she said. "I feel guilty that I make it worse than it is. I feel guilty that I baby him too much so he isn't as independent as he might be."

Her eyes were wide, and she blinked several times.

"Are you ready to go over to the side of earned rewards?"

She nodded.

"I feel grateful that he is such a fine person. . . . I feel grateful that we have gotten such wonderful help for him. . . . I feel happy that he is doing so well, that he is enjoying so many things in life. . . . I feel secure that I have done the best that I could do in a very difficult situation. . . . I feel proud that our family has all supported him, and I feel proud of myself for . . . being a good mom."

She had popped herself above the line, and her face was simply radiant.

"Emily, that was wonderful! All you did was the two natural flows of feelings, and look what happened!"

Emily was blushing and laughing, and several in the group couldn't wait to give her Tender Morsels, but all I could see was that look of life in her face, the beauty of emotional balance.

As I left the session that evening, Emily was on my mind, mainly because her skills in nurturing and limits were getting amazingly strong, but her lifestyle surgery was lagging behind. I knew that what she most wanted was balance, but that she would never have it unless she got her whole body above the line. She wasn't there yet, and I questioned whether she would be committed to personal balance enough to do what was unavoidably necessary to have vibrancy.

At the same time, Tom was making the climb and doing well. His relationship with Michelle had its bumps, but they were more trusting of each other every day. He still wasn't drinking, and they were spending most evenings together. I had worried that this "in love" stage would drastically reduce his threshold of need for the skills, and that he'd get a false sense of being above the line and leave the training—and that, when the first blush of love had left, he would find that he was nearly as below the line as he had been with Karen.

Fortunately, Michelle's child came to the rescue, although I don't think that is what Tom would have called it. Michelle had a daughter by her first marriage, a sixteen-year-old named Nicola who lived with her half the time. Nicola had taken an instant dislike to Tom and was perfectly comfortable saying such things to him as, "You're so old. My mother has dumped men far younger than you."

Nicola was small and pretty and had been remarkably indulged with material possessions—a new car for her sixteenth birthday, shopping trips to New York each summer, and at least three closets full of clothes, nearly all of which were on her bedroom floor most of the time. What triggered Tom to go right below the line was when Nicola blatantly sassed her mother and

Michelle simply ignored it, saying that her daughter would learn to speak to her more respectfully as she got older.

Tom said to the group one night, "I really love Michelle, but her daughter is so rude and obnoxious. I've had it with her, but Michelle forbids me to talk back to Nicola or set any limits whatsoever. I'm sick of arguing with Michelle about it, and I don't think I can take Nicola's rude behavior anymore."

"What do you do when she's rude to you?"

"I go numb. I go numb because if I don't, I'd feel like smacking her one. Well, I wouldn't really smack her, but I'd *feel* like it. I'd yell at her and tell her what a selfish little witch she is."

"Is she?"

"Without question."

"What else is triggering you to go below the line these days?"

Tom blinked and was silent for a moment. Finally, he said, "Actually, nothing."

"How often do you feel numb?"

"Not at work anymore. Not at night when I'm at home. I'm exercising and not working too much, except one evening last week. I would say just around Nicola."

"Well, I think you should consider thanking God for Nicola."

He snorted. Then he coughed. "Just tell me, Laurel, why should I be thankful for this little terror?"

"Because as you and Michelle continue, as the 'in love' stage passes and you start actually being what one would call interdependent . . ."

"You mean married?"

"I mean some arrangement that amounts to a marriage, an arrangement that will trigger your emotional trash about Karen to come up, and Michelle will start looking exactly like Karen in ways that are almost scary, and you start acting like the person you were when you were married to Karen . . ."

"Stop. I don't want to hear this. I wish I hadn't come to group tonight."

"Well, I feel very happy that Nicola is being impossible, because it's an opportunity to muscle up on your skills, so there is more chance that as you and Michelle get closer, she won't look like Karen to you and you won't act like the guy you were."

"That feels better. Okay, you win. I'm extremely grateful that Nicola is driving me crazy."

Several people laughed. Even Tom was smiling.

"Tom, she throws you below the line. That kid can take a grown man who weighs . . ."

"Two hundred and five pounds," he said.

". . . two hundred and five pounds and completely control his emotional balance! Your job is to hold on to yourself, to use the skills to stay above the line. If you're above the line and it's a reasonable expectation that making a request of Nicola or Michelle will bring something good for you, then you give her a Solution Sandwich. If not, you don't. Would you pick someone to role-play it with?"

Tom nodded. "Yes. Drew, will you work with me on this?"

"Sure," Drew said. She was fond of Tom and loved role-playing with him while he practiced using the skills.

"Would you please set up Drew for what happened?"

"It happened last evening. I was over at Michelle's house, and we were having a great evening. We were listening to music and reading, and I was thinking about how beautiful she was. Nicola burst into the room with three of her equally spoiled, obnoxious friends. She interrupted what we were doing, flipped off the CD player, never acknowledged my presence, and started yelling at her mom about her favorite sodas not being in the house. Total and complete disrespect!

"I went right below the line, and as soon as Nicola and her friends left the room, I lit into Michelle, saying, 'How could you let your daughter talk to you like that?' Things went downhill from that moment, and I ended up going home and sleeping in my own bed last night."

"So you're sitting in the chair numb, then you explode into hostility."

"Correct."

"So you need to muscle up on your skills that produce emotional balance."

"Supposedly."

"Why don't you do a cycle first?"

"I feel angry that she is such a bitch. . . . I feel furious that Michelle lets her daughter treat her with disrespect. . . . I hate it that Michelle won't discipline her own daughter. . . . I feel angry that there is nothing I can do. . . . If I yell at her I'm wrong, and if I don't I can't live with myself. I feel sad that she is such an awful parent. I feel afraid that my life is going to be miserable on

> ## Essential Pain and Earner Rewards: Balance
>
> - It is hard work.
> - I will have personal balance.
>
> - I must feel my feelings.
> - Some of my feelings will be good.
>
> - I can't be numb.
> - I can be more alive.
>
> - Emotional imbalance is familiar. Change is difficult.
> - I will have a new life.
>
> - I can't hide from my emotional trash.
> - I can heal my emotional trash and feel better.
>
> - Life is difficult and unfair.
> - Life can be wonderful, too.
>
> - I am alone.
> - I have myself. I have the spiritual.
>
> - Nobody will rescue from unhappiness.
> - I can rescue myself.

account of Nicola. . . . I feel afraid that I will blow it and lose Michelle. . . . I feel guilty . . . there is no guilt. The kid is a bitch, and nobody could stand her, not even her schoolmates. She is a walking disaster."

"If part of your dark side is being a little bit . . ."

"Arrogant?"

I winced. "Well, yes, arrogant . . . then if you don't have a robust 'I feel guilty' skill, more bad things will occur."

"I feel guilty that I've botched my relationship with Nicola. She knows I can't stand her. . . . I feel guilty that I either go numb and am passive, or get hostile and aggressive. My unreasonable expectation? That it will be easy to be in love with someone who has a very temperamental daughter. A reasonable expectation?"

He thought for several moments.

"I expect myself to do my best to stay above the line, and when I am above the line, to talk it through with Michelle. I need to deal with her daughter, whether I want to or not."

"Tom, you've been working on your most basic expectations, right?"

"Right, for a few months now."

"How is it coming?"

"Really great. I've ground in a few really basic ones, and it makes all the difference. I feel really secure that I don't abuse my body. I feel very clear that I don't abuse other people, which is why there was no question in my mind that although I feel like lighting into Nicola, I wouldn't do that."

"What is your most basic expectation about an intimate relationship? The risk of intimacy is that they may reject you or you may surrender to them."

"I surrendered to Karen. I put up with her denigrating me, drowning my fury in wine for years. I'm confused, though, because when I was a kid, I fled. One of my basic expectations is that I feel my feelings and don't run away."

"So how can you create a very basic expectation that will be like a backbone for you, solid but flexible, so that you do not abandon what is most important to you, even when life is difficult?"

"I don't know. I'd have to think about it."

"There is no rush."

"The essential pain of staying in an intolerable situation like this one is that I will lose myself. I will start drinking again. I know I can't handle what's going on now. It's not essential pain, but self-neglect. Maybe other people could handle this situation, but I can see myself clearly. I cannot."

"So what would the most basic expectation be?"

"Hmmmm. My most basic expectation is that I feel my feelings and do all I can to connect with Michelle, stopping short of abusing or seriously neglecting myself." He stopped and thought for a moment, then said, "That's it!"

"And the essential pain of life you would have to face in order to follow through with that new, most basic expectation?"

Again he paused, his face sober.

"I may lose Michelle."

"The earned reward?"

"I won't lose myself."

I breathed deeply, amazed at how much the skills had become part of Tom, a man who, eighteen months earlier, had a short fuse and virtually no skill in accessing his feelings. He was not the same person he had been before.

"Tom, that was so wonderful. And I know that you know what to do . . ."

"Yes," he said. "Say it ten times per day every day until it is part of my bones."

I nodded, still savoring the work he had just done and its meaning with regard to where he was in his climb.

I asked him, "Is it a reasonable expectation that after Nicola left the room last evening, you would be in enough balance to give a Solution Sandwich to Michelle?"

"No. I should have just said that I needed some time to myself and gone home, rather than getting into a fight with her."

"Do you want to practice a Solution Sandwich that you could give her when you are ready to?"

"Yes, I really need the practice."

"Drew, are you ready?"

She smiled. "Yes. I'm playing Michelle, right?"

I nodded and turned to Tom. "White bread, Tom. The softness of honest empathy. Tom, do you want coaching from Drew?"

"Yes, I do."

Tom began, "I understand you really love Nicola, but I feel that she is so spoiled and rude."

Drew said, "That was melba toast, not white bread. Also the meat, it needs to start with a real feeling, not an 'I feel . . .' that is not a feeling."

Drew had mastered the art and science of Solution Sandwiches. Having been a very bratty teenager herself, she was the perfect person to coach Tom.

Tom tried again. "I understand that you really love Nicola and that she is at a hard age."

"Not bad," said Drew.

"I feel . . . ," Tom looked confused. "I don't know how I feel. I feel angry . . ."

I interjected, "Tom, it's reasonable to expect you to feel all the feelings—angry, sad, afraid, and guilty—but you need to communicate only the *honest* feelings that won't send Michelle below the line. If you say that you feel angry, how will that be for her?"

"I've been so hostile about Nicola in the past that she'd go straight out of balance," he said. "Okay, let me try again." He turned back to Drew. "I feel very sad and afraid when I hear Nicola speak to you that way. I need you to know that it's not easy for me to hear that."

He paused for a moment and closed his eyes a little, then said, "I need you to know that what you allow her to do is your decision, but if she is rude to me when I am here, I will excuse myself and leave for the evening. If it continues, it would make me sad to do it, but I would only want to see you at my house, or to come here when Nicola was with her dad. Would you please tell me how that is for you to hear?"

Drew was aghast. "Incredible, I'm blown away. I don't even need more white bread. You have me out cold. Whatever you want, I'll do!"

Tom smiled, obviously pleased with himself. Several people clapped.

Both Tom and Emily were close to having mastered emotional balance and were busily picking fruit near the very top of the tree.

26. Sanctuary

The inherent strength, goodness, and wisdom—your intuition—with which you were born reside in your sanctuary. So do your nurturing inner voice and a wealth of love, security, and connection to yourself and the spiritual. Your sanctuary is your essence, your soul, your true center. Your sanctuary is *you*.

You could see it as your feeling brain, but I suggest that you consider going lower, to the place in your body that feels like your essence, the spot you are aware of when you bring up a nurturing inner voice or are alone in the dark with yourself, or the place within where you find solace when there is danger around you.

That is your sanctuary.

The idea of a sanctuary is tough for some people to accept, especially if they were raised with chaos, negativity, confusion, or harshness. Oddly enough, it is also hard to fathom for those who were raised with indulgence, the underside of which is powerlessness, encroachment, and disappointment. Deprivation and indulgence are two sides of the same coin.

If you don't have a warm, accepting, knowing place within, your job is to build one, because the only real source of security in life comes from within. As you take out emotional trash and bring up a nurturing inner voice, that sanctuary will become warmer and stronger. We say that you build your own sanctuary, brick by brick by brick. Even if you came to this method with a warm sanctuary within, caring for it to keep it that way will require your attention.

It's really just like cleaning house. Mainly, you do it yourself, taking out emotional trash when it invades, cleaning the cobwebs off a nurturing inner voice when it slips into harmful tones, and attentively repairing any disconnects between yourself and your sanctuary. Sometimes, or even often, you might decide you need a housekeeper, dear friend, cycle buddy, or counselor to help you keep that place within warm and safe and clean.

All that really matters is that you develop a deep commitment to doing whatever internal housecleaning is necessary to keep your fingers on the pulse of your inner life and to be continually, deeply, and lovingly connected to yourself.

If you could picture your sanctuary right now, it would have a certain shape, color, size, and texture. Or perhaps your sanctuary is not a place you can imagine right now. If that is the case, please store the idea until a later time when it might make more sense, and recognize that since the nature of this work is developmental, when you read some chapters a few months or a year from now, it will seem as if you had never read them before. The concept of sanctuary is often like that. At some point, as you make this climb, you are likely to understand that you own your sanctuary, and that having it changes everything.

Like most of life's sweetest rewards, sanctuary builds slowly at first. By the middle of the journey, most people are sometimes aware of their sanctuary. But it is not until you begin to reach the top of the tree—when so many of the rewards of life somehow appear—that sanctuary becomes the ever-present connection to all that is good and all that is more.

Drew's sense of sanctuary was dramatically wiped away at the age of eight by the traumatic changes that coincided with the birth of her twin brothers. After that event, she suffered an onslaught of emotional trash, and the development of her skills to nurture and set limits from within came to a virtual standstill.

Reasonable Expectations: Sanctuary

I expect myself to do the best I can to:

- Trust that there is a sanctuary within me, and that it belongs to me

- Build a sanctuary, brick by brick by brick, that is larger and warmer and safer for me

- Take out emotional trash as it arises, to keep my sanctuary safe and warm

- Be aware of my sanctuary when times are good

- Be aware of my sanctuary when life is difficult

Drew found no warm, welcoming sanctuary within, but rather a very cold, rejecting void.

It didn't matter how proficient Drew became at using the skills; unless she used them within the security of a sanctuary, they would be shallow and ineffective. Using the skills from the void would do as little to create balance as sponging down a sinking boat instead of grabbing big buckets and bailing the water out.

About halfway through her climb, Drew felt discouraged, and she shared that feeling with our group.

"I have no sanctuary. I abandon myself right and left. In fact, there is no 'me,' there is just the person who is way too good at school and way too bad at home. If I were to be perfectly truthful," she looked around the room, "I would say that I have no inner life, no inner life worth having."

Obviously, Drew's threshold of need had gone up, and *plunk!* she had been tossed below the line. In reality, she had built quite a bit of sanctuary within, but when you're below the line, you're below the line. Once the plug has been pulled and you have disconnected with yourself, there is no past or future, there is no rational perspective or accurate memory. You are just below the line, and it is very difficult to see that you have ever had sanctuary or ever will. Later, after Drew reached her Solution, even at times when she was way below the line, in the very back of her mind she would hear the quiet whisperings of that sanctuary within. She would begin to know, nearly all the time and no matter what, that that safe place was within her, even if she could not fathom it for that moment.

"Drew, would you like to do a cycle?"

She glared at me. "Would I like to? No! Do I need to and am I willing to? I guess."

"Start with your Thinking Journal."

People in the room seemed to settle into their chairs, preparing to listen to a deep cycle, knowing that Drew was now capable of going right to the roots of her emotions and popping herself above the line. They had observed her skills strengthening slowly over the months.

Drew said, "I have no sanctuary, and I'm sick of it. Nobody loves me, and I don't love myself, and there is so much confusion in me, and I feel so rotten inside. Last night I had a pizza binge for the first time in months, and I have this horrible food hangover and my face . . . do you see how bloated I am?"

Everyone looked at her face, which looked perfectly normal, and said nothing. But then, she wasn't really looking for them to.

"I feel so ugly inside, and I'm so sick of doing cycles, and I can't stand it . . ."

"Natural flow of feelings?" I suggested.

"I feel angry that I am so alone. I feel furious that nobody can make me feel better. I am so angry that I can't have what I want. I hate it that life is so hard. How could God make life like this? He must be a guy . . ."

The ends of her mouth curled up a little, then her face turned serious again:

"I can't stand it that I am so empty right now. I feel sad that I am alone, and sad that my life is so empty. I feel afraid it always will be, and guilty that I am so lazy and so incredibly self-destructive at times."

I stopped her. "Drew, I haven't seen you so out of balance for a long time. I'm worried about you! Your threshold of need must have gone up."

She nodded.

"What happened?"

Then she started to cry. "Well, it's my best friend from college, Jane. She came to town, and we went out to dinner. She has the perfect life: a husband who loves her, two children who are about as beautiful as any children I've ever seen, and a great job as a mortgage broker, easily making a six-figure income. She has a gorgeous wardrobe, a beautiful body, and a face that looks like she's never had an evening lost to eating, drinking, and smoking in her life. I felt like this defective . . . animal around her, a creature from a different planet . . ."

Again, I interrupted her. "Drew, you could do a cycle on this, but right now I'm angry."

She was startled. "You are?"

"And sad."

"Why?"

"You've been building a sanctuary within you, a nurturing inner voice, using the skills to stay connected to yourself now and cleaning out truckloads of emotional trash, and then this woman . . ."

"Jane."

". . . Jane comes into your life and blows apart your sanctuary. In one meal."

Drew pulled at the tendrils of hair at the back of her neck and looked sad for a moment. Then she said, "I completely lost my boundary to her. I stopped seeing myself. All I could see was myself in comparison to her."

"Which suggests an expectation . . ."

"My expectation was that her way was the right way. Anything different than being perfect, beautiful, loved, and immaculate was wrong, and made me wrong. More than that, it made me a big nothing."

"Where was your sanctuary, your nurturing voice, your use of the skills that would create a limit that would have made you safe?"

"Nowhere," said Drew.

"Perfect. This is exactly the practice you need, so let's do it now."

She nodded.

"It's easy to have sanctuary when you're on easy street, but seeing Joan . . ."

"Jane."

"Seeing Jane popped up your threshold of need and whoosh, there you went, below the line, your warm sanctuary practically evaporating."

Essential Pain and Earned Rewards: Sanctuary

- I have to go inside.
- Inside will become a safe place.

- Connecting with myself is scary.
- I can feel the fear and let it fade.

- Building sanctuary takes work.
- It's worth it. I will have a deep security.

- I must take out emotional trash. It hurts.
- My sanctuary will stay safe and warm.

- Nobody can build a sanctuary for me.
- I can do it for myself.

"Exactly," said Drew.

"Let's get it back."

"I don't know how to."

"You have a tool kit of these skills. There's no one right way to do it. Just be curious. Try one tool. If that doesn't work, try another and another until you're aware of the sanctuary within yourself."

The expression on Drew's face matched the one I would have expected if I'd told her she had to have a root canal. She groaned, and even whined a little.

"Ohhh . . . This is so hard."

"It's not the hardest thing you'll ever do. Besides, Drew . . ."

She looked up at me, a little more hopeful, so I continued. "Your job at this point in the climb is to pump up the skills, to expect to go below the line at times and then to observe yourself down there in the playpen, whether it is dripping with self-pity, depression, or hostility, or even eating, drinking, smoking, or spending. Then, with a compassionate eye, you reassure yourself that you are not bad or wrong—you are just below the line. At times, people go below the line. But you need to know that it's only a matter of time before you get out your tool kit and do what you need to do to get yourself back above the line."

Drew took a few deep breaths.

"Please don't rush yourself, Drew."

She took a few more breaths, then out of her mouth came:

"I hate it that I have to do this myself. . . . I can't stand it that nobody can get me above the line but me. . . . I'm sick of checking in. I'm tired of being an adult. . . . I hate it that I have to grow up and take care of myself. I'd rather piss my life away and have someone else clean it up!"

After saying those words, she let out a gasp of surprise at herself, but went on:

"I feel sad that I am so insecure. . . . I feel sad . . . no, I feel angry that I let Jane blow away my balance. . . . I can't stand it that I lost any sense of my own personal worth just because she is . . . PERFECT! I HATE THAT MY LIFE IS NOT PERFECT!"

By now she was yelling her words and her face was bright red.

"You're doing great, Drew. Keep going."

The anger had turned into sadness.

"I feel sad that my life hasn't been better. . . . I feel sad that

I'm just a teacher. . . . I feel sad that I'm not married. . . . I feel sad that nobody loves me. . . . I feel afraid that I'll never have a beautiful face. . . . I feel afraid that I'll never have a perfect body, a loving husband, and two immaculate children . . ."

Then a flood of light filled her face, and she started to laugh. It was a rich, low laugh that came from deep in her chest and rolled and rolled on, quite decadently, for several minutes.

Then she said, still very loudly, "God, how I'd HATE to have her life! How I'd hate to have all that perfection."

And her face turned soft and loving.

"God, how I *love* my life, my stupid little problems and all the ways that I'm not perfect. How I cherish my little house with all my clutter and all that old furniture and a life that is unique and my very own. Phew. I feel so much better!"

Drew had popped herself above the line, but what had just happened only happens when one nears the top of the tree. Drew had practiced the limits cycle so effectively and so often that it was becoming integrated and automatic. She could feel her feelings deeply, and more often, the limits cycle would spontaneously wrap its arms around those feelings and pop her above the line.

It was a sign to me that she was nearer her Solution than she had known. If Drew had so much as gone near those very painful, intense feelings just a year earlier, she would have triggered the release of so much emotional trash that she would have been wiped out for days, engaging in as many external solutions as she could lay her hands on. Now her internal limits were essentially holding her, much the way, in the best of all worlds, she would have been held when she was eight and ten and twelve. The difference was twofold: She was doing it for herself, and it was occurring automatically.

"So what I need . . . ," I encouraged her to continue.

"What I need is to appreciate how far I have come and that I do have a sanctuary inside me. Laurel?"

"Yes."

"I think I may be near my Solution."

I smiled. "I wouldn't be surprised at all, Drew. I'm happy for you."

She smiled back, looking very secure and rather radiant.

"The support you need?" I asked.

"I don't know that I need any right now. The support is . . . inside me."

27. Intimacy

I was so proud of myself. I had read in the paper that the runner carrying the Olympic torch was coming through our town at 9:00 A.M. on a Sunday morning, passing just four blocks from our house. I managed to wake my thirteen-year-old son and his friend, and I put the dog on the leash. We all walked down the street, planning to pick up bagels, milk, and juice at the corner shop that was on our way.

I was in my element, feeling like the "good mother," intimate with myself, close to my child, and very happy and excited about the day. Then, when I was in the bagel shop, at the moment I was the most relaxed, I realized that my son and his friend had vanished.

In our little hamlet and at their age, it wasn't likely that they'd been abducted, but I began a somewhat heated search for them anyway, walking up one block, now crowded with onlookers and strewn with Olympic pendants, then down another.

After about fifteen minutes, in my own below-the-line-ness, I concluded that the boys had ditched me and no matter how hard I looked, I wouldn't find them. Moreover, I felt rejected, for I had extended my love to them but they "clearly" didn't want it. For in the midst of this bucolic setting and bright sunny day, a whole slew of emotional trash about being ditched as a kid had come flying in my face!

There I was, with the dog pulling at the leash and my arms full of milk cartons, juice containers, and a bag of hot, fresh bagels—all by myself and with all that emotional trash in the air. I was definitely below the line. And just the way it usually does when you are below the line, things got worse. Everywhere I looked, everyone seemed to be with *someone*. I'd been looking forward to sharing this monumental occasion with my child and his friend, and there I was, alone.

A few Chevy trucks went by, handing out American flags. I stood at the corner on the appointed street, took a few flags to save for the boys, and, now feeling very sorry for myself, made a small pile of my parcels. I still tried to catch a glimpse of the boys, but otherwise, I stood there waiting for the torch.

More precisely, I stood there *looking* as if I were waiting for the torch. What I was actually waiting for was my nurturing inner voice to arise. When it did, an expectation appeared, seemingly in neon:

I expect myself to do the best I can to give love to others. Sometimes people will take that love, and sometimes they won't.

That little expectation found its way to my awareness and immediately took the sting out of being "ditched." Even though I had been knee-deep in the muck of self-pity, smarting from the imagined pain of rejection, the bulk of the pain stopped. I was able to take care of my health and my happiness, still keeping an eye out for the boys and having some loving moments along the way. I caught up with a friend I hadn't seen in a long time and we chatted warmly. I met someone who was also sitting alone and shared some laughter, and I had a long conversation with a neighbor.

Later, when I connected with the boys, they said emphatically that they had not ditched me but had been looking for me all that time. They hadn't even seen the torch!

Some days are like that.

I certainly didn't have the kind of intimacy that I had intended that morning, but in my own imperfect way, I had done what I could to stay above the line and receive the intimacy that the universe had provided.

In The Solution, intimacy is not seen as narrowly as romantic love, parental love, or the love of soul mates. Rather, it is a reflection of the reality that we can only control our *readiness* for intimacy with another, but not the moment of intimacy itself. There is something very honest and stabilizing in acknowledging that all we can do is be out in the world, living our lives and holding ourselves accountable for staying above the line, grounded in intimacy with self and connected to the compassion of the spiritual. The rest we must watch unfold, knowing it is not completely within our control. Intimacy with self and the spiritual are within our control; intimacy with others is less so. This makes us appreciate each moment of human closeness more, as it is elusive, more like unexpected gifts than personal possessions.

We all have needs for intimacy; closeness with others has been shown to foster health and happiness. Two feeling brains

---

Reasonable Expectations: Intimacy

I expect myself do the best I can to:

- Be present in the current moment

- Cultivate a nurturing voice toward myself and others

- Be as closed as I need to be in order to create safety

- Be as open as I feel safe being in order to encourage love

- Acknowledge that other people have needs, just as I do

- Be willing to give and receive

- Risk the possibility of rejection or surrender

---

becoming attuned to each other, or "resonating," can have a tremendously balancing effect, and most of us naturally seek emotional connection with others when we are blue. We do our best to develop enduring relationships of various sorts.

In The Solution, the way we approach intimacy is to suggest that we become "intimacy catchers": We develop and nourish relationships that meet our enduring needs but also become skilled at catching intimacy in a child's laugh, a chance exchange with a stranger, a shared moment with a friend, or an unexpected sensual moment with our lover. Oddly, in this stance of holding ourselves accountable for doing the best we can to stay above the line and intimate with ourselves and with the spiritual, we have more love in our lives, even if this intimate connection is not returned.

At one time, one of my children was going through a period of questioning the spiritual, and I commented, "Well, let's be practical about it. What the Bible says is that you are supposed to love other people, and if you love other people, who gets the good feeling?"

My child said, "You do."

I said, "Right. So even if the Bible is wrong, how can you knock a belief that, when you follow it, makes you feel better?"

My comment was met by a silence that connoted that I might, in fact, have a point.

We all have a dark side, and we won't always be able to stay above the line in love. However, by staying intimate with ourselves and with the spiritual, we may experience more loving feelings. In fact, we may even feel love for another when they do not feel love for us—what I call soul-touching love that is not returned. That doesn't mean we lay ourselves open to perpetual hurt from a rejecting other, but we can keep the safe distance we need and still love them. Can you think of someone you love even though they do not have the skill to feel love for you?

Two of the most common relationship problems are staying in a relationship that is seriously harmful and losing sexual desire in a committed relationship. Both are less likely to occur when we are above the line.

If we are grounded in intimacy with ourselves and intimacy with the spiritual, it is far easier to endure the admittedly colossal pain of separating from a loved one in a relationship that would cause us to lose our spirit if it continued. A relationship cannot become an external solution to our distress if we have a sanctuary within. We want the relationship, but not enough to sell our soul.

The same is true for lasting desire. The intense attraction of new love fades in six months or so, and as the relationship becomes committed, that attraction is apt to continue waning. The threshold of need for the skills is higher when the relationship is committed, so there is a greater tendency to go below the line—you know, merging, distancing, and getting into control struggles. When we are below the line, soulful, loving, creative, and rewarding sex is less likely to occur. Our wish for lasting desire can motivate us to hold on to ourselves and stay above the line, even when our partner is not.

A tool you can use to maintain balance in a relationship is the Intimacy Cycle. When we go below the line in a relationship, one of two things happens: We either lose sight of our own feelings and needs, or we lose sight of the other person's feelings and needs. For intimacy to occur, we need to pump up the cycle that is stopping. When both cycles are running at once, like two bicycle tires moving, there is often intimacy.

If you're the kind of person who tends to lose sight of your own feelings and needs when you are close to others, you're probably apt to merge, rescue, and people-please. If you're the kind of person who tends to lose sight of other people's feelings and needs when you are close, you're likely to distance, persecute, or control. Neither of these positions is very loving or intimate, but the Intimacy Cycle has a way of nudging you to have both bicycle tires moving at once and experience more intimacy in your life.

Drew said, "I'm getting out more, and I have more intimacy in my life. But no sex."

"Why not?" I asked.

She looked at me somewhat aghast.

"Laurel, I don't have a partner, that's why!"

"You own your own sexuality, and it's your role to take care of it, regardless of whether you are in a relationship. There are lots of ways to meet your needs for passion, eroticism, orgasm, and sensuality."

Drew paused for a moment. Then she said, "I haven't been taking care of myself. I don't feel very sexual."

"Overdrinking and overeating don't help your desire."

"But I haven't had a binge in months."

"Good, then how would you go about honoring your needs?" I asked.

She shook her head. "I don't really know. Perhaps having a massage or starting to take care of my skin or . . ."

". . . engaging in erotic pleasures that bring you to orgasm?"

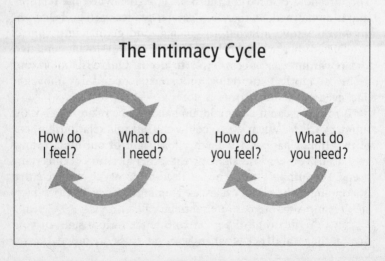

The Intimacy Cycle

How do I feel?   What do I need?   How do you feel?   What do you need?

Several people in the room smiled. So did Drew.

"Yes, I could pleasure myself more, definitely." She paused, looking up at the light in the classroom, seemingly in another world. "But I don't think there is anything as good as really loving someone and making love with them," she said.

The energy in the room vanished.

"It is sad to be alone sometimes," I said.

"Yes, it is sad," said Drew.

"There is one more essential pain."

"What is it?" asked Drew. "That not *all* of our needs are met *all* of the time?"

Several people laughed, including Drew.

"Great. If I accept that pain, what kind of a reward could there be?" Drew was exasperated at this point, but Emily spoke up brightly. "I know!"

Drew just glared at her, but she went on.

"The earned reward is that you've experienced the pleasure and fulfillment that you're capable of at that time."

Drew was not impressed.

"How many people here honored their needs for sexuality, sensuality, and passion during the last week?" I asked.

In a room of twelve people, Tom raised his hand. Mark half raised his, and Emily held her hand up high.

"Drew, if you don't meet your needs that are most basic, such as emotional intimacy and sexual fulfillment, there is a greater chance that those needs will go underground and . . ."

"I know," she said, "come up as external solutions. Okay, Laurel. Leave me alone! I'm going to work on it. I promise. You've reached me!"

She was laughing, and so were many in the group, but during the weeks after that session, Drew spoke a good deal about her progress with intimacy. She had deepened friendships with two coworkers, Craig and Sandra, and with her next-door neighbor, Tillie. Tillie and Drew had been friends for years, but Drew was only now opening up to her. She spoke often about her growing Body Pride, her interest in her sensuality, and how using the two bicycle tires of the Intimacy Cycle was helping her to capture more moments of closeness with others.

One day, Drew said, "I've been using the Intimacy Cycle, and last Sunday it really worked. Tillie and I got into the car to go to an estate sale. She looked rather glum, but I immediately started talking a mile a minute about my school project, and I just wouldn't shut up. Then the picture of those bicycle tires came into my brain, and this lightbulb went off."

I smiled, as I myself am a person who goes on and on at times. Drew continued her story.

"I said to myself, 'I wonder how Tillie feels, with me going on and on? I know how I feel. I feel happy about my project and proud that it is going so well, and I know what I need—to talk about it. But how does she feel and what does she need?' I realized that I hadn't even given it a thought."

Drew shrugged. "So I just asked myself the questions. How might she feel? She looks glum. I really can't know for sure what she needs, but she might need to be asked about how she is doing."

Drew took a deep breath.

"So I stopped jabbering, and I asked her how she was, and she started talking about having a headache. So we ended up going to

---

Essential Pain and Earned Rewards: Intimacy

- Others could reject me.
- I won't reject myself.

- I could surrender to their will.
- In time, I would reclaim myself.

- I can't *always* have it my way.
- There are times when I get what I want.

- They won't love me perfectly.
- I can love myself perfectly.

- I may fail.
- At least I will have tried, and I may succeed.

- Giving and receiving brings up past hurts.
- As they are brought up, I can heal them.

- Our relationship will end, somehow or someday.
- I will cherish the moment more.

a coffeehouse nearby and getting a cup of coffee and, after a while, talking and laughing in a closer way than we have ever done before. And I've lived next door to this woman for five years!"

Several people gave Drew Tender Morsels, including Emily.

She said, "Drew, I loved your story, particularly because I do the opposite. When Clay or my kids are around, I know how they feel and what they need before they do." She laughed, which she was doing more and more these days. "They say I have X-ray vision, that I can see into them and it gives them the willies!"

She sighed. "But the trouble is that I am really not intimate with them during those moments. I am only honoring them, not myself, and I think there's a price I've paid."

She pushed her glasses up on her nose. "It's been a loss of authenticity and intimacy. If I am not aware of my own feelings and needs, I'm taking care of them, but the intimacy is lost. There is no *me*."

"Emily, would you like a suggestion?" I asked.

She nodded.

"When you're with them, pretend that the bicycle tire 'How do I feel? What do I need?' is in neon. In the moment, pump up that skill and see what happens. Get that bicycle tire moving."

She lifted her eyebrows and said, "Okay. I can do that."

I began to go on to the next person when Emily interrupted.

"Wait—one more thing. It's my sex life."

"Yes?"

"I'm not rescuing anymore, not the kids or Clay. Clay's been different, too. I'm above the line with him, giving him Solution Sandwiches and not rescuing him sexually, and our desire is incredible."

All were listening.

"We are having sex that is so creative and loving and alive. I think it's the best lovemaking I've had since . . . a man I was involved with before Clay. I desire him, and I can sense his desire for me. It's wonderful, just wonderful."

Both Drew and Emily had made progress with intimacy, and Tom had made some progress as well. He was using the Intimacy Cycle regularly, was skilled at giving Solution Sandwiches, and had taken out a lot of emotional trash about his childhood and about Karen. He had done some lifestyle surgery to stop drinking and to leave work by six.

Yet intimacy was his sweetest fruit, and having it in abundance was still beyond his reach. There was, of course, a blessing in that; it would motivate him to continue the work, to focus on retraining his feeling brain enough to have all the other rewards, and to turn off the drives for the whole range of external solutions.

When I first met Tom, I thought for certain his good looks, success, and wealth would make him "slippery"—that is, that it would be easier for him to find escapes from life's pain and not want a Solution enough to do the work to get it. I worried that he didn't have enough fire-in-the-belly "hunger" for his sweetest fruit.

As it turned out, Tom had done exceptionally well with The Solution. He had stayed on the pathway, more or less, and had practiced the skills, even becoming proficient at the Intimacy Cycle much of the time. But he did not yet have an *abundance* of intimacy, and the more I listened to Tom's cycles, the more convinced I became that he would have to struggle harder, go deeper, and heal more before he would receive intimacy in abundance.

Although the story of Tom's childhood seemed normal in some ways—a small town, playing outdoors—on an emotional plane, it seemed quite out of the ordinary. If Tom had acted out—breaking windows, driving drunk, shouting obscenities— he might have been better off. Someone would have given him counseling or noted that he was in need, then helped him! But because he had been the "good boy," doing well in school, playing sports rather than screaming out his needs in one way or another, the isolation continued.

Karen loved him, but the love never penetrated. He "knew" she loved him, but he didn't *feel* her love. The foundation for love of self, nurturing, and limits had not been laid, and the neural networks in his feeling brain took her loving gaze and sent it careening out of balance into a fear of rejection that was paralyzing at times. Sometimes he had longings for love that he could not name. Other times, he was just too numb to feel.

As I listened to his cycles over time, it seemed he sometimes regretted not getting help for his drinking earlier. He was ashamed of some of the ways he had acted and some of the scenes his sons had witnessed—a glass pitcher broken in fury, the recycling bin stacked with wine bottles, and some ugly arguments with Karen. Now he had built within him, brick by brick by brick, a depth of intimacy with himself. He was above the line enough to be intimate with another and was deeply pleased at his growing intimacy with Michelle. But one evening, Tom came to the group looking stricken. His face was uncharacteristically pale, and he looked somehow smaller.

When I opened the session for people to do cycles, Tom did not volunteer. So I checked with him. "Tom, do you need to do cycles?"

He nodded. When he spoke, his voice was so flat that I knew something was very wrong.

"It's Michelle," he said as he rubbed his face with both hands and covered his eyes. "She's being hard on me."

"Your Thinking Journal . . ."

"We've been seeing each other for more than a year—well, nineteen months, and she's putting the squeeze on me to move forward."

"To move forward . . ."

"She wants to either get married or have some commitment to each other. I keep telling her that it's like we're married and that I want to spend the rest of my life with her, and then she starts to cry and I feel like a total bastard."

Everyone in the room was silent.

"I can't put myself in a powerless situation again. I can't leave myself open to another ugly divorce and a woman taking away all my power. I have this nearly uncontrollable urge to run as far away as I can get . . ."

He began rubbing his neck and looked as if he was in as much agony as a person could be. Whenever the pain goes that deep, it often pays to look around and see if there's some emotional trash.

"Do you want to take out emotional trash?"

"From Karen?" he asked.

"From the earliest time, if you can," I responded.

"That would be my mother," he said. "God, I can't stand doing another cycle on my mother. I've spent a zillion hours in therapy about my mother and the death grip she put on me with her tacit rejection and being out-to-lunch emotionally."

"I'm not suggesting insight," I said. "I'm suggesting that for deep hurts, you have to do a lot of very deep natural flows of feelings until the splinter comes out, until the crack in your heart heals."

He sat up in his chair and said, "I need to take out emotional trash about both of them."

"When you're ready . . ."

"My mother. I don't feel angry. I've felt angry at her for decades for being so removed. What I feel is sad, sad that I was alone. . . . I feel afraid that if I ever started to open up about my sadness, it would overwhelm me. . . . I feel afraid that Michelle will be put off by my neediness. . . . I feel afraid that she will reject me, too. . . . I feel afraid that I will still be alone. . . . I feel afraid that she will start looking like my mother to me . . ."

Tom stopped for a moment, then said, "Actually, she *is* looking like my mother to me. I feel afraid that I can never get away from my mother. . . . I feel like she's going to fuck up the rest of my life . . . which makes me angry. . . . I feel angry that I've let a bumbling woman, who was trying the best she could but did a bad job of it, mess up my life. . . . I feel afraid that I'm going to continue to have her haunt me. . . . I feel guilty that I haven't taken care of this before now."

"Use the limits cycle to separate Michelle from your mother. You know how to do it. They're like a pair of closed scissors now; the expectations are merged. Open the scissors and separate the expectations."

Tom nodded. "My unreasonable expectation is that Michelle is my mother. My unreasonable expectation is that Michelle is going to be as removed and unloving as my mother was."

"Separate now from before, your mother from Michelle. In the past, it was a reasonable expectation, as a child, that . . ."

"In the past, as a child, I had a mother who was unloving, and I was dependent upon her for love."

"Fantastic. In the present . . ."

"In the present, I have more skill and . . . ," he was searching for the words, ". . . and I get the love from myself . . ."

". . . and the spiritual?" I asked.

"Not really. Why?"

I shrugged. "That intimacy comes in handy when it is hard to forgive, when it is difficult to pull yourself out of a control struggle . . ."

He shook his head slightly and went on with his expectation. "I expect myself now to get my love from myself and from Michelle, who is not my mother."

"Separate your mother and Michelle."

"My mother *did not* have the skills to be loving to me. I did not have the skills to leave. Michelle *does* have the skills to be loving to me. I do have the skills to leave."

"Great. Positive and powerful?"

"I am not the same person I was. Michelle is not my mother."

"The essential pain?"

He looked perplexed and took several moments to respond.

"The essential pain is . . . I was powerless in the past." He was squinting. "My childhood was very lonely."

"The earned reward?"

"I am not powerless now. Making a commitment to Michelle doesn't mean I give up my power."

His face was peaceful, and the color was back.

"Do you feel above the line?"

He nodded.

"So what I need is . . . ," I nodded toward him.

"What I need is to begin to trust myself more and trust Michelle more. I need to take this slowly, but I need to begin to move forward."

"The 'Would you please . . . '?"

"I need support from Michelle and from the group. That's it!"

I looked at him. "Tom, so you're going to continue to keep your fingers on the pulse of your inner life, feel your feelings, grieve your losses. You're going to take the small steps you need to take in order to begin moving forward with the relationship, even though it brings up emotional trash and requires you to face the essential pain of rejection or surrender."

He smiled and said, "Precisely."

28. Vibrancy

You may have already started using the method, doing cycles, and watching yourself pop above the line for a moment or an hour or longer. When people get the hang of using the cycles, they usually say, "Wow, it really works!"

But quite frankly, it doesn't work that well at first, at least in comparison to what occurs later on—and the journey can be rather long. Sometimes it feels like you're barely taking baby steps, or that you're sludging through mud. That slow grind goes on for at least the first half of the climb, and sometimes longer.

Then, often when you least expect it, the pace of the journey irreversibly quickens. People feel as though, overnight, they've moved from the middle of the climb to the branches near the top of the tree. It's as though the feeling brain's neural networks that supported imbalance have given way, and the new neural networks that support balance are dominating. When people begin to use the skills more deeply, more often, and more effectively when they near the top of the tree, they usually reap their sweetest fruit soon thereafter—typically, within three to six months.

Vibrancy doesn't usually occur until you approach the top of the tree. What vibrancy *is*, precisely, I am still not completely certain. All I can tell you is how it *looks* and what other changes accompany it.

It all starts with the face.

As people approach the top of the tree, their faces change, and often their voices do too. That's because the feeling brain affects contractions in the many small muscles of the face, which are directly connected to the skin. So when your feeling brain changes to favor balance, that transformation will be apparent on your face. Voices are imbued with emotion, and as your emotional balance changes, you may find a new voice—one that is more authentic, stronger, and more warm. Other changes appear, often in posture, movement and skin.

Of Emily, Drew, and Tom, it was Emily's face that changed first. She had never had a harsh expression, but still, her face softened

---

Reasonable Expectations: Vibrancy

I expect myself to do the best I can to:

- Take excellent care of my health
- Take pride in my body and myself
- Avoid external solutions
- Create a happy, healthy lifestyle for myself
- Stay above the line, connected to my spirit

---

somehow. She looked far more alert and happy, her skin glowed more and her voice had a new strength and authenticity to it.

When Drew began her journey, her expression was usually either vacant or full of animated upset. Soon after Emily's face began to change, Drew's face grew to have a look of innocence. I imagined that she had looked much like that when she was a child, still in balance and still the primary object of her parents' affection. Her voice grew up, too, and sounded more authoritative and balanced. It was right around that time that her external solutions began falling away. She had only a couple of drinks a couple of nights a week and had largely stopped overeating, but for the occasional handful of chocolate cookies. The drive to go to excess wasn't completely turned off, but it was nearly gone.

Tom's transformation took longer. I kept waiting to see a change, but it wasn't coming! There were clearly other signposts of changes in him—the fading away of his overworking, his drinking, and his overthinking was an obvious sign of progress. But when his change in facial expression and voice, and the vibrancy it heralded, didn't come, I worried.

One evening at least six months after Drew and Emily began looking more vibrant, Tom walked into the session and was clearly *different*. The change was by no means subtle—*everyone* could see it.

I could hardly contain my pleasure. "Tom, you look different!"

He frowned. "I do?"

Everyone laughed.

Drew said, "C'mon, Tom. Yes! You do. Your face looks warm and relaxed and peaceful."

Emily said, "You look ten years younger."

Mark spoke up cautiously. "Tom, I can see a change, too. A big one."

That change in facial expression and voice often marks the time when the method begins to snowball, and the retraining of the feeling brain begins to have a deeper effect. What once seemed impossible to accomplish now happens spontaneously, or with a modicum of planning and effort. The threshold of need for the skills comes crashing down, for we are taking better care of our health, setting limits with external solutions, and having more Body Pride. We are eating in a more balanced way and creating a lifestyle that is active, rewarding, and restorative.

Vibrancy is what it looks like to have a Solution, and it is nothing short of beautiful. People look radiant, as though light and beauty are coming off their bodies, perhaps the synergism of emotional balance, spiritual connection, more intimacy, and a healthy lifestyle.

When I first met Emily, she believed that her sweetest fruit was balance. In fact, it was what she most wanted when she was at the base of the tree. But she had actually picked that fruit near the middle of the tree. She had mastered the skill of taking out her tool kit and using the skills to pop herself above the line. As her climb continued, external solutions had lost their power over her. As she stopped wanting all that sugar, she had lost some weight, though one could never have thought of her as heavyset.

But of course, there was one last reward that Emily simply could not reach, and it vexed her to the point that she was beside herself.

One evening, as she was nearing her Solution, she came to a group session screaming mad. As soon as the group began, she asked to do a cycle and went right into it without even doing a Thinking Journal. The feelings were that hot.

"I HATE it that my body is so sickly. . . . I CAN'T STAND it that I am so fragile. . . . I am FURIOUS that my body is giving out on me. . . . I feel angry that I have one illness after another, one medical problem which causes another, and I am nearly always feeling GOSH AWFUL. IT'S NOT FAIR!"

She wasn't done.

"I feel sad . . . I don't feel sad. I feel petrified. . . . I feel scared out of my mind that I am going to be this pathetic, sickly person for the rest of my days, that I will NEVER feel vibrant and I will

NEVER feel strong and free, and that my whole life will turn into this nightmare of pills and doctors and chronic pain, lethargy, nausea, and misery. I am scared to death.

"And I'm sick of it! I'm sick of feeling bad. . . . I am furious that I have let it go on for so long, and I'm sad that my body is sick, and I feel guilty that I've not taken my health seriously. . . . I feel guilty that I take better care of my houseplants than I do my body."

With that, she covered her face and started to laugh and cry at the same time.

She patted her chest. "That was exhausting! But I feel so much better."

There it was again. Emily's limits had been ground in so deeply during the second half of her climb that they automatically lifted her above the line. More and more often, she could be totally authentic with her feelings, and then when the Natural Flow of Feelings ended, she felt acceptance, safety, and power. She was above the line.

All she needed to do was complete the nurturing cycle.

"What do you need?"

Essential Pain and Earned Rewards: Vibrancy

- It takes time, money, and hard work.
- More vibrancy! More joy!

- I have to do things I don't want to do.
- I will get stronger.

- My body is not perfect.
- I am human and perfect in my own way.

- I am not in complete control of my health.
- I will use the control I do have.

- I have neglected myself.
- I can start honoring my body now.

- Nobody will do this for me.
- I can do it myself.

"What I need is . . . to take my health seriously. To find better doctors. To exercise more." She grabbed her thin but shapeless arms. "See these arms? They have NO muscle in them. I've been so lazy about my body, and I am furious enough now to do whatever it takes to have an abundance of vibrancy. An *abundance*!"

"The 'Would you please . . .'?"

"I need support from . . . I would say Clay, but I really don't want to get him involved. Part of his dark side is to be extremely controlling. When he puts away the dishes from the dishwasher, he insists that everything must line up perfectly, even the flatware! When I talk to him about my health, he either tunes me out or gets so overly involved and controlling that I feel like I must be a total imbecile. I love the man, but it's not reasonable to expect that he can give me the support I need.

"I can't share health information with my social friends because most of them have no limits whatsoever. If I told even one person I was going to have a colonoscopy, nearly every human in San Francisco would know within twenty-four hours!"

She looked around the room. "Actually, I could do cycles. I would love support from the group."

Drew responded, "I'd love to do cycles with you."

Emily was known for doing cycles that went on and on, sometimes for an hour. Tom said, "I'll do Community Connections with you, but I max out at thirty minutes."

She smiled. "Okay, my friend. Thirty minutes. I always knew you were a lightweight."

He smiled back.

Emily did just what she said she would do. She took her health seriously, got all the support she needed, went to the gym and started lifting weights, and kept herself emotionally balanced and spiritually connected.

About two months later, she was done. She had her Solution, and her whole body and soul were above the line. She certainly had what she had thought was her sweetest fruit, emotional balance, but she most cherished the true touchstone of her development: vibrancy.

She spoke about her life to come, and I asked her about her piano and her dreams, what she most wanted in her life now.

Emily spoke slowly. "Right now, I'm not making any particular plans. I'm very, very happy. I feel extremely solid in the skills, and I know I will never lose sight of myself again. I love my piano classes and am somewhat relieved to see the children go to college. Clay and I are closer than ever, and I am at peace with the moment."

She was just so happy and had that *look* of joy that comes with having a Solution. "Emily, I'm so happy for you and would love it if you would allow me to check your Solution."

She was shining with vibrancy. "I would love it if you would."

"Do you have any external solutions?"

Emily said proudly, "No. Not one."

"Do you have an abundance of integration?"

"Yes!"

"Balance?"

"YES."

"Sanctuary?"

"Very much so."

"Intimacy?"

"Yes. It's never been better."

"Vibrancy?"

"YES!"

"Spirituality?"

"Yes. I've always had it, but now it has deepened. That connection is more solid."

I folded my arms across my chest, feeling very happy and proud of her, and said, "Emily, it sounds as if you have a Solution. Congratulations!"

There, next to me, in this circle of people who were all on the same pathway, was a happy, healthy, sensual, vibrant woman! She was *beautiful*, and she had created this transformation herself, by building the skills within her—brick by brick by brick.

29. Spirituality

Spirituality usually arrives after the other five rewards have been secured. Even those who begin the climb with a spiritual base find that their spirituality deepens. For those whose early environment contained missteps of a greater magnitude, spirituality may be their sweetest fruit. At the very least, it is a reward that must be felt, if not in abundance, then with some depth if their sweetest fruit is to be reached.

Spirituality, as this work draws upon it, has little to do with religion or dogma or anything cognitive. It is more like desire than intellect, in that it is about connection—something the thinking brain is ill equipped to provide. Spirituality is the capacity to keep your fingers on the pulse of your inner life so deeply that you touch something more, however you experience or define it. It results in knowing that you are not alone, that there is a sense of the universe, a natural presence, a mystical connection, or personal rapture that embodies the spiritual dimension of life.

We can talk about how spirituality nourishes us the way external solutions never could. However, to get practical for a moment, without a spiritual connection, it is very *hard* to do the cycles deeply and well. You can do them "all right," but all right is often not enough, especially if the cards life has dealt give you a high threshold of need for the skills. Without the immense sense of safety having a spiritual base brings, feelings simply don't go very deep. Moreover, our "reasonable" expectations may have an attachment to overcontrol, whether it is expressed or not. As long as we can act as if we're God and can determine what will be, we may not willingly submit to the essential pain of life. Instead, we fight it. Our cycles go round and round but may not result in the feeling of personal harmony that people experience when they are above the line.

People who tend to think rather than feel often have more difficulty reaping the reward of spiritual connection. If spiritual connection is a feeling-brain affair and we're accustomed to relying on our thinking brain for processing daily life, we're likely to run into trouble. That is why people in this training who are highly thinking-oriented and have done enough hourly feelings checks to bring themselves to a nearly constant awareness of their feelings often go back late in training and practice that skill once again. For without a deep emotional connection to ourselves it is unlikely that we will have a deep emotional connection to the divine.

Some of us have been hurt deeply early in life and are likely to find it more challenging to feel a spiritual connection. It's only logical, for how could we believe there is a universal safety net if we weren't afforded that net as a child? Yet, beyond that logic, there is a biological basis for how difficult it can be for those of us with the most unresponsive early lives to feel a spiritual connection. It turns out that if you are exposed early in life to severe physical or emotional abuse or neglect, some of the early development of the feeling brain's neural structures may be affected. The normal developmental process that involves clipping some structures rather than others may clip those that favor a life of connection.

Knowing that can be a relief in some way. If we experienced severe early abuse or neglect, it means that we would expect to work harder and take longer to reach our Solution. Moreover, that Solution may be defined slightly differently, that is, within the limits of our biological destiny. We may find it harder to connect. We may find that the connection isn't as strong. But accepting our losses in life is part of having a Solution, for we are all, in our own ways, handicapped. It is a matter of seeing ourselves accurately, grieving the losses, accepting our limitations, and going on.

This last reward is the one that is the most difficult for some people, and many people have all the rewards except this one. If their spirituality is a large pool of water, they may have walked up to the edge, look into the water, then turned around and retraced their steps. They have not reached a true Solution.

So if you hate religion, by all means, hate it. If you can't stand the word "God," don't use it. If you define spirituality in your own way, as nature or the common goodness or whatever, then do that. But consider giving some attention to finding a way that is honest, acceptable, meaningful, and rewarding to you to receive spiritual connection in life.

By the time Emily had her Solution, both Drew and Tom were close to their sweetest fruit but could not yet pluck it from the branches. It would stay just beyond their reach until they had

Reasonable Expectations: Spirituality

I expect myself to do the best I can to:

- Be aware of what I need from the spiritual and ask for it

- Be aware of what the spiritual needs from me and do my best to do it

- Expect to receive from the spiritual just what I *need*, even if it is not what I *want*

- Forgive myself, forgive others, and forgive God

everything in their lives that they needed—an abundance of all the rewards, including a spiritual connection.

Drew said in group, "I am so near my Solution that I can taste it. I've been working hard on expectations, and the one I'm trying to grind in right now is, 'I am not a bad person.' "

"Drew, are you sure that's a reasonable expectation?" I asked.

She dropped her jaw and choked a little. "You mean, I'm a bad person?"

I shook my head. "No, Drew. It's the other way around. Saying you're not a bad person sounds like, 'No, really, I'm not the most evil person who ever walked the streets!' "

Several people laughed. Drew didn't.

She hunched over in her chair. "It's not that I don't appreciate my light side. I do now more than I ever have. But part of me feels unlovable, like I *am* a bad person."

Her tone was so sober that the room turned quiet.

I said, "You feel unloved by God."

Her eyes were slightly moist, and she nodded, looking at the floor.

"Drew," I went on, "a defect in the relationship with one's parents can cause a defect in the relationship with the spiritual. The love that is there for you becomes blocked. But the nourishment of that love is important to your capacity to do what you came to Earth to do and to experience a full life."

She looked up slightly.

"Your skills are very strong now, and it may be that doing a cycle on this most sensitive and important piece of emotional trash will help."

She said quietly, "I'd like to."

"Begin when you are ready."

She furrowed her brow. "I don't feel angry at my parents. They were only human, and the situation they were in was tough. I've really forgiven them."

"But the hurt remains, the leftover learnings that harm you."

She nodded.

"More than anything," she said, "I hate God for putting me in that situation. I hate Him."

"When you are ready . . ."

"I HATE YOU, God, for ruining my life. . . . I hate you for making me miserable. . . . I can't stand it that I was stranded in that horrible family with no place to go. . . . I hate it that you didn't protect me. . .

"I feel sad that you don't love me. . . . I feel sad that I am not important to you. . . . I feel afraid that I will trust you and you will abandon me again, and I feel guilty for hating you."

She looked at me and said, "I'm actually not feeling that so mad at God anymore. I've been feeling more of a sense of grace. It's just this one part of me . . ."

"I know."

Drew took a deep breath. "My unreasonable expectation? I don't really know." She looked to me.

"Drew, as children, it is a reasonable expectation that when our parents don't have the skills to be responsive to us, we don't feel loved. There may be a blurring of parent and God, and as a small child, we don't feel loved by God either and assume that we are bad."

Drew said, "My unreasonable expectation is that if I don't feel loved, God doesn't love me."

I nodded.

"A more reasonable expectation is that God always loved me but I couldn't feel it."

I nodded again.

"Positive and powerful? I'm *not* bad. The love was there. It's just that I couldn't feel it."

"And the essential pain? Drew, this is very difficult. Please take your time."

She was quiet for several moments.

"The essential pain of accepting that God always did love me is that . . . well, that I don't believe he did."

"Let's go back to the Natural Flow of Feelings."

"I feel angry that that son of a bitch screwed up my life."

She was on to something.

"I feel furious that He hated my guts enough to give me such shitty parents. . . . I can't stand it that I've made a cesspool of my life. . . . I HATE what I have done to myself. . . . I can't stand it that I've screwed with my body with drinking and smoking and eating, and that I've lived this depressed, isolated, miserable life, all while putting on a happy face and being Mother Teresa at school. . . . I JUST HATE IT!"

And with that, she screamed. It was the scream she had been pushing down since the age of eight, and it echoed through the empty hallways outside that basement classroom that late evening, with only a janitor or two to hear.

"Pheeew," said Drew. "Oh, that felt good! Pheew."

She let out a few more deep breaths, and several moments passed. The group was completely attentive. No one moved. Finally, she took a deep breath, looked at me, smiled, and said, "That's it. That's it. I'm above the line."

I smiled and chuckled, "Wow!"

Then I waited to hear what was next.

"What I need is to love myself and to appreciate that God has always loved me. I just couldn't feel it, but I can now."

Again, I waited. The room waited.

"The support I need? Probably to do cycles, but for now, I need to just sit with this and feel this deeply."

Then she looked directly at me. "I never realized that it wasn't me. I didn't know that the love was always there, just that what happened with my parents blocked it from me. I can see that now." She paused and clarified herself. "Actually, I can feel it now."

After a monumental cycle like that one, no one in the room is left untouched. There were lots of Tender Morsels, but only after several moments of quiet as each individual's own raging feelings began to calm.

Mark said, "Amazing. I can't believe you did that cycle. I will never forget it. Thank you, Drew."

Emily said, "Thank you for trusting us enough to do that work. I love you."

Drew smiled, "I know. I love you, too."

Tom said, "Your cycle was nothing less than inspiring. Thank you, Drew."

We took a break for a few minutes, as we do when a cycle has been very intense. Someone opened the windows that looked out on a cement wall, a pathway that led to the busy street. Several went to the restroom and others sat in their chairs, still recovering from the emotional power of Drew's cycle.

Weeks later, I would look back on that cycle as what completed Drew's Solution for her. When she clearly had her Solution, about a month later, she said what I supposed she would say, which was, "I can't believe it! I have no external solutions, none! Plus all of the rewards—an abundance of them. I saw it happen to other people, but I never thought it would happen to me!"

But it did. She had worked hard, and she had earned it.

After people had taken a break on the day Drew did that cycle, we still had a whole hour of group time left in the session. When we were all seated in our chairs again, I asked the group, "Who would like to do a cycle?"

Tom's hand shot up.

I nodded at him, then noticed that Emily's hand had been raised, too.

"Emily?"

"I just want to share something with the group. It's brief."

"Okay," I said.

"It's an expectation that is working very well for me that has to do with the spiritual."

"What is it?"

"It is: *I expect that the spiritual will give me just what I need when I need it, even if it's not what I want.*"

I thought about that one for several moments.

"Tell me more, please," I said.

She told about Rob and his speech problem, and how tormented she had been about it, how close she had been to becoming bitter about such an unfathomable loss. She spoke about that tight fist of overcontrol, and how her expectation had allowed her to open her hand to receive more in life—and to forgive.

Even in one life, there are two worlds: above the line and below. We have moments in which we are below the line, disconnected from ourselves, from others, and from the spiritual. We have those in which we are above the line, and connected. Some people understand that their life will move between the two worlds: "I will go below the line when my threshold of need for the skills goes up. But I don't have to be perfect to be wonderful. I will use my skills to move myself back to the world above the line." But most people live a pattern: They are either mainly above the line or mainly below.

The noted psychologist Wayne Dyer has spoken of our choice to be a slave to the ego or a servant of the spiritual. I think of that as a shift in expectation, an expectation that colors our entire life force. It is either

I expect to get what I want when I want it,

OR

I expect God to give me precisely what I need when I need it, even if it is not what I want.

As people make the climb, they often experience a cluster of seemingly impossible losses, changes, and upsets. Some seem torturous, as if God is intentionally inflicting on them the pain that they can least tolerate. The magic of it is that with their tool kit in hand, in response to those challenges, they dig deeper. When they do, a spiritual shift often occurs, which changes everything.

Emily said, "I realize now that I had to make a decision. What game was I playing, the world of this world or the spiritual world? Was I furious at God for not giving me what I wanted when I wanted it: three totally "perfect" children? Or was I ready to accept that it was all perfect, that there would be blessings from this loss that I could not now fully understand? It was then that I opened that tight fist of overcontrol, stopped wanting it my way, and accepted my life and accepted Rob's."

Emily's Solution was continuing to evolve, and it would do so in the coming years. Getting a Solution does not mean that your development stops, but that the full complement of skills and rewards is in place so that you continue to evolve and your life continues to unfold as it should.

Essential Pain and Earned Rewards:
Spirituality

- I am not in complete control.
- I don't have to be.

- I have responsibilities to fulfill.
- The spiritual will help me fulfill them.

- I don't always get what I want.
- I always get precisely what I need.

- I am not perfect. I have done bad things.
- I am human. I have been forgiven.

- I must stay above the line.
- I will be aware of the grace and mystery of life.

After the group gave several Tender Morsels to Emily, Tom was still restless in his seat and ready to do cycles. He began:

"My relationship with Michelle brings me more happiness than I have ever had, and I feel very grateful . . ."

". . . and proud?"

He smiled, "Yes, proud that I have the skills, and happy that I have so much love in my life."

He paused, and his face turned cloudy as he shook his head.

"I still have this horrible problem with her daughter, Nicola . . . and quite truthfully, with Michelle, too, about how she parents Nicola. I've supported Michelle in parenting Nicola the way she sees fit, and since I set a limit on Nicola's behavior—that I'd leave if she sassed me—things have gotten better. Michelle has been asking more of Nicola, so I really can't complain too much. But I still find it very difficult to be around Nicola. When Michelle isn't around, Nicola pulls some fast ones on me, like asking me for money that her mother forgot to give her or calling me to come pick her up at the mall because she locked herself out of the car. All of this is fine, but it bothers me that all she does is take! She is as selfish and self-centered with me as she is with her mother. Michelle and I are getting married . . ."

The room erupted with excitement.

'd around the room, smiling. "I didn't tell you that,

..ily shook her head. "No, Tom, somehow you left out that piece of information."

He looked sheepish. "Well, I asked her last Saturday night. She came over, I had some French champagne open, and the fire was blazing in the fireplace, and I asked her."

The cycle was now completely stopped, and the normal structure of the group went out the window.

No one was surprised to hear that Tom had popped the cork on a bottle of champagne. About a month before, Tom had had a glass of wine socially and found that he didn't want more, that he was able to have one glass and no more. But everyone was quite excited that he'd popped the question to Michelle, and Tom was clearly enjoying telling his story.

"Yes, she made me get down on my knee, and I gave her a ring, and we're going to be engaged for as long as we need to. There's no rush, but I love this woman, and I want to spend the rest of my life with her."

Mark said, "Congratulations, my man."

Tom nodded and beamed.

"I'm happy for you," said Emily.

Drew spoke up, "It's about time! Too bad you're off the market now."

He shared more details, and the mood in the room was festive and self-congratulatory. Everyone in the room had done cycles with Tom about Michelle, and all felt as if they shared a piece of the glory, that this man whom they had first seen in so much pain was now joyously fulfilled in love, anticipating a deepening commitment with the woman of his dreams.

Tom's attention eventually returned to his cycle.

"I feel totally incompetent in this area, and my relationship with Nicola could spoil what I have with Michelle. I've done a million cycles to get above the line with her, and people in the group have been great at listening, but I still can't stand the kid, and I hate living with her."

"Want to try the Intimacy Cycle?"

"I did. All I could get is: How do I feel? Angry that she is such a selfish kid. What do I need? To get away from her."

"What happened when you asked, 'How does she feel and what does she need'?"

"She feels . . . mixed up the way all kids do. She feels angry at me for stealing her mother's attention. What does she need? She needs to punish me every chance she gets!"

"Have you used the Spiritual Cycle on it?"

"No. I haven't used that cycle at all."

"It mirrors the Intimacy Cycle—two bicycle tires. You consider the situation in which you find yourself, then ask: *How do I feel? What do I need from the spiritual?* and *How does the spiritual feel? What does the spiritual need from me?*"

"I could try it."

"Most people are resistant to using it, but when they do, the power of it often amazes them. Like the Intimacy Cycle, they find that typically one of those bicycle tires isn't spinning."

I opened it up to the group, knowing full well that those who were new to the group wouldn't necessarily find what I was about to say very helpful. A sensitivity to this skill typically only appears very late in training.

"How many people find that it's easy for them to be aware of how the spiritual feels and what the spiritual needs from them, but forget to consider their own feelings and what they need from the spiritual?"

Several hands shot up.

"How many people do the opposite—are only aware of their own feelings and what they need from the spiritual, but the feel-

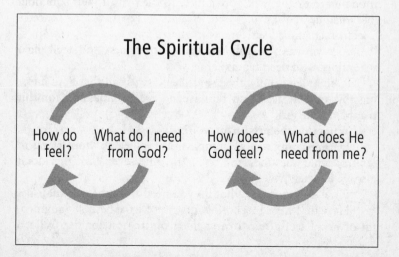

The Spiritual Cycle

How do
I feel?

What do I need
from God?

How does
God feel?

What does He
need from me?

ings and needs of the spiritual dimension of life completely escape them?"

More hands shot up.

"How many think that what I'm saying makes no sense at all and they would prefer me to go away and stop talking about it?"

Several laughed, and four hands shot up.

"Great. Are you ready, Tom?"

"Yes," he said, sitting up tall in his chair.

"Here you are, loving Michelle and building an intimate relationship with her. You have the skills to access the strength, goodness, and wisdom with which you were born more and more often, and from a loving relationship comes so much that is good for you and for those around you."

He nodded.

"Nicola is there, trying to grow up and find her way, throwing darts at you when she can, and generally being selfish and self-absorbed and miserable to be around."

He nodded.

"Imagine the spiritual in any way that you want to . . . God, the universe, nature, the force . . ."

"The universe."

I nodded.

"No, not the universe. Use God," he said.

"There you are in this situation, and I want you to use your imagination, your intuition, your feelings—go under those thoughts to the belly of your brain, to the seat of your soul, and just imagine . . ."

His face looked serene.

"Ask yourself, in this situation, how does God feel? And what does God need from me?"

He breathed deeply, then said, "God feels sad that I am messing this up. He feels sad that I can't feel compassion for this troubled little girl."

"What does he need from you?"

"He needs me to feel compassion for her, to stop trying to control what she does and to . . . love her even though I don't always like her."

"How do you feel? What do you need from the spiritual?"

"How do I feel? I feel . . . guilty that I have been so judgmental of her. I feel afraid I can't find compassion for her. What I need is for God to help me love her even when she is not acting very lovable."

His face looked so serene and beautiful. I knew that Tom had his Solution.

"Tom, you have your sweetest fruit, don't you?"

He smiled and said, "Yes, I do."

The most important step you can take is to begin. Following are a few strategies to make your first cycles easier. Once you've popped yourself above the line a few times, you will easily recognize the feeling and probably want to have more of it. Though your first cycles won't be nearly as powerful as those you'll experience later on, you will probably be amazed that the method, in fact, works!

Try any of the following to begin:

1. Use the Nurturing Cycle

One easy way to start using the method is to ask yourself the questions of the nurturing cycle. Do it once a day for five days. Notice how much easier it becomes by the fifth day.

Just ask yourself:

- How do I feel?
- What do I need?
- Do I need support?

If you don't know the answer, don't worry. Just keep doing it once a day, and you will be likely to begin to notice a change.

2. Check Your Solution Pocket Reminder

Clip the Solution Pocket Reminder on page 369, and keep it with you. Once a day, take out the reminder and read the questions. Take note of the answers that appear in your mind. If you like, enlist a friend to ask you the questions. Either way, start asking; the answers will begin to be clear to you.

3. Use "The Instant Connection"

On the Internet, there is an Instant Connection that poses the questions of the cycles to you in the correct order. All you have to do is click, without thinking about what question to ask next. It's available to all members of our website. For more information about it, go to www.sweetestfruit.org.

4. The Natural Flow of Feelings

Another way to begin that can have a rather immediate positive effect is to do the Natural Flow of Feelings once each day.

Just take time once each day to complete these statements:

I feel angry that . . .

I feel sad that . . .

I feel afraid that . . .

I feel guilty that . . .

AND

I feel grateful that . . .

I feel happy that . . .

I feel secure that . . .

I feel proud that . . .

These are four easy ways to begin. Use them, or any other methods that work for you. What is most important is that you take a big, deep breath and muscle up the courage to start. It will only get easier and easier.

Appendix B
The Solution Pocket Reminder

Below is the Solution Pocket Reminder, which will help you use the method as you begin your journey. Carry it with you or paste it where you can see it much of the day. Please enjoy this little bit of added support.

The Solution™

Am I *above* the line or *below* the line?

If I am *above* the line:
How do I feel?
What do I need?
Do I need support?

If I am *below* the line:
I feel angry that . . .
I feel sad that . . .
I feel afraid that . . .
I feel guilty that . . .
Are my expectations reasonable?
Is my thinking positive & powerful?
What is the essential pain?
What is the earned reward?
What do I need?
Do I need support?

The Pathway (2003), *The Solution* (1998), ReganBooks
The Institute for Health Solutions   www.thepathway.org
©Laurel Mellin 2003

*You don't have to be perfect
to be wonderful.*

Earned Rewards

grateful　　happy　　secure　　proud　　rested
satisfied　　loved　　healthy

Essential Pain

angry　　sad　　afraid　　guilty　　tired　　hungry
full　　lonely　　sick

What is your sweetest fruit?

integration　　balance　　sanctuary　　intimacy
vibrancy　　spirituality
freedom from external solutions

Regardless of whether you are a joiner or a loner, you may want to receive more support with your journey. Fortunately, whether you prefer community or professional support, many options are available to you.

Community support

1. Join or Start a Solution Circle

Several years ago, we began receiving telephone calls from people who were meeting informally to use the method. They were getting together regularly with a few friends, neighbors, or coworkers to "do cycles"—that is, to practice these skills. Their enthusiasm for these gatherings was contagious, so we began listening very carefully to learn more about what made their Solution Circles so successful. Using what we learned from their experiences, we've included a guide for creating your own circle in the appendix "Solution Circles" (see page 375). People in these circles use Solution Kits, but otherwise this support is absolutely free.

2. Find a Solution Buddy

Saying to yourself, "I feel sad," yields a certain kind of experience. Saying those same words to another person yields an experience that's quite different, and typically far more riveting. The questions of the cycles, which create an intense intimacy with yourself, can also create satisfying intimacy with others. These skills grow best in the warm, moist soil of love. If there is someone trustworthy in your life with whom you would feel safe speaking about your feelings and needs, consider asking that person to listen to you do cycles.

The conversation may go something like this: "I'm doing The Solution, and I'm worried that I'm not practicing enough. I need to be listened to while I practice doing cycles. Would you be willing to listen to me do them? What I would need from you is to simply listen to me without interrupting until I am done. When I'm through, please say nothing at all or say something positive (nothing negative or critical, and no unasked for advice). Again, all I really need you to do is to listen to me. Would you be willing to do that?"

There is also a Solution Buddy Finder on our website that lists those members who want to connect with others.

3. Take The Solution Course

The complete course involves Solution Kits, which help you muscle up on the skills and take out emotional trash in a graduated way. The kits take much of the guesswork out of using the method and guide you in deepening your nurturing inner voice, staying balanced, staying on the present, and doing gentle but effective lifestyle surgery. They include a journal/workbook, CDs of visualizations, and the advice and examples I give my own participants in each phase of the training. All professional Solution programs use these kits, and they are recommended for those in Solution Circles. The kits are so integral to the method that even in my own groups, in which I do my very best to nudge each participant to their Solution, if participants do not do their kit work, they do not progress. The kits are:

- Solution Kit 1—Launching Your Solution
- Solution Kit 2—Popping Above the Line
- Solution Kit 3—A Deeper Level of Healing
- Solution Kit 4—Staying Above the Line
- Solution Kit 5—A True Solution
- Solution Kit 6—Reaping Your Rewards

All kits are used in conjunction with this book. They are also compatible with the weight-solution book based on this method: *The Solution: 6 Winning Ways to Permanent Weight Loss* (ReganBooks, 1998).

4. Join Our Internet Community

The Solution Kits include membership in our Internet community. The site is interactive, so you can communicate with others who are on this journey worldwide. The community is restricted to those people who are currently using The Solution

Kits, so everyone you connect with on the site will be experiencing the method and working toward their sweetest fruit and having a Solution. It's an exciting and dynamic community. There are discussion boards on the site so you can communicate with others who are in various phases of the training. Solution Providers and program graduates (Solution Supporters) visit the site often to answer your questions and give their support.

Professional support

5. Coaching or Groups with Certified Solution Providers

Professional support from certified Solution Providers is available to help you reach your Solution as easily, safely, and rapidly as possible. All Solution coaches are licensed health professionals who, in addition to their professional training, have completed an eighteen-month certification program in this method. They have mastered the skills personally and clinically and provide groups in your community, support by telephone (telegroups and coaching), and periodic seminars and retreats. Check the Group Finder on our website for the providers in your area.

6. Other Professional Support

You may already have a counselor you trust and may be inclined to ask that person to coach you on these skills even if the person is not certified in the method. *We recommend that you not do this.* In our experience, most health professionals, including psychotherapists, have not mastered these skills in their own lives. As you can imagine, *you can't teach these skills with any depth unless you have them yourself.* Our experience has been that most therapists also tend to blend The Solution with insight-oriented methods that may slow or stop the pace of your journey along this pathway. Trying to "figure it out" directly conflicts with seeking to be in the present moment and using the method's tools to stay above the line.

If you are now seeing a therapist, we suggest using his or her services for general emotional support. If your therapist relies on insight or analysis, please consider the option of finding a new therapist who will simply be responsive to you rather than guiding you to analyze your life. With respect to your Solution training, we recommend that you do not ask for advice on the method or coaching in the cycles from your therapist. Instead, we suggest that you access the services of a professional trained in the method: a Solution Provider. Solution Providers will answer your questions if you post on our website in the Members section. In addition, you can access their services for personal coaching or group training in your community or by telephone.

7. Support from the Institute for Health Solutions

If you have questions about the method, contact the Institute for Health Solutions at 415–457–3331. The staff there will do their best to respond to your needs. If you prefer, visit www.thepathway.org or e-mail support@thepathway.org.

A Solution Circle is a small group of people—usually three to six—who meet together much the way a book club meets; regularly and with a common purpose. Their common purpose is to create a Solution in their own lives and a safe community in which to practice the cycles and watch one another transform. Most groups meet weekly for two hours.

The safest and most effective support during this work can be found in a Solution Group, but as of this writing, there is far more demand for these groups than there are certified providers to conduct them—and the sessions are not free.

If you are following Pathway 1 or 2—that is, you do not require professional support—you may want to get involved in starting a Solution Circle. There is something very wonderful about these groups. They're done the old-fashioned way: in neighborhoods, in homes, in community, in . . . circles.

Forming a circle

All you really need in order to start a Solution Circle is a copy of this book and the courage to call a few acquaintances, coworkers, or friends and suggest getting together to experiment with forming a circle. Just lending a copy of your book to those you'd like to have in your circle will probably be enough to give them a sense of whether or not they would like to become involved.

Ask anyone who is considering joining your circle to take the Solution Inventory to find out if a Solution Circle might provide the safety and support they require—that is, if they are on Pathway 1 or 2. If they are on Pathway 3, their needs may be better met by receiving support from health professionals certified in the method.

Effective support

The good news about Solution Circles is that they are free and can be started by almost anyone who is reasonably balanced and interested in organizing a small group. They can be conveniently located as your own living room, a church basement, or work. The not-so-good news is that there is no one there who knows the method intimately and has the professional skills to make your journey as safe, easy, and quick as possible.

Some Solution Circles function rather well on their own, but most find that they want some contact with a Solution Provider. If those in your circle feel that way, there are several options we've developed that are low in cost. The most popular one is to arrange for Circle Coaching. Once a month, your entire group meets by telephone on our conferencing line with a Solution Provider and asks questions, does cycles, or uses the time in any way the group wants. Since there are several people sharing the expense, the cost is low and everyone benefits.

In response to requests from Solution Circles, we have also developed Solution Mini-Groups, CDs of real groups that I lead. Some Solution Circles circulate them among members or listen to them as part of the Circle meeting. They provide a model for how to do cycles and how to run a Circle. You can hear how participants progress, the questions they ask, and the cycles they do. The coaching I give them may be helpful for you, too, plus the enthusiasm is contagious and infuses your circle with more vibrancy. Last, there are Solution Retreats: weekend intensives on the method that give you a chance to improve your skills, receive coaching from a Solution Provider, and have some fun.

Creating safety

Some of these circles are exceedingly casual, meeting monthly for a warm gathering and some cycles practice. However, most are seriously directed toward reaching a Solution, with weekly meetings and use of the Solution Kits. Regardless of which style you prefer, I strongly encourage you to use the format I've suggested. It has been tested thoroughly and often gives circle members the right blend of nurturing, community, skill practice, and structure to create a joyful and effective experience.

Although Solution Circles can be wonderful, they are not without risks, including unsafe behavior such as giving unasked-for advice or being intrusive, judgmental, or aggressive. Another risk is that the group starts blending The Solution with other methods, which generally dilutes Solution work to the point that it loses its effectiveness.

Another risk of Solution Circles is that members reinforce one another in being below the line and/or using the method ineffectively. You know that the program is not being used effectively if participants engage in self-destructive behavior, do not pop themselves above the line when they do cycles, or are below the line emotionally for a prolonged period. If that occurs in your group, ask yourselves whether the group members need professional support and should consider that they are not on Pathway 2 (community support) but on Pathway 3 (professional support). Perhaps you all are on Pathway 2 but even that pathway benefits from some professional support.

Safety is so central to each participant's progress that we recommend that any group member who does not stay within safety guidelines is asked to leave the group. If you find yourself in a circle that is not both safe and effective, consider separating from the group and accessing support that meets both of those needs.

A supportive setting

The setting you choose for your meetings should be safe, nurturing, and accessible. Many circles meet in church or temple meeting rooms, library seminar rooms, or after-hours conference rooms at work. Most meet in homes. If you're meeting at a home, be sure that any other people living there are not at home during your meeting, or that they understand that this is sacred time and you must not be interrupted.

Regardless of where you meet, the recommended room setup is the same. Move the chairs into a circle, with no table in the middle to block your connection. Consider having water and a pot of tea or decaffeinated coffee available—this adds to the nurturing atmosphere of the circle. You might also have a box of tissues, some Solution Pocket Reminders, and a copy of this book in the middle of the circle.

A session plan for a Solution Circle follows. The role of reading the plan may either rotate or be assigned to one person. Each part of the session is important to its success. If you need to plan for a shortened session at times, consider having just one person do cycles rather than two or three. Enjoy the session!

The Solution Circle Plan

1. Housekeeping

> A circle member checks for Housekeeping needs:
> "Does anyone have housekeeping, any announcements, or administrative details they want to mention now?"

Any administrative matters are taken care of or noted.

2. Statement of Purpose

> A member of the circle reads this Statement of Purpose:
> We come together to create a safe, loving community to practice the skills at the roots of health and happiness and to create a Solution in our own lives. Although we are all very different, the pathway is the same, and we respect each person's journey to reap what they most want in life, whether it be to end a common excess or to receive one of life's sweetest rewards: integration, balance, sanctuary, intimacy, vibrancy, or spirituality.

3. Safety Guidelines

> Next, a circle member reads the following Safety Guidelines:
>
> 1. **Confidentiality**—Anything shared in this circle is confidential and is not shared with others, including our spouses and best friends. Participation is confidential.
>
> 2. **Positive and Compassionate**—We are positive and compassionate toward one another, and gentle but honest with ourselves. We do not give unasked-for advice and do not interrupt others when they are doing cycles.

3. **Taking Turns**—We take turns doing cycles so that everyone has an opportunity to listen and be listened to.

4. **Tender Morsels**—After a person has completed a cycle, several people give that person a brief nurturing statement that reflects their own reaction to the cycle and typically starts with "I."

5. **Creating Safety**—If we do not feel safe in this circle, it is our responsibility to create safety for ourself right away, even if that means leaving this room. If a circle member commits a safety violation, he or she agrees to remove themselves from the group.

6. **Cooperation**—Our circle is cooperative. All members take part in room setup and cleanup and share in any administrative activities, support, or materials expenses of the group.

7. **No Blending**—Other programs or methods are not discussed in this circle. Blending The Solution with other methods decreases its power.

8. **Commitment to Safety**—We are all committed to creating a safe, loving, and joyful community that supports each of us in reaching our Solution.

4. Feelings Check

Next, a circle member reads the Feelings Check:

Please settle back into your chair and take a nice, deep breath. Be aware of your body and begin to go inside yourself. You may feel afraid, and if you are, just remind yourself that fear is just a feeling and it will fade. Go inside anyway, with a sense of curiosity (I wonder what I will find there!), strength (I am gaining the skills to feel back to balance), and a growing commitment to spending more moments of the day above the line.

Go inside past the smokescreens and the thoughts, right down to the most basic feelings, always checking for both essential pain and earned rewards.

Please check first for essential pain. Notice feeling angry, sad, afraid, guilty, tired, hungry or full, lonely, or sick.

When you are ready, please check for earned rewards, knowing that they feed us in ways that external solutions never could. Notice feeling grateful, happy, secure, proud, rested, neither hungry nor full but satisfied, feeling loved, and feeling healthy.

Please take all the time you need to feel the feelings that are true for you right now. Then, when you are ready, please rejoin the group.

Pause for about a minute.

If you need more time, please raise your hand.

The person reading the Feelings Check interlocks his or her index fingers.

The person who read the Feelings Check continues:

We've connected with ourselves so we can better connect with one another.

Let's go around the circle, each sharing at least one earned reward and at least one essential pain. If you prefer to pass, please say so.

The person reading the Feelings Check then says, "I feel . . ." Then the next person in the circle does the same, until all circle members have had an opportunity to state their feelings. If someone passes, no one comments. If someone does it incorrectly, no one comments. Circle members focus on themselves unless a person acts in a way that is not consistent with the safety guidelines, in which case they use the skills to get themselves above the line, then give that person a Hamburger Sandwich.

5. Cycles

> Someone asks: "Who would like to do cycles?"

Typically, two or three people will do cycles during a circle meeting. Some people *never* want to practice cycles, and others *always* want to. Please keep this in mind and find a way to give everyone the opportunity to participate. When a person does cycles, this is the format that has proven safe and effective:

The Thinking Journal—If you are the person doing cycles, describe something that you want to do a cycle about. If you are not below the line about something, you do not need to do cycles. Cycles can be done on anything that is driving your imbalance, whether it is a hurt from the past or a present source of stress.

You state the situation simply and briefly, resisting the urge to turn the session into a general support or psychotherapy group. Practicing the skills is what creates a Solution, not insight or compassion alone.

This verbal Thinking Journal typically takes one to three minutes. Its purpose is to enable you to get out any facts that you want the group to know so that you won't feel the need to explain yourself as you go through the Natural Flow of Feelings. Another purpose is to bring up the thoughts that will elicit strong emotions. When you can feel the emotions strongly in your body, it is typically time to move into doing cycles.

The Cycles—You then move through the Natural Flow of Feelings (I feel angry, sad, afraid, guilty), then a limits cycle. Then, when you are above the line, you complete the nurturing skill by answering the questions: What do I need? Do I need support? You keep asking yourself the questions of the cycles until you are above the line.

Listening to cycles can be very challenging for circle members. Their job is to use the skills within themselves and to avoid detaching or merging with you as you do cycles. It is not easy, but they must not interrupt you, must not give unasked-for advice, and must not correct you in any way. This is *your time* to do very intimate work, and you are very vulnerable as you do it. Your willingness to do these cycles in the presence of others is a tremendous gift to them, and an act of trust on your part.

Tender Morsels—When you feel above the line and are ready to stop, time is allowed for nurturing support. Others in the room reflect for a moment on the cycle that was done and on what they experienced, then one or more make a personal statement of caring and recognition.

Tender Morsels usually start with "I," such as, "I really care about you, and I loved watching you move yourself above the line," or, "I appreciate all the courage it takes to do a cycle that is so deep. Thank you." Since the focus of the circle is practice, Tender Morsels are sincere but brief, allowing more time to do cycles—that is, to truly practice the method.

6. Accomplishments and Challenges

> Someone reads:
> "It's time for Accomplishments and Challenges. Please focus on your training in these skills—not your general accomplishments and challenges in life—but the ways you have continued to move along this pathway. Please state your biggest accomplishment in mastering these skills in the last week and what you believe to be your biggest challenge in mastering these skills in the next week."

Examples:

- "My biggest accomplishment is that I did three Community Connections. My biggest challenge is to do them again this week."

- "My biggest accomplishment is that I didn't use any external solutions. My biggest challenge is to take out more emotional trash."
- "My biggest accomplishment last week was staying above the line in a discussion with my spouse. My biggest challenge in the next week is to do hourly feelings checks."

7. Progress Check

> Someone in the circle reads the Progress Check:
>
> - "If you attended the session, would you please raise your hand?"
> - "If you were physically active for an hour or more each day, would you please raise your hand?"
> - "If you stayed above the line with food most of the time, would you please raise your hand?"
> - "If you made three or more Community Connections this week, would you please raise your hand?"
> - "If you completed at least one chapter in The Solution Kit, would you please raise your hand?"
> - "If you met your goal for your external solution, would you please raise your hand?"
> - "If you stayed on the pathway, would you please raise both your hands?"

8. Closing Ritual

> Someone in the circle leads the Closing Ritual.

The exchanges that go on during a Solution Circle are often very precious and important. Just the act of coming together to do such intimate work is a tremendous accomplishment. As a result, we close with a brief ritual as a way of honoring our time together and our circle.

If you're not much on rituals, just say at the end of the session, in unison: "I take care of my health and my happiness."

If you like the idea of doing something more, consider closing your session the way we close all Solution Groups:

Stand in a circle, holding hands. One person says, "I take care of my health and my happiness," then squeezes the hand of the person on his or her left. That person repeats the process. This continues until the hand-squeeze is returned to the person who started the ritual.

Then, all together, everyone in the group does two things:

1. Stomp their left foot, then their right foot, then their left foot (stomp, stomp, stomp), because we all need to be close to the Earth.

2. Then put both hands in the air over their head in a "V" and shout "Yes!"—because nobody can be depressed with their hands in the air shouting "Yes!"

Stomp, stomp, stomp, YES!!

Stomp, stomp, stomp, YES!!

Appendix E
The 3-Day Balancing Plan

The Solution Three-Day Balancing Plan is a good way to quickly pop ourselves above the line if our bodies are accustomed to overeating, oversitting, or certain chemical pleasures. If it sounds too difficult for you, consider speaking with your physician about a more comprehensive plan, particularly if you are bulimic, anorexic, alcoholic, or addicted to drugs.

Coming off a caffeine overload will take about a week, and in fact, most excesses take more than three days to find their way out of our bodies. However, starting with a Three-Day Balancing Plan usually helps people turn the corner and cleanses their bodies of a fair amount of imbalance. Given enough encouragement and awareness of the consequences of continuing to use food or chemical pleasures, most of us can make it for three days. Keep in mind: It's only three days!

You don't have to make a lot of decisions on this plan. You won't be using chemical pleasures during these days, so check with your physician about how to safely stop or wean yourself off of any chemicals, from caffeine to psychotropic drugs. You will have two food plans to choose between, a Nurturing Food Plan that involves eating when hungry or a Clear Limits Food Plan that suggests what you should eat. Choose the one that you find most appealing. In addition, you will be exercising for sixty minutes per day, and sleeping or resting with the lights out between 10:00 P.M. and 6:00 A.M. At 6:00 A.M., you arise.

The evening before you begin your Three-Day Balancing Plan, have a balancing meal, then wake up the next morning and use this plan for three days. Get as much support as you can from friends, family members, coworkers, and people from your Solution community. This is not easy, but it is something that you can do. *It's only three days*.

Again, this plan is not safe for everyone. Before using the Three-Day Balancing Plan, please check with your physician to be sure it is safe and appropriate for you.

The evening before you begin . . .

When your body is out of balance, it feels awful—bloated, either overly hungry or overly full, or very slow. You may have trouble sleeping or interrupted sleep, or you may sleep too much. Your normal sensuality may be blocked, and your mood may be on a false high or an unnecessary low, or you may be emotionally numb.

To rebalance your body as rapidly as possible, begin your Three-Day Balancing Plan with a balancing evening the night before your first day on the plan.

After 5:00 P.M. that evening, do not use any chemical pleasures. No caffeine. No alcohol. No marijuana. No designer drugs.

Eat a meal that will stabilize your blood sugar: plenty of raw or cooked vegetables with healthy oils. Drink nothing but water, mineral water, or caffeine-free tea or decaffeinated coffee. Think of it as your cleansing meal.

Do calming activities before going to bed, or whatever rituals make for a good night's sleep. Unless your family responsibilities or work schedule require otherwise, go to bed by 10:00 P.M. and do not arise until 6:00 A.M. If you are awake during the night, do cycles. After eight hours in bed, get up and start the first day of your Three-Day Balancing Plan.

Begin the Three-Day Balancing Plan

On the first day of the plan, continue the work you began the night before. Do not use any chemical pleasures (or continue following the plan your physician recommended). In addition:

- Exercise for sixty minutes (but not more than ninety minutes).
- Go to bed by 10:00 P.M., and awake and get out of bed by 6:00 A.M.
- If you are awake during the night, do cycles.
- Eat according to the Nurturing Food Plan or the Clear Limits Food Plan. If you have been using chemical pleasures, the best choice for a food plan is often the Clear Limits Plan. If you are an emotional overeater, the best choice is often the Nurturing Plan.

The Balancing Meal

The Fresh Salad Option

green lettuce and sliced fresh vegetables
(as much as you would like)
3 tablespoons salad dressing
at least 2 glasses of water, drunk with your meal

The Vegetable Stew Option

vegetables, cooked (as much as you would like)
2 tablespoons olive or canola oil and
herbs of your choice
at least 2 glasses of water, drunk with your meal

Choose from these vegetables

artichoke hearts (water-pack canned or fresh)
asparagus   broccoli   Brussels sprouts
cabbage   carrots   celery   cucumbers
eggplant   garlic   green beans   green onions
jicama   leafy greens   leeks   lettuce
mushrooms   onions   peppers   sprouts
tomatoes   zucchini

The Nurturing Food Plan

Do not eat in the morning until you feel *body* hunger. When you eat, keep your fingers on the pulse of your inner life and stop eating when you are just satisfied, not full. After ten minutes, you will feel full. Turn your attention away from food, and do not eat again until you are aware of body hunger again.

Here are the basic ideas of this diet:

1. Eat Only When You Feel Hungry

Eat only when you are hungry. If a mealtime comes and you are not hungry, do not eat. If your pattern is to skip meals, then feel ravenous and overeat, instead of skipping a meal, consume something very small, such as a glass of milk, a piece of fruit, or a bowl of veggies.

2. Stop Eating When You Are Satisfied, Not Full

Stop eating when you can no longer feel sensations of hunger. It is easy to confuse emotional hunger with body hunger, so to be sure that you feel true body hunger, consider doing cycles often during the day, perhaps hourly. It's also helpful not to put too much food on your plate. Only go back for more if you feel body hunger.

3. Establish a Hunger Rhythm and Stay with It

Eat lightly in the evening so you awake feeling hungry again. Then follow your hunger throughout the day, eating when you are hungry and stopping when you are just satisfied, not full.

That's it! Just be responsive to yourself, allowing your hunger to be your guide.

The Clear Limits Food Plan

This food plan is simple to follow because it all comes down to the number three. You're only going to stay on it for a few days, so even if it's a little healthier than you'd like, you can manage. You will feel *so much better* after three days!

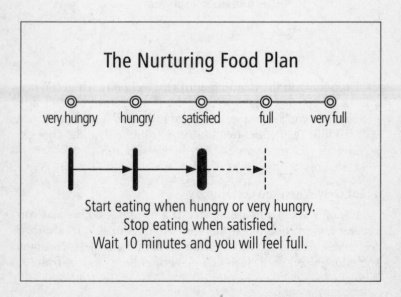

The Nurturing Food Plan

very hungry　　hungry　　satisfied　　full　　very full

Start eating when hungry or very hungry.
Stop eating when satisfied.
Wait 10 minutes and you will feel full.

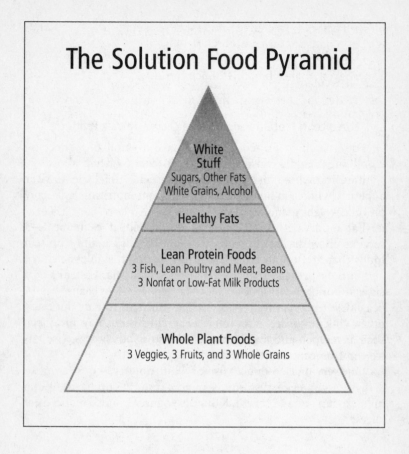

Whole plant foods

Three Veggies—Three Fruits—Three Whole Grains

These foods are attached to their natural fiber. They contain more nutrients—particularly micronutrients and phytochemicals—than processed and refined foods. They keep your blood sugar more stable and fill you up on fewer calories. Whole plant foods are the mainstay of healthful eating.

Eat fruit rather than drinking fruit juice. Eat bread and grains that are made of ingredients that look like bark off a tree (high protein sprouted wheat berries or 100-percent stone-ground whole-wheat flour), not the white stuff or pseudo-brown products based on such ingredients as enriched wheat flour or unbleached flour. Eat lots and lots and lots of vegetables: vegeta-

bles for snacks, vegetables for appetizers, vegetables on sandwiches, salads for lunch or dinner.

One serving is: 1 cup uncooked vegetables or ½ cup cooked,
1 piece fruit, 1 slice bread, 1 ounce cereal.

Lean protein foods

Three Lean Protein Foods—Three Low-Fat Milk Products

Foods high in protein can also have a stabilizing effect on
blood sugar and a positive impact on energy. They allow the
calories you eat to last longer and, as such, can decrease your
appetite. Milk products provide important nutrition and may
prevent weight gain.

Eat moderately high amounts of protein at each meal—a
serving about as big as your fist—and choose mainly protein
foods that are low in fat, such as fish, seafood, skinless chicken
and turkey breasts, lean meats (beef round, flank steak, veal
cutlets, pork tenderloin), and low-fat legumes (soybeans, beans,
peas). Use eggs sparingly—opt for egg whites, throwing out every
other yolk or using a scrambled-egg substitute. Soy products,
such as tempeh and low-fat tofu, are also good choices. Use fat-
free or 1 percent milk products.

One serving is: 6 ounces fish or white poultry, 4 ounces meat,
2 eggs, ½ cup egg substitute, 4 ounces tofu, ½ cup beans, 1 cup
milk, ¾ cup cottage cheese, 8 ounces yogurt, 1 ounce reduced-fat
cheese.

Healthy fat

Three Olive or Canola Oil, Oily Fish, Avocados, or Nuts

Include a little "healthy" fat in your diet. Healthy-fat foods
are high in monounsaturated fatty acids (MONOs) and/or
omega-3 polyunsaturated fatty acids (OMEGA-3s). They
improve the flavor of the food without adding saturated fat or
sugar, and they decrease the bad cholesterol (LDL) without low-
ering the good (HDL). They also replace the saturated fats and
trans fats that increase the risk of heart disease and the polyunsaturated fats that increase the risk of cancer and heart disease.
OMEGA-3s also reduce the risk of heart disease and may
improve emotional balance.

Oils like canola oil, olive oil, flax oil, wheat germ oil, soy oil,
high-oleic safflower oil, and high-oleic sunflower oil are a good

source of healthy fats, as are nuts such as almonds, cashews, hazelnuts, macadamia nuts, peanuts, and pecans. Fish that contain these good fats are salmon, bluefish, mackerel, sardines, and anchovies.

One serving is: 1 tablespoon olive or canola oil (or other oil mentioned above), 6 nuts, 3 ounces oily fish, ½ avocado.

White stuff

Three or Fewer Servings of Sugar, Refined Carbohydrates, Fats, or Alcohol

Life and food are to be enjoyed. Sometimes the "white stuff" tastes better than the brown, and nobody ever said that your diet has to be perfect to be wonderful. During these three days when you are rebalancing your body and getting your insulin levels down, limit your intake of white stuff to no more than three servings. The point is for this plan to work, and consuming more may cut into the plan's effectiveness. For these three days, do not consume any alcoholic beverages. If you are taking drugs that you consider external solutions and have obtained your physician's approval that is it safe to stop them, do so.

One serving is: 1 small cookie, 1 slice white bread, 2 crackers, ½ cup white pasta or white rice, 1 teaspoon butter or regular (non-canola-oil-based) margarine, 1 regular soda.

If at any time you don't feel well during your Three-Day Balancing Plan, or if you worry that this plan is not right for you, stop using it and contact your physician. Otherwise, continue using it for three days.

After three days, notice how your body feels. Notice your emotional response: pride, security, happiness, and joy. Make decisions about which of these practices you will continue and which you will not.

Use this plan, with your physician's approval, whenever your body is out of balance and needs some lifestyle surgery to regain the balance you need.

Of course, drink as much water as your thirst dictates. Drink plain water, seltzer water, or mineral water and other liquids that are free of sugar, caffeine, and alcohol. Limit aspartame-containing "diet" sodas to no more than two daily.

If you need more information about nutrition, consider having a private session with a registered or licensed dietitian to personal-

The Solution™

The Three-Day Balancing Plan Checklist

Obtain your physician's approval before beginning.

The Evening Before You Begin

☐ Eat a balancing meal.
☐ Use no chemical pleasures after 5:00 P.M.
☐ Use balanced sleeping: Go to bed by 10:00 P.M. and arise at 6:00 A.M. If you are awake, do cycles.

Days 1 to 3

☐ Follow a food plan: Nurturing or Clear Limits.
☐ Use no chemical pleasures.
☐ Continue balanced sleeping.
☐ Exercise for sixty—but no more than ninety—minutes daily.
☐ Receive support from others to make this easier.
☐ Consult with your physician if you don't feel well.

After Day 3

☐ Feel your earned rewards: vibrant, proud, happy.
☐ Continue the parts of this plan that work well for you.

ize your food plan and be sure it meets your needs, nutritionally and emotionally. To find a registered dietitian in your community, visit wwww.eatright.org or contact the American Dietetic Association at 800–366–1655.

Move for one hour daily

It will be easier to stay with the Three-Day Balancing Plan if you're in a good mood, not irritable or depressed. Exercise works as well as antidepressants for elevating mood and is as effective as psychotherapy for feeling good, so it is essential to this balancing program. In addition, although the eating plan will decrease your insulin levels and your appetite, adding exercise will make it even more effective. This plan includes one hour of exercise daily.

If you have not been exercising, consider walking. Walk for an entire hour or break it up into twenty- or thirty-minute strolls. If you are already physically fit and have been exercising regularly, continue your current program, but be sure that you exercise for at least one hour. Don't begin any exercise program without the approval of your physician. To find an exercise specialist in your community, visit www.acefitness.org or contact the American Council on Exercise at 800–825–3636 ext. 3.

After three days, feel your earned rewards: pride, vibrancy, and balance. To the extent that this plan is healthy and responsive to you, stay with it, or move to a more moderate plan if that is best for your health and your happiness.

Observations in this book about the effectiveness of the method were based primarily on my clinical experiences, reports from other Solution Providers about participants in their groups, and the small amount of research designed to study the method's effectiveness.

Only three studies have been conducted on the method's effectiveness; none offers the scientific merit of a large-scale, controlled clinical trial, because we have tried for years without success to obtain funding for more rigorous research. Funding has been sought from the National Institutes of Health (NIH) by researchers John Foreyt, Ph.D., and Kenneth Goodrick, Ph.D., and their colleagues at Baylor College of Medicine in conjunction with University of California-San Francisco (UCSF) researchers. A small group of UCSF researchers, in collaboration with officials from the State of California Department of Health, are preparing another grant that will be submitted to NIH in 2003. Larry Dickey, M.D., M.S.W., M.P.H, Mary Croughan, Ph.D., Gail Aultschuler, M.D., and Seleda Williams, M.D., are involved in the project, which will be submitted through UCSF's Department of Family and Community Medicine, School of Medicine. A University of Illinois-Chicago grant application is in preparation for the purpose of developing measurable assessments of these developmental skills.

The small amount of research that has been conducted has met with some significant methodological limitations. Samples in all three studies underrepresent men, minorities, and low-income participants, and two of the three lack a comparison group. In addition, there has been reliance to a greater or lesser degree on self-reported data.

Yet the research does have some strengths. The first study is current and involves 134 subjects with an unusually high response rate. The second study followed participants for six years, with repeated measures, including objective measures of blood pressure and weight. And the third study included the study of a comparison group.

Perhaps the most important finding is not based on any one study but on what these three studies show collectively: that participation in the method is, for many, associated with persistent improvements in mind, body, and spirit.

The first study summarized here is the Solution Method Survey, which surveyed 155 program participants who had completed much or all of The Solution complete course. The second study, the Solution Six-Year Follow-up Study, assessed various aspects of health and happiness in a small number of program participants at UCSF over the long term. The last study, the Adolescent Shapedown Study, evaluated the effectiveness of the method applied to adolescents in four communities in Northern California over a period of fifteen months.

More complete information about each study is available at www.solutioninstitute.org. Information about the adolescent program is available at www.childobesity.com.

The Solution Method Survey

A researcher from the University of Illinois, Chicago, Nancy Bates, Dr.P.H., R.D., C.H.E.S., conducted an independent survey of participants in The Solution to assess program effectiveness. The Institute for Health Solutions staff identified program participants who had purchased Solution Kits 5 or 6 during the previous year and provided that information to her.

A questionnaire was developed by Dr. Bates in consultation with researchers at the University of Illinois, Chicago and the University of California, San Francisco, and the research was approved by the Human Subjects Institute Review Board at the University of Illinois, Chicago. The questionnaire was sent by mail to eligible program participants in June 2002, returned to Dr. Bates by August 15, 2002, and analyzed by her staff. The Institute for Health Solutions had no access to these data but was provided with the following summary of the findings. All the changes were highly statistically significant, at the $p = 0.000$ level.

Of the 155 individuals who were sent questionnaires, 134 returned them, a response rate of 86 percent. Respondents were largely middle-aged white women. Mean age was forty-nine years, and 75 percent of the respondents were forty to sixty years of age. Ninety-eight percent were female, which reflects the past gender composition of Solution Groups. During the last year, far more men have sought Solution training. Ninety-five percent of respondents were Caucasian, which is consistent with the trends nationally for group health promotion interventions.

Forty-four percent of respondents had completed four Solution Kits, and 46 percent had completed five or more kits. The Solution Kits are the coursework of the method; however, participants can choose various forms of support. Forty-three percent had completed at least a year of Solution telegroup support (audioconferencing group with a Solution Provider). Thirty-three percent had completed at least one year of Solution Group support (in-person group with a Solution Provider). Seventeen percent completed the program through self-study or with Solution Circles. At the time of questionnaire completion, respondents had used The Solution for an average of about two and a half years, and all respondents had used the method for at least one year.

Participant satisfaction was high, with 96 percent rating the program as excellent or good and 91 percent responding that they would recommend The Solution to someone they cared about. Perceptions of improvements in health, happiness, and a range of related variables were also high:

The Solution Method Survey:

Perceptions of Improvement in Health and Happiness

- 68 percent reported improved health.
- 91 percent reported improved happiness.
- 83 percent reported improved personal relationships.
- 58 percent reported improved work relationships.
- 76 percent reported improved coping with work stress.
- 56 percent reported improved work productivity.
- 69 percent reported improved exercise.

The charts shown present the responses of subjects to questions about how often they engaged in an external solution or experienced a life reward prior to starting their Solution training and after receiving the training. There was a trend toward improvement in all rewards and all excesses. Participant responses were highly significantly different before The Solution compared with after participating in The Solution.

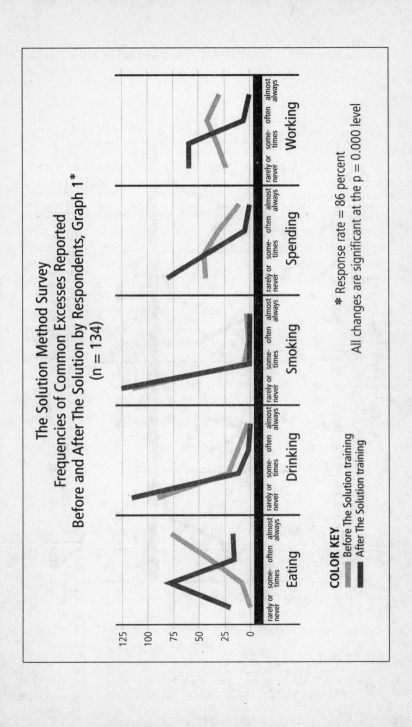

The Solution Method Survey
Frequencies of Common Excesses Reported
Before and After The Solution by Respondents, Graph 1*
(n = 134)

COLOR KEY
Before The Solution training
After The Solution training

* Response rate = 86 percent
All changes are significant at the p = 0.000 level

The Solution Method Survey
Frequencies of Common Excesses Reported
Before and After The Solution by Respondents, Graph 2 *
(n = 134)

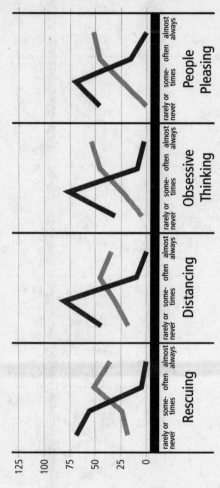

	rarely or never	some-times	often	almost always	rarely or never	some-times	often	almost always	rarely or never	some-times	often	almost always	rarely or never	some-times	often	almost always
	Rescuing				Distancing				Obsessive Thinking				People Pleasing			

Scale: 0, 25, 50, 75, 100, 125

COLOR KEY
— Before The Solution training
— After The Solution training

* Response rate = 86 percent
All changes are significant at the p = 0.000 level

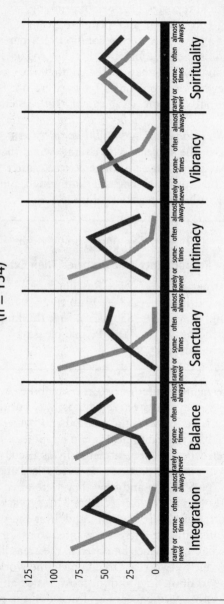

The Solution Method Survey
Frequencies of Life's Sweetest Rewards Reported
Before and After The Solution by Respondents, Graph 3*
(n = 134)

COLOR KEY
Before The Solution training
After The Solution training

* Response rate = 86 percent
All changes are significant at the p = 0.000 level

The majority of respondents engaged in the external solutions of overeating, rescuing, and obsessive thinking, and only a minority of them reported excesses of drinking, smoking, spending, working, distancing, and people-pleasing. We considered participants to have an external solution in a particular area if they indicated on the questionnaire that they engaged in it "often" or "almost always." If they indicated that they engaged in it "rarely or never," or "sometimes," they were not considered to have an external solution. *Of particular interest to us was the percentage of respondents who had an external solution when they started Solution training but did not after using the method.* For example, of the subjects who overate when they started the training, what percentage no longer overate after the training. This finding turned out to be remarkably high, and reasonably consistent regardless of external solution:

The Solution Method Survey:

Percentage of Respondents Who Resolved Their External Solution

Overeating	92	Rescuing	97
Excessive drinking	88	Distancing	86
Smoking	83	Obsessive thinking	86
Overspending	90	People-pleasing	72
Excessive working	82		

There are many limitations to the reliability and generalizability of this survey; however, this report was positive regarding participant satisfaction with the method and perceived improvements in variables related to health and happiness.

First, a retrospective pretest method was used, which means that at one point in time participants were asked about how they were before The Solution and how they were after being in The Solution. Although it would have been better to ask participants these questions before the program and after the program, two issues made this difficult. First, we wanted to ask program completers what their experience had been in the areas just discussed. Since it takes one to two years to complete the work, we did not have the time to do it. In addition, most, if not all, of the skills and rewards have specific meanings learned in the program. It is very possible that someone asked before starting the program how often he or she experienced integration might realize after being in the program, and experiencing a deeper integration, that he or she really hadn't experienced true integration before starting the program.

Second, when looking at the effects of an intervention, comparing the results of the participants to those of nonparticipants gives a better sense of whether the general public is changing or whether the change can be attributed to the intervention. Although we could not use a control group in this survey, the dramatic changes seen in rewards and excesses seem unlikely to be happening in the general population.

Third, the survey has not yet been tested for reliability and validity, so we don't know how well the questions that are about similar things, such as skills, rewards, and excesses, relate to one another. In addition, we have not tested the validity of the survey, or how well it measures what we want to measure.

Finally, generalizability, or the confidence we have that we would see the same results in other groups of people, is limited to white women. It has been our clinical experience that men and minorities respond in the same way, but this survey did not include data that would either support or refute that observation.

The results from this report, which were collected, on the average, two and a half years after participants began using the method, were similar to the results reported at two years in the six-year follow-up study described in the next section. This is an important strength of these findings.

The Solution Six-Year Follow-up Study

A small study of The Solution was conducted at UCSF and included participants in our groups. This group was similar in age and gender to the more recent survey. A complete description of it has been published,[1] and its methods were approved by the UCSF Committee on Human Research. All subjects entered Solution training for weight loss and received an average of eighteen weeks of Solution Group training conducted by a psychotherapist and a registered dietitian trained in the method. The initial sample involved twenty-six people, and at two years, complete data were available for twenty-two participants, and at six years, for sixteen participants.

The initial report of the findings of this study was based on data collected in the first two years of observation. Participants

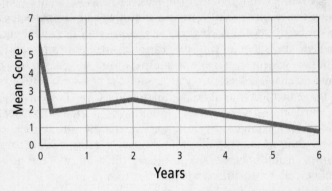

*Mean Beck Depression Inventory (Short Form) scores for participants in a group program. Measure taken at baseline, three months, six months, one year, two years and six years. Change significant at the $p < 0.003$

lost weight, increased their exercise, lowered their blood pressure, and felt less depressed at three and six months and at the one- and two-year follow-ups. When this study was published, it marked the first time in the medical literature of which we are aware that a nonsurgical intervention for weight management had shown continued weight loss after the program ended.

The six-year follow-up results were presented during a talk at a scientific meeting in 1999,[2] and these data suggested that either most of the improvements at post-treatment were sustained or further improvements occurred. These research findings prompted *Health* to name The Solution one of the ten top medical advances of 2000. Despite the small sample size, the changes, in most cases, were statistically significant ($p </= 0.05$).

In the sample of sixteen who had completed the program and participated in the intervention enough to have mastered the skills, an average twenty-two-pound weight loss was sustained compared with baseline values ($p = 0.02$). This compares favorably to behavioral, diet, exercise, or drug therapies in which initial weight loss typically is regained within one to two years after treatment ends, resulting in no mean reduction in weight in the long term.

Mean physical activity in minutes per week increased 165 minutes compared to baseline (p < 0.001). Again, the physical activity literature mirrors the weight literature in that typically when the intervention to promote physical activity (the external sources of nurturing and limits) stops, physical activity practices return to baseline levels.

Both systolic and diastolic blood pressure improved by a mean of 11 mmHg for systolic blood pressure (p = 0.06) and 16 mmHg for diastolic blood pressure (p = 0.004).

Perceptions of improvement in health, happiness, and a range of related variables were also positive:

The Solution Six-Year Follow-up Study:

Perceptions of Improvement in Health and Happiness

- 69 percent reported improved health.
- 88 percent reported improved happiness.
- 88 percent reported improved personal relationships.
- 88 percent reported deepened spirituality.
- 100 percent reported improved coping with work stress.
- 88 percent reported improved work productivity.
- 88 percent reported improved physical activity.
- 54 percent of those with spending problems reported improvement.
- 80 percent of those with substance problems reported improvement.

The finding that was of greatest interest to us was the apparent impact of the method on depression. Most participants improved their extent of depression significantly early in the intervention. Although training ended, their depression scores continued to improve, even at six-year follow-up (p < 0.003). Depression was measured by responses to the Beck Depression Inventory (short form). Initial mean depression scores suggested moderate depression of about five, and the mean score at six-year follow-up was less than one, suggesting no significant depression.

These data are consistent with clinical experience with the method, that is, depression levels improve rather rapidly for most people. It is also consistent with the concept of the sweetest fruit, that is, emotional balance typically comes during the first half of training, whereas the most primitive drives begin to abate during the second half of the climb.

The Adolescent Shapedown Study

The method was first developed to treat adolescent obesity, then modified for childhood obesity treatment. It was not until the early 1990s that the program was adapted to adults and later to problems other than overeating. During the early development of the program, it was a family-based behavioral intervention that stressed parental nurturing and limit-setting skills. One study was conducted using the third edition of the program materials, which reflected this behavioral-improved parenting paradigm.[3] Subsequently, the program materials were revised to more fully reflect The Solution Method (the fourth edition), with greater influence on teaching children and adolescents, as well as their parents, the skill to nurture and set limits from within.

With the current epidemic of pediatric obesity, schools and the government are trying to reverse that trend. Unfortunately, the interventions that are often selected stress diet and exercise without also increasing the internal skills that turn off excessive appetites: nurturing and limits. Changing behavior without turning off the drives to go to excess poses the risk that weight loss may be only short-term or that if overeating abates, another substitute external solution will arise.

The Shapedown Program stresses healthy eating and activity but supports the development within the whole family of the skills to nurture and set limits from within. It is only a ten- to twenty-week program because the feeling brain of the young is far more easily retrained than that of adults.

The Shapedown Program continues to be given in clinics and hospital settings, and a new program recently became available for use in the schools. The Institute for Health Solutions plans to sponsor the development of a school-based health education program not just for weight but for health, happiness, and the prevention of external solutions. However, at this time, only the school-based weight program is available.

A study of sixty-three overweight and obese adolescents was conducted in four sites in Northern California and involved a study design that was approved by UCSF's Committee on Human Research. Health professionals who had been trained in pediatric obesity through a forty-hour interdisciplinary course provided fourteen weekly sessions to the test group of thirty-four adolescents and their parents. The control group of twenty-nine subjects received no treatment.

Baseline, post-treatment, and one-year follow-up measures were taken. The mean changes at three and fifteen months of the control group were not significant except for self-esteem. Those participating in the Shapedown Program significantly improved in knowledge, self-esteem, depression, weight-related behavior, and relative weight.

Research on the method is very important in order to describe program effectiveness and to guide further program development. It is not always easy to conduct Solution research because the method must be administered by health profession-als who are trained in the method and have both the personal and professional skills to bring participants to a Solution. The basic certification program takes eighteen months for licensed health professionals (mental health professionals, physicians, registered dietitians, and nurse practitioners) to complete. Our experience has been that after certification, health professionals require at least two years of clinical experience with the method to have the clinical skills to bring most participants to a Solution.

The program outcomes shown in these three studies were dependent upon course materials developed for program partici-pants and support provided by licensed health professionals who have received specialized training in the method. Our clinical impression is that those who do not use program materials that guide their practice of the method and have the professional sup-port of method providers experience outcomes that are less favorable.

If you are a researcher interested in exploring the possibility of conducting Solution research, please contact the Institute for Health Solutions for information about established protocols for training and program evaluation (415–457–3331, or research @thepathway.org).

Notes

1. Mellin, L. M., Croughan-Minihane, M., and Dickey, L. "Two-Year Trends in Weight, Blood Pressure, Depression, and Functioning of Adults Trained in Developmental Skills." *Journal of the American Dietetic Association* (1997), 97:1133–38.

2. Mellin, L. M., "Developmental Skills Training for the Treatment of Obesity: Integration of Decades of Research." Presented at annual meeting of the American Dietetic Association, Denver, October 1999.

3. Mellin, L. M., Slinkard, L. A., Irwin, C. E., Jr. "Adolescent Obesity Intervention: Validation of the Shapedown Program." *Journal of the American Dietetic Association* (1987), 87:333–38.

Recommended Reading

American College of Sports Medicine. *ACSM's Guidelines for Exercise Testing and Prescription*. New York: Lippincott Williams & Wilkins, 2000.

Anderson, S. R., and Hopkins, P. *The Feminine Face of God: The Unfolding of the Sacred in Women*. New York: Bantam Books, 1992.

Bridges, W. *Transitions: Making Sense of Life's Changes*. Reading, Mass.: Addison-Wesley, 1980.

*Bruch, H. *Eating Disorders: Obesity, Anorexia Nervosa, and the Person Within*. New York: Basic Books, 1973.

Dwyer, W. *There Is a Spiritual Solution to Every Problem*. New York: HarperCollins, 2001.

Goleman, D. *Emotional Intelligence: Why It Can Matter More Than IQ*. New York: Bantam Books, 1994.

Gray, J. *What You Feel, You Can Heal: A Guide for Enriching Relationships*. Mill Valley, Calif.: Heart Publishing, 1994.

Janov, A. *The Biology of Love*. New York: Prometheus Books, 2000.

LeDoux, J. *The Emotional Brain: The Mysterious Underpinnings of Emotional Life*. New York: Simon & Schuster, 1996.

Leonard, G. *Mastery: The Keys to Success and Long-term Fulfillment*. New York: Penguin Books, 1992.

†Lewis, T., Amini, F., and Lannon, R. *A General Theory of Love*. New York: Random House, 2000.

McArdle W. D., Katch, F. I., and Katch, V. L. *Exercise Physiology: Energy, Nutrition, and Human Performance*. New York: Lippincott Williams & Wilkins, 2001.

McCann, E., and Shannon, D. *The Two-Step: The Dance Toward Intimacy*. New York: Grove Press, 1985.

†Mellin, L. *The Solution: 6 Winning Ways to Permanent Weight Loss*. New York: ReganBooks, 1998.

‡Mellin, L. *The Shapedown Child and Adolescent Weight Man-*

agement Program. San Anselmo, Calif.: Balboa Publishing, 2000.

Miller, J., and Stiver, I. *The Healing Connection: How Women Form Relationships in Therapy and in Life*. Boston: Beacon Press, 1997.

Moore, T. *The Soul of Sex: Cultivating Life as an Act of Love*. New York: HarperCollins, 1998.

Muuss, R. *Theories of Adolescence*. New York: McGraw-Hill, 1996.

Nestle, M. *Food Politics: How the Food Industry Influences Nutrition and Health*. Berkeley: University of California Press, 2002.

Newberg, A., D'Aquili, E., and Rause, V. *Why God Won't Go Away: Brain Science and the Biology of Belief*. New York: Ballantine Books, 2001.

Northrup, C. *The Wisdom of Menopause: Creating Physical and Emotional Health and Healing During the Change*. New York: Bantam Books, 2001.

Ornish, D. *Love and Survival: 8 Pathways to Intimacy and Health*. New York: HarperCollins, 1999.

Peeke, P. *Fight Fat After Forty*. New York: Viking, 2000.

Pert, C. B. *Molecules of Emotion*. New York: Scribner, 1997.

Sapolsky, R. *Why Zebras Don't Get Ulcers: An Updated Guide to Stress, Stress-Related Diseases, and Coping*. New York: W. H. Freeman, 2000.

Satir, V. *Conjoint Family Therapy*. Palo Alto, Calif.: Science and Behavior Books, 1983.

Schnarch, D. *Passionate Marriage*. New York: W. W. Norton, 1997.

Sizer, F. S., and Whitney, E. N. *Nutrition: Concepts and Controversies*, 9th ed. Belmont, Calif.: Wadsworth, 2002.

Schwartz, J. M., and Begley, S. *The Mind and the Brain: Neuroplasticity and the Power of Mental Force*. New York: Regan Books, 2002.

[†]Thayer, R. *Calm Energy: How People Regulate Mood with Food and Exercise*. New York: Oxford University Press, 2001.

Vaillant, G. *The Natural History of Alcoholism Revisited*. Cambridge, Mass.: Harvard University Press, 2000.

Watters E., and Ofshe, R. *Therapy's Delusions: The Myth of the Unconscious and the Exploitation of Today's Walking Worried*. New York: Scribner, 1999.

Notes

*The original inspiration for the method came from Bruch, H., and Touraine, G. 1940. "Obesity in Childhood: V. The Family Frame of Obese Children." *Psychosomatic Medicine* 11:142–206.

†These books are highly recommended:

> *A General Theory of Love* provides interesting information about the limbic brain.

> *Calm Energy* presents a thoughtful discussion of mood regulation, food, and exercise.

> *The Solution* will be of particular help to those applying the method to eating and weight concerns.

‡More information about the method's application to child and adolescent obesity is available from Balboa Publishing, 1323 San Anselmo Avenue, San Anselmo, CA 94960, or at www.childobesity.com.

About the Author

Laurel Mellin is an associate clinical professor of family and community medicine and pediatrics at the University of California, San Francisco School of Medicine. She is the founder and director of the Institute for Health Solutions, a nonprofit organization that trains and certifies licensed health professionals to provide this method and sponsors method research. The organization also distributes materials and facilitates support for individuals using the method, including:

The complete Solution course (The Solution Kits 1 through 6)

Referrals to Solution Groups and coaching in the community

Referrals to Solution telegroups and telecoaching

The Solution Orientation by telephone (free) for an easy start on the pathway

The Solution Great Start Groups (four-week introductory groups by telephone or in your community)

The Solution Buddy List for Community Connections

The Solution weekend retreats

The mission of the Institute for Health Solutions is to develop, evaluate, and disseminate programs that support the mastery of the skill to nurture and set limits from within for the prevention and treatment of health problems and the promotion of personal happiness.

The Institute for Health Solutions is committed to bringing this method to those who need these skills the most or who face special challenges. Many who use the method experience such a transformation in their lives that they want to bring this experience to others. If, at some point, you have the desire, we welcome you to contribute to this mission. If you have a particular expertise or other resource that could benefit this work, please let us know. If you would like to make a tax-deductible contribution in any amount to either our Solution Scholarship Fund or our Solution Development Fund, we welcome you to do so and will feel grateful for your contribution.

The Solution Scholarship Fund provides Solution Kits and Solution training to those with severe economic disadvantages. To inquire about contributing, please e-mail: scholarship@the pathway.org.

The Solution Development Fund supports pilot research and program development for prevention and for specific high-risk populations. Current project priorities include: alcoholism, family violence, foster parenting, diabetes, inner city youth and school-based health education. To inquire about contributing your expertise or making a donation, please e-mail: development@ thepathway.org.

The Institute for Health Solutions
415–457–3331
www.thepathway.org

Laurel provides workshops and lectures on the method at health professional meetings and courses, has conducted more than eighty national conferences for health professionals on The Solution Method, has authored numerous research articles, and practices the method clinically. She also developed the Shapedown Program, an application of this method to child and adolescent obesity. Laurel lives in Marin County, California, with her three children.